Turgenev

His Life and Times

I. S. Turgenev in 1846.
A water-colour portrait by K. A. Gorbunov

Turgenev

His Life and Times

LEONARD SCHAPIRO

Harvard University Press
Cambridge, Massachusetts
1982

This Harvard University Press paperback is published by arrangement with
Random House, Inc. It contains the complete text of the original
hardcover edition.

Copyright © 1978 by Leonard Schapiro

Printed in the United States of America

Library of Congress Cataloging in Publication Data

Schapiro, Leonard Bertram, 1908–
Turgenev, his life and times.
Originally published: New York: Random House, c. 1978.
Bibliography: p.
Includes indexes.
1. Turgenev, Ivan Sergeevich, 1818–1883—Biography.
2. Authors, Russian—19th century—Biography. I. Title.
PG3435.S3 1982   891.73'3 [B]   82-9368
ISBN 0–674–91297–7 (pbk.)

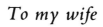

To my wife

CONTENTS

ILLUSTRATIONS

(found in the insert, appearing in sequence between pages 176 and 177)

PREFACE

The appearance of yet another biography of Turgenev calls for some justification. My defence is simply the fact that in the past decade (and therefore since the appearance of such an admirable biography as that by Avram Yarmolinsky) much new material has come to light, both in France and in Russia. Many hitherto unknown letters, mainly to Pauline Viardot, have at long last been made public in France. In the Soviet Union a complete edition of Turgenev's works and letters has been published under the auspices of the Soviet Academy of Sciences, the fruit of laborious and meticulous scholarship. Eight volumes of miscellaneous research and documentation have also appeared.

It cannot be claimed that this new information changes the familiar picture of Turgenev: weak, uncommitted politically and unhappy about it, critical of the radicals but an admirer of their courage and honesty, humane and unpompous. But although he was always talking about himself, Turgenev still remains something of an enigma. So the considerable amount of detailed information which has now become available may help to shed some light on a man whose fascination both for Russians and non-Russians time does not seem to diminish.

I must emphasize that I have made no attempt to 'interpret' Turgenev. I thought it right to portray him as best I could, his thought, his actions, and his work, on the basis of the most reliable evidence available to me, and then leave it to the reader to decide what kind of man he was. However, as Goethe said (and as Turgenev was fond of quoting), a man remains what he is. This applies not only to those who are being judged, but also to those who do the judging. So I suspect that those of my readers who were charmed by Turgenev before will find their view reinforced by my book; while those who detest him (if they get so far as reading what I have written about him) will find more disreputable incidents and opinions to support their judgement.

Turgenev frequently denied that he was a politician. In the sense that his primary activity was not concerned with the political sphere this was true – with some little-known exceptions, to which I have drawn attention. In the sense that he was not interested in political events this disclaimer was quite untrue. His letters bristle with comments on Russian and French public events, and firm opinions are voiced. Besides, while it is true that the human problem always predominated for him in his fiction, it was quite impossible to write about contemporary Russia in the nineteenth century (or at any time, for that matter) without becoming deeply involved in the current controversies. Indeed, Turgenev was well aware of this in writing *Virgin Soil*, as his years of preparatory study for his last novel demonstrate. I have therefore tried to provide sufficient information on the relevant political background in Russia to illuminate his position.

There have been attempts to claim Turgenev as a radical at heart. I am not convinced by these attempts – though there was a short period in his life when this was almost true. What makes him remarkable and exceptional on the Russian scene is that he cannot be readily labelled – unless love of liberty, decency, and humanity in all relations can be called a 'label'. Everything in Russian conditions conspired to force people into categories: if you were critical of the radicals, you belonged in the same box with Katkov and the other avowed reactionaries; if you attacked inhumanity and obscurantism in government policy, you were for practical purposes a Red. Turgenev was one of the very few nineteenth-century Russian figures who rejected this typically Russian tyranny of categories and labels, which is one reason why his political outlook is more acceptable to a Western European liberal than that of Dostoevsky, or Tolstoy. But Turgenev was no Western European liberal in the accepted sense.

Because of the close connection between many of Turgenev's works and political questions I have, of course, dealt with the stories and novels in the course of my narrative. Moreover, some of his fiction or articles, while of no political relevance, are important because they reveal the development of his general outlook. But I make no claim to offer a work of literary analysis – there are others much more qualified than I to do that. Among recent works in English I should mention Richard Freeborn's *Turgenev: a Study*, the imaginative book by Eva Kagan-Kans entitled *Hamlet and Don Quixote: Turgenev's Ambivalent Vision*, and V. S. Pritchett's study, *The Gentle Barbarian*. For readers of Russian there are the classical works of Gershenzon and Ovsianniko-Kulikovsky, among many, many others.

Nor have I been able to ignore Turgenev's emotional life. In spite of April FitzLyon's definitive *The Price of Genius*, I had to take account of letters to Pauline Viardot which were not available to Mrs. Fitz-Lyon. Besides, to omit Pauline (and, for that matter, a few other quite important ladies) from a biography of Turgenev would be to produce a caricature, not a Life.

Lastly, I should emphasize that this is a book about Turgenev, not a book about the books about Turgenev. The literature on Turgenev runs to many thousands of books and articles; a recent Soviet bibliography of works published between 1918 and 1967 alone lists over two thousand items. A great quantity of reminiscences about Turgenev appeared in the thirty years or so after his death. I cannot claim to have done more than indicate some points of importance in the vast literature which discusses the works from all angles – artistic, political, social, and psychological. But I have tried to use all the memoirs which were accessible to me, even if I have only been able to quote a fraction of the total.

I have had much assistance in the preparation of this book which I gratefully acknowledge. The libraries of the University of Indiana, Bloomington, of the University of Washington, and of the School of Slavonic and East European Studies among others have been particularly helpful. I am indebted to Professors Leon Edel and Patrick Waddington and to Dr. Georgette Donchin for information and advice. Mrs. April FitzLyon and Mrs. Ellen de Kadt were kind enough to read the whole manuscript and to make most valuable comments. Mrs. Ann Kennedy not only typed the manuscript with great skill and patience, but made most helpful suggestions for its improvement. The editors concerned at the Oxford University Press, and especially Miss Judith Chamberlain, showed great skill, tact, and patience in polishing the manuscript. The encouragement, editorial skill, and imaginative advice of my wife Roma have done more than I can express to try to give this book any elegance of form which more charitable readers may detect in it.

LEONARD SCHAPIRO

London School of Economics and Political Science
January 1978

Turgenev

His Life and Times

CHAPTER ONE

Family and Childhood

Ivan Sergeevich Turgenev was born in Orel, the capital of the province of that name, on Monday 28 October 1818 and christened on 31 October.*[1] According to a note recorded by his mother, the time of his birth was twelve noon, and he was twenty-one inches long. His parents' home, in which he first saw the light, has long since been destroyed by fire, as were so many of the wooden houses of Orel in the course of the last century.

His father, Sergei Nikolaevich Turgenev, who was twenty-five years of age when his son Ivan was born, was descended from a family which was well established in the Russian minor nobility. The founder of the family, Lev Turgen, came over from the Golden Horde in 1440 to join the court of Grand Prince Vasilii Ivanovich, and was received into the Christian faith. His descendants, as the official record shows, served the Russian throne as ambassadors, military commanders, and in other high ranks, and were rewarded by the tsars in 1530 and at other times with estates.[2] Turgenev himself expressed particular pride in two ancestors: Peter, who exposed the false Demetrius and was executed the same day; and Jacob, the court jester of Peter the Great, who helped to cut the beards of the boyars, and 'in his own way furthered the cause of enlightenment'.[3]

Ivan's father served with distinction as an officer, attained the rank of lieutenant-colonel in the Ekaterinoslav Cuirassier Regiment, and in 1821 was retired at his own request. He was decorated for courage

---

* In the nineteenth century, the Russian calendar was twelve days behind that which was in force in Western Europe. Considerable confusion is caused because Russians living abroad tended to use the Western or the Russian date indiscriminately. The practice followed in this book is to date events which happened in Russia, or letters written in Russia, in the Russian style, and events which happened in Western Europe or the United States, and letters which emanated from those areas in the Western style.

at the battle of Borodino. In 1816, aged twenty-three, and renowned for his handsome looks and his success with women, he had married the twenty-nine-year-old Varvara Petrovna Lutovinova, a rich land-owner, said to have been worth the enormous fortune of 5,000 serfs. In a letter, dated 1838, she stated her fortune to be only 3,000 serfs, but, of course, there may well have been sales during these twenty-five years.[4] Sergei Nikolaevich's modest estate scarcely exceeded a hundred serfs. It was commonly believed that the match had been entered into, on his side, for mercenary reasons, and he certainly con-tinued his amorous adventures unrestrained by matrimony. Varvara Petrovna, on the other hand, apparently adored him, and after his early death in 1834, preserved his study as a shrine which no one was allowed to enter, and spoke of him in terms of superlative praise – how sincerely is another matter.

Turgenev was well aware of the strain which existed between his parents and has recorded it in his story 'First Love', written in 1860, which on a number of occasions he referred to as completely autobio-graphical. In 'First Love' the fifteen-year-old boy tells us of his feel-ings for his father (as they appeared to him in retrospect) a year before the latter's death:

Strange was the influence which my father had on me, and strange were our relations. He hardly ever took any part in my education, but he never insulted me: he respected my freedom, he was even, if one can so express it, courteous in his behaviour towards me. But – he would never let me approach him. I loved him, I fervently admired him, he seemed to me a model of all that a man should be – and, my goodness, how passionately I would have become attached to him if I had not always felt his hand push-ing me away! When he wanted to he knew how to arouse in me limitless trust towards himself, almost on a moment, with one word, one move-ment. My whole being opened up – I chattered as I would to a sensible friend, to a condescending mentor. And then, just as suddenly he would leave me – and his hand once again thrust me aside – in a gentle and kindly manner – but thrust me aside nevertheless. ...

Once – and only once – he caressed me with such tenderness that I nearly burst into tears. ...[5] Sometimes, I recall, I would begin to study his intelli-gent, beautiful, illuminated face, while my heart trembled and my whole being yearned for him ... he seemed to sense what was happening inside me, and would casually fondle my cheek – and then either go away, or occupy himself with something, or freeze up as only he knew how to freeze up, and I would immediately seize up and go cold as well. ... 'Take what you can yourself, and don't let yourself fall into someone else's hands; to belong to oneself – that is the whole trick of life', he said to me once. On another occasion I began, in my capacity as a young democrat, to discuss freedom in his presence. 'Freedom', he repeated, 'but do you know what can give one freedom?'

'What?'

'Will, your own will, and it will give you power which is better than freedom. If you know how to want, you will be free, and you will be in command.'[6]

A longing for decisiveness of character, for strength of will and determination, which he was never able to achieve, remained with Turgenev all his life. Perhaps this strange relationship with his father played its part in keeping alive the sense of privation, of having missed something in life. However, virtually all our knowledge of Turgenev's childhood is based on reminiscences recorded by him many decades later. In the account just quoted, for example, the statement that his father hardly took any interest in his education is belied by some letters dated between 1830 and 1834 from the father to his two sons, Ivan and Nikolai, which have been preserved, and which display a real and affectionate interest in the boys' progress, and, what is of particular relevance so far as the future writer is concerned, and, incidentally, somewhat unusual for one of the senior Turgenev's background and upbringing in the Russia of the time, meticulous insistence on application to the Russian language.[7] Turgenev's father seems to have been a man of some education, with knowledge of French, German, mathematics, history, and geography; but, to judge by what has survived of his library, he was not a great reader.[8] The letters also display a warmth and affection which are again not quite consistent with the son's picture as drawn in 1860.

Of Turgenev's mother, Varvara Petrovna, we have considerably more knowledge and do not have to rely solely on the son's recollections: we possess the detailed memoirs of her natural daughter, who lived with her from her birth in 1833 until the death of Madame Turgenev in 1850; several accounts by neighbours and friends; and numerous diaries and letters, mostly unpublished. The Lutovinov family was of humbler and more recent origins than Sergei Turgenev's. Land records show that in the seventeenth century two ancestors of Varvara Petrovna were rewarded for their military service to the tsar with the grant of lands in Spasskoe, a village some five or six miles away from the town of Mtsensk in Orel Province. Thereafter the estate remained in the hands of the family until it was inherited by Varvara Petrovna in the early years of the nineteenth century. Tradition ascribes great savagery and brutality of character to the Lutovinovs, and especially to the three sons of Varvara Petrovna's grandfather – Ivan, Alexei, and Peter. It is recorded of one of them, probably Alexei, that he conducted a fixed battle with his armed domestics against the landowners of one of his villages who had tried to take him to court over a land dispute, killing fifteen in the process. The other brothers were similarly renowned for their brutality towards their serfs.[9]

The last of the brothers, Ivan Ivanovich Lutovinov, inherited Spasskoe, built the manor house, and laid out the gardens and park. Turgenev has left us a description of the park at Spasskoe in 'Faust'. This story consists of a series of letters; in the first letter to a friend the author describes his return to his estate after some years' absence.

The alleys of lime trees have become particularly fine. I love these alleys, I love their grey-green delicate colour, and the delicate scent of the air beneath their canopy; and I love the multicoloured network of light circles on the dark earth – I have no sand, as you know. My favourite baby oak-tree has grown into a young oak. Yesterday I sat for over an hour in its shade on a bench. I felt very well. The grass spread around me so merrily, all bathed in golden light, gentle, strong light, which even penetrated into the shade ... and the birds that could be heard. ... The turtle doves cooed incessantly, now and again an oriole would emit its whistle, a chaffinch would execute its charming pattern, the thrushes chattered angrily, a cuckoo called from afar. Suddenly, a woodpecker uttered a piercing cry ...'

The house was two storeyed, with twenty-one rooms and a stone gallery adjoining the house. There was a vast orchard and an orangery; a multitude of stables, baths, coach houses, barns, mills, shoe-makers' and tailors' workshops and domestic servants' quarters, an infirmary and a building for music and song.[10] One must cast one's imagination back to Russian life in the eighteenth century as it still survived in the nineteenth, to picture what it must have been like in Spasskoe when Turgenev was a child. 'This little serf-world, this miniature state' (as the poet Polonsky called it many years later), teeming with countless human beings supported by it, all 'gossiping, whispering, intriguing'. 'Think only', says Polonsky, 'of the innumerable tales, traditions and superstitions, the fears and the petty passions' which made up the atmosphere in which the infant Turgenev grew up.[11] The manor house was burned down in 1839 but a large wing survived, which Turgenev continued to occupy after his mother's death on his periodic visits to Russia.*

---

* The wing in turn was destroyed by fire in 1906. But fortunately the distant relative of Turgenev who had inherited Spasskoe after Turgenev's death, had in 1905 removed much of the contents, and in particular the Lutovinov family library as well as Turgenev's own books and other personal belongings, to her

Varvara Petrovna's childhood and youth were certainly not of a kind to bring out the best in a young girl. Her father died young and her mother remarried. Not only did the stepfather detest Varvara, but her mother turned against her as well. Her childhood was a time of brutality and humiliation at the hands of her stepfather. When she was sixteen he began to make advances to her, and forced his attentions with the threat of most degrading punishment if she did not comply. The girl decided to escape, which she achieved with the aid of her devoted nurse, seeking refuge with her uncle Ivan, the owner of Spasskoe. Ivan did not ill-treat her, but was mean, and kept her virtually a prisoner at the estate. According to one account he actually drove her from the house intending to disinherit her, but death intervened before he could achieve his purpose. She was nearly thirty when he died, and she inherited the vast estate. The only portrait of her known to exist does not suggest any beauty. Her features are mean, her complexion is said to have been marred by smallpox, and she was short of stature. In spite of her lack of formal education her library, mostly in French, (now in the Turgenev Museum in Orel) suggests that she was a woman of cultured tastes. It comprises quite a large collection of works of travel and descriptions of nature in all parts of the world, as well as books on botany and gardening and the serious French novels of the early nineteenth century, such as those of Chateaubriand and Madame de Staël.[12] This was the woman who fell in love with and married Sergei Nikolaevich Turgenev.

Two and a half years after the birth of Ivan, the Turgenevs removed from Orel to Spasskoe, where they remained until 1827. The family at the time of the move to Spasskoe consisted of two sons—the other son, Nikolai, was two years older than Ivan. (A third son, Sergei, was born in 1831, but died as a boy.) In the course of 1822 and 1823 the whole household undertook a vast journey through Germany, Switzerland, France, and Austria, spending some six months in Paris. The journey seems to have been frequently interrupted by the illness of Varvara Petrovna. Turgenev records of this journey—of which he remembered little—that while in Bern he all but fell into the famous bear pit, and was only rescued at the critical moment by his father.

Life at Spasskoe during these early years was one of true Russian

---

house in Orel, where the Soviet authorities in 1918 opened up a Turgenev Museum which seeks to reproduce the setting and atmosphere of Turgenev's life in Spasskoe.

magnificence, in the old style of a princely country house. The Turgenevs spent the whole year on their estate, without moving to Moscow for the winter. They entertained lavishly, enlivening the company with music, theatre, and ballet performed by specially trained domestic serfs. In one of his conversations late in life Turgenev recalled a theatrical evening in the park at Spasskoe with music and coloured lanterns and a multitude of guests. Turgenev's recollections of his early childhood in Spasskoe are derived almost entirely from his accounts in conversation many decades later. The only earlier record, made at the age of seventeen, is an autobiographical sketch which states that 'of my years as an infant I only know that I was spoilt – that I was an ugly child – and that I nearly died when I was about four, but was revived by Hungarian wine'.[13] The later recollections paint a very different picture. So far from being 'spoilt', he related that his upbringing was spartan in the extreme, and that he was beaten by his mother severely, frequently, and often without cause. On one occasion, at the age of six or seven, he suffered a beating for his literary opinion. He recalls that he was presented to an old and venerable man, and on being told that this was I. I. Dmitriev, the poet, promptly recited one of his fables. Then, to the horror of the assembled company, he pronounced: 'Your fables are good, but Ivan Andreevich Krylov's fables are much better' – a judgement which was beyond dispute sound, but did not save him from a severe thrashing which, as he said, fixed forever in his memory his first meeting with a distinguished author.[14] But not all the punishments he suffered were so rational. There was one incident which he recalled in conversation with Polonsky a few years before his death, when he was beaten by his mother for no reason which he could discover; when he begged her to tell him why he was being punished, she only said, 'You know very well why you are being whipped, and what is more you will be whipped every day until you admit your offence.' The poor child was so terrified that he planned to run away at night. His kindly German tutor found him about to leave the house, comforted him and promised him that he would not be beaten again. The promise seems to have been kept, after the tutor had had a long conversation with Varvara Petrovna behind closed doors.[15]

But though the young Turgenev may have himself escaped further brutal treatment from his mother after this incident, her tyrannous behaviour towards her household serfs made an indelible impression upon him, and complicated his relations with her. But this question belongs mainly to a later period, when Turgenev, no longer permanently living in Spasskoe, was a frequent visitor there and witness of his mother's behaviour.

We know little about Turgenev's first encounters with literature. According to his own testimony he became a voracious and indiscriminate reader from an early age, acquainted from childhood with the fables of I. I. Dmitriev and I. A. Krylov.[16] Dmitriev (1760–1837) really belonged to the eighteenth century in his manner and in his choice of subject; his elegant, if sentimental, style exercised some influence on the formation of the modern Russian language. Krylov (1769–1844) was a literary figure of much greater importance. The first collection of his fables appeared in 1809 and became an outstanding success overnight. They were learned by heart and repeated throughout educated Russian society, and enjoy a well-deserved popularity to this day. The first collection was followed by others. As Belinsky rightly pointed out, Krylov's fables are often miniature comedies, excelling in humour, in characterization and, above all, in that profound knowledge of Russian peasant life which may well have influenced the future author of *A Sportsman's Notebook*.

We know also that as a boy Turgenev was introduced to the poetry of Kheraskov by one of the serfs in his mother's household, the major-domo Fedor Ivanovich Lobanov – an incident which later formed the basis of the story entitled 'Punin and Baburin'. M. M. Kheraskov (1733–1807) was an important and influential eighteenth-century literary figure, and one of the creators of modern Russian. The *Rossiada* is a long poem in the heroic style devoted to the capture of Kazan by Ivan the Terrible, and redolent with patriotic sentiments.[17] Of the rest of Turgenev's reading at this early age we have little information. 'I grew up on the classics', he wrote in later life;[18] and on another occasion he describes how, as a child, he used to rummage among the dusty literature of the late eighteenth and early nineteenth centuries – of which there was indeed a good collection in Spasskoe, including Kantemir, the *Rossiada* of Kheraskov, Sumarokov, Derzhavin, Fonvizin, Karamzin, Dmitriev, and Krylov. Varvara Petrovna, who in spite of her reluctance to speak Russian was able to read the language, also added to the Spasskoe library authors of the early nineteenth century like Venevitinov, Zhukovsky, and Zagoskin.[19]

It is also clear that from an early age Turgenev was reading the English romantic poets and the novels of Dickens and Bulwer Lytton. Many of these authors are represented in what survives of the library of his brother Nikolai who apparently taught Ivan to read English. The young boy was also frequently fascinated by the study of a strange book entitled *Symbols and Emblems* which is still in the (rehoused) Spasskoe library, and which is minutely described – from memory, since the novel was written abroad – in *A Nest of the Landed Gentry*. The library at Spasskoe included some of the early editions of Pushkin's poems – *Ruslan i Liudmila* which was published in 1820, and the early chapters of *Eugene Onegin*, which appeared between 1825 and 1828, in other words during Turgenev's infancy and childhood. But we do not know of the impression left on the boy by the poetry of Pushkin, which was to exercise a profound influence on him throughout his adult life.

We likewise know little of the kind of instruction that he had while living in his parents' home at Spasskoe, except that many tutors were employed to educate the boys. In his application for admission to Moscow University of 4 August 1833, Turgenev recorded that he was taught the following subjects in his parents' home: arithmetic, algebra, geometry, physics, history, and geography.[20] But this, presumably, relates to the whole course of his education, including the time after he had left Spasskoe, for, early in 1827, the Turgenevs moved to Moscow. Ivan remained with them, in his parents' house, until August 1829 when he and his brother Nikolai were lodged for a few months in the educational boarding establishment of the Armenian Institute, and his education entrusted to one Inspector Krause. He left the Armenian Institute in November and returned to his parents' home, where his education was continued by visiting tutors, except for about a year during 1830–1 when he was lodged in the educational boarding establishment of Weidenhammer.[21] On 20 September 1833, at the early age of fifteen, he was accepted as a student in the faculty of literature of the University of Moscow.

Five letters, dated in March and April 1831, from Ivan to his uncle Nicholas Nikolaevich Turgenev, a retired officer, have survived. As a boy Ivan had a great affection for his uncle, with whom in later years he was destined to quarrel. At the time when the letters were written he was back in his parents' house in Moscow, having left the Weidenhammer establishment. His father was still abroad, having gone there for reasons of health, and was only due to return in the summer, ostensibly cured. These missives to his uncle, which record the uneventful life of a boy, his enthusiasms, his lessons, and occasional family matters, are written with a vivid directness of description, humour, and whimsicality in which it is not too imaginative to discern the future master of the epistolary art that Turgenev was to become. Here is a sample:

Sunday, 22 March. That day I rose just after six, dressed and went to church. After the service we drove in a hired vehicle to the Sparrow Hills. When we had reached the city limits, we asked permission to walk along the road and were allowed to do so. I had hardly left the vehicle and gone a few steps when with my usual clumsiness, I slipped, and went bang into the mud. I dirtied my fur coat and trousers and tore the latter. Well, there was nothing to be done, I got up and walked on. When we arrived at Anna Ivanovna's I was taken into the study, where my trousers were removed, and, while I was waiting for them to be sewn up, I sat alone in a dressing gown. Alone! It would have been all right if they had put me somewhere upstairs. But I was separated only by a partition from the room in which they were breakfasting. Very annoying and very boring! I had to breakfast there, and, from nothing to do, picked up some book or other which was lying there. What do you think it was? A German prayer-book. I started to read it, when they brought me my trousers. I went out, and we soon drove home, where there was no dinner by the kind favour of the cook.

And so on. The letters also reveal a certain rather affected emotionalism, which may have been the result of the boy's reading of the romantic writers. 'Ah! If only I had wings I would fly to you, and would press you tightly, so tightly, to my bosom, and cover you with kisses.' And more in the same style.[22]

This boyish correspondence also tells us something about the subjects which the two brothers studied with their tutors – German, Russian grammar and literature, history, French, mathematics (with some examples, for the benefit of his uncle, of the problems set), philosophy, geography, rhetoric, and Latin. The standards certainly seem high for a boy of thirteen, and his enthusiasm for his lessons is evident throughout. We are also told something of the various tutors, several of whom Turgenev was to recall in later years with affection and respect.

He was especially devoted to his tutor of Russian, D. N. Dubensky, who was the author of a study, 'remarkable for its time' according to Turgenev in later life, on 'The Tale of Igor's Host'. Dubensky strongly disapproved of Pushkin, and 'brought us up on Karamzin, Zhukovsky and Batiushkov';[23] he referred to Pushkin as 'a snake, gifted with a nightingale's song'.[24] However, in spite of his tutor's disapproval, Turgenev was already well acquainted with the works of Pushkin, which he quotes in these early letters – *Rusalka* and *Boris Godunov*. But he also expresses enthusiasm for the more orthodox and classical poetry of Derzhavin and Zhukovsky. The only novel referred to, and with enormous approbation, is *The Traitor* by Bestuzhev-Marlinsky. Bestuzhev-Marlinsky was active in the

Decembrist rising, and was exiled to Siberia. He influenced the development of Russian literature considerably through the medium of *Polyarnaia zvezda*, a periodical almanac which he edited jointly with the leading Decembrist, Ryleev, from 1823 to 1825. Marlinsky's short novels are on historical subjects and are of a romantic character, belonging in spirit to the eighteenth century. Shortly before this time, while still at Weidenhammer's institution, the boy had been enormously impressed by another historical novel, *Iurii Miloslavsky* by M. N. Zagoskin, published in 1829,[25] which had earned the author the reputation of being the Russian Walter Scott, and was indeed one of the first (if not the first) detailed representations in fiction of the Russian past and national character.

There is one reference of particular interest, where the boy has compared the reviews of two books in the *Moscow Telegraph* and the *Telescope* and is amused to find that the judgements expressed are diametrically opposed. Now these two were the important literary and general periodicals of the day; the *Telegraph* was edited by the historian N. A. Polevoi from 1825 to 1834, the *Telescope* by N. I. Nadezhdin from 1831 to 1836. Both were solid in content, dealing not only with literature, art, and the theatre, but with science, history, economics, and subjects of general interest. Both were of high quality, and if indeed this precocious boy was by now reading them regularly they could have opened up to him a whole world of knowledge. The main bone of contention between the two journals, which is reflected in the difference of opinion which amused the young Turgenev, was that the *Telegraph* was a staunch defender, and the *Telescope* a staunch opponent, of romanticism in literature and in art.

It was during the summer of 1833, while at the dacha of his parents near Moscow, that Turgenev experienced the trauma of adolescent first love, which he later (in 1860) described in detail in the story of that name – the sufferings of an adolescent whom the object of his admiration treats as a child, and the shock of discovering that his father is having an adult affair with the girl, who adores him slavishly. From the recently published autobiographical note or 'Memorial', written by Turgenev in 1852 or 1853 for his own use and not intended for publication, we know that the lady was a Princess Shakhovskaia, but nothing more.[26] It was also during this summer, according to an account said to have been given by Turgenev to the brothers Goncourt in Paris some forty years later, that the fifteen-year-old boy had his first sexual experience. In what are stated to be his own words, Turgenev related that

I was quite young, a virgin, and with the desires that are normal at the age of fifteen. My mother had a chambermaid, good-looking, with a stupid expression – but as you know, there are some stupid faces which acquire some majesty from a stupid expression. It was a damp, gentle rainy day, one of those erotic days that Daudet has described for us. It was getting dark. I was walking in the garden. Suddenly I saw this girl coming straight towards me – I was her master, and she was my serf. She seized me by the back hairs and said 'Come on'. After that there followed a sensation like the one we all know.[27]

Some doubt is thrown on this story, in which the romantic imagination either of the brothers Goncourt, or of Turgenev, may have played a part, by the entry in the autobiographical 'Memorial' under the year 1837, when Turgenev was nearly nineteen – 'Had a woman for the first time, Aprakseia in Petrovskoe' – though many years later he described this first sexual experience as having happened when he was seventeen.[28] But the sexual side of love was to play a small part in Turgenev's life and episodes of the kind which he here describes, though they occurred, were comparatively rare.

CHAPTER TWO

University and Foreign Travel

The year 1834 found Turgenev still in Moscow; he was now at the university, where he remained only until the early summer. This short stay was mainly due to domestic circumstances. Varvara Petrovna had had to go abroad for reasons of health, possibly not unconnected with the birth of her natural daughter in 1833. His father had become anxious about his son Nikolai, who was alone in St. Petersburg, not very happily embarking on his military career, and decided to move his family to the capital. For a short time, until he could join his father in St. Petersburg, Turgenev was lodged with Krause, who had looked after him some years before. He has left a description of his life as a student in Moscow at the house of Krause and his wife in a story entitled 'Andrei Kolosov'. After Turgenev had successfully completed his first-year examinations at Moscow University and become entitled to be entered for the second year courses, he applied for transfer to St. Petersburg University, in order to join his father[1] – whose letters of this period, incidentally, like the earlier letters already referred to, are full of concern for the welfare of the two boys and do not bear out Turgenev's later account of his father's indifference and aloofness.[2]

Moscow University seems to have made little impact on Turgenev. Among his older contemporaries there were Herzen, Stankevich, and Ogarev, but there is no indication anywhere that Turgenev became acquainted with them. Not many years after leaving the university he referred to it in conversation as 'full of nit-wits'.[3] Of lecturers there he recalled only Pogodin the historian, Pavlov, who 'lectured on physics according to Schelling', and Pobedonostsev, 'who nurtured his students on Lomonosov panegyrics'.[4] He also remembered with affection in later years the poet I. P. Kliushnikov, a member of Stankevich's circle, who was one of his tutors in Moscow before he entered the university.

In St. Petersburg he joined the faculty of history and philology. On 30 October his father died – his mother was then still in Italy. We have no record of the impact on him of his father's death. A short time before, while already in St. Petersburg, Turgenev had begun work on his first literary effort, which he completed at the end of the year. This was a dramatic poem, in conscious imitation of Byron's *Manfred*, entitled *Steno*. Of no great poetic merit (and never highly esteemed by Turgenev) it was not published until thirty years after his death.

His first year in St. Petersburg seems to have been uneventful. The 'Memorial' records domestic matters – the return of his mother after a successful operation, meetings with friends in Moscow, where Turgenev and his mother moved for the summer. There is also a first reference for the year 1835 to what was to become Turgenev's predominant passion – shooting game – and an entry which suggests that he was beginning to frequent the theatre.[5] The records for these years in St. Petersburg which he spent with his mother, so far as they are available, do not yet suggest any of the friction which was to mar their relations some years later. No doubt it required Turgenev's experience of his mother's rule in Spasskoe (where the family had not lived since he was a young child) to cause the beginning of their estrangement.

But regular life in Spasskoe during the summer months was not to begin until 1837, after Turgenev had successfully completed his studies at the university. His first attempt at his final examinations, in 1836, was unsuccessful, in the sense that he was only awarded the degree of 'actual student', and not the higher grade of 'candidate'. He accordingly applied for, and was granted, permission to be re-examined in the following year, when he obtained the higher qualification. There is an amusing account by one of his contemporaries of the reason for his failure at the first attempt. At his oral examination in general history he was asked a question on trial by ordeal by Professor I. P. Shulgin. He replied that in addition to ordeal by fire and water, there also existed a form of it in which a calf's tail was smeared with grease, and the subject of the test had to grasp the tail, while the calf was hit with a stick. If he did not lose his grip of the tail, he succeeded in passing. Turgenev had apparently read about this somewhere, but Shulgin obviously thought Turgenev was making a fool of him, and marked him as 'unsatisfactory'.[6] But his undoubted abilities as a student were fully recognized the following year when, in addition to awarding him the degree, the university offered him the opportunity of remaining on in order to pursue an academic career. Turgenev was attracted by the idea, but, as he later recalled, went to the country, became absorbed in shooting, and gave up the thought of writing a dissertation – the first step towards obtaining a university post.[7]

We can trace something of Turgenev's intellectual development during his time at St. Petersburg University. Of the professors who impressed him he mentions, at different times, A. A. Fisher, who lectured on philosophy, F. G. Greffe, the classicist, and P. A. Pletnev, the professor of Russian literature. Pletnev, a poet and critic of repute, who had been one of the first to recognize the significance of Gogol, was a friend of Pushkin, and succeeded him after his death as the editor of *Sovremennik* (the *Contemporary*), the leading literary journal, founded by Pushkin in 1836. Pletnev seems to have been well disposed towards the young Turgenev, who submitted *Steno* for his judgement – and had the dubious satisfaction of hearing his poem mercilessly, though anonymously, criticized by Pletnev in one of his lectures. However, this does not seem to have spoiled relations between them, and Turgenev, in his literary reminiscences, has left a record of a 'Literary Evening at P. A. Pletnev's' in which he recalls Pletnev with respect and affection.[8] This party took place in January 1837. As he entered the flat a young man, in hat and cloak, was taking leave of his host with a laugh and the remark 'Yes, yes! Our ministers are certainly a fine lot!' It was only later that Turgenev learned that the young man was Pushkin, who was killed in a duel a short time after. Turgenev saw him once again a few days before his death, at a concert – and seems to have irritated Pushkin by staring too fixedly.

Turgenev was undoubtedly an admirer of Pushkin by that date, and had been since his boyhood. He continued to venerate the poet for the rest of his life: 'My idol, my teacher, my unattainable model', he called him in 1874.[9] But the rest of his literary taste seems to have been for a time uninformed and conservative. He was a fervent admirer of Bestuzhev-Marlinsky's novels, which had fascinated him as a boy; and wept in ecstasy over the vapid and rather talentless poems of Benediktov, which enjoyed an enormous, if short-lived, popularity.[10] He records the indignation with which he encountered Belinsky's devastating, but well-merited, attack on Benediktov's poetry which appeared in 1836; but likewise how, before long, he began to see the justice of the onslaught.[11]

Turgenev was now beginning to mature in judgement and to associate himself, if only tentatively, with the new, exciting trends in Russian thought and literature – of which Gogol was the leading exponent. In March 1837, in a letter to A. V. Nikitenko, another professor of literature at the university with whom Turgenev was friendly, he refers to a work upon which he had recently embarked in 'a fit of angry resentment at the despotism and monopoly of certain people in our literature'[12] – by whom he clearly meant the conservative literary 'establishment' of the time, Bulgarin, Grech, and Senkovsky. However, if by 1837 Turgenev's intellectual awakening was already beginning, the process was a slow one, and a recent one at that. The first performance of Gogol's *The Government Inspector* on 10 April 1836, was to prove a milestone in the history of the Russian theatre, comparable only to the first performance of Griboedov's *Woe from Wit* in 1831 – though the influence of that play was achieved more through the circulation of the text in manuscript, in nineteenth-century 'samizdat'. Turgenev attended the performance of *The Government Inspector* but, though he laughed a great deal, its real significance left no impression on him, as he records himself.[13] In this respect he differed little from the general public in St. Petersburg, which received the play coldly. Its subsequent success and the recognition of its importance were largely due to Belinsky's praise. Incidentally, while a student at St. Petersburg, Turgenev met Gogol during the short time in 1835 that he was engaged to lecture on history at the university, and left a most amusing account of this supremely unsuccessful episode in Gogol's career.[14]

It is therefore not, perhaps, surprising that Turgenev nowhere mentions the most momentous episode in the intellectual history of 1836 – the publication of P. Chaadaev's 'First Philosophical Letter' in the *Telescope*, of which Turgenev was by now an assiduous reader, particularly of Belinsky's articles which appeared in it regularly after 1835. With its downright dismissal of Russia's past, present, and future as being without any value or hope because of the separation of Russia from the mainstream of European culture, the 'First Philosophical Letter' caused a furore. If the 'Letter', as Chaadaev later agreed, was somewhat exaggerated, the reaction of the Emperor was even more so: the *Telescope* was closed down, the censor dismissed, the editor exiled, and Chaadaev declared insane and ordered to be visited regularly by a doctor. Although Chaadaev was far from being a revolutionary, in the absence of other critical literature the 'First Philosophical Letter' was welcomed by young, liberal-minded Russians – notably Herzen – as a blow for freedom. In view of the fact that Turgenev did not, apparently, react in any way to the 'Letter', statements by him in later life that he was already a 'democrat' or a 'republican' by the time he went to university must be taken with a grain of salt.

Of Turgenev's daily life in St. Petersburg with his mother we have little information. There is a cryptic reference in the 'Memorial' under the year 1837 to 'unhappy evenings' at the house in which they lived, which may refer to early clashes with his mother. On 13 June 1837 mother and son moved to Spasskoe, where Turgenev was to remain until the winter. Except for a short visit with his uncle in 1835, he had not lived at Spasskoe since he was nine, and this summer gave him an opportunity to observe his mother in action as mistress of the estate.

There are several accounts of this extraordinary woman's behaviour. Turgenev himself was to portray her in his stories, including 'Punin and Baburin' and 'Mumu', and in the only fragment which he published from a novel which he planned and wrote in part but never completed, *The Privy Office* (1853).[15] She was despotic, capricious, and severe in her treatment of her vast household of domestics. Although on occasion capable of acts of kindness, her general practice was to maintain a rule of terror under which complete subordination was exacted from her peasants, who were never allowed to forget that they were serfs or to think of themselves as human beings. Turgenev's story 'Mumu', which relates how the mistress of an estate insists, for no discernible reason, on her deaf and dumb giant of a porter being deprived of a small dog which he had befriended, was strictly based on fact, and describes an incident at Spasskoe which Turgenev must have witnessed, or had related to him. Punishment for transgressions, real or imaginary, was severe: most often it took the form of exile to some remote village in her possession, involving separation from family, but floggings were not unknown. The regime which she imposed at Spasskoe was bizarre. Her household was modelled on what she imagined to be the style of crowned heads: her main servants were not only provided with titles, but even with the names of ministers – the head butler, for example, was known as Minister of the Court, and called Benckendorff. No one dared speak to her without her permission. She maintained a private police force for internal discipline, and the female servants were placed under the iron rule of an old woman, described as particularly repulsive.[16] As Turgenev's friend Annenkov, who knew Varvara Petrovna, was later to record, 'She herself, in inventiveness and in far-sighted and calculated malevolence, was far more dangerous than her hated favourites who carried out her commands. No one could equal her in the art of insulting, of humiliating, or of causing unhappiness, while at the same time preserving decency, calm and her own dignity.'[17]

Although it appears that Varvara Petrovna modified some of her excesses when Turgenev was at Spasskoe, the effect of her behaviour on the boy can easily be imagined. All accounts agree that he was kind and gentle, and abhorred violence in all forms from an early age. From childhood he had always felt instinctive sympathy with the domestic serfs as fellow human beings. As his mother's natural daughter, who lived at Spasskoe, recalled, 'All loved him, everyone felt that he was "one of us" and was devoted to him, with faith in his kindness, which, however, he did not dare to display openly in anyone's defence.' Two incidents in which he was directly concerned have been recorded by eye-witnesses, though it is not certain whether they date from this first stay at Spasskoe, or from a year or two later. One concerned the major-domo, Lobanov.* On one occasion Varvara Petrovna lost her temper with him while he was making his daily report to her, took up a riding switch and made to attack him. He seized the whip from her hand and threw it across the room. Blind with rage, Varvara Petrovna summoned her private police, and ordered Lobanov's removal. There followed in the next few days agitated appeals by Turgenev, apparently to no avail, since Lobanov was exiled for a time to a remote village and separated from his wife and children – to Turgenev's evident horror.[19] The second incident arose when Turgenev, hearing that his mother had sold one of her young girl serfs, announced that he would not tolerate the sale of human beings, and hid the girl with a peasant family. The purchaser applied to the police, and the local police chief, with a posse armed with clubs, arrived to demand the girl. He was greeted by Turgenev with a gun, who threatened to shoot. The affair was patched up by Varvara Petrovna's intervention, and her agreement to rescind the sale.[20]

In 1837 or 1838 Varvara Petrovna agreed to let Turgenev go abroad to complete his studies in what was then the mecca of all young Russian intellectuals – Berlin. The intention was that he would spend two years there, and on his return to Russia would take the examination for his master's degree as the first step towards an academic career.[21] At the end of 1837 he left Spasskoe for St. Petersburg, and set sail for Germany on 15 May 1838. His mother, brother, and half-sister saw him off, after a special service held in the Cathedral of

---

* Lobanov, it will be recalled, had taught Turgenev as a small boy his love for Kheraskov's *Rossiada*; he was a man of good education, with an excellent knowledge of French. His wife and his mother also held responsible posts in the Spasskoe household. After Varvara Petrovna's death the family were given their freedom, but continued for a time in salaried service to Turgenev.[18]

Our Lady of Kazan. On the way back his mother fainted. Turgenev's journey was far from uneventful. Within sight of Lübeck the ship in which he was sailing caught fire and the passengers had to be rescued in lifeboats. Turgenev's account of this incident was dictated by him to Pauline Viardot some months before his death, forty-five years after the event, and while it does not attempt to suggest that he behaved with any particular heroism or courage in what must have been a very frightening situation, it does not bear out the rumours of his supposedly outrageously cowardly behaviour which were spread in Russian society, and which caused him considerable pain. He denied them in the public press when they were later repeated in a review of a volume of memoirs by Prince P. V. Dolgorukov.*[22] It was on board ship, incidentally, that Turgenev conceived some kind of romantic attachment for the first wife of the poet Tiutchev, Eleonora, who was returning to Munich with her four daughters, and who died the following year. His correspondence with his mother suggests that he was in love with her, or fancied himself to be so, but that is as much as we know.[23]

The first years abroad were exciting and stimulating for the young Turgenev who, except for the last eight or nine months of 1839 when he returned to Spasskoe, spent his time between 1838 and 1841 travelling in Germany and Italy, and at the university in Berlin. In Italy in the spring of 1840 he visited among other places Rome, Genoa, and Naples. He was overwhelmed by the works of art he saw:

A whole world unknown to me, the world of art, flooded into my soul. Yet how much of what was beautiful and great escaped my gaze, how unformed was my understanding of fine art. But, in spite of this, the sense of form and colour awoke within me, and developed; I began to find delights in art which hitherto had been unknown to me ...

he wrote to Granovsky shortly after his Italian journey. He stayed six or seven weeks in Rome – long enough to fall half in love with the daughter of a Russian couple resident there. He was appalled by the state of the Italian people, 'the feigned sanctity, the systematic enslavement, the absence of real life ... all the movements which have been shaking Northern and Central Europe do not cross the Appenines'. Unlike the Russians, the Italians were finished.[24] He returned to Berlin via Switzerland, Mannheim, Mainz, Frankfurt,

* An unsavoury character who, in 1927, was proved by graphological evidence to have been the author of the scurrilous anonymous letters sent to Pushkin and his friends which led to the duel in which the poet was killed.

Marienbad, and Dresden, where he fell ill. In Frankfurt an incident occurred which was to form the basis, thirty years later, for his short novel, *Spring Torrents*. A young girl of extraordinary beauty suddenly emerged from a tea-room to plead for his help in reviving her brother who had fainted. But, unlike Gemma in *Spring Torrents*, the girl was a Jewess, not an Italian; and, unlike Sanin, Turgenev had the sense to leave Frankfurt the same night without becoming involved with her (see Chapter 14).

Turgenev's foreign travel in the years between 1839 and 1841 was also of great importance to him for the friendships he formed. Most influential among these were those with T. N. Granovsky and N. V. Stankevich, who were both about five years his senior. Granovsky was already a professor of history at Moscow University, and was shortly to win wide fame with his public lectures. He was indeed one of the most remarkable minds in Russia in the first half of the nineteenth century. No very intimate friendship seems to have developed between the two in Germany, any more than it had in St. Petersburg. Granovsky is said to have dismissed Turgenev as a lightweight and as lacking in character, which did not diminish the younger man's deep veneration for him which lasted until Granovsky's death in 1855. Turgenev then wrote of him, recalling Berlin days, 'We were never close. Truth to tell I did not at that time merit his close friendship.'[25]

Stankevich, who exercised a quite extraordinary influence on the members of his 'circle' in Moscow through his exposition of German philosophy, came to Berlin at the end of 1838 and was introduced to Turgenev by Granovsky. His feelings for Turgenev were warmer than those of Granovsky, especially during the time they spent together in Rome. In his letters, Stankevich often referred to the younger man with what appear to be condescension and affection rather than respect: 'There is nothing remarkable about his gifts, but he does not entirely lack them. He is kind, and honourable ...'[26] Indeed, the general impression that the young Turgenev created around this time was of a somewhat vain dandy, amusing, a marvellous raconteur, brilliant, but of little real substance intellectually or otherwise. Turgenev's loving admiration for the older man, with whom he spent much of his time in Italy, in Rome and elsewhere, was never in doubt, and Stankevich's death from consumption in 1840 at the age of twenty-seven was a shattering blow to him as it was to countless others. 'Sometimes it seems to me that with his death our last link with Heaven has been severed', Bakunin wrote to some friends.[27] Turgenev was to write a remarkable sketch of Stankevich

in 1856, which was, however, not published until 1899. Apart from
the light it sheds on Stankevich, this obituary also allows one to
glimpse something of the intellectual discipline which he exacted
from the young Turgenev, as he did from all those contemporaries
who formed his 'circle'. Once, when they were in the catacombs
in Rome and were passing the niches in which are preserved the relics
of Christian worship in the first centuries of Christianity, Turgenev
exclaimed that they were the blind instruments of Providence. Stankevich remarked fairly severely that there were no such things as
'blind instruments' in history, or indeed anywhere else.[28] In a letter
to his friends Bakunin and Efremov, shortly after Stankevich's death,
Turgenev wrote rhetorically: 'Stankevich! It is to you that I owe
my rebirth. You stretched out your hand to me and pointed out the
goal ...'[29] There was probably a good deal of sincerity in this
remark, for Turgenev was beginning to shed some of the frivolity
which so much disturbed his friends. He also paid a tribute to Stankevich in his first novel, *Rudin*, in the character of Pokorsky.

Among other friends who gathered at the Berlin flat of a Russian
couple called Frolov – he was a minor writer, a translator of von
Humboldt, while his wife seems to have been a lady of very remarkable intellect – were Karl Werder and Bettina von Arnim, with both
of whom Turgenev was on close terms. Werder was professor of
philosophy at the university, an inspired exponent of Hegel, who
stimulated Hegelian enthusiasm in dozens of young Russian intellectuals who came to Berlin in the forties to drink at the pure fountain
of all wisdom. Werder was enormously popular – the publicist M.
N. Katkov has described in detail a special evening of celebration
arranged for Werder by his students early in 1841 – and is recorded
as having expressed a high opinion of Turgenev's abilities.[30] Bettina
von Arnim, then in her mid-fifties, was idolized by most young Russian intellectuals, who were at the time the willing victims of German
romanticism. She had conducted a juvenile love affair with the great
Goethe, and had recorded this with quite nauseating sentimentality
in a work which appeared in 1835 entitled *Goethes Briefwechsel mit
einem Kind (Goethe's Correspondence with a Child)*. This, along with
the works of Goethe and Schiller, and of such authors as Novalis,
Chamisso, and Hoffmann, formed at that date the staple intellectual
pabulum of every educated young Russian. Turgenev was no exception and possessed a copy of the famous book. He had many meetings
with Bettina, no doubt devoted to lengthy discussions on the true
meaning of nature, beauty, love, and the like. The draft of a long
letter from Turgenev to her has survived. It is full of discourse on

these noble subjects—and is quite fatuous. Perhaps he never sent it.[31] His enthusiasm for Bettina (whom Madame Frolova treated with ill-disguised contempt) was enhanced by the fact that at this time he was studying intensively the works of Goethe—indeed his first serious publication a few years later was to be a critical essay inspired by a Russian translation of *Faust*. Another Berlin friend was G. H. Lewes, the future biographer of Goethe, and companion of George Eliot.[32]

The closest friendship which Turgenev formed in Berlin was with Michael Bakunin, who was four years his senior. The eldest of a large family of brothers and sisters, Michael was for a time for Turgenev an object of veneration comparable only to Stankevich.

On the title page of my [Hegel's] Encyclopaedia there is inscribed: 'Stankevich died on 21 June 1840'; and below that 'I got to know Bakunin on 20 July 1840'. Out of all my former life I do not wish to retain any other memories. I have only had two friends—and the first was called Michel. He died ... but you will live.[33]

For some months Bakunin and Turgenev shared a flat and spent their time studying Hegel, often listening to Beethoven in the evenings. Annenkov, who had not yet met Turgenev, recalls noticing one evening in a Berlin café renowned for its enormous stock of German and foreign newspapers, two tall Russians, 'with remarkably handsome and expressive faces'. These were Turgenev and Bakunin, 'who were at that time inseparable.'[34]

The Bakunins were a united and affectionate family. Much of their correspondence has been preserved and published—it is romantic, highly emotional, and egocentric. Michael's letters in particular are affectionate and full of concern for the details of family life and emotions, to a degree which seems scarcely credible in a more robust and matter-of-fact age. When Turgenev met Michael the Bakunin family was much dispersed. His brothers were engaged on study or military service in Moscow and elsewhere. Of the sisters one, Liubov, had died young in 1838 – Stankevich had been in love with her. The second sister, Varvara, was married but separated from her husband (Michael, who always interfered in his sisters' lives, had played a part in the separation) and was living in Berlin, and Turgenev and Michael spent many of their evenings with her either alone, or in the company of Werder, Bettina von Arnim, and others. Alexandra and Tatiana, who was three years older than Turgenev, were living with their parents at Priamukhino, the family estate, which a few years earlier had been a centre of attraction for the leading intellectuals

of the day; along with Stankevich and others, it had drawn to
it Belinsky and V. P. Botkin, who had been in love with Alexandra. Tatiana was Michael's favourite sister: his letters to her reveal
an emotional, almost erotic, attachment, which at one time caused
him to have fits of jealousy, directed against her admirers. Turgenev,
who on his return to Russia was to be absorbed into the Bakunin
family and much implicated in its affairs, would shortly embark on
a serious romantic attachment with her. Michael at this date had not
yet adopted the political faith which was to become one of the causes
of estrangement between him and Turgenev. But Turgenev always
retained affection (if not respect) for the Bakunin whom he had
known in Berlin, and later portrayed him sympathetically, if critically, in the character of Rudin.

Turgenev's studies at the university were mainly concentrated on
history, classics, and philosophy, especially Hegel. In later years he
listed as teachers who influenced him in Berlin other than Werder,
the classicists Zumpt and Böck, and the historian Ranke.[35] The
heavily annotated works of Hegel in Turgenev's library leave no
doubt that he studied them seriously.[36] The leading Soviet scholar
on the young Turgenev, Gorbacheva, has concluded that he was at
this time under the influence of Werder and so-called 'right' Hege-
lianism, whose followers regarded Hegel's philosophy as compatible
with belief in the existence of God, and indeed as strengthening belief
in God. Her main evidence for this view is an essay on 'Pantheism'
which Turgenev wrote on 5 May 1842 as part of his examination
for the degree of Master in St. Petersburg University. It is true that
this essay reflects a 'right' Hegelian interpretation and reproves and
rejects Feuerbach for whom, of course, God and religion were pro-
jections of man's insecurity and misery:[37] the difficulty in accepting
this picture of Turgenev at this time as a man of orthodox religious
disposition is that there is no evidence at all that he ever went to
church while abroad, although he did so regularly while staying with
his mother; that there is ample evidence in his letters, especially from
Italy, of his distaste for the church; and that a recently discovered
letter to Granovsky of 30 May 1840 from Berlin refers to Feuerbach's
Philosophy and Christianity in terms of the highest praise.[38] It may
be that the essay did not represent Turgenev's views, but was written
with the authorities in mind – and the need to express orthodox views
if he was to succeed in his examination. 'Pantheism' around this time
was identified in official Russian circles with 'communism' and
'socialism' and regarded as a most dangerous doctrine: in the forties,
when the journal *Otechestvennya zapiski* (*Annals of the Fatherland*) was

subjected to attack and denunciation by the literary 'establishment' as represented by Bulgarin and Grech, one of the charges made against it was the propagation of 'communism, socialism, and pantheism'.[39] This judgement on the essay on 'Pantheism' is further confirmed by the fact that a few years later, in 1847, in his letters to Pauline Viardot, Turgenev expresses himself in the language of romantic atheism. For example, referring to Calderón's play *La Devoción de la Cruz*, on 10 December 1847, he says: '... I prefer Prometheus, or Satan, who typifies the revolt of the individual. Atom as I am, I am my own master, I want the truth, not salvation, and I look for it from my intellect, and not as an effect of grace.'[40] It is true that in 1843 Turgenev wrote a poem entitled 'When I pray', which refers to his fervent prayers to 'my living God'[41] – but it is unlikely that this, like some other occasional outbursts of religious fervour, represented a consistent state of mind.

During these years signs appeared of the ill health which was to pursue Turgenev all his life – though it is not easy to decide whether the illnesses were always as serious as Turgenev, who had a tendency towards hypochondria, was inclined to make out. But the 'Memorial' has several references to diseases – inflammation of the bladder at the end of 1838, and some unspecified, 'terrible' affliction in 1840 in Dresden, which resulted in his spending over a month there, instead of the five days he had intended. The illness did not prevent him from writing a series of most entertaining and frivolous letters to his friends. His correspondence throws little light on the subject of health: in one letter from Dresden, for example, in September 1840, there is only a reference to a suggestion by his doctor that Turgenev had caught a cold and another similar reference to a doctor's comforting opinion. But our information is obviously incomplete for these early years, and complacent doctors are not, presumably, the monopoly of the twentieth century. As the 'Memorial' shows, Turgenev certainly took these two illnesses very seriously.

The 'Memorial' records that he arrived in St. Petersburg on 14 May 1839. This is certainly wrong, because we know from his correspondence that on 20 June he was still in Berlin, where news of the fire which had destroyed the greater part of the house at Spasskoe had reached him. He also seems to have been involved in some claim over the birth of a child which cost him 200 thalers – presumably someone other than a serf girl, who would have had no right to make a claim. Be that as it may, the summer and autumn of 1839 were spent at Spasskoe, where his half-sister was now growing up.

Varvara Nikolaevna Bogdanovich-Lutovinova, born in 1833, was brought up by Varvara Petrovna, ostensibly as her adopted daughter, who scarcely concealed the fact that the child was her natural daughter: the evidence suggests that the father was Dr. A. E. Bers, the father of the wife of Leo Tolstoy.[42] We know nothing of the reaction of Turgenev's father, who did not die until 1834. If Turgenev knew of little Varvara's true origin, as must be presumed, he never referred to it. His rare contacts with her after she had grown up remained formal and remote and only became friendly late in life: there was a serious conflict over some money question after Varvara Petrovna's death in 1850, which led to estrangement. But the easy and happy relations with the young Turgenev described by Varvara Bogdanovich-Lutovinova in her memoirs are fully borne out by a poem which he dedicated to her in 1843, which breathes deep affection and sympathy.[43]

As for Ivan and his mother, whatever cause for friction there may have been between them, there is nothing to suggest that during the summer of 1839 in Spasskoe he was anything other than the devoted and considerate son described by little Varvara in her memoirs. For the period of Turgenev's stay in Germany, between 1839 and 1842, we possess the evidence of numerous letters written by his mother to him: his infrequent letters to her have not survived, but we can guess at some of their content from references and quotations in hers. There are in all 175 letters for the period 1838–44, enough to fill a volume, because Varvara Petrovna was anything but laconic. They have not been published, but have been extensively drawn on for the purposes of two long analytical articles.[44] The correspondence is all in French – Varvara Petrovna used Russian only for speaking to her serfs. The mother writes to 'Jean' in the familiar *tu*, he replies in the respectful form, *vous*. She makes no attempt to hide the fact that he is the favourite of her two sons. The letters are a strange mixture, reflecting the unique amalgam of qualities and defects which Varvara Petrovna exemplified. In the words of a scholar who has made an intensive study of her,

Love of power, egoism, unrestrained malice, sometimes towards persons most devoted to her, a desire to humiliate, to insult, not to forget an offence – on the one hand; and on the other, impulses of generosity, of kindness, of passionate devotion, tenderness, an ability to forgive – were all mingled in her in a bizarre fashion.[45]

The impression left by the correspondence is of a deeply unhappy woman, with an almost morbid love for her sons (and particularly for her favourite Ivan) and a longing for this love to be returned;

yet at the same time driven by impulses which she cannot control to do everything to alienate them. The letters are, in the main, a long catalogue of complaints and resentment: that he does not write frequently enough, that he does not provide details of his illnesses, that he makes too many requests for money. So far as money was concerned, her main ground for displeasure was not the amounts, which she did not grudge, but the fact that her son never provided any accounts to show how his allowance had been spent. Since Turgenev was always extravagant and improvident with his money, this demand was not unreasonable. Madame Turgenev may certainly also have had good cause for complaint about the infrequency of his letters. There was one occasion, for example, in 1841, when she was driven by anxiety, after a silence of over two months, to send over to the Bakunin sisters and to Granovsky in an endeavour to extract some news of Turgenev.[46] Some of the complaints are less justified – that he does not provide enough detail about his new friends or that he sends her bad verses. A little self-restraint would surely have enabled her to realize that her son, plunged into the excitement of a new life abroad, would find it irksome to write the kind of detailed letters she expected; and would have shown more consideration for a young man's literary vanity. It must also have been very wounding for Turgenev to discover that his mother had believed all the rumours which were circulating about his supposed cowardice on the occasion of the fire at sea, and was full of reproof. At the same time, she was aware of her own shortcomings, and wrote, rather pathetically: 'My life depends on you. ... I am sometimes afraid that I will drive you to fury with my reproaches and injunctions. But – you must accept my justification. All my life I have had nothing but enemies, people who envied me. I had to pay dearly for all the blessings which the Creator bestowed on me ...' Yet for all the nagging, glimpses of mutual affection and intimacy are occasionally revealed – where he apparently disclosed to her his infatuation for Madame Tiutcheva, and she counselled him to read a novel by Alphonse Karr, '*Une femme de 40 ans*'; or his occasional concern for her loneliness; or her unrestrained delight when at the end of October 1840 he wrote to tell her that he had decided to become a professor at Moscow University. The letters certainly reveal some friction between them. But there is no suggestion as yet of any break or quarrel.

CHAPTER THREE

Return to Russia

On 2 June 1841 Turgenev sailed from Lübeck to St. Petersburg. He was preceded by a letter from Michael Bakunin addressed collectively to all his brothers and sisters in which he wrote of Turgenev in the most enthusiastic and affectionate terms: 'There were no secrets between us; and so you see, my friends, he cannot be a stranger to you. He will tell you a great deal about us. . . . And he is a masterly story-teller . . .'[1] According to Michael, Turgenev intended to spend some time in Priamukhino, but in fact he went first to join his mother in Moscow. Shortly afterwards they left together for Spasskoe, where Turgenev was to stay until the middle of October.

As usual he spent much of his time on shooting expeditions in the neighbouring countryside, lasting several days. He was acquiring his knowledge of peasant life and of the Russian landscape which was to be so well reflected a few years later in *Sketches from a Sportsman's Notebook*. He records in the 'Memorial' the name of his favourite dog at the time (Napol the Second: Napol the First was now past it), as well as the names of two serfs – Porfirii Kudriashev and Afanasii, with whom he went shooting. Porfirii Kudriashev was a young serf who had accompanied Turgenev on his travels and they were close friends. (He was, incidentally, Turgenev's half-brother – an illegitimate son of his father, Sergei Nikolaevich.) An educated man, who spoke excellent German, Porfirii had received some medical training – partly in Berlin, where he accompanied Turgenev – and subsequently acted as Varvara Petrovna's personal house 'physician'. He was freed after her death, and remained for many years in service at Spasskoe. He later left the estate, and fell on evil days. In 1862 Turgenev was successful in arranging settled employment for him as an excise officer, but by 1869 he was once again living in Spasskoe, and drinking heavily. Afanasii Timofeevich Alifanov (with whose daughter Turgenev had some kind of an affair)[2] was a great expert on game, 'a sportsman from head to toe', according to Turgenev. He was a serf belonging to a neighbour, and figures as 'Ermolai' in the *Sketches*. When he could afford it, Turgenev bought him, and gave him his freedom. He stayed on in Spasskoe and, in his old age, having taken to the bottle, was given a small pension. He died in 1872.

Turgenev's warm relations with the peasant serfs must certainly have been in marked contrast to his mother's inhuman severity. But he was not immune from the common practice of serf-owners of looking to serf girls for the satisfaction of his sexual desires. At least one instance has been referred to from the 'Memorial' entry for 1837, and there had probably been others. This summer of 1841 an affair with a serf girl, Avdotia Ermolaevna Ivanova, was to have consequences. As he wrote later to Madame Viardot, 'I was young ... it was nine years ago ... I was bored in the country, I noticed a fairly pretty sewing maid whom my mother had taken into service, I spoke a couple of words to her, she came to visit me, I paid, I left – there is the whole story for you.'[3] When Avdotia became pregnant, Varvara Petrovna was, as could be expected, furious, but the girl seems to have escaped anything worse than exile to Moscow. (According to one account she was whipped 'a little' first.) For the time being Turgenev seems not to have concerned himself about the matter, and some years were to pass before he was to become aware of and to take an interest in the daughter whom Avdotia bore him on 26 April 1842,[4] though, as the 'Memorial' shows, he knew of the pregnancy. But he never denied the paternity, and looked after Avdotia financially. She called on Turgenev whenever he visited Moscow, until her death in 1875.

In the middle of September he joined his mother, who was by then back in Moscow. A few weeks later, on 10 October, the long-delayed visit to Priamukhino took place. It lasted six days, long enough for the impressionable Tatiana to fall desperately in love with him. It was the beginning of a romance which was to go on for some six months. We can follow the course of this sad little love affair from Tatiana's letters to Turgenev and to her brothers, from the one letter from him to her which has been preserved and from several poems which he wrote to her.[5] For the time being, Turgenev, like so many before him, fell in love with the whole remarkable Priamukhino family. Somewhat later, when the excitement of the new friendship had worn off and been absorbed by other interests, his judgement was perhaps less clouded. As Belinsky recorded (in April 1843),

This is what Turgenev says about the Bakunins, both brothers and sisters, with the sole exception of Michael: 'They are all destined to be nothing but unhappy. Their natures are fiery and impulsive, they lack any deep religious feeling, and are therefore always inclined to become half reconciled, both to themselves and with reality, on the basis of some kind of a little moral sentiment or principle. They haven't the strength to look the Devil straight in the eye.'[6]

Tatiana was twenty-six when Turgenev met her. Her portrait suggests an intelligent and interesting, rather than beautiful young woman; her letters reveal a deeply introspective, emotional and, above all, serious nature. Some three years before, when he had been in love with the whole family, Belinsky had written of Tatiana's eyes, that they were 'dark blue and deep as the sea, her look – sudden, like lightning, long as eternity, to use Gogol's expression, her face meek and saintly, on which it seemed as if the traces of passionate prayer still lingered. . . .'[7] Tatiana fell in love with Turgenev madly, unrestrainedly, unreservedly. (A few years later, however, when she had completely recovered from her infatuation, she wrote to her brother Paul that her feeling for Turgenev had never been 'true love', but only the 'fantasy of a heated imagination'.[8]) Turgenev was for a time, or fancied himself to be, in love, but it was an emotion that did not last. The love affair between the two was not only short-lived, but interrupted; a few days in Priamukhino, a few days at the end of 1841 in Torzhok (another Bakunin estate) and thereafter, during the first few months of 1842, in Moscow, where Tatiana had been sent by her parents who were disturbed by her declining health – apparently caused by Turgenev's failure to respond to her exaggerated declarations of love.

Tatiana's letters are an amalgam of romantic, passionate love and sheer bewilderment, of veneration tinged with despair. She accepts in the end that Turgenev cannot return her feelings, rationalizing the situation with the wisdom of several years' seniority: 'You are still a child. You have not yet grown up sufficiently to face the serious and terrifying things in life, the things of major significance.' Or again:

As yet you cannot give, you are like a child in whom are concealed many embryonic qualities, both good and bad, but neither the ones nor the others are as yet developed – therefore one can only hope or fear. But I do not wish to fear for you. No! You will not destroy any one of the gifts with which you are endowed. All these riches will develop within you, all the beauty of a divine life, and you will be a man – but when?

On Turgenev this experience evidently made a deep impression because the theme of a woman, giving and passionate, on the one hand, and a man, weak and indecisive and missing an opportunity for happiness which he later regrets, on the other, recurs in many forms in his fiction. 'Give me your hand, and, if you can, forget all that was difficult, all that was half-finished in the past. My whole soul overflows with deep sorrow, and it is hateful and terrible for me to look back. . . .', he wrote to her in his farewell letter on 20 March 1842. 'Listen – I swear by the name of God . . . I never loved any woman more than you – even though I did not love you fully and securely. . . .'[9] In addition to the farewell letter there was also a farewell poem, written some months later, at the end of May 1842, but not published until 1925. It reads like a last appeal to try to renew the love affair, and provides further evidence of the ambivalent state of Turgenev's emotions.[10]

For some time to come, as his early writings show, Turgenev remained absorbed with the question of how to end a love affair where one partner (always the man, incidentally) has ceased to be as fully in love as the other person. It is the theme of his long poem *Andrei*, published in 1846, where the generous and unselfish acceptance of the situation by the woman recalls Tatiana's behaviour, and the verses actually echo some of her letters.[11] The argument that it is the moral duty of the lover, when he feels his passion cooling, ruthlessly to break off all relations (which Turgenev, of course, did not have the courage to do) is the theme of the first short story which he published, in 1844, 'Andrei Kolosov'.[12]

It is probable that an anonymous article in *Annals of the Fatherland*, No. 2 for 1843, based on recently published letters of Goethe to Countess Stolberg, was written by Turgenev, who was by then a regular contributor to this journal. Stylistic evidence supports the supposition that he was the author, and we know that Turgenev had been reading these letters before 3 April 1842 when he forwarded copies of two of them to Aleksei and Alexander Bakunin. His enthusiasm for Goethe around this time is well established. If Turgenev was the author of this article, Goethe's platonic and rather anaemic correspondence with a woman whom he had never met may have suggested some parallel with Turgenev's less than full-blooded relations with Tatiana. The editors of Turgenev's correspondence have noted some similarities of expression between his letters to Tatiana and these letters of Goethe, but do not suggest that the essay was his work.[13] This was first conjectured by N. L. Brodskii, the editor of Tatiana's letters to Turgenev.

The winter of 1841–2, which Turgenev spent in Moscow, was a time of new impressions and friendships. He was on close terms with the Bakunin brothers at this time; like Michael, they took Turgenev warmly to their hearts. In Michael Bakunin's correspondence with Turgenev there are many references to money matters, and to Michael's disastrous financial situation, in which Turgenev's help was invoked. Though he did provide a sum of 1,000 roubles at one stage, he seems to have been pretty lavish with promises which he had little prospect of fulfilling, including one to discharge debts to the sum of 8,000 roubles over two years. On 21 July 1843 he forwarded 2,000 roubles to Bakunin and his creditors, but we do not know whether he ever paid the remaining 6,000.[14] Turgenev's own financial position was not good: Varvara Petrovna, who had supported him generously enough while he was on his foreign tour, seems to have become very reluctant to do so once he was back in Russia, and the testimony of his friend Annenkov suggests that he was at times literally penniless, subsisting on loans and editors' advances in anticipation of his future inheritance from his mother.[15] There is ample evidence in Turgenev's own correspondence of his frequent dependence on advances from his editors, until his mother's death in 1850.

According to his entry in the 'Memorial' he became a 'lion' in Moscow that winter – a term which, in the slang language of the time, denoted a fashionable dandy with a certain air of 'demonic' mystery.[16] Among the houses we know he visited was that of Granovsky, where Botkin and M. S. Shchepkin – with both of whom Turgenev was to remain friendly thereafter – were frequent guests. He was also a welcome visitor in the house of M. F. Orlov (once a close associate of the Decembrists), where the leading intellectuals of Moscow gathered; it was here that he met Chaadaev.[17]

Among those he mentioned as friends at this period are the future leading Slavophiles, Iurii Samarin and Konstantin Aksakov. These, as well as Khomiakov, he met at the house of A. P. Elagina, who was the mother of the Kireevsky brothers (also Slavophiles), who maintained a salon in Moscow, at which on two occasions, as he later recalled, he met Gogol.[18] Turgenev's reception by the Slavophiles, according to Annenkov, was not very warm. They suspected him from the first of rabid 'Westernism', and did what they could to spite him. 'A whole collection of vapid anecdotes about his statements, expressions and remarks was carefully assembled by his enemies and put into circulation with appropriate distortions and additions.'[19] On the other hand, there is no doubt that at this time Turgenev was anxious to impress, in the knowledge that he was a superb talker, and above all to appear original. It was not, therefore, to be wondered at if he made enemies and prompted malicious outbursts. 'He considered at that time that the most shameful condition which could beset any mortal was that of resembling others.'[20] To those who knew him only slightly he gave the impression of being an empty dandy. 'A Khlestakov [Gogol's fake government inspector], educated, clever, superficial, with a desire to express himself and *fatuité sans bornes*' was Herzen's verdict on him when they met in 1844.[21]

But Stankevich had some years before warned his friends that Turgenev should not be judged by first appearances.[22] As yet he had not made any significant mark as a writer, and it was in his writings, in which sincerity always prevailed, that the real man was to be revealed, rather than in his conversational exhibitionism. For a time Turgenev was to return the compliment to the Slavophiles, especially under the influence of Belinsky whom he was to meet in 1843; Belinsky encouraged his 'Westernism' and was delighted with his vicious verbal attacks on Konstantin Aksakov, the most exaggerated of the Slavophiles.[23] Turgenev's poem 'The Landlord', published in 1845, contained a quite disgraceful caricature of what was plainly meant to be Aksakov, of which he was in later years thoroughly ashamed, and ensured its excision in subsequent editions of the poem.[24]

At this point, Turgenev seems to have turned his thoughts to the possibility of a university career. The first step towards a professorship was admission by the university to the master's written and oral examinations. If the examinations were successful, this was followed by the submission of a dissertation which, if approved, would normally lead to an appointment to a chair. Turgenev made an attempt to persuade the Moscow University authorities to accept him for the master's examination in philosophy. This was refused, ostensibly because the chair of philosophy had been vacant for fifteen years and there was no one to examine him. A conversation with Count Stroganov, who had ministerial responsibility for Moscow University, convinced him that the Moscow chair was unattainable.[25] He therefore transferred his attentions to St. Petersburg, where he was accepted for the master's examination and completed it in May 1842. In addition to the essay on 'Pantheism', he was examined with success in Greek and Latin literature and antiquities.[26] The next step towards a chair in St. Petersburg was now therefore the dissertation. But, as Turgenev later recalled, he had by then become absorbed in writing fiction and abandoned all thoughts of an academic career.

Turgenev spent the summer of 1842 in Spasskoe. His stay there included a visit to neighbouring Shashkino where he went shooting with the owner of the estate, Beer. The Beers were close friends of the Bakunins. Tatiana was staying in Shashkino, and in the 'Memorial' Turgenev records meeting her there. This was evidently the occasion when the attempt to renew the affair, hinted at in the poem he wrote to her, was made. The poem was sent to her a few days before her arrival at Shashkino, on 4 June.[27]

At the beginning of July he left the country for St. Petersburg and shortly afterwards embarked on a second journey to Germany.[28] It is not clear why he went, but it may well have been for reasons of health, since Turgenev first went to Marienbad, a well-known watering resort which he had visited for his health in September 1840.[29] From Marienbad he went on to Dresden, presumably to see his doctor, Dr. Hedenus. There he met Michael Bakunin and his brother Paul, who was visiting. Turgenev and Paul left together for Russia on 22 October, but their journey was interrupted in Berlin, where Turgenev caught a bad chill.

The first half of December found Turgenev in St. Petersburg, where he now intended to settle permanently.[30] From a letter to Paul Bakunin (in which, incidentally, he sends greetings to Tatiana) we learn that he had made a new acquaintance, L. P. Yazykova, a friend of Michael Bakunin who was, like Turgenev, involved in raising money to rescue the future anarchist from his creditors. Yazykova was a sister of the Decembrist V. P. Ivashev and a future supporter of Bakunin's revolutionary activities. In spite of enthusiastic references to Yazykova in the letter, there is no evidence to suggest that the friendship was enduring or influential. The 'Memorial' also refers to 'Herwegh' – presumably Georg Herwegh the German poet and revolutionary. Turgenev was to meet him frequently in Paris in 1848, and had got to know him on his second visit to Germany. The fact that he recorded these two names in the 'Memorial' suggests that revolutionary friends were of some particular significance to Turgenev and may reflect his preoccupations around this time.

It was evidently in the course of this second German visit, possibly influenced by Bakunin, that Turgenev conceived the idea of entering government service. His choice of the Ministry of the Interior was, no doubt, dictated by the fact that it was at the time concerned with the peasant question and with projects of reform. The Minister, L. A. Perovsky, had been close to Decembrist circles in his youth and was reputed to be an energetic and outspoken critic of serfdom. The Special Office, to which Turgenev was to become attached, was headed by V. I. Dal, the distinguished lexicographer, who was then engaged in compiling materials for new legislation on domestic serfs. Although Turgenev in a brief 'Autobiography', written in 1875, states that he entered the Ministry in 1842, there is no doubt that the official order of the Minister of the Interior assigning Turgenev to the Special Office was dated 8 June 1843.[31] Government records also show that the Minister of the Interior inquired of the Minister of Education on 7 February 1843 whether Turgenev was qualified to join his Ministry, and received an answer on 19 February which implied that the appointment had better be postponed until he had successfully defended his dissertation at St. Petersburg University.[32] Yet a note of his entitled 'Some Remarks on the Russian Economy and the Russian Peasant', dated 23–25 December 1842, has been preserved and is endorsed by its owner, a colleague of Turgenev's in the Ministry, as having been written while Turgenev was engaged in the service of the Special Office; and it was indeed the case that such essays were demanded of new entrants to the Ministry as a form of examination of their capabilities.[33] The explanation may be that Turgenev was unofficially attached to, or on probation in, the Ministry for some six months before the official posting took place. Yet the 'Memorial' records quite explicitly for the beginning of the year, 'Desire to enter the public service. It does not succeed', and refers to entry into service around the middle of the year. So the note may, after all, have been connected only with an unsuccessful effort to enter the Ministry at the beginning of 1843.[34]

The note, which extends to some fourteen printed pages, is a remarkably perceptive analysis of serfdom, indicating that this young man of twenty-four had already studied the subject and thought deeply about it. Of his early hatred of serfdom he was to write in 1868, when explaining his decision to go to Germany as a young man: 'That way of life, those surroundings ... to which I belonged ... the sphere of landlords and serfs ... did not represent anything that could detain me. On the contrary, nearly everything that I saw roused in me feelings of shame and indignation – of revulsion in fact.' So, he relates, he plunged headlong into the German sea:

When at length I came to the surface of the waves I found myself a 'Westerner' in spite of myself, and have always stayed one. It would never enter my head to condemn those of my contemporaries who achieved the kind of freedom of consciousness which I sought to achieve by a less negative path ... I only wish to announce that I saw no other way open to me.

I could not breathe the same air, stay in the proximity of something which I hated: for that, probably, I lacked the endurance and the character. It was necessary for me to put a distance between me and my enemy in order to attack this enemy the more vigorously from afar. In my eyes this enemy had a definite image, had a well-known name: it was serfdom.

And he goes on to say that he would never have written the *Sketches from a Sportsman's Notebook* (which were almost all written in France) if he had not left Russia.[35] However, some doubt is thrown on his claim that he was determined to fight serfdom as early as the Berlin years of 1839–40 by the recollection of a German Berlin University friend: 'In all our conversations he never departed from the purely historical soil, and I never heard him express ardent hopes or wishes on the subject of the abolition of serfdom, as many now assert.'[36]

Plainly a note written to test his abilities as a civil servant was not the place for a young candidate to produce a revolutionary tract demanding the abolition of serfdom. What Turgenev tactfully tried to do was to lay stress on the minor reforms to the condition of the serfs which had emerged in the reign of Nicholas I, and to put the blame for the defects of serfdom squarely on the landlords.

In discussing the defects of our economy, I deliberately did not mention the condition of serfdom of our agricultural labourers. Their so-called slavery has been the subject of many fairly empty-sounding pontifications which often reveal complete ignorance of the real needs of Russia. We wish for legality and firmness in relations between landlords and peasants: legality excludes the arbitrary whim of the serf-owner, and therefore also excludes what is called slavery. Slavery is an un-Christian notion and therefore cannot exist and never has existed in a Christian state. . . .

Since the whole note is devoted to showing the *absence* of that legality which is said to be inconsistent with slavery, this remark must have been intended as irony.

Turgenev lists seven 'inconveniences' of Russian agriculture. These are first, the absence of certainty and legal principle in ownership of land: the determination of the boundaries of estates (which was then proceeding) would be the first step towards encouraging landowners to undertake improvements. Second, the absence of legality in the relations of landlords to peasants. Third, the very unsatisfactory state of agricultural science. Fourth, the lack of equilibrium between agriculture and industry and the need for grain storage in years of good harvest in order to prevent famine in bad ones. Fifth, the very weak sense of citizenship or of a sense of law among the peasants: the peasant is cunning as a fox is cunning, but this is unworthy of a citizen. And, says Turgenev, it is remarkable that a peasant who will go to extremes to cheat a landlord whom he does not trust, becomes 'a rational, understanding and efficient human being under the guidance of a landlord who cares for his welfare'. Turgenev therefore welcomes the recent legislation on the education of village youth. Sixth, the antiquated institutions inherited from the former patriarchal way of life. And seventh, 'the insufficiency of a spirit of social duty among the landed nobility' – a pregnant sentence, which is not expanded. But elsewhere in the note there is further criticism of the landed gentry – for example, of landowners who neglect their estates, and of patriarchal attitudes in the peasant communes which ought to be replaced by courts of law.[37]

It was not necessarily hypocritical to lay the emphasis on the need for the reform of the institution of serfdom rather than its abolition. Since the Decembrist fiasco of 1825 the call for the abolition of serfdom had become submerged in a wave of official reaction which regarded even discussion of the subject as almost equivalent to violent revolution. Besides, it was widely recognized, even by the more liberal-minded, that abolition of serfdom would not of itself solve Russia's problems (as indeed proved to be the case after 1861) and that it raised new problems no less insoluble than the old. Turgenev undoubtedly felt the revulsion against serfdom that was to prompt Herzen and Ogarev a decade later to raise the cry for 'Land and Liberty' from London. He may have genuinely felt at the time that more was to be hoped for from enlightened reform than from revolutionary abolition. There were good landlords as well as bad: if the bad could be made good by legislation and education the main evils of serfdom could be avoided. By 1845, however, he seems to have become convinced of the need for serfdom to be abolished (see Chapter 4).

Turgenev was not happy in government service and, according to his own statement, not very efficient. On 29 July 1843 he was confirmed in the rank of 'Collegiate Secretary' with seniority from the date of the beginning of actual service in the Ministry, but his period of government service was of short duration.[38] His break with official life was influenced by his progress as a writer, and the realization that literature was his real vocation.

Up to 1843 his publications had been minimal: a few lyrical poems published in periodicals and a juvenile book review of no importance. The lyrics have a freshness and simplicity, and lend themselves particularly well to musical settings – though Turgenev in later life wrote disparagingly that he felt towards them 'a very nearly physical revulsion, like from bugs or beetles'.[39] But in the second half of April

1843 there appeared as a separate slim volume a verse romance entitled *Parasha*, which established his reputation as a writer. Though published anonymously, signed with the initials 'T.L.' (Turgenev–Lutovinova) it did not take long for the identity of the author to become known. His own estimation of the poem is hard to assess: a letter of 4 April 1843 states, 'I have prepared much. You will, perhaps, soon hear of me,' which clearly refers to *Parasha*. Two months later, however, he says that he doesn't wish to talk about the poem because 'all joking apart, I don't like it'.[40]

Parasha, subtitled 'A story in verse', is short and simple: sixty-nine stanzas long, its content is slight. It tells of the marriage of a young woman to her dull and very unromantic neighbour, and how she settles down fairly happily to a humdrum life. The epigraph to the poem, a quotation from Lermontov, provides a clue to the moral of the story – 'We hate, and love, by chance.' *Parasha* is written with irony and humour, and in verse of great facility and elegance – including, incidentally, and quite irrelevantly, one stanza (XVI) of outstanding beauty, which recalls the author's experience of a hot day in Naples.

The success of the poem, which was in large measure due to Belinsky's enthusiastic long article praising it in the *Annals of the Fatherland*,[41] was not unconnected with the state of Russian literature at the time. Pushkin – whose style in such poems as *Graf Nulin* and *Eugene Onegin, Parasha* very much recalls – had been dead since 1837, although some of his works continued to appear posthumously. Critics were quick to spot the debt owed by the author of *Parasha* to such narrative poems by Lermontov as *Sashka* or *A Children's Story* – the similarity is, indeed, quite obvious. But Lermontov had died in 1841, and had left a void. In prose, Gogol had conquered the imagination of those members of the reading public who were longing for a voice in literature that did not speak in the tones of what Turgenev and his friends used to call the 'pseudo-majestical school' – by which they meant such writing as that of Bestuzhev-Marlinsky, Zagoskin, or the highly popular dramatist Kukolnik, or the earlier romances of Karamzin. These were the idols of the literary 'establishment' of the day, whose views were voiced in the journal *Biblioteka dlia chtenia* (the *Reader's Library*), edited by O. I. Senkovsky, which was hostile to the new, unromantic influences exemplified by Pushkin, Lermontov, and Gogol. *Dead Souls*, published in 1842, had taken the young reading public by storm: for *Biblioteka dlia chtenia* it was merely coarse and dirty, 'the vilification of the Russian people'.

In short, by 1843, when *Parasha* appeared, the young Russian reader was longing for ironical, unpretentious, and unpompous writing about real people and real things, and there was already discernible a division into 'we' and 'they'. The 'we' were the enthusiasts for Gogol, Pushkin, Lermontov, Griboedov; the 'they' were the staid and unimaginative literary 'establishment' of the reign of Nicholas I, always on the alert for subversive views and for any hidden criticisms of the regime, eager to denounce them to the authorities (and indeed free with their denunciations), looking for a literature which in its artificiality, its lack of realism and its pseudo-patriotism presented no conceivable threat to the established order. It was to the mission of purifying language from the artificial encrustations which had become part of the literary style of authors of the first quarter of the nineteenth century that writers such as Pushkin, Lermontov, and Gogol had dedicated themselves. *Parasha* was the first clear signal that Turgenev was also going to be of that company.

Turgenev was certainly a committed 'we' man in his literary taste – his declaration of faith to Nikitenko at the early age of eighteen was proof of this (see p. 15 above). But the undisputed leader of the enthusiasts for the new voices in literature, and the scourge of the 'establishment', was V. G. Belinsky, at that time at the height of his fame as a critic on the pages of the *Annals of the Fatherland*. Turgenev had been an enthusiastic admirer of his articles for years past. According to Turgenev's account, when *Parasha* was printed he delivered a copy to Belinsky, but they did not meet then, though they had met, fleetingly, twice before. After the appearance of the article in praise of *Parasha*, Turgenev called on Belinsky, their closer acquaintance began, and was cemented in the summer of 1843 when they occupied neighbouring dachas near St. Petersburg.* Turgenev recalled years later the long hours of conversation in Belinsky's austere and comfortless dacha. These were mostly about philosophy (mainly Hegel) and literature. The following winter, back in St. Petersburg, Tur-

* Belinsky confirms that he met Turgenev before *Parasha* was published. In a letter to the Bakunin family of 22–3 February (*Parasha* only appeared in mid-April) Belinsky relates that he had 'recently made the acquaintance of Turgenev. He was so kind as to express the wish to meet me. We were brought together by Zinoviev. It seems to me that Turgenev is a good man.'[42] (P. V. Zinoviev was an acquaintance of Turgenev.) But it seems clear that Turgenev got the year of their close friendship wrong and that the residence at neighbouring dachas was in fact in 1844, because Belinsky, as we know from his correspondence, spent the whole summer of 1843 in Moscow, and the adjacent dachas were near St. Petersburg. Moreover, the 'Memorial' states that Turgenev spent the summer of 1844 in Pargolovo, which is in fact a summer resort near St. Petersburg, and near Belinsky, who was at Lesnoe.

genev naturally became a member of Belinsky's 'circle'. This included Annenkov, the historian K. D. Kavelin, the poet Nekrasov, for a short time Dostoevsky, and the novelist I. A. Goncharov. Botkin, Herzen, and Ogarev 'often came over from Moscow'.[43]

Turgenev has left an outstandingly vivid and penetrating sketch of this brilliant, tragic, and meteoric figure in the Russian literary firmament, who was to die of consumption five years later, at the age of thirty-seven. Of Turgenev's affection and genuine admiration for him there can be no doubt. He gives full credit to Belinsky's sincerity, integrity, and passion in the pursuit of what he believed to be the truth. He dismisses with indignation the calumnies which were spread abroad by the many enemies of this chaste, monastic, and ascetic figure. He awards him the highest tribute as a critic when, in discussing the succession to Pushkin, he speaks of Gogol and Lermontov in the world of creative art, and of Belinsky in the sphere of thought and criticism. He stresses Belinsky's seriousness in everything he wrote. He justly emphasizes the fact that Belinsky, while a convinced admirer of the West, never lost his instinct for Russia and things Russian. Above all, Turgenev (writing in 1869, during the period of Alexander II's reforms) stresses the influence of Belinsky at a time when life for the young intellectual was grim, and when Belinsky and his group of friends provided some escape from the oppressive reality:

I often used to go to him in the afternoon. .... Times in those days were difficult: our present young generation does not have to experience anything like what it was then. Let the reader judge for himself: in the morning, perhaps, you have had your proofs returned to you, all scored and disfigured by red ink, as if covered with blood. You may even have to pay a visit to the censor, offer him vain and degrading explanations, or justifications, and listen to his verdict, often derisory, from which there is no appeal. ... Then perhaps, in the street you have chanced to meet Mr. Bulgarin or his friend Mr. Grech; some general, not even the director of your department, but simply a general, interrupted you, or worse still, gave you encouragement. .... If you were to cast a mental glance around you, you would see bribery flourishing, serfdom standing firm as a rock, the barracks on top of everything, no courts, rumours rife that the universities are to be closed ... trips abroad becoming impossible, impossible to send abroad for a sensible book, some kind of a dark cloud hanging constantly over the whole so-called learned and literary administration. And then on top of that, the hissing of denunciations creeping along their way. Youth without common ties and a common interest, all terrorized and subdued. ... Well, you come to Belinsky's flat, a second, a third friend appears, a conversation is struck up, and it becomes easier.

He adds that conversations were seldom political: 'the uselessness of such conversations was too strikingly evident'.[44]

However, through the perfectly sincere praise of Belinsky, some differences of temperament, some friction possibly, can be glimpsed. Turgenev was always inclined to frivolity. The heavy seriousness of Belinsky (' "We have not resolved the question of the existence of God" – he once said to me with bitter reproachfulness – "and you want to eat!" '; this was after two or three hours of argument) was not quite Turgenev's style. But Turgenev hastens to add that his object in recalling this incident is not to mock Belinsky, and that the recollection rather invokes in him a sense of being moved and surprised. It was, of course, the case that no one could have been more passionate in 'the pursuit of certainty' than Belinsky. The 'certainty', however, was not always the same. At the outset of his career, for example, it was Hegel, whose works Belinsky – who could not read German – knew only at second-hand, most probably from the expositions of Stankevich and Michael Bakunin. Belinsky's enthusiasm for Hegel led him for a time to the view that because 'the real is rational', so the regime imposed on Russia by Nicholas I had to be regarded as 'rational'. (Turgenev was particularly impressed with the way in which, during their long discussions at Lesnoe in the summer of 1844, Belinsky talked about his 'aberration' without any false shame.) Towards the end of his life socialism became the object of Belinsky's overwhelming enthusiasm.

More serious for Turgenev, perhaps, for whom human relations always took first place, were Belinsky's violent personal attacks on the Slavophiles, whom he hated with a burning, passionate hatred (and referred to in correspondence as 'the Slavofarts'). Turgenev did not agree with the Slavophiles, and was not above mocking them: but he was on cordial terms with Konstantin Aksakov and Iurii Samarin, for example.[45] He supported Belinsky's derision of the Slavophiles in private, and indeed delighted his friend with his own mockery of them,[46] but it is improbable that he could have supported Belinsky in the violence of his personal attacks on the Slavophiles for long, or that he sympathized with the strong prejudice with which Belinsky's judgements were often coloured. 'In general, Belinsky, who was wonderfully perceptive as a critic, was fairly weak in the realistic understanding of living people, whom he judged to a large extent on the strength of preconceived ideas', he wrote in 1877.[47] Above all, Turgenev could have had little sympathy for Belinsky's overwhelming sense of the priority of social over aesthetic criteria which led him, for example, to criticize Pushkin for his supposed lack of civic principles. For Turgenev, political questions always had to yield to art – except that in some of his very early writings, which show traces of Belinsky's influence, he got very near to sacrificing his art to the desire to point a social moral (see Chapter 4).

As for Belinsky's attitude to Turgenev, his letters around the time when he met him stress his wit, his good-heartedness, and his great intellectual gifts. But there were also certain reservations on Belinsky's part about the younger man's vanity and flippancy. As I. I. Panaev, who was one of Belinsky's circle, recalled,

Turgenev soon became close friends with Belinsky and with all our circle. All, beginning with Belinsky, grew to love him very much, having convinced themselves of the fact, that along with his brilliant education, his remarkable mind and talent, he had a very kind and very gentle heart. . . . Turgenev was at that time not free of that petty worldly vanity and frivolity which are usual in youth. Belinsky was the first of us to notice these weaknesses in him, and sometimes laughed at them mercilessly. I must say that Belinsky was only merciless to the weaknesses of those for whom he felt great sympathy and love.

Turgenev very much respected Belinsky and submitted to his moral authority without question. . . . He was even a little afraid of him.[48]

Turgenev went to Spasskoe early in the year, according to the 'Memorial', to present a copy of *Parasha* to his mother. He then returned to St. Petersburg, and spent some part of the early summer in Pavlovsk, a nearby summer resort, then, as later, distinguished for its excellent concerts. It was while he was in Pavlovsk that he made the acquaintance of A. Ya. Panaeva, at whose house he was to become a frequent visitor for a time. Madame Panaeva was the author of vivid and amusing memoirs, which were written more for effect than out of any regard for the truth.[49]

Varvara Petrovna had treated her son's early excursions into literature – mainly the lyrical poems published in *Annals of the Fatherland* – with undisguised contempt. She did not regard writing as a suitable occupation for a gentleman, and did not conceal her opinion. The appearance of the slim volume of *Parasha*, however, seems to have caused her great pride and joy. A neighbour recalled how Turgenev presented his mother with a copy of the pink-covered poem. She wept with joy, while her son stood by her, bathed in happiness.[50] Somewhat later, having read both *Parasha* and Belinsky's article about it in *Annals of the Fatherland*, she wrote to him in what for her were glowing terms.

Indeed, I see talent in you. There are spots too, as on the sun, and you are my sun. Joking apart – it is beautiful . . . I am like Voltaire's cook, I don't know how to express myself. But ... I am proud that such thoughts came to my son, such new thoughts ... Wild strawberries are just being served. We, country people, love everything that is real. And so, your *Parasha*, your story, your poem ... smells of wild strawberries.[51]

For the time being all was harmonious between mother and son. It was not long to remain so. One of the disturbing factors was to be Turgenev's widely-known infatuation for the singer Pauline Viardot, whom he met before the year 1843 was out.

CHAPTER FOUR

Pauline Viardot

Pauline Garcia Viardot was twenty-two years old when, on 22 October 1843, she appeared for the first time on the Russian stage, in the Imperial Opera, in the role of Rosina in *Il Barbiere di Siviglia*. She came from a distinguished musical family. Her father, Manuel Garcia, had been a great singer, and her sister, known as La Malibran, had acquired a legendary reputation in her tragically short life. Pauline, who had made her debut in London in 1839, had captivated her audiences with her voice, which was universally acclaimed as superb, her dramatic sense, and above all her charm; neither portraits nor contemporary descriptions suggest that she was beautiful, though she had expressive black eyes, a slender figure, and she moved with elegance. A shrewd observer, Heinrich Heine, writing a year later, discerned a certain exotic, even barbaric quality, in the great singer:

She is ugly but with a kind of ugliness which is noble, I should almost like to say beautiful. . . . Indeed, the Garcia recalls less the civilized beauty and tame gracefulness of our European homelands than she does the terrifying magnificence of some exotic and wild country. . . . At times, when she opens wide her large mouth with its blinding white teeth and smiles her cruel sweet smile, which at once charms and frightens us, we begin to feel as if the most monstrous vegetation and species of beasts from India and Africa are about to appear before us . . .[1]

At the age of eighteen Pauline had married Louis Viardot, twenty-one years her senior. He was Director of the Théâtre Italien in Paris, an author of some repute, a lover and student of Spain, and a passionate shot. She was not in love with him, but he was devoted to her, and provided her with security and protection, which she rewarded with genuine affection and with reasonable fidelity. One daughter, Louise, had been born to them on 14 December 1841.[2]

Turgenev was probably present at Madame Viardot's Russian début, and he certainly heard her sing in the course of her triumphant season. At the end of October he met Louis Viardot at the house of an acquaintance, Major A. S. Komarov, who was an occasional visitor to Belinsky's circle. Turgenev and Viardot, who shared an interest in literature and in shooting, and, probably, the same political inclination, since Louis was a free-thinker, a rationalist, and an ardent republican, struck up a genuine friendship which was to survive considerable strains in the years that lay ahead. On the morning of 1 November, accompanied 'by the little Major Komarov', Turgenev called on Pauline Viardot at the house where she was staying in St. Petersburg.[3] If there is such an experience as love at first sight, Turgenev became a victim of it on that morning. He immediately fell in love with her (or so it seemed) and loved her quite literally until the last conscious hour of his life, with unquestioning, submissive, undemanding devotion.

Turgenev was, at this time, an unusually handsome man, to judge by numerous contemporary descriptions, and a portrait by Gorbunov dated 1846. (A painting by the same artist, which was done in Berlin in 1838, was said by several contemporaries, including his mother and half-sister, to be a remarkably good likeness.)[4] He was very tall and broad-shouldered. His eyes were dark blue-grey, and thoughtful. His hair, worn rather long, was chestnut coloured. He may already have grown the moustache which is shown in the portrait of 1846, but he was otherwise clean-shaven. His features were large and somewhat rugged. His smile was one of remarkable charm. His voice was not attractive: he had a slight defect of speech, almost a lisp, and he tended to squeak when he got excited. But there was great gentleness and kindness in his manner of speaking, and his conversation, in spite of an occasional hesitation in choosing the right word, had a quality which enraptured his listeners. Pauline Viardot accepted him as one of her many admirers, but does not appear to have shown him any particular favour at this stage. Judging by many contemporary accounts, he was among her most assiduous followers. He attended her performances, he taught her Russian, he was a frequent visitor at her house. As we know from his friends' accounts, his vanity, his desire to talk for effect, to shock and to be original were at this time among his more irritating qualities. Before very long, and probably as the result of falling deeply in love for the first time, he was to acquire a new seriousness and sincerity of manner. Meanwhile, in the winter of 1843, he made himself somewhat ridiculous (and possibly displeased Madame Viardot) by proclaiming his devotion to her and singing her praises from the housetops, often to the embarrassment of his friends.[5]

Madame Viardot's visit to St. Petersburg also had the effect of arousing in Turgenev a passionate, lifelong devotion to music in general, and to opera in particular. Music had hardly been mentioned in his early correspondence, although, as already noted, he used to go to listen to Beethoven with Bakunin and his sister in Berlin; and while staying at Pavlovsk in the summer of 1843, he attended the evening concerts. Pauline Viardot's repertoire during her triumphant St. Petersburg season, which ended with a concert on 25 February 1844, would have been much to his liking – Rossini's *Otello* and *Tancredi*, Bellini's *La Sonnambula* and *I Capuletti ed i Montecchi*, Donizetti's *Lucia di Lammermoor* and Mozart's *Don Giovanni* – the last an otherwise poor production in which she sang the role of Zerlina. Writing a few years later Turgenev complained of the decline in quality – from Mozart and Gluck to Rossini; from Rossini to Donizetti and Bellini; and then to Verdi.[6]

Somewhat surprisingly, Turgenev left St. Petersburg before the end of Madame Viardot's season. On 14 February he was granted twenty-eight days' leave from his duties at the Ministry, which must have been applied for some days before, at least, and left for Moscow to join his mother.[7] Before leaving he arranged some shooting expeditions with Louis Viardot, who later described them for publication. 'Your wife', Turgenev wrote to him, 'is, I will not say the greatest, she is, in my opinion, the *only* singer in the world.'[8] Turgenev fell ill while in Moscow with inflammation of the lungs and did not return to his work at the Ministry until 17 May.[9] His mother seems to have cared for him affectionately during his illness, and even went to the lengths of organizing a great party for him, since, as she wrote, he had expressed the desire to see some of his 'learned apes'.[10]

Four days after his return to St. Petersburg, he sent what appears to have been the first of the many letters he was to address to Pauline Viardot. He makes some excuse for writing, and fills the letter with musical and other gossip. Had his departure from St. Petersburg perhaps been caused by Madame Viardot's annoyance at his flamboyant flaunting of his feelings for her? Or had it not been love at first sight, after all, but youthful exhibitionism which, on reflection, had turned into the real and deep love which it was thereafter to remain? We have no way of knowing, but the serious note on which he closes his letter leaves little doubt that by this date his love was unselfish, undemanding, and submissive, as it would remain to the end of his life. 'Be happy,' he closes his letter. 'You know, when I say these words to you, I have nothing more to add, since I speak them from the depths of my heart. ... Your devoted friend, J. Tourguéneff.'[11]

Turgenev continued his literary activity on an increased scale after the appearance of *Parasha*. Most of the 1843 and 1844 issues of *Annals of the Fatherland* included one or more of his lyrics. No. 10 of October 1843 contained a short play, set in Spain, entitled *Carelessness*. Not in itself remarkable, it is notable as indicating Turgenev's interest in the stage: in the next few years he would seriously devote himself to writing for the theatre. Some of his publications are of particular significance, because they clearly indicate Belinsky's influence on him at this period. At least three of Turgenev's works were written during the summer of 1844, when he and Belinsky were spending much time together near St. Petersburg: a long poem entitled *The Conversation*, published as a separate edition at the beginning of January 1845; the story called 'Andrei Kolosov', published in the *Annals of the Fatherland* No. 11, at the beginning of November 1844; and a long review of a new translation of Goethe's *Faust*, published in the *Annals of the Fatherland* No. 2 for 1845, in February.

All these works are characterized by an emphasis on the social as opposed to the human side which is dominant in all of Turgenev's later works. He sent a copy of the proofs of *The Conversation* to Belinsky for comment. Belinsky dissected the verse in his characteristic manner, of which the following is an example: 'What is "haughty silence"? "Magnanimous cranberry fool"?' Turgenev replaced the offending words in the final version with 'misty heights', and also took Belinsky's other criticisms into account.

The Conversation is cast in the form of a long dialogue between an old hermit and a young man who visits him. The poem is clearly open to the interpretation that the hermit represents the past generation of seekers for truth – the Decembrists and their many intellectual followers – while the young man typifies the disillusioned and bewildered idealists of the forties whom Turgenev was later to portray as the 'superfluous men'. The old hermit reproaches his visitor with his lack of determination and manhood – 'in the full vigour of youthful strength you are like an old man, dejected and weak. ... It is fitting that men should labour long and hard for the glorious pursuit of the Good.' The young man pleads that he too had burned with desire to serve his people, only to find that there was no place for him in the world; and that he was a stranger among his own people and could not come close to them. This brings down further reproofs on his head from the stern old hermit. But the young man has the last word: 'Now let me ask you, oh ancestors, what did you do for us? Come, tell us: "there, thanks to our valiant labours, look how our nation has grown! There is the clear and unmistakable trace of great and genuine victories!" Well, answer us! Alas, like your grandsons, you hurried from difficult but vain labour, to senseless repose. But we are no better – the same fate awaits us ...'

The poem closes on this note of deepest pessimism, which reflected the mood of the young idealists of the early forties. The poem also deals with two of Turgenev's favourite themes on the subject of love. One is that love between man and woman is an enslavement of the man, a view which was to recur again and again in much of his fiction. The other motif is a man's bitter regret when he realizes that he has failed, through his own indecision, to seize a proffered opportunity of happiness in love.[12]

But although *The Conversation* is devoted to burning social questions of the day, its artistic quality does not suffer because of it – the verse is noble and there are no jarring notes. The same cannot be said of Turgenev's first story 'Andrei Kolosov'. The scene is set in Moscow student circles. Kolosov is introduced by the narrator in terms of such exaggerated praise that one's highest expectations are aroused – he is a 'genius' (at least in the first edition: in the first collected edition of 1856 he is merely described as 'unusual'), his influence on others is said to be irresistible, and so forth. The narrator, who is Kolosov's friend, is persuaded to accompany him on his nightly visits to a house on the outskirts of the town, where lives a preposterous, selfish old humbug with his daughter Varia. Kolosov is in love with Varia, who adores him. The narrator's function on these evening calls is to entertain the old father at cards, while Kolosov talks to Varia. In the fullness of time Kolosov tires of the girl. The narrator (who has meanwhile fallen in love with Varia himself) is induced by Kolosov to convey this news to her; and, in consoling Varia, he finds himself engaged to be married to her. But his love is very half-hearted, and he soon liberates himself by the simple device of never visiting her again. As for Kolosov, the 'genius' in truth turns out to be little more than a self-centred prig who, like thousands before him, extricates himself clumsily from a love affair which is beginning to cloy. But Turgenev was so concerned to strike a blow against romantic and sentimental love that he elevated Kolosov's conduct, in hyperbolical terms, to the heights of nobility: 'Oh gentlemen,' exclaims the narrator, 'a man who parts from a woman whom he has once loved, in that bitter and great moment when he recognizes against his will that his heart is not wholly and entirely immersed in her, that man, believe me, understands the sanctity of love better than those pusillanimous people who from boredom or weakness continue to play on the half-live strings of their weak and sentimental hearts.'[13] (Was Turgenev thinking of himself and Tatiana Bakunina?)

The nobility of Kolosov's character remains in the author's imagination. The story is flat and, as a work of art, a disappointment. 'Andrei Kolosov' includes some touches of genius, such as the picture of the horrible old father, and, if not to the same extent, of Varia. But one of the main weaknesses of the story is that we never feel Kolosov to be a real human being at all, or capable of loving anyone. He remains an almost Soviet type of hero, a coat-hanger for supposed civic virtues. (It was, perhaps, not accidental that 'Andrei Kolosov' was Lenin's favourite Turgenev story.) The story pleased Belinsky – with qualifications.[14] It is not too fanciful to suggest that on this occasion Turgenev sacrificed his art to the temptation to preach a moral homily. He would never do so again. (Thirteen years later he warmly agreed with the critic Druzhinin that Kolosov, contrary to what his author had intended, had turned out a trivial egoist.)[15] Some years were to pass before he returned to fiction, in the *Sketches from a Sportsman's Notebook.*

Turgenev's long review of the new translation of Goethe's *Faust* is only in part devoted to a discussion of the translation. In the main, he used the occasion to analyse the significance of *Faust*. The work of Goethe had been one of his great enthusiasms. In returning to *Faust*, however, Turgenev was now, very probably under the influence of Belinsky, concerned to make certain assertions of primarily social significance on contemporary Russia. Turgenev seems to have left Goethe behind him for the time being – at any rate he describes *Faust* as 'the sharpest and most decisive expression of romanticism', and, of course, there was no worse word of abuse in his and Belinsky's vocabulary at this time than 'romantic'. Faust is a romantic – an egoist who thinks only of himself. Mephistopheles is only a small-scale devil:

he is the personification of that denial which arises within a soul which is exclusively preoccupied with its own doubts and uncertainties; he is the devil of solitary and abstract people who are profoundly confused by any little contradiction in their own lives and who will walk past a whole family of artisans dying of hunger with philosophical indifference.[16]

Turgenev sees the greatness of *Faust* in the fact that it does not resolve its hero's problem: in the terms of romanticism there was no solution. 'Any reconciliation of Faust outside the sphere of human reality would be unnatural, while of any other form of reconciliation we can as yet only dream'; presumably he meant by 'any other form' one which involved a transformation of human society on socially just lines.

Let me repeat: as a poet Goethe is unequalled, but what we need now are not poets alone ... we (and, I am sorry to say, not all of us) have become like people who at the sight of a beautiful painting of a beggar are incapable of admiring the artistic qualities of the representation, but are sadly troubled by the thought that there are still beggars around in our times.[17]

It is difficult to imagine Turgenev writing such a passage a few years later.

Madame Viardot returned to St. Petersburg for another season, to the delight of the Russian musical public, and of Turgenev. The audience welcomed her back with wild enthusiasm at her opening performance, on 9 October 1844, in *La Sonnambula*. Turgenev continued to frequent her house and to give her Russian lessons. 'It seems clear that at this period Pauline accepted Turgenev's adoration, gave him her friendship, but did not greatly encourage his love.'[18] The Viardots left St. Petersburg just before Holy Week for Moscow, where Pauline was to give several concerts. One of them was attended by Varvara Petrovna who, as can be imagined, was not over-pleased by her son's infatuation with a singer. Turgenev had on 5 February 1845 applied for two months' leave by reason of his mother's illness, and this leave was granted four days later.[19] He was therefore in Moscow at this time and presumably accompanied his mother to the concert, which took place in the morning. Having returned home, Varvara Petrovna was very angry to discover that her son had not come back for the midday meal, which was consumed in complete silence with Varvara Petrovna frowning crossly. 'At the end of the meal, she struck the table angrily with her knife and, as if talking to herself, not addressing anyone in particular, said, "One has to admit it, that damned gipsy sings well!"'[20]

Early in 1845, Turgenev decided to leave Russia. In a letter of 9 January to Alexei Bakunin (in which he expresses the hope that the Bakunin family will understand why the intimacy of the past had ceased), he states his intention of leaving Russia 'in about two months' time, perhaps for a long while' in order to attend to his failing eyesight.[21] Turgenev's eyesight was bad, so the excuse may not have been wholly untrue. But it is fair to assume that he had already decided that he must free himself from government service so as to be able to travel abroad and to be near Pauline. He never returned to the Ministry from the sick leave granted him in February. On 3 April he petitioned the Emperor to allow him to retire from the public service on the grounds of poor eyesight;[22] the petition was granted on 18 April.[23] A passport for foreign travel 'to Germany and Holland for medical reasons' was granted on 10 May and soon after, in the company of the Viardot family, he left St. Petersburg by sea for France, having returned to the capital from Moscow with them.[24]

Before his departure for France, Turgenev and another friend of the Viardots (and admirer of Pauline), S. A. Gedeonov, had dictated at Louis Viardot's request a translation into French of five of Gogol's stories. These were published by Viardot, with acknowledgement to Turgenev and Gedeonov, in Paris at the end of the year. On 19 July 1845, some months before this volume appeared, an unsigned article on Russian literature was published in the journal *Illiustration* No. 125. There are reasons to believe that it was written by Turgenev: certainly, the views expressed in it are very close to his. The anonymous author stresses the importance of Pushkin as the first national Russian author, and of Lermontov as his short-lived successor. But a special place is assigned to Gogol, not only as a national Russian author, but as a master of comedy, a talent which Pushkin lacked. Gogol is equally at home in describing all classes of society. He is, says the author of this article, the most popular, the most influential, and the most frequently imitated writer of the day.[25] If indeed, as seems probable, Turgenev wrote this article, it is an early example of his attempts to make Russian literature better known to the Western European reader.

The next few months of life in France were described by Turgenev in the 'Memorial' as 'the happiest time of all my life'. June and early July were most probably spent in the Viardot household at Courtavenel. As frequent references in his letters of 1846 reveal, his attachment to the house and the family knew no bounds; he returns to details of life in Courtavenel with affectionate remembrance. During his stay there he met George Sand, an intimate friend of Pauline. Since Turgenev, along with most of his educated contemporaries, much admired the works of George Sand (one of them, *Consuelo* published in 1842, was a portrait of Pauline), this was an occasion of sufficient significance for him to record in the 'Memorial'. Relations with Pauline were now harmonious and, for Turgenev at any rate, satisfying. He could adore her in her own surroundings and he seems to have demanded no more. They had not yet even exchanged kisses – they were to do so for the first time the following winter, in St. Petersburg, according to the 'Memorial'.

Before returning to Russia in time for the Viardots' next visit, Turgenev spent several weeks touring France, which as yet he hardly knew. In company with two friends, V. P. Botkin and N. M. Satin, he travelled by stage coach to Orléans, Tours, Poitier, Angoulème, and Bordeaux. From there they went on to the Spanish border, where they separated. Botkin went into Spain,★ and Turgenev wandered around in the Pyrenees. From an unpublished letter to Pauline, dated from Paris 3 October 1845, we know that he paid a second visit to Courtavenel in the autumn, after Madame Viardot had already left for Russia.[26] It was, presumably, on this occasion that he developed his warm attachment for Pauline's mother, Madame Garcia. He returned to Russia overland, reaching St. Petersburg around the middle of November.

It was on this visit to St. Petersburg that he first met Dostoevsky. Although Dostoevsky's first novel, *Bednye liudi* (*Poor People*), was not published until January of the following year, it was already widely known and had been extravagantly praised by Belinsky and many others. Dostoevsky's first impression of Turgenev was highly favourable: 'A poet, a talent, an aristocrat, superbly handsome, rich, clever, educated, twenty-five years old – I can't think what nature has denied him. Above all, a beautiful character, straight as a die, schooled in kindness', he wrote to his brother after their meeting in November.[27]

His enthusiasm was short-lived. By the summer of the following year, if not before, there was a turbulent scene in which Dostoevsky turned on Turgenev and abused him roundly.[28] In the course of a few months the members of the Belinsky circle had ceased to be on good terms with Dostoevsky. For one thing, Dostoevsky's story, 'Dvoinik' ('The Double') which followed on *Poor People*, had been very badly received by Belinsky and his friends. Early in 1846, probably in January, a satirical poem in the form of an address by Belinsky to Dostoevsky had been composed and circulated by Turgenev and Nekrasov.[29] In general, the satire was fairly gentle and good-natured. But the last stanza must have touched Dostoevsky on the raw, since it referred to a story freely circulated in St. Petersburg even by quite reliable witnesses, like Annenkov, as well as by Turgenev, to the effect that in offering *Poor People* for publication in a collective volume called *The St. Petersburg Symposium*, Dostoevsky

---

★ He was to publish a volume, *Letters from Spain*, in 1847.

had insisted that his novel must be printed either first or last, and decorated with a special border. The gossip was widely believed although it was probably untrue: there is certainly no border in the volume as printed, even though *Poor People* was indeed placed first. Of course Turgenev was at that time always ready with a witticism at someone else's expense; on the other hand, Dostoevsky was very vain and morbidly sensitive to criticism, real or imagined. According to his daughter, the real cause of the estrangement between the two men was Turgenev's inordinate jealousy at the success of *Poor People*, but this seems a very improbable story.[30] These incidents in Dostoevsky's early career, soon to be interrupted by penal servitude, inaugurated a lasting dislike and contempt for Turgenev the man (though not always the writer). Though neither may have realized it at the time, the cause for the antipathy lay deeper, in the widely divergent outlooks of the two authors.

The Viardots came once again to St. Petersburg for the season of 1845–6, and Pauline was rapturously received. But her stay in the city, where the weather that year was particularly severe, had to be cut short early in February. She had contracted whooping cough; the doctors advised an immediate change of climate, and she applied for leave to break her contract.[31] The more intimate friendship between Pauline and Turgenev which had started in the summer in Courtavenel had continued in St. Petersburg. The 'first kiss', recorded in the 'Memorial' as having occurred at the end of 1845, is eloquent testimony of this: given the more formal customs of St. Petersburg at that time, a kiss meant very much more than it would today.

The deepening of the friendship is reflected, if somewhat one-sidedly, in Turgenev's letters to Pauline in 1846: we have no letters from her to him, except for a few dated between 1850 and 1881. Turgenev still hoped in his early correspondence that she would return for the season, but she could not face another Russian winter, and the two could not meet until early in the following year. There is a new tenderness and sincerity in his letters to her. 'Ich bin immer derselbe und werde es ewig bleiben' ('I am still the same, and will always remain so'), he wrote in what seems to be the first letter written after her departure from St. Petersburg,[32] and German phrases were to recur frequently in his letters for the more intimate expressions of his love for Pauline; since German could have had no special meaning for her, its use in this manner may well have been for reasons of privacy. Reading letters aloud was a custom in the Viardot household and one can well imagine that Turgenev's

letters were also read out by Pauline, to Viardot or to the whole
family. The German phrases could either be omitted in the reading
(especially if Louis, as seems probable, did not know the language)
or, if need be, freely and harmlessly paraphrased. 'Adieu! Be happy,
and deign sometimes to think of your most devoted friend.'[33] Or
again: 'I have so many things that I could say to you that I prefer
to keep quiet, besides, you can guess most of them.'[34] All the letters
of this period contain messages for Viardot, and one, of 8 November,
is addressed to them both and is in reply to a joint letter.[35]

Sometime in May Turgenev left for Spasskoe, where he spent
five months writing and shooting. The 'Memorial' records, in
brackets, the names of two girls, Fifina and Nastia – presumably a
reference to casual affairs with serf girls, which nevertheless Turgenev found worth remembering and recording. But we have little
evidence with which to assess the importance of sexual intercourse –
as distinct from the grand, if still somewhat abstract, passion for Pauline – in his life at this time.

This visit to Spasskoe was to be the last occasion when Turgenev
was to spend any length of time with his mother. Causes of friction
between them had by now multiplied. There was his friendship with
Pauline Viardot. The question of money must also have loomed
large, particularly if we assume that Turgenev had by now determined to travel abroad in order to see Pauline, if she decided not
to come to St. Petersburg for the winter season of 1846–7. A further
cause of friction was connected with Turgenev's brother, Nikolai,
who had formed an attachment for Anna Yakovlevna Shvarts, a companion employed by his mother. He insisted on marrying her, against
his mother's wishes: she rewarded this defiance by withholding all
further financial support for him, and persisted in insulting him to
the end of her days, in a mean and petty manner. Turgenev had
always taken his brother's side in this affair (though there never was
very close intimacy between them) and had aroused his mother's rage
when he was a student in Berlin by daring to 'give her advice', as
she put it, on the subject of Nikolai's love for Anna Yakovlevna.[36]
Now, on the occasion of his last visit to Spasskoe, there was further
friction between Ivan Turgenev and his mother (as recalled by Varvara Bogdanovich-Lutovinova, who by then was thirteen years old)
on the subject of her behaviour to Nikolai.

Another source of disagreement between mother and son was the
old subject of Varvara Petrovna's treatment of her peasants. The
question of serfdom was much in Turgenev's mind this summer
because the 'Memorial' records (in the only instance of a reference

to any of his writings) that 'Khor and Kalinych', the first story out of which the *Sketches from a Sportsman's Notebook* was to grow, was written in Spasskoe in 1846. Little Varvara recalls that she overheard a heated argument on serfdom. Varvara Petrovna insisted that her serfs were well fed and housed, and even – something that was most unusual – paid a wage. Turgenev argued that they lived in a constant state of terror. This his mother regarded as right and proper, just as she saw nothing wrong in the fact that she had absolute power over them, and could exile a serf for quite capricious motives.

A final cause of friction was Turgenev's clear intention to go abroad again. His mother strongly disapproved of this. She also deplored his abandoning his career in the Ministry of the Interior for the unworthy occupation of a writer. That summer there were frequent outbursts of hysteria, sobbing, and rage.[37]

One reason for Turgenev's intense preoccupation with writing while in Spasskoe was the projected appearance of the *Contemporary* (*Sovremennik*) under new management. The *Contemporary* had been founded by Pushkin; after his death in 1837, it had gradually gone into a decline under Pletnev, the editor who succeeded him. In 1846 Pletnev agreed that the journal should be jointly taken over by the poet Nekrasov and I. I. Panaev, publicist and journalist. Both of them were friends of Belinsky whose collaboration as principal critic in *Annals of the Fatherland* was becoming difficult owing to disagreements with its editor, Kraevsky. Belinsky expected to be one of the editors of the refurbished *Contemporary*, but he was disappointed in this, which caused a certain amount of bitterness among him and his friends. The *Contemporary* soon became the leading journal for intellectually lively circles, and attracted a whole company of writers who were associated with Belinsky, including Annenkov, Botkin, Herzen, Grigorovich, and Kavelin.

Turgenev was involved in the new journal from the first, though possibly somewhat on its fringes. His reputation as a real writer still remained to be made, and an aura of flippancy and irresponsible vanity still hung around him.[38] On 8 November, back in St. Petersburg from Spasskoe (he returned on 18 October), he informed Viardot and Pauline of the new journal with which he was much preoccupied, though as a contributor, not as an editor.[39] When the first number under new auspices appeared at the beginning of January 1847, it included nine poems by Turgenev, a long review of a tragedy by the 'pseudo-majestical' Kukolnik, an article on musical and artistic life in the capital and 'Khor and Kalinych'. At the same time, Turgenev's second story, 'The Swashbuckler', a slight tale in which there is no trace of the crudeness which marred 'Andrei Kolosov', appeared in the first issue for 1847 of the *Annals of the Fatherland*. Possibly this was because he was still paying off advances to the editor, Kraevsky. But it is also likely that his instinctive reluctance to commit himself to what was, after all, an embryo political demonstration – given the conditions of the time – had made him reluctant to appear to be too closely tied to the new *Contemporary*. At any rate he did not accept Nekrasov's offer to buy off his indebtedness to Kraevsky so that he could contribute exclusively to the new journal.[40]

Meanwhile, it had become clear that Madame Viardot was not coming to St. Petersburg that year, and Turgenev began to make arrangements to go abroad. On 28 November he wrote to Pauline, who was then in Berlin, to say that he hoped to arrange his affairs in such a manner as to be able to leave St. Petersburg in the New Year.[41] On 26 December the Ministry of the Interior issued a passport valid for foreign travel for I. S. Turgenev 'who is going to Germany and Italy for medical reasons'.*[42] On 12 January 1847 he left St. Petersburg for Berlin.

* Passports for foreign travel on medical grounds were issued relatively freely to members of the nobility.

CHAPTER FIVE

Life Abroad: 1847–50

Turgenev stayed a few months in Berlin and then moved to Paris, and he remained there (with occasional absences) until his return to Russia in the summer of 1850. Two daguerrotypes of him dating from the late forties have survived: both depict a young man of striking good looks. A short beard has now been added to the moustache. The dark eyes shine with unusual lustre, as in the Gorbunov portrait of the late thirties, but a greater melancholy is reflected in them, perhaps a new seriousness. Such, at any rate, was to be the impression of some of his friends during those years abroad. Herzen, whose attitude to Turgenev was always tinged with a slight degree of patronizing contempt, records that 'Turgenev has developed morally to a considerable extent and I am pleased with him.'[1] Herzen's wife, Natalie, observed that for all his entertaining gifts as a story-teller, Turgenev had a reserved side to him: 'For me he is like a book; when he is telling a story it is interesting, but as soon as the soul is touched on, there is neither greeting nor answer.'[2] (There was, it is true, little love lost between them.)

Natalie Tuchkova, who was then nineteen, the future wife of Herzen's close friend the revolutionary Ogarev, saw Turgenev frequently in Paris in 1848. He formed a fatherly attachment for her, and dedicated his play, *Where it's thin, it tears*, to her. In her memoirs, written in later life, Natalie recalled his moodiness – long, obstinate silences alternated with animated arguments. She also recorded his performance of amusing parlour tricks at which he was a master, such as realistic imitations of a cock, or of a madman. Like most of the Russian community in Paris, Natalie blamed Pauline Viardot for keeping Turgenev away from Russia, where he belonged.[3] His friend Annenkov, who probably knew him best (after Pauline, who kept quiet on the subject), says in a memoir of the young Turgenev, published in 1884, that

> he was an unhappy man in his own eyes: he lacked the love and attachment of a woman which he sought for from his early youth. It was not for nothing that he repeatedly remarked that the company of men without the presence of a kind and intelligent woman was like a great cart with ungreased wheels, which shatters the eardrums with its unbearable, monotonous screech. . . . He suffered from the awareness that he was incapable of subduing and directing a woman's heart: he could only cause her torment.

And Annenkov goes on to refer to 'First Love', and Turgenev's horrified fascination with the, for him, unattainable domination over women which his father was able to achieve.[4]

Turgenev found the intellectual climate of Berlin much changed during the six years he had been away. Of the former idols, he wrote in March 1847, Schelling, Stahl, Bettina von Arnim, Max Stirner, Bruno Bauer – even the great exponent of Hegel, Werder, were forgotten. Only Feuerbach was, if anything, more than ever in fashion.[5] Was this judgement, perhaps, a reflection as much of a change in Turgenev as in Berlin intellectual life? In one of his stories, published in 1847, there is a scathing reference to Bettina;[6] while his enthusiasm for Feuerbach, first expressed in 1840, was reiterated in a letter to Pauline Viardot of 8 December 1847: he was, he wrote, 'among all the German scribblers' of the day 'the only talent'.[7] He paid a call on Varnhagen von Ense and impressed him with his judgement on Russian literature – although little appeared in print, there was much talent. A few weeks later he called again, bearing a poem which he had dedicated to the great man.[8] Turgenev was planning to translate into German an article by K. D. Kavelin on juridical relations in ancient Russia, and to publish it with Varnhagen von Ense's help.[9] In this essay, which appeared in the first issue of the newly managed *Contemporary* in January 1847, Kavelin argued that the emancipation of the individual in Russia was the result of the emergence of the centralized Muscovite state under Ivan the Terrible, and that in the person of Peter the Great individuality 'entered upon its absolute rights' in Russia – a thesis which outraged the Slavophiles.[10] Nothing came of this project. It was perhaps significant that this was already the second, if not the third, occasion on which Turgenev had planned to write critically on the Slavophiles, but did not carry out his intention. This failure (if not simply due to a natural tendency to procrastinate) was more likely to have been occasioned by his personal relations with leading Slavophiles than by any admiration for their theories.★

Pauline Viardot and her husband were in Berlin for her German tour when Turgenev arrived, and naturally he spent as much time with them as he could. Belinsky was also due in Berlin for what was to prove a vain attempt to restore his failing health. The expenses of his journey were generously met by his friends, including V. P. Botkin, who was well-off and could afford it, and Annenkov who could not, and who, in addition to providing 400 francs, changed his plans in order to travel to Germany to join Belinsky. Turgenev was delighted to hear of Belinsky's proposed visit, confident that it would benefit his health, and promised without fail to meet his friend in Stettin. However, he did not keep his promise (through no fault of his own, he claimed, though he did not specify the reason) and on 21 May returned home to find Belinsky sitting in his lodgings, draped in a Tartar dressing-gown.[12] After spending three days in Berlin, which Belinsky did not enjoy, they left together for Dresden – it was still too early for taking the waters at Salzbrunn, their ultimate destination and Dresden was a convenient centre for walking in the Saxon mountains.

For Turgenev, Dresden presented an added attraction – Pauline was now there. Belinsky was an unwilling attendant at the opera to hear her sing in Meyerbeer's *Huguenots*. A couple of days later the two Russians visited the Zwinger to see the pictures: Turgenev irritated Belinsky by insisting on waiting for the Viardots, urging as an excuse Louis's great knowledge of painting; and Belinsky had a brief encounter with Pauline, who enquired if he felt better – to which Belinsky replied, in the kind of French 'that even horses don't use', that he was. Belinsky's trials were not over: he was forced, obviously much against his will, to attend, at Pauline's invitation, a concert which she gave, and to be 'dragged' by Turgenev to thank her for the invitation afterwards.[13] Belinsky's attitude to Pauline was not untypical of the reaction which Turgenev's absorption with the Viardots provoked from his Russian friends. The Viardots left Dresden the day after the concert, and the two Russians, after walking in the mountains, set off for Salzbrunn, where they arrived on 3 June. Annenkov was due there in a week's time.

Annenkov, who later wrote an account of their stay in Salzbrunn, discusses Turgenev's attitude towards his Russian friends. His refusal,

★ It was on this visit to Berlin that he met Ludwig Pietsch who in later years was to become his translator and close friend, and an intimate in the Viardot household.[11]

he says, to commit himself wholeheartedly to one or other of the 'camps' into which intellectual life was divided at the time, gained him many enemies, as well as an undeserved reputation for frivolity. Annenkov stresses that Turgenev's preoccupation with the need for fairness in making judgements about people was neither understood nor appreciated by his Russian contemporaries, but was later to earn him his well-merited reputation for real understanding of Russia.[14]

Turgenev stayed in Salzbrunn for some weeks, and left for London (following Pauline) early in July.* It was after his departure that Belinsky wrote his notorious 'Letter to Gogol'. This 'Letter', which aroused the wild enthusiasm of the 'progressive' intellectuals, among whom it freely circulated in manuscript, was one of Belinsky's most intemperate and least creditable outbursts. In 1847, Gogol, who had published nothing since *Dead Souls* had astounded the reading public five years earlier, and had been undergoing a spiritual crisis (as well as suffering from severe physical illness), published his *Select Passages from My Correspondence with Friends*. This tortured, self-questioning book bears all the marks of the work of a man who is beset with doubts about his function and duty as a writer; no fair-minded reader, however disconcerted by some of its contents, could have had any doubt about its burning sincerity. Much of it is taken up with self-searching about *Dead Souls*, and about Gogol's own duty to his readers in the projected second and third parts of this work (he had already burned the first draft of the second part). Many of the letters consist of moral injunctions to his correspondents. There are some literary excursions which show strongly conservative leanings. There are some passages with enthusiastic, and exaggerated, praise for the Russian Church and priesthood; and advice to landowners which, if not actually approving of serfdom, certainly expressed no disapproval. For Belinsky, who, like many young Russian intellectuals, had welcomed *Dead Souls* as a straightforward and devastating satire on the regime of Nicholas I, and Gogol as a fellow 'oppositionist' in the 'we-they' confrontation of the period, the new product of Gogol's pen appeared as nothing but a dastardly betrayal, and he promptly said so in a review of the book which did not mince words. It is true that much more moderate writers than Belinsky also wrote critically of the *Select Passages*, but no one else was as emotionally involved as he: in a private letter, he refers to Gogol's 'artistically calculated baseness',[15] which was arrant nonsense. Gogol

---

* While in Salzbrunn he completed a story entitled 'The Serf Manager', which was eventually to form a part of the cycle known as *Sketches from a Sportsman's Notebook*.

was hurt by the review, and enclosed a message for Belinsky in a letter he wrote to Annenkov: the Salzbrunn 'Letter' was the result. If its purpose was to shatter a sick and deeply disturbed man, it could not have been better contrived. 'Preacher of the Knout, apostle of illiteracy, protagonist of obscurantism, panegyrist of Tartar mores, what are you doing? Look under your feet: for you are standing over·an abyss', is a fair sample of its style.[16] Annenkov did not approve of *Select Passages*, but was apprehensive about the effect of Belinsky's letter on Gogol. He tried unsuccessfully to restrain his friend.[17]

Belinsky and later Chernyshevsky, laid the foundations for the radical tradition in Russian literary criticism which turned Gogol into the arch-realist critic of Russian life, and relegated his deeply religious side to the realm of aberration, if not lunacy. Most critics only later began to notice that so far from being an eccentricity, Gogol's religious outlook was the dominant force of his life, and that his supposed 'realism' was more in the nature of a moral parable than a portrayal of actuality.[18]

Turgenev certainly did not welcome the *Select Passages*, and years later expressed disapproval of the book in the strongest terms in his reminiscences of Gogol.[19] Indeed, it would have been very surprising if Turgenev, who disliked equally religious trappings, serfdom, and sentimental attachment to traditional 'old Russian ways' should have reacted to it other than negatively. However, he did not make any public pronouncement on the book at the time, though he is reputed to have welcomed in private the fiasco of *Select Passages* as one of the comforting manifestations of contemporary public opinion.[20] That Turgenev understood Gogol's book is suggested by a remark in a letter to Annenkov in 1853 where he points out that his intention had been to counterbalance and 'smooth out some of the savagery of *Dead Souls*'.[21] It is quite certain that he would not have approved of the violent tone of Belinsky's 'Letter' to a writer whom he considered, along with Pushkin and Lermontov, to be the greatest of his generation.

During this European visit Turgenev's constant preoccupation with Pauline Viardot came between him and Belinsky. The two Russians met once again in Paris, where Belinsky spent most of August, and where, to judge by Belinsky's letters to his wife, they seem to have been friendly enough. Belinsky's health improved somewhat, and he planned to return to St. Petersburg. Turgenev promised to see him off as far as Berlin, or even Stettin. 'But it is no good relying on Turgenev – he turned up for a few days in Paris, and then sneaked off again to the country to the Viardot', as Belinsky wrote to his wife. It was indeed from Courtavenel that Turgenev wrote to Belinsky on 17 September regretting that he could not take leave of him personally. A somewhat penitent couple of sentences feature in the letter. 'I don't have to assure you that any good news about you will bring me joy. I know I am an "urchin", as you call me, and generally a frivolous person, but I know how to love good people, and become attached to them for a long time.'[22] The two were not destined to meet again: Belinsky died in the following year, before Turgenev's return.

Turgenev's life in Paris (and in Courtavenel) during the next two and a half years, until his return to Russia in the summer of 1850, centred largely on Pauline Viardot, and, in her frequent absences on tour, on her family. He also did a substantial amount of writing, and firmly established his literary reputation. His main Russian friends during these years were Alexander and Natalie Herzen, in whose apartment he was a very frequent visitor. His friendship with Herzen became fairly warm and close – although Herzen's mocking attitude persists in his references to him in correspondence with common friends in Russia. Natalie never grew to like him at all. Turgenev also saw much of the Tuchkov family in the course of 1848, and in particular young Natalie Tuchkova, although without any suggestion of romance. (Natalie recalled an incident when Turgenev pressed her jokingly to say whom she would prefer to marry – Annenkov or him? Natalie laughingly replied that if forced to such a choice she would throw herself in the water. 'But what if there were no water?' – 'Well, I would choose you' – much to Turgenev's delight.)[23]

Other friends in Paris were Georg Herwegh and his wife Emma. Herwegh was a German poet and a revolutionary, and a family friend of the Herzens whom Turgenev had first met in 1842, and seems to have formed an attachment for – somewhat surprisingly, since Herwegh was the kind of extreme romantic for whom Turgenev usually had little time. In the revolutionary excitement of 1848 Herwegh led a detachment of French workers across the frontier into Germany, with the object of stirring up a rising. They were promptly massacred – though Herwegh himself escaped. Turgenev strongly disapproved of all this.[24] By the summer of 1849 Herzen had moved to Geneva, soon to be followed by his wife and the Herweghs – Herwegh's love affair with Natalie Herzen shortly afterwards was all but to wreck Herzen's life.

Michael Bakunin reappeared for a few months in 1847. He talked at length to his old friend of student days about his political plans and ambitions. This was before Bakunin was banished from Paris for delivering an inflammatory speech in favour of Polish independence. In 1863, when Turgenev was summoned by the Russian authorities to give evidence about his contacts with revolutionaries (see Chapter 12) he successfully concealed these meetings with Bakunin, and only referred to a casual encounter in the street.[25]

Throughout his stay in France Turgenev was often ill. He had been ill in Salzbrunn when staying with Belinsky, and Herzen's letters from Paris in 1848 contain a number of references to Turgenev's illness, which apparently was connected with his bladder and a suspected stone. There is even a statement about a 'cauterization' due to take place on 7 November 1848,[26] but no further mention of the operation is made. The illness which required such treatment may well have been a long one, because he was taken ill while travelling in the South of France in mid-October and, after recovering, returned to Paris, once again ill, on 6 November. In May 1849 he contracted the prevalent cholera (a disease of which he, not unnaturally, retained a morbid fear for the rest of his life) and was nursed back to health in the Herzens' flat.

While in Paris Turgenev was an enthusiastic visitor to the Opera, and described in detail to Pauline Viardot his impressions of other singers and the music of new operas, when she was absent. We can only surmise that when she sang in Paris he was in constant attendance: he heard Meyerbeer's *Prophet*, in which she appeared, ten times for example, and did not tire of it – unlike Pauline who, after ninety-nine performances, not unnaturally grew somewhat bored with it.[27] His taste for Rossini remained unchanged and he did not learn to like the music of Verdi.[28] Among new enthusiasms acquired in the years 1848–50 was the music of Mendelssohn, Meyerbeer, and above all Gounod, whose career was only starting, but whose appearance on the musical scene Turgenev characterized as 'something so unusual that one's happiness in welcoming it cannot be too great'.[29]

The theatre absorbed Turgenev all his life, and presumably during his Paris stay he spent long hours there, at a time when he was devoting much of his energy to writing plays. His taste in drama was classical. Shakespeare remained a lifelong enthusiasm, frequently quoted and studied, and Goethe second only to Shakespeare. He liked Corneille and Racine, and detested Victor Hugo. He was a voracious reader, especially of works of history, which are frequently mentioned in his letters at this time: Michelet on the French Revolution, for example, or works on Napoleon. Turgenev repeatedly

expressed admiration for the work of Michelet. But the two men
did not meet until 1872, despite an attempted introduction by Herzen
in 1857.[30] At the end of 1847 he began to study Spanish:[31] his remarkable facility for languages, which had distinguished him from
an early age, ensured rapid progress. The plays of Calderón aroused
his particular delight, especially *La vida es sueño* (which he compares
to and contrasts with *Hamlet*) and *El mágico prodigioso* ('Le Faust
espagnol ... je suis tout encalderonisé').[32]

We know of these intellectual activities from the long and detailed
accounts of his daily life which Turgenev wrote to Pauline whenever
she was away. In all, forty-seven letters from this period have been
published, dated between 22 July 1847 and 26 July 1850, some of
them extending to many printed pages. They are written in a spirit
of easy confidence and sincerity, and help to illuminate the development of his opinions and outlook.

There is a word in Russian, *poshlost'*, which has defied all translators
because of the many notions it embodies, including vulgarity, meanness, small-mindedness, banality, pettiness. It was with *poshlost'* that
Gogol was concerned when he wrote *Dead Souls*, and Pushkin (to
whom Gogol read the first part of *Dead Souls* some years before its
publication) constantly praised him for his unique ability to analyse
and expose this human disease.★ It was precisely with this quality
of the mean, the vulgar, the pettily vicious that Turgenev was concerned in so many of his writings, beginning with *Parasha* – the hero
of which, we are told, believed in *poshlost'* 'firmly and unremit-
tingly'.

Turgenev was to hate *poshlost'* above all else throughout the whole
of his life. His detestation of serfdom was now beyond question.
There was no longer any sign of the ambiguity which had still been
discernible in 1842. This development in his attitude may have been
influenced by the Decembrist N. I. Turgenev (see Chapter 8). His
dislike of the Church and of the whole system of religious ritual is
also very evident in his correspondence during this period[34] – indeed,
his continued enthusiasm for Feuerbach suggests that at this stage
of his life he may have been more inclined towards atheism than to
the agnosticism which usually characterized him.

Turgenev's letters also reveal the view of nature which was to recur
frequently in his writing, as something 'indifferent', as a blind force

★ Gogol, who did not intend *Dead Souls* as a satire, but as a diagnosis of the baseness which dwells within every human soul, designed the second part, of which
he burned the draft after five years' work, to show the way to redemption from
poshlost'.[33]

which causes suffering and destruction because it pursues its own course without any regard for the consequences to individuals. 'This does not prevent this rascally nature from being wonderfully beautiful. The nightingale can produce enchanting ecstasies in you while at the same time an unfortunate insect half-devoured is dying painfully in its gizzard.'[35] Another letter pays tribute to scientific progress which, in view of its increasing success in subjugating nature to man's intelligence will, perhaps, liberate and transform humankind. The greatest poets of the day are the Americans who are 'about to pierce the isthmus of Panama and to set up an electric telegraph across the ocean'.[36]

The most consistent feature of Turgenev's outlook at this time, which was to remain with him throughout, was loathing of violence in all its forms. This becomes particularly evident in his many references to the revolutionary events in France and elsewhere in the course of 1848. Turgenev's basic liberalism always placed him firmly on the side of democracy and against authoritarian repression in all its aspects:

I have from a reliable source two pieces of news, of which one is good and the other bad; Haynau has been crushed by the Hungarians beneath the walls of Pressbourg, and much more thoroughly than has been stated in the newspapers – but the Russians have defeated Dembinski [who held a command in Hungary]. The devil take all nationalistic feelings! There is only one country for any man who has a heart – democracy – and if the Russians should be victorious it will be dealt a death blow.[37]

The facts – which related to the Russian intervention to suppress the Hungarian rising – were not quite accurate, but the sentiment is clear. There are several similar outbursts against violence in the letters. He denounces a bloodthirsty Frenchman whom he encountered on a train and who described with relish the shooting in cold blood of seventeen insurgents – 'and drig, drig, drig, there they were, kicking in the road'.[38] And a few days later comes a remarkable outburst against the army in general, which Pauline Viardot withheld from publication in 1907:

What a nauseating and vile institution the army is! These African Chasseurs, who according to the statement of their own captain never give quarter, kill unarmed people, rape and plunder. ... May perdition take the lot of them! ... This old captain with his simple face and his jolly smile had the effect of an ogre on me. How he lamented the fact that one had not shot *all* the Paris insurgents![39]

But it would be wrong to infer that Turgenev was wholeheartedly on the side of the revolutionaries – indeed, he is careful not to take sides, except against brutality wherever it is to be found. His detailed description, in a letter to Pauline, of what he witnessed in Paris on 15 May 1848, is essentially impartial. One of the things that struck him particularly, he writes, was the impossibility of telling what it was that the population wanted: were they revolutionary, or reactionary, or simply friends of order?[40] But even if he did not sympathize with revolution, he respected what he considered to be the moral integrity of the revolutionaries, contrasting them, in reminiscences written twenty-six years later, with what he regarded as the tyranny of the *communards* in 1871.[41] He showed little sympathy for Louis Blanc, the leading socialist figure in France until he was forced to flee his country after the failure of the insurgency of 1848.[42] As for freedom, he writes after the events of 1848, 'If it comes to that, who said that man is intended to be free? History proves the opposite.'

Turgenev's dislike of violence extended to exaggerated expression and imbalance in literature, as we discover from some of the passages restored after Pauline's censorship. The most remarkable instance of this is his stricture on Grigorovich, a most forceful, if melodramatic, novelist whose main theme was criticism of serfdom, and whose powerful novel *Anton the Hapless* was published in 1847. Talent, he wrote to Pauline on 19 December 1847 with reference to Grigorovich, was of no avail if it disdained wit.[43] A few days later he was complaining that French society, in its present form, could not be expected to produce new and vital writers, but would produce authors like Scribe, Ponsard, and Hugo, 'or, at the very most, powerful, but tortured and sick prophets, like George Sand'.[44] To meet with Turgenev's approval, literature had to show the kind of moderation in outlook of which he was before long to become a master.

Turgenev's letters must have been a delight to receive. They are witty, charming, graceful, and imaginative, and far from the petty-mindedness and vulgarity (if allowance is made for the occasional spiteful or anti-semitic remark) which he so deplored in others. A picture of the young Turgenev would not be complete without some further examples of his epistolary style. Here is a sample of his charm, sentimentality almost:

Ah! Madame, what a good thing long letters are! (Like the one which you have just written to good Mamma, for example.) With what delight one begins to read it! It is as if one were, in summertime, entering a long alley, very green and very fresh. Ah! One says to oneself, it is good here; and one walks with short steps, one listens to the birds prattling. You prattle much better than they do, Madame. Please, go on like that: for you must know that you will never find more attentive readers, or more avid.[45]

And here is a somewhat more robust extract, written when Turgenev was recovering from cholera at Herzen's flat:

Speaking of cholera, if only I dared. . . . Ah bah! I'll chance it. Now you must know that when one is afflicted with this illness, one has to have many enemas, it is indeed one's only form of taking food. In this smiling land of France it is the custom for old women to administer them. My nurse accordingly was getting ready to perform her mission and I had already 'opened my bosom' to her, when, to my great surprise, instead of the rigid beak of the bird in question I got a finger being inserted. Startled, almost frightened, I withdrew hastily. 'What are you doing there, Madame?' 'Ah, Sir, I always begin like that, I can't see very well.' I ended up by holding the lamp for her – it was very difficult – I had to embrace her head with my arm. What a scene![46]

★   ★   ★   ★   ★

The most significant (and far and away the most popular) writing achieved by Turgenev during these years was his *Sketches from a Sportman's Notebook*. The present canon, based on an edition of 1874, includes three stories written very shortly before that date. Of the remaining twenty-one sketches, two (including 'Khor and Kalinych') were written in 1846, before Turgenev left Russia. One was written in Salzbrunn, twelve were written in France in 1847, two in France in 1848, and four after he had returned to Russia, in 1850 and 1851. 'Khor and Kalinych', which was never intended to become the first of a series, was published in the January 1847 issue of the *Contemporary*. It won wide acclaim, even from Konstantin Aksakov, in spite of its complimentary references to the policy of Peter the Great which the Slavophiles deplored. Belinsky praised it highly, as well as 'Petr Petrovich Karataev', which appeared in the following month, and expressed his opinion that this type of sketch from real life was Turgenev's true literary bent, rather than imaginative literature. Somewhat later, Gogol wrote to Annenkov in terms of highest praise for the stories. Annenkov showed the letter to Turgenev, who was naturally delighted.[47] Thus encouraged, and motivated by the belief that he was doing something to open the public's eyes to the evils of serfdom, Turgenev continued with the sketches, which were all published in the *Contemporary*.

In spite of some omissions dictated by the censor (and it was surprising that the censor should have allowed some of them to be published at all) most of the tales carried, directly or by implication, a picture of the arbitrariness, incompetence, and cruelty of serf-owners towards their serfs. There were exceptions. A story like the very popular 'Bezhin Meadow' contained no social message at all, while 'The Hamlet of Shchigrov District' was mainly a satire on the Moscow intellectual 'circles' of the forties. Another story, 'The District Doctor' was based on what Turgenev had heard about the death of Liubov Bakunina, and 'Kasyan' on what he had learned locally in Spasskoe about the life and trials of the sectarians. Several other stories were projected, but never written, and are known mainly from memoirs which record Turgenev's conversation – such as a terrifying encounter with a madwoman, related to Maupassant; or an account of the crushing to death of one of the Spasskoe house-serfs who fell into a bear or wolf pit on a hunting expedition and was killed when his horse fell on top of him.[48]

Of the effectiveness of the stories as a weapon against serfdom there can be no doubt. This was not only due to their great artistry, their humour, their realism, and the author's skill in understatement, but also because Turgenev had, for the first time probably, shown members of his own social standing that peasants were individual human beings, with intellectual and spiritual potentialities – a fact which very few landowners were accustomed to recognize. Annenkov points out that the *Sketches* contributed in no small measure to a change of attitude towards the peasants and their mental processes. They put an end to a tendency among 'Westernizing' intellectuals to treat the peasant with a certain degree of derision and contempt.[49] It is also quite certain that the future Emperor Alexander II was influenced by the *Sketches* in his final decision to put through the emancipation of the serfs,[50] and Turgenev regarded this as his main achievement in life.

In addition to 'Andrei Kolosov' and 'The Swashbuckler' Turgenev had completed for publication three further stories before leaving Russia. 'The Jew' was a dramatic story of the execution of a Jewish spy by the military authorities. 'Three Portraits' was based on a legend current in the Lutovinov family and is of interest as the first appearance of a supernatural theme in Turgenev's writing. The third story, 'Petushkov', is very reminiscent of Gogol in its depiction of types. The theme, however, is characteristic of Turgenev: the degradation and humiliation which the desire of a man for a woman brings in its train. This recurrent theme in his writing (*A Month in the Country* and *Spring Torrents* are notable examples) is also central to 'The Diary of a Superfluous Man', written in France during this visit, and published in April 1850 in *Annals of the Fatherland*. It was written at intervals in 1848 and 1849, and completed in Paris on 15 January 1850.

The story takes the form of a diary of the last days of a dying man, who reflects bitterly that his entire life has been 'superfluous'. The hero, Chulkaturin, is the human failure, the man who is ignored and passed over by life: Turgenev had already portrayed such a man in one of the *Sketches from a Sportsman's Notebook*, 'The Hamlet of Shchigrov District'. So Chulkaturin, in his bashful courting of Liza, the daughter of a locally important official, is completely displaced and outshone by a dazzlingly attractive, successful, and confident prince, who captivates her completely, only soon to discard her. But the heart-broken Liza does not even turn for consolation to Chulkaturin, but marries instead a dull and solid admirer in order to escape. The peak of Chulkaturin's humiliation comes when he insults the prince, and is challenged to a duel. He fires first, and inflicts a scratch wound on the prince's hand. The prince, entitled to fire in return, magnanimously declares the duel over, and fires into the air. The 'superfluous man' (or so it seems to Chulkaturin) is not even considered worth killing.

The 'superfluous man' was to preoccupy Turgenev as a political figure and a victim of the Russian social background, at least from *Rudin* onwards. But there is nothing political about the fate of poor, consumptive Chulkaturin, who is destroyed by his own temperament, or unassertive character. It is interesting to observe that the 'superfluous man' emerges in Turgenev's work in the first instance as a human problem, a problem of temperament – Turgenev's abiding concern in virtually all of his writing. The contrasts of 'The Diary of a Superfluous Man' – the dull, virtuous failure set against the dazzling, determined but morally rather reprehensible winner in the pursuit of a woman – occur in various forms in Turgenev's fiction, notably in 'First Love'.

Apart from *A Month in the Country*, Turgenev wrote four other plays while he was in France. One of them was a slight, comic, one-act sketch, *Lunch with the Marshal of the Nobility*, a satire on *poshlost'* among the landed gentry, which was staged in 1849, and frequently thereafter. Of his more substantial plays, the longer one-act *Where it's thin, it tears* was published in the *Contemporary* for November 1848, and was staged in 1851, and occasionally thereafter, though without great success. It is a bookish rather than a dramatic work. The two-act *Alien Bread* is in quite a different category. A newly married St.

Petersburg high civil servant returns with his wife in order to settle on her estate. An old, degraded nobleman has been living there free of charge for years. He is, in fact, the father of the young wife, though neither the wife nor her husband – nor, for that matter, anyone else – knows this. After being derided, teased, humiliated, and encouraged to get drunk by the civil servant and his despicable neighbours, who are guests at luncheon, the old man blurts out the truth. After explaining the whole story to his daughter, he endures for her sake the humiliation of being bought off by the husband and enabled to end his days elsewhere. The play combines Turgenev's intense sympathy for the human tragedy of the father with bitter satire on the grand husband from St. Petersburg and the local gentry, and on their despicable ethical standards.

Intended for performance at the benefit of the actor M. S. Shchepkin, it was rejected by the theatrical censor – not surprisingly, perhaps, in view of the fact that the censor was S. A. Gedeonov, about one of whose plays Turgenev had published a scathing article a few years before. But the play was also rejected for publication on the grounds that it was prejudicial to the good name of the landed gentry, and it did not appear in print until 1857.*

The three-act comedy *The Bachelor*, a satire on the *mores* of St. Petersburg officials, was performed in October 1849. It was the first play of Turgenev's to be staged, and was given a mixed reception. It had been published in *Annals of the Fatherland* in September 1849.

Turgenev was thus contributing both to Nekrasov's *Contemporary* and to Kraevsky's *Annals of the Fatherland*, to both of whom he owed money. By the time he had paid off all advances, in the shape of contributions, Turgenev was desperately in need. Many years later he claimed that his mother had provided him with no financial support at all during the whole of the time that he was in France.[52] But since his correspondence in 1849 shows that he had heard from his brother in August that there would be no payment for that year, or in future, of the 6,000 roubles which his mother normally allowed him, it is fair to assume that he received 6,000 roubles a year from Varvara Petrovna (around £270 sterling) in 1847 and 1848.[53] There are, incidentally, no letters from either year urgently requesting advances from his editors, which also suggests that until 1849 Turgenev had had enough to live on. Whatever the

---

* One of the fair copies of the manuscript of this play was dedicated to P. Ya Chaadaev 'as a mark of sincere friendship by the author' – Turgenev had met Chaadaev at M. F. Orlov's house in 1842, but there is no evidence of any close friendship between them.[51]

true position, in August 1849 the news reached him that there would
be no money from Russia at all for that year, or in the future, and
Turgenev was forced to borrow 400 francs from Louis Viardot,[54]
as well as to press his editors for further advances against future contributions. Evidently Varvara Petrovna was growing tired of her
son's long absence, and was no doubt not best pleased by his continued association with 'the gipsy'. There was also friction because
of his brother's intended marriage, in which matter Turgenev took
his brother's part, to his mother's fury. All that he received from
his mother before his departure from France for Russia was,
apparently, 600 roubles, which would scarcely have paid for his fare,
let alone his debts.[55] By the end of his stay Turgenev's earnings, debts
apart, were not entirely negligible. He was being paid 50 (silver)
roubles for a printer's sheet by the *Contemporary* and 200 (paper)
roubles by the *Annals*, the equivalent of around 60 silver roubles (in
sterling equivalents: £8 and £9.10),[56] and the plays and the longer
stories ran to several sheets each. But Turgenev was never very provi-
dent with his money and was certainly still in debt when he left
France.

★ ★ ★ ★ ★

During the years which Turgenev spent in France, Pauline Viardot
was absent a good deal from Paris (or Courtavenel) and the time
which they could spend together was restricted. She was away for
about six months in the winter of 1847–8, on tour in Germany. In
1848 she spent a short summer in London, returning to Paris to prepare for her long season there, in the course of which she was to
appear in a new opera by Meyerbeer, *Le Prophète*. The summer of
1849 found her once again in London; Turgenev spent the time of
her absence in Courtavenel, much of it alone. Pauline returned to
Paris in October 1849 and stayed there or at Courtavenel (apart from
a visit to Berlin) until her departure for London and Turgenev's
return to Russia in the summer of 1850.* His letters during these
periods of separation, which are often more in the nature of diaries,
also tell us much about the course of their friendship. They contain
a detailed account of how he spent his time in her absence, which
shows how much he sought to interweave his own life with those
of Pauline's mother, Madame Garcia, her brother, and other relatives. They all foregathered regularly for an almost ritual cult of the

---

* On 30 October 1849 she sang in a performance of Mozart's Requiem on
the occasion of Chopin's funeral when Turgenev was present.

absent Pauline, to rejoice over her repeated stage triumphs. Conversation was in Spanish. A feature of many evenings was Turgenev's ceremonial reading aloud of Pauline's letters to her mother, giving details of her successes. The foreign newspapers were also scanned for reports of her performances: on one occasion in 1849, Turgenev made the journey to Paris from Courtavenel, with the sole purpose of reading what the English papers had to say about her appearances in London.[57]

Turgenev kept Pauline supplied with detailed accounts of the merits of other singers who appeared in the operas which he attended. It will not cause surprise to learn that the accomplishments of other ladies did not, in Turgenev's view, measure up to Pauline's. Jenny Lind, for example, whom he heard in London in July 1847 (who by all contemporary accounts had a superb voice) was 'a charming singer, who can do certain things better than anyone but... but... I don't have to tell you "but" what'.[58] Evidently she consulted him in her letters on how to perform certain roles, and he gave her very perceptive advice. In advising her on the dramatic performance of the role of Romeo in Bellini's *I Capuletti ed i Montecchi* (which is scored for a female voice) he says that while one cannot imagine deeper despair than to be faced with the corpse of the one whom one loves above all, stifled cries, sobs or fainting 'are nature, they form no part of art'. What is required is 'the calm which derives from a ... deep emotion; yet one must at the same time avoid extreme calm since there is the risk of appearing cold'.[59] Occasionally he gave her advice of a more practical nature, unrelated to the theatre:

Please forgive the great liberty which I am going to take in talking about your apartment [in Berlin] but – why are certain areas, which are only referred to in English, probably because the English are the most modest of all people in their language, exposed to the inclemency of the seasons and to the severity of the cold air? Take care in such places, I beg of you, and do something to remedy this state of affairs; it is a greater danger than may appear at first sight in this time of influenza and rheumatism.[60]

Were Turgenev and Pauline lovers, in the accepted usage of the word? It is impossible on the available evidence to know, but it seems probable that their love was consummated on some occasions in 1849 and 1850. In the 'Memorial' Turgenev records under the year 1849: '14/26 June I was for the first time with P.'* In May 1849 he had fallen

* The entry is followed immediately by a reference to the purchase of Diana – his favourite bitch, who was thereafter to remain, even after her death, unrivalled by any other sporting dog or bitch.[61]

ill with cholera, in Paris, at the Herzens' apartment. Pauline was in Courtavenel, and, as he began to recover, he wrote to her frequently with accounts of his progress. He planned to join her there as soon as possible, but was not able to do so until after 12 June, probably on 13 June. By 19 June however Pauline had left Courtavenel, since in a letter to her from there Turgenev writes 'after your departure'.[62] This must mean departure from Courtavenel, since Pauline, whose next destination was London, only left Paris for London on the night of 8–9 July, as we know from a letter of 9 July from Turgenev, who was by now in Paris. ('It is now 4 o'clock – you have been in London for six hours'.)[63] Since the last known letter from Turgenev written from Courtavenel was dated 20 June it was possible for Turgenev to have returned to Paris by 26 June, and to have been with Pauline. It may be that the danger of death which Turgenev had so recently faced brought them together more intimately than hitherto.

The passages of endearment, usually in German, with which Turgenev often embellished his letters to Pauline, suggest two dates when there was special intimacy and devotion on Turgenev's side (though, of course, in the absence of their complete correspondence, any inference must remain very tentative): October 1848, when, after a reunion with Pauline on her return to Paris from London, Turgenev went off on a short tour of the South of France, was, perhaps, one such period. 'Guten Tag, liebste, beste, teuerste, Frau, guten Tag, einziges Wesen' ('Good morning, best loved, best and dearest woman, good morning, you only being') he begins his letter from Lyon. After recounting details of the journey, he tells her that he had tried to write some poetry for her, but that nothing had come of it, and ends this day's instalment (it continues on the following day), 'May God bless you. Dearest angel. ... May God and all his angels watch over you'.[64] Even greater endearment is to be found in his letters of July 1849 – those written after 26 June, the date he noted down in the 'Memorial'. In one from Paris, immediately after her departure for London he writes: 'Gott segne Sie Tausend mal, Sie einzige Teuerste' ('God bless you a thousand times, you only one, and dearest one'). And two days later from Paris: 'Liebes, teueres Wesen, jede Minute denke ich an Sie, an den Vergnügen, an die Zunkunft. ... Sie sind das Beste, was es auf der Erde gibt' ('I think of you every minute, of the pleasure, of the future. ... You are the best that there is on earth').[65] And on 23 July he writes from Courtavenel, where he had returned from Paris: 'Liebe, Theuere! Gott sei mit Dir und segne Dich!' ('Most loved and dearest! God be with

you and bless you!'). This is the only known instance in his letters
to Pauline where Turgenev uses the intimate 'Dich' in place of the
usual, formal 'Sie'. And later comes the sentence: 'Ich bin zu auf-
geregt, um Ihnen weiter zu schreiben' ('I am too excited to write
to you any more'). There also occurs in this letter (again in German)
a curious reference to her husband: 'What is the matter with Viardot? Does he perhaps dislike the fact that I am living here?' (i.e. in
Courtavenel).[66]

However, having noted for what it is worth the evidence of correspondence in support of the view that the two became lovers in June
1849, it is probable that for Turgenev the physical side of love was
never of the greatest importance, so far as the three or four women
in his life with whom he was on terms of most intimate friendship
were concerned. If his own feelings on the subject are mirrored in
Smoke, *Spring Torrents* and elsewhere, then for Turgenev sexual
passion was above all a disease, a madness almost, beyond man's control and little related to the true love and devotion which a man can
feel for a woman. Late in life, at a time when such confidences are
most likely to be sincere, Turgenev told a woman friend that, to
him, 'the physical side of his relationships with women had always
mattered less than the spiritual side, that consummation was always
less important to him than the emotions which preceded it. ...'[67]

Early in 1850 Turgenev decided that he must return to Russia,
however little he relished the prospect. To Herzen the reason for
his decision was quite clear – he was returning to Russia because Pauline had demanded it. 'Turgenev is mad', he wrote to Herwegh on
1 April, 'to go at a time like this to die in the clutches of Nicholas,
for the Garcia.'[68] The evidence suggests that the reason was not quite
so simple. It is clear that the subject of Turgenev's departure was
discussed at length between him and Pauline: 'You are good as an
angel', he wrote to her on 7 May 1850,

but it is really too painful to return to this subject once again. My decision
causes me too much distress as it is. I will only tell you one thing. You
counsel me to be prudent. But prudence urges me to return straightaway:
to stay any longer in Europe would be highly imprudent. But I have already
told you all my reasons in the letter which you must have received yesterday
[This letter is not known]. I am in despair (and this is no mere phrase)
at causing you distress: I beg of you, my good friends, to spare me and
not to make my task more difficult: believe me, it is difficult enough.

His plan at this date was to leave Paris on 16 May, and reach Berlin
on the 20th. The arrangement was that he would meet Pauline in
Berlin on his way to Russia, and say goodbye to her there.[69]

One of the reasons urged by Turgenev we can guess from a letter from Pauline written between 29 June and 3rd July 1850 from London (written after his departure): 'If you believe that your departure has done me good, you deceive yourself vastly.'[70] Another reason may, perhaps, have been (as Mrs. FitzLyon suggests) Pauline's apparent infatuation with young Charles Gounod, who was composing his opera *Sappho* with a part for her; as a result, she spent a great deal of time with him and had installed him, with his mother, at Courtavenel. As against this, however, there is ample evidence in Turgenev's correspondence of his genuine, affectionate, and continuing friendship for Gounod, right up to 1852 when Gounod married, and his wife insulted Pauline. After that, friendship between the Viardots and Gounod was ended until 1871. Turgenev, naturally enough, took the Viardots' side. 'All is over between us', he wrote to Pauline.[71]

Whatever emotional reasons may have been involved, there were good practical reasons calling Turgenev back to Russia at this time. His financial situation was very precarious, and Varvara Petrovna was in no mood to come to the rescue to any significant extent. Moreover, her relations with her other son had reached breaking point over his marriage. But, most significantly of all, important as Turgenev's attachment to Pauline Viardot was for him, his literary vocation was at least equally vital. Prolonged absence from Russia, without even an occasional visit, could have had a devastating effect on his work as a writer. He may also, with justice, have feared that if he stayed away from Russia much longer he could be forced to become a permanent exile, like Herzen. The Russian authorities would certainly have known of his meetings with radicals and liberals in France, and might well have decided before long to prohibit his return.

In spite of his original intention to leave early in May, Turgenev delayed his departure on the strength of advice from a friend in Russia (probably Annenkov) that the moment was not politically propitious, since the Emperor, Nicholas I, was in a particularly bad temper.[72] On 20 June 1850 he wrote to Pauline of his decision to leave in a few days' time,[73] and confirmed his decision in a letter written the following day. 'Twenty-four hours of reflection have only strengthened my resolve. ... You can imagine that without some pretty serious reasons I would never have taken such a decision. I leave – but with what sadness of spirit, with what a weight on my heart!'[74] Possibly Pauline had not been convinced by his earlier professions of his determination to leave France, especially as he had

already postponed his departure once before. At all events her letter
to him, written from London, undated but evidently in reply to his
letter of 20 June, expresses consternation at his decision, although
'Louis and I had entertained some suspicions when we saw you
remove Diana [his favourite bitch], and all your belongings and your
money from Courtavenel.' In a postscript, both she and her husband
in effect accept his decision with regret, and urge him to come back
to France as soon as possible.[75] The long letter of 29 June/3 July,
again with a postscript by Viardot, followed him to Russia; it is,
like the earlier one, couched in terms of warmest friendship and affection, but nothing more.[76] Of course, there may have been other letters from Pauline in different terms (and without postscripts by her
husband) which have not been revealed to us. But on the evidence
it is clear that by this date, June 1850, there was little left on Pauline's
side of the passionate relationship suggested by Turgenev's correspondence in July 1849. The tone of Turgenev's letters, however,
remains unchanged, with insertions of endearments in German as
before, if not quite as intimate as they had been earlier.

There is a certain mystery about the circumstances of their parting.
According to Turgenev he said goodbye to Pauline on 17 June
1850.[77] Since the Viardots left for London on 14 June Turgenev may
have been mistaken about this date and meant 14 June (there is no
doubt that he wrote 17 June – the original manuscript is quite
clear).[78] Or, alternatively, since Paris was only twelve and a half
hours away from London, he may have travelled to London to see
her. But whatever day they parted, his letters of 20 and 21 June, in
which he announced his imminent departure, and her reply, suggest
that Turgenev had said nothing definite about going back to Russia.
Did his courage fail him? Or was he still debating the issue with
himself, and hoping against hope that he would somehow succeed
in postponing the evil day? It is more likely that Turgenev was right
about the date – 17 June – and that there was a parting which was
kept secret from Louis; and that the letters from London, written
in effect jointly with Louis, were a device to allay the husband's suspicions. And there are hints in Turgenev's later letters to Pauline which
suggest that there was some intimate discussion between them when
they parted: for example, on 8 December 1850, he writes: 'Are we
going to meet this [coming] year?' And then, in German: 'But even
if I were able to come to you, I would only do so if you were to
summon me.'[79]

The longest of the plays which Turgenev wrote while in France,
which eventually came to be known as *A Month in the Country*,

suggests, as do so many of his works, a basis in personal experience. Originally called *The Student*, Turgenev started work on it early in 1849. By 14 April one of its five acts had been written; the fourth act had been completed by 25 December, and the work in its entirety was completed on 22 March 1850, copied and sent off to the *Contemporary*. The censor promptly banned its publication. It was forbidden again later in the year when submitted under the new title *Two Women*. It was not licensed for publication until 1855 (with its present title), and then only on condition that the central character, Natalia Petrovna, should be transformed into a widow, thus destroying much of the point of the play. The censor also cut out a number of rude remarks about the gentry, and the lecture on love quoted below.[80]

As Turgenev told the actress Savina many years later, 'Rakitin is myself. I always portray myself as the unsuccessful lover in my novels.'[81] And indeed Rakitin's predicament in some respects resembles Turgenev's situation in the spring of 1850. He is in love with Natalia Petrovna, whose husband is his close friend. Rakitin has lived for the past four years in Natalia Petrovna's country house, in constant and devoted attendance on this capricious lady. During his temporary absence Natalia Petrovna has engaged a student as tutor for her small son. When Rakitin returns he sees a change in Natalia Petrovna, and it soon emerges that she has fallen in love with the rather uncouth (and socially inferior) student. So has her seventeen-year-old ward Vera – and the rivalry between the two women, which gave the play its second title, is its central point. (This idea was probably derived from a play by Balzac, *La Marâtre*, which ran on the Paris stage in 1848.) Rakitin, discovered with Natalia Petrovna in his arms by her husband when he is trying to comfort her lovesick despair, is forced into a very friendly explanation with the husband about his 'innocent' relations with Natalia Petrovna and decides that he must leave. The student, somewhat bewildered by the two women who have fallen in love with him, also reluctantly leaves, but not before Rakitin has lectured him on the deceptive joys of love – a constant theme in Turgenev's works.

In my opinion, Aleksei Nikolaevich, every love, happy as well as unhappy, is a real disaster when you give yourself over to it entirely. ... Wait! You will perhaps still discover how these delicate little hands can torture you! ... You will remember me when you are thirsting for peace as a sick man thirsts for health, when you are thirsting for the most senseless, the most banal peace. ... Wait! You will learn what it means to belong to a skirt, what it means to be enslaved, infected – and how shameful and oppressive this slavery is![82]

Finally, the ward, who from being a child has become a grown woman almost overnight, decides to accept an offer of marriage from a grotesque, middle-aged neighbour in order to escape from Natalia Petrovna. In the course of a few days the peaceful, humdrum life of the country house, with Rakitin content to trail his undemanding devotion at the feet of Natalia Petrovna, has been completely shattered by passionate love.

The publication of *A Month in the Country* aroused little interest. Those critics who did notice it dismissed it as too much concerned with psychology, and too much devoted to long and elaborate conversations to make a play. It had comparatively little success when it was first produced on the Russian stage in January 1872, though rather more when Savina acted in it after 1879. Many critics complained that it was really a novel, and not a play. Later generations have taken a different view, and *A Month in the Country* has now established itself as a play which can attract both large audiences and first-class actors and actresses. It is beyond question Turgenev's only play with a claim to dramatic distinction. The charge of bookishness can justly be levelled at the earlier plays, but *A Month in the Country* is of absorbing psychological subtlety, and rivets the attention, even if its action is limited. It stands out as a drama of emotions, in the manner made familiar by Chekhov – but composed some forty years earlier. Indeed it may be that the popularity of Chekhov's plays has made modern audiences more ready to admire a play of this kind than would have been the case in the 1870s.

Of course *A Month in the Country* does not describe what happened at Courtavenel when Turgenev decided that he must leave for Russia. It makes little sense to try to identify Gounod, and Pauline's infatuation for him, with the student tutor and Natalia Petrovna's passionate attachment to him, if only because much of the play had been completed, and therefore the main outlines of it already planned, before Gounod came into Pauline's life. The central theme of the play is the rivalry of the two women, which has no bearing on Turgenev's own experience. It is not impossible that Turgenev had to offer up some explanation to Viardot of the kind that Rakitin made to Natalia Petrovna's husband, because in his farewell letter to Louis, Turgenev thanks him for his good advice – 'de vos bons conseils'.[83] Did this mean 'advice' to moderate his attentions to Pauline? What can be said with certainty is that the play mirrors a predicament which must have occupied Turgenev's thoughts a good deal while he was writing it – that of the close family friend in love with the wife, and forced to ask himself how it will end.

We still do not know exactly how it all did end. Did Turgenev decide that he must go, as his letters suggest, because weighty reasons drew him to Russia? Did Pauline in fact decide to put a stop to the kind of friendship which had existed between them in the summer of 1849? For there is no doubt that their relationship had changed by 1850, and Turgenev knew it. 'We will remain friends, will we not?' he writes in one of the two sad farewell letters that he sent to her from Paris on the eve of his departure for Stettin, to set sail for Russia.[84] Is it really possible that he could have doubted even this? Even after the lapse of a century and a quarter, his last words from Paris are still deeply moving. They come from the heart of a man for whom a luminous and happy phase of his life has reached its end, leaving an uncertain future before him, hidden in the dark maze of reactionary Russia. 'If you were willing to promise me in return that you will remember me – I believe I could more easily bear this absence – with a less heavy heart. ...' And next morning: 'I have hardly slept; I awoke every few minutes, and I felt my sorrow continuing in my sleep'. Two hours later, he is packing and weeping: 'Adieu – adieu. I embrace you all, you, Viardot – blessings on you – my dear, good friends, my only family, whom I love above anything in the world. ... I commend you to God. Be happy. I love you and I will love you to the end of my life.'[85] He kept his promise.

The clue to the relationship between Turgenev and the Viardots lies in those three words, 'ma seule famille'. He had interwoven his life with theirs, with that of the whole family. For this warm-hearted man always sought affection and friendly intimacy with his fellow humans, looking for the kind of family life which he had never known in Varvara Petrovna's household, or for that matter, while his father was alive. Of the suffering which this break caused him there can be no doubt. When he arrived back in Russia, though he was not yet thirty-two years of age, he looked old and haggard, and his hair was beginning to turn grey.[86]

CHAPTER SIX

Arrest and Exile

It was not only sorrow at parting from Pauline that sent Turgenev back to Russia with a heavy heart. Life for an intellectual of even mildly liberal inclinations had not been easy when he left Russia in 1847: it had become much harder since the events of 1848 in Europe had thrown Nicholas I and his advisers into a panic fear of contagion from revolutionary ideas. In 1849 the so-called Petrashevsky conspiracy had been 'unmasked'. Over thirty-five men were arrested, of whom twenty-one, including Dostoevsky, were sentenced to death. After having been put through the elaborate farce of a pretence to carry out the executions, the 'conspirators' were graciously pardoned by the Emperor, and their sentences commuted to various terms of penal servitude. Only in Russian conditions of 1848 and 1849 could these young men, who gathered in private to discuss social and political problems and critically to examine Russian internal affairs, have been treated as conspirators – though there is some evidence that a few of them, including Dostoevsky, may have been involved in a clandestine conspiratorial nucleus within the organization. From 2 April 1848 until the accession of Alexander II in 1855, the efforts of the existing censorship were reinforced by a kind of super-censorship, usually known as the Secret or Buturlin Committee. The liberal-minded, but very far from revolutionary or even oppositionist censor and scholar Alexander Nikitenko, noted in his diary a few weeks after 2 April that terror gripped everyone who thought or wrote.

'Secret denunciations and spying complicated the situation even more. People began to fear for each day of their existence, thinking that it might be their last among their loved ones and friends.'[1] Annenkov's *Diary* for the period 1849 to 1851 bristles with anecdotes of arrests and interrogations of intellectuals on the kind of suspicion which could arise only in the minds of not very literate policemen.

The historian, Professor O. M. Bodiansky, for example, was arrested for publishing Giles Fletcher's *Of the Russe Commonwealth* – the impressions of Queen Elizabeth's Ambassador to Muscovy; and the Slavophile Iurii Samarin was confined to the fortress as the author of an *unpublished* manuscript criticizing the Baltic Germans. There were many more such instances.[2] All this took place under the personal supervision of Nicholas; the circle of intellectuals was small, and almost entirely drawn from the nobility. Turgenev had already, while he was in France, experienced difficulties with the censor, particularly over the production and publication of his plays. But this was to prove relatively trivial in comparison with the events of 1852.

After a short stay in St. Petersburg, Turgenev travelled on to Moscow, where he arrived on 3 July. Writing on board ship to Pauline Viardot he had begged to be allowed to pour out his troubles to her, and the request was repeated from Moscow on 4 July 1850. Henceforth, for the years during which he was to remain separated from her, he filled his letters with minute details of the tribulations which beset him. In Moscow he found his brother Nikolai married to Anna Yakovlevna Shvarts. For a long time his mother had opposed the marriage, and Nikolai and Anna had eventually dispensed with the ceremony and lived together. Varvara Petrovna's consent to the marriage had been made conditional on Nikolai retiring from the army. But since she did not provide him with enough to live on he had to subsist as best he could on giving lessons, and the like. She also refused to receive Anna in her Moscow establishment, or at Spasskoe, and insulted and humiliated both her son and his wife in the most petty and irrational manner, which even the birth of their child did nothing to abate.[3]

The final break between the two sons and their mother came soon after Ivan's return and was occasioned by Varvara Petrovna's refusal to make any kind of financial provision for them, other than doling out pittances when the humour took her. If the account of little Varvara is to be believed (who by this time was seventeen years old and much involved in the disputes as go-between from mother to sons), both men behaved with respect and restraint and did everything they could to avert the last, decisive quarrel. On the other hand, Turgenev would shortly afterwards describe little Varvara's character in terms of scathing condemnation of a kind which he rarely used. This was after his mother's death, when arrangements had to be made to find a home for her. He was apparently outraged by what he believed were her mercenary intrigues. She was 'false, wicked, wily and heartless.... What a vile and perverted nature at seventeen years of age!'⁴ They did not meet again until near the end of his life – in Moscow, in May 1880 – a meeting which was to be their last. By that date no trace of past enmity remained.⁵ Strange to say, there is no indication in his correspondence or elsewhere that Turgenev knew of the blood relationship between them. He would certainly have discovered the true situation when he read his mother's diary after she died,⁶ but he never referred to it.

There was a further matter which poisoned relations between Turgenev and his mother – his rediscovery of his daughter, whose existence he seems up till then to have forgotten. One day, while at Spasskoe, he observed through the window a small and poorly dressed young girl, being forced by a coachman to carry a pail of water. He remonstrated indignantly with his mother. Varvara Petrovna called the child in, and, roaring with laughter, asked the assembled guests to say whom the child resembled, and then, turning to her son, said 'Why, it is your daughter.'⁷ Turgenev gave Pauline a brief account of his newly discovered child and asked her advice on how to educate her, stressing the fact that her mother, who was of loose morals, took no interest in her, and he was anxious that the child should forget her. Pauline generously offered to bring the little girl up in her own household⁸ – an offer which Turgenev readily accepted. For the moment the Viardots had to advance money for the child's keep. Later, after the death of his mother, Turgenev provided an annual income of 1,200 francs for her.⁹ Early in October he took her to St. Petersburg and made arrangements for her to travel to Paris in the care of a Madame Robert. Paulinette, as she became known (she had been christened Pelageia), left St. Petersburg with her companion on 23 October.¹⁰ Turgenev blamed himself for the ravages which the character of this eight-year-old had suffered as the result of her upbringing, and which appalled him. In place of the little savage he had expected to find, he discovered a very intelligent, very cold and calculating little person. She shocked her father on one occasion when she told him that she never felt pity for anyone. '"But if you should see someone suffer?" – "Oh well, what about it? I only have pity for myself. ... I am small, but I have seen the world. I know everything – I have seen everything."'¹¹

Having broken with their mother, the two sons and Nikolai's German wife, Anna, settled in Turgenevo, their father's former estate, some ten miles away from Spasskoe where Varvara Petrovna was now established. It was a modest property, quite inadequate to support two families, and much neglected. But the efficient Anna

Yakovlevna made life as comfortable as possible.* For a time there were the consolations of country life, including peasant festivities and, of course, shooting expeditions with his much loved bitch, Diana. Turgenev by now seems to have been able to support himself by a combination of his literary earnings and editors' loans on account, so he ceded to his brother his own 'share' of Turgenevo. Legally Varvara Petrovna was the owner of her late husband's property, but she does not, somewhat remarkably, seem to have done anything to persecute her two sons while they were there, beyond immediately recalling her peasant huntsman Afanasii, Turgenev's favourite companion on shooting expeditions. Having settled affairs at the estate, Turgenev moved to St. Petersburg where it was his intention to spend the whole winter. But the death of his mother in Moscow forced him to change his plans.[13]

He was not in time to find her alive when he arrived in Moscow on 20 November: she had died four days earlier. According to the account left by her daughter, she had been ill for some months before, and her doctor, Inozemtsev, had pronounced her incurable. Her sons wrote to her: she read their letters, but did not reply, nor, until the very end, express any wish to see them. She made (again, according to Varvara) certain dispositions of her property – a legacy of 15,000 silver roubles (£2,300) and much jewellery to her daughter (which, according to Turgenev, was obtained by Varvara by dishonest influence), their freedom and pecuniary bequests to several serfs. Towards the end she did receive Nikolai, and begged him to send for Ivan. This was immediately done, but the journey from St. Petersburg to Moscow in 1850 (one year before the railway was opened) took five days and so he arrived too late.[14]

Varvara's picture of her mother's peaceful and orderly end must be treated with caution: if Turgenev's strictures on her mercenary behaviour are right, she had a strong interest to portray the old lady as calm and in full possession of her faculties right up to her death. A very different description of the last hours of this strange, unhappy woman was given by Turgenev in a detailed letter to Pauline Viardot, dated 24 November.

My mother died without having made any provisions of any kind: she left all this multitude of lives who depended on her as it were in the street. We shall have to do what she ought to have done. Her last days were really

---

* Turgenev spoke quite warmly of her at this time, though only a few years later he described her to his friend Fet as 'hideous . . . cruel, capricious . . . and extremely depraved' and could not understand his brother's attachment to her.[12]

sad – God preserve us from a similar death. Her only desire was to deafen herself. On the eve of her death, and indeed when the rattle of the death agony was beginning, there was – by her orders – an orchestra playing polkas in the neighbouring room.

He adds an account of her final and precise instructions to her estate manager to take steps to reduce as much as possible the value of the property which her two sons would inherit.

Well, all this must be forgotten, and I will willingly forget, now that you, who are my confessor, know all about it. And yet, I feel it, it would have been so easy for her to make herself loved and missed by us all. Ah, yes – may God preserve us from a death like hers! And may God grant her peace![15]

Turgenev portrayed his mother in his fiction ('Mumu', 'Punin and Baburin', 'The Privy Office') as a tyrannous and unreasonable domestic despot. Yet this letter, written with obvious deep emotion, suggests that he understood her real tragedy – that she desperately wanted to be loved by her sons, but the actions to which her warped character drove her repelled them. An entry in her diary, made shortly before her death, suggests that she had realized this herself: 'Mother of God, my children, forgive me. And you, oh Lord, forgive me as well – for pride, this mortal sin, was always my sin.'[16]

Turgenev had not yet experienced any kind of triumph as a playwright. Two slight plays, *The Bachelor* and *Lunch with the Marshal of the Nobility*, had been staged in 1849, and fairly frequently thereafter, without attracting much notice. *A Month in the Country* and *Alien Bread* were still forbidden by censorship, and two sketches (*Carelessness* and *Lack of Money*) and the light comedy *Where it's thin, it tears* were known only on the pages of the journals where they had been published, and had been quite coolly received. A minor success now awaited him with a new one-act comedy. In October 1850 he offered to write a short play for the actress N. V. Samoilova and her actor brother. The offer was accepted and *The Provincial Lady* was first staged in Moscow on 18 January 1851, and in St. Petersburg (when N. V. Samoilova's actress sister and her brother appeared in it) on 22 January. It was very popular with the audiences, and was frequently revived thereafter. The serious critics, however, and especially those of Slavophile tendency, dismissed it as frivolous and without relevance to the social problems of the day – as indeed it was. Turgenev was present, more or less by accident, since his departure for St. Petersburg had been delayed by illness. He was overwhelmed. 'Just imagine,' he wrote to Pauline, 'I was recalled with such shouts

of enthusiasm that I ran for my life as if pursued by a thousand devils.'
The uproar lasted for a quarter of an hour and only subsided when
the audience were told that Turgenev was not in the theatre.[17] He
reached St. Petersburg in time to witness the first performance of
The Provincial Lady in the Alexandrine Theatre.[18] Although there
was no repetition of the wild excitement shown by the Moscow
audience, the play became firmly established in the repertoire of that
famous theatre. Except for two further dramatic sketches (*Conversation on the Highway* and *Evening in Sorrento*), written in 1851 and 1852,
this was to be the end of Turgenev's activity as a playwright. He
came to the conclusion that writing for the stage was not his true
vocation. When *A Month in the Country* was eventually staged, without great success, in 1872, Turgenev wrote to his brother that he
had been convinced all along that his play would be a failure. 'That
is why I gave up writing for the stage after 1851: that is not my
type of work.'[19] The success of the play when it was revived in 1879
with Savina in the role of Vera, came too late to make him change
his mind. As far as his comic plays and sketches are concerned, he
was probably right: they owed too much to the influence of Gogol
on the one hand, and were not redeemed by profundity or originality
on the other.

Apart from the revolution on the Russian stage which had been
inaugurated by Gogol with *The Government Inspector* in 1836, a new
genius had appeared in the person of A. N. Ostrovsky, whose first
important play, *We are ourselves, we can settle it* was published in 1850,
but had been widely known through private readings in the literary
circles for some years. It is a play about Moscow merchants, whom
it portrays as unmitigated rascals and swindlers. Ostrovsky, who was
at the outset of his career as the leading modern Russian playwright,
had joined the so-called 'young editors' of the journal *Moskvitianin*,
who included A. F. Pisemsky, Apollon Grigoriev, B. N. Almazov,
and L. A. Mei. This group, which was joined by Dostoevsky on his
return from exile, became known as the 'Native Soil Men' ('Poch-
venniki'). It believed that the function of art was primarily to portray
Russian life, in all its aspects. Unlike the Slavophiles the 'Pochven-
niki' did not idealize Russian life, dark sides and all. On the contrary,
they believed in the need to exhibit Russia's faults fearlessly, the
better to bring out her virtues, and thereby to help to find a true
meeting point between the authentic Russian tradition and the influences of the West.[20] The 'young editors' therefore welcomed the
appearance of Ostrovsky. Turgenev was one of his early admirers
but, with characteristic refusal to be drawn into literary cliques,

rejected some of the extravagant praise which was showered on him by Apollon Grigoriev and others, as the author who had replaced and surpassed Gogol.

When Ostrovsky's second full-length play *The Poor Bride* appeared, it was greeted with exaggerated and undeserved approval by the 'young editors' of *Moskvitianin* and in particular by Apollon Grigoriev, for whom it was a matter of policy to build up Ostrovsky; and also by the 'progressive' writers, who saw a deep social message in its theme – the girl forced to marry for money in order to save her family from disaster. Turgenev, who was neither involved in 'Native Soil' politics nor particularly well disposed to crudely expressed social messages in art, exposed the very real shortcomings of *The Poor Bride* in one of his rare essays in literary criticism published in the *Contemporary*, No. 3 for 1852. He drew attention to the poor characterization, the lifelessness of the monologues, and the other defects of this generally drab and unattractive play.[21] Possibly one of his motives was to get even with Apollon Grigoriev, who had not very long before severely criticized *The Provincial Lady* in the pages of *Moskvitianin*,[22] and whom, according to what he allegedly told Leontiev, he 'hated'.[23] In March 1853 the veteran actor M. S. Shchepkin, an old friend of Turgenev who had appeared in the Moscow production of *The Provincial Lady*, visited him at Spasskoe, and read to the assembled company Ostrovsky's new play *Don't Get into Someone Else's Sleigh*. Turgenev, as he wrote to Annenkov, recognized the 'remarkable dramatic talent' of the author, but had some reservations about the play's exaggerated emphasis on what was supposed to be the true Russian spirit.[24] Again, a very fair judgement.

Turgenev published very little during the first few years after his return to Russia. In the course of 1852 and 1853, substantially all that appeared in print were reviews of a novel, of Ostrovsky's *Poor Bride* and of S. T. Aksakov's *Memoirs of a Sportsman with a Gun in Orenburg Government*, and a few stories. Although Turgenev preferred to spend as much time as he could in St. Petersburg, he also stayed occasionally in Moscow, usually with his brother and sister-in-law. When in Moscow he was a frequent visitor in the salon maintained by a literary lady, the Countess Sailhas de Tournemire. Sister of the playwright Sukhovo-Kobylin, the Countess was a somewhat eccentric figure (she would later be portrayed by Turgenev in *Smoke* in the person of Sukhanchikova), but her salon became a centre in the fifties for the surviving Moscow liberal intelligentsia, which included Botkin and Granovsky. Her rather disreputable husband, having long squandered the dowry he had received from his wife, was by now back in France.[25] Turgenev, as his correspondence shows, was very friendly with her, and wrote of her to Pauline: 'She is witty, kind and outspoken: she has something about her way of behaving that reminds me of you. We are great friends.'[26] The Countess wrote very long novels (under the name of Evgeniia Tur) and it was one of these, *The Niece*, which Turgenev reviewed. Although generous in recognizing some merits in this work, Turgenev's gently expressed criticism could not conceal the fact that he found the book much too long-winded and the characterization weak. The review attracted a great deal of, on the whole, unfavourable attention in literary circles and, naturally enough, did not please the poor Countess – though she and Turgenev remained on good terms.

The author of the *Memoirs of a Sportsman* was S. T. Aksakov, then over sixty years old and still to win fame with his *Family Chronicle* and *The Childhood of the Bagrov Grandson*, to be published in 1856 and 1858. He was the father of the leading Slavophile writers, Konstantin and Ivan Aksakov. Turgenev, when he returned to Russia, was already well acquainted with the sons. At the end of 1850 he met the father and in spite of the difference of age, a close friendship, much helped by a common passion for the gun, sprang up between the two men. Turgenev always made the effort to see Aksakov when a visit to Moscow made this possible, and maintained regular correspondence with him. Forty-two letters from Turgenev to him are known, dated right up to the year of his death, 1859. Turgenev much admired Aksakov's *Memoirs* and the latter in turn was enthusiastic in his praise of Turgenev's prose writing. Turgenev wrote two reviews of Aksakov's book, both of which appeared in the *Contemporary*, in 1852 and 1853. The first consists mainly of high praise for his descriptions of nature, illustrated by very long extracts from the work. The second is more concerned with the contents as a whole and contains a wealth of highly expert technical information on sporting dogs, guns, cartridges, and the like. This article also contained a long digression on nature, which was a central theme in much of the German philosophy to which Turgenev had devoted his student days, and, of course, in the work of Goethe. For reasons best known to himself the censor excised this excursus from the review. While it is true, Turgenev wrote, that nature forms one great, harmonious whole, at the same time it is also the case that nature strives to ensure that each separate unit within it should exist solely for itself, and should concentrate solely on its own aims and needs – the mosquito which sucks your blood is solely concerned with you as food; while the interest of the spider in the mosquito

is in turn, the same. How it comes about that out of all this frag-
mentation, in the course of which each fragment seems to live only
for itself, there arises that infinite harmony in which everything that
exists, on the contrary exists for someone else and only achieves
reconciliation or resolution through that someone else, is 'one of
those "open" secrets which we both see and do not see'. And he
quotes Goethe in conclusion: 'Nature ... divides everything in order
to unite everything ... it can only be approached through love ...
it seems only to be concerned to create individuals – and yet individuals mean nothing to it.'[27]

Of the stories, two ('The Singers' and 'The Tryst') belonged to
the series of *Sketches from a Sportsman's Notebook*, and were written
and published after Turgenev's return to Russia. 'The Singers' is a
vigorous account of a contest held between two peasant singers,
which, as he wrote to Pauline, he had witnessed himself and which
made him think of Homer, since 'all peoples resemble one another
in their infancy'.[28] The other is a sad little story in which a corrupt
and westernized house-serf (of whom Yasha in Chekhov's *Cherry
Orchard* is in many ways reminiscent) abandons the simple servant
girl he has seduced. Of the remaining three longer stories, two,
'Mumu' and 'The Inn', also deal with serfdom and belong in spirit
to the group which comprises the *Sketches*, though they are longer
and more elaborate than any of them. 'Mumu', which was written
while Turgenev was under arrest in 1852, is based on an incident
which happened in Varvara Petrovna's lifetime – a giant deaf and
dumb household porter is forced by his capricious and tyrannous
mistress to get rid of a little dog which he has befriended and to which
he is deeply devoted. The man drowns the dog, and after a period
of wandering returns to his post and continues to serve his mistress
with complete fidelity. 'The Inn' is a longer and more ambitious
story. A serf is nominal owner of a prosperous inn – in fact the legal
owner of the inn is the woman who also owns both the innkeeper
and the much younger domestic serf girl whom he marries. The
young wife falls in love with a travelling salesman, and steals her
husband's savings to enable the salesman to buy the inn from the
serf owner over her husband's head.* The dispossessed landlord, after
a wild drinking bout, attempts to set fire to the inn, is caught by
the new landlord, but set free on a promise to forgive the past and

---

* The legal position, namely that the ostensible property of a serf remained in
law that of his owner, and could be disposed of by that owner over the head
of the serf, was incidentally correctly described by Turgenev, though it surprised
some critics.

abandon all thoughts of vengeance. He forgives his wife as well, accepts the situation with complete humility, and becomes a pious wanderer across Russia, begging his way. Both stories are, therefore, studies of the submission and humility of the Russian peasant in the face of injustice, an essentially Slavophile view of the peasants which struck a new note in Turgenev's writing. Like 'Mumu', 'The Inn' was based on events which had actually occurred in a village not far from Spasskoe.[29] The third story, 'Three Meetings', is an imaginative, somewhat fantastic tale, written with consummate skill, which hints at an undisclosed mystery.

For some time before 1852 Turgenev had the notion of publishing the *Sketches* which had appeared over the years in the *Contemporary*, in volume form. He made several requests to Pauline for permission to dedicate the volume to her anonymously, in other words to replace the name with three asterisks. Her reply is unknown, and although the manuscript submitted to the censor contained such an anonymous dedication, this was in the end omitted. There was also, originally, a preface to the volume which apparently took issue with some of Apollon Grigoriev's criticisms of Turgenev's work, but this too did not appear in the volume as published. The manuscript was submitted to Prince V. V. Lvov, one of the Moscow censors with whom Turgenev was acquainted, and was passed for publication in March. The following month Turgenev was arrested and eventually exiled for publishing an article on Gogol but the arrest did not hold up publication of the *Sketches*, which came out at the beginning of August. The book was sold out within six months.

Events soon showed that Prince Lvov had been somewhat unwise in authorizing the book for publication. No sooner had it appeared, than the Minister of Education ordered an investigation into the circumstances in which the censor had passed it. The official who reported to the Minister pointed out that the book would be read by literate peasants and would do more harm than good, since it not only idealized the peasants but showed them to be oppressed, while landlords appeared as 'vulgar savages and half-wits' who behaved in an arbitrary and illegal manner, the village clergy as servile, and the police as corrupt. The Minister of Education passed these comments on to the Emperor, who personally ordered the dismissal of the censor, Prince Lvov, with loss of pension.* Turgenev frequently maintained that the real cause of his arrest and exile was the publication of the *Sketches*, but since he was arrested two or three

---

* Lvov died soon after. Turgenev remained friendly with his widow and family for years.

months before the report was submitted to the Emperor, this seems improbable.[30]

Sketches from a Sportsman's Notebook won almost universal acclaim. Except for right-wing critics with close links to officialdom, the thinking literary public welcomed the book, if not always for the same reasons: the radical liberals saw it as a kind of Russian *Uncle Tom's Cabin* (which also appeared in 1852), while the Slavophiles, though critical in many respects, still valued it as a true picture of the life of the people. Turgenev seems at this period, possibly to some extent through the influence of the Aksakovs, to have been more sympathetic to the Slavophiles' point of view than at any time of his life. He did not accept their interpretation of Russian history, such as their unqualified veneration for Muscovite Russia and rejection of Peter the Great, but he seems to have shared their view of the Russian people. For example, writing to Ivan Aksakov, on 28 December 1852 (and incidentally apologizing for the fact that a passage in 'Khor and Kalinych' which could be interpreted as a satire on Ivan's brother Konstantin had, by inadvertence, not been excised from the publication of the *Sketches* in book form), he fully endorses his interpretation of 'Mumu'. Ivan Aksakov had written to him that he regarded the deaf mute Gerasim as the personification of the Russian people, 'its terrifying strength and its inscrutable humility. . . . It will, of course, raise its voice in the course of time, but at present it appears to be deaf and dumb.' Turgenev wrote in reply, that 'the idea of "Mumu" is so truly grasped by you'.*[31] A few months before, he had written to Ivan Aksakov, with reference to his brother Konstantin: 'What a strange thing! We agree in our view of our people, but each of us draws a different deduction from it.'[33] Turgenev was unable to go along with enthusiastic elevation of everything Russian in order to show its immense superiority to Western Europe.

There was one aspect of Slavophile dogma in particular that Turgenev could never accept – their veneration for the peasant commune. In a letter to S. T. Aksakov, written three years later, in 1856, he says that he will never agree with his son Konstantin on this question.

He sees the *mir* as a general . . . panacea . . . and I, while ready to acknowledge

---

* However, in a letter to Annenkov of 2 April 1853, he admits to being somewhat 'embarrassed' by the praise showered on 'The Inn' and especially on the character of the dispossessed Akim, by the Aksakovs. 'Russian man', they wrote, 'has remained pure and saintly' and will perhaps, by his saintliness 'humble the proud, correct the evil, and save society.'[32]

its peculiarity and indeed appropriateness ... for Russia, see it only as no
more than ... the form *on* which to build and not the form *into which* the
state must be poured. ... Say what you will, the right of the individual
is destroyed by the *mir* – and I have fought for this right up till now, and
will continue to fight for it to the end.[34]

By this time Turgenev had turned against the *Sketches* and his
similar writings, and was searching for what he could recognize as
his, as yet undiscovered, true style. 'I can indeed assure you', he wrote
to Ivan Aksakov on 28 December 1852, 'that it sometimes seems to
me as if this book [the *Sketches*] had been written by someone other
than myself, so far removed do I feel from it. The tenseness and stiff-
ness which occur in it too frequently can in part be excused by the
fact that when I was writing the book I was abroad, surrounded by
life and by elements which were not Russian, and hence I involun-
tarily drew the pencil twice over every line.'[35] He was, no doubt,
also influenced by the advice of some of his friends that he had gone
far enough with his *Sketches*, and it was time for him to discover
a new kind of writing.[36] His search for his true style had begun to
preoccupy him not long after his return to Russia when he discovered
that he was incapable of writing, or of writing in the way that he
felt he ought to write, but yet without being able to define or describe
this new way. As far back as 2 April 1851, he had written to his friend
E. M. Feoktistov (a very young man, recently out of university, a
protégé of the Countess Sailhas de Tournemire, and at the threshold
of a minor literary career): 'I give you my word of honour that
Sketches from a Sportsman's Notebook is over and done with forever.
I intend to have nothing printed for a long time to come, and to
devote myself if possible to a long composition, which I will write
con amore and without hurrying – and without any kind of thought
at the back of my mind of the censorship. ...'[37] 'It is neither apathy
nor tiredness,' he wrote to Ivan Aksakov on 4 December 1851, 'it
is that waiting, that longing for real and concrete impressions. ...
Actually, the literary itch has long calmed down within me. When
I take up my pen again I will do this as a result of different prompt-
ings, and different inner necessity.'[38]

A year later he had still not found the way that he sought. He
was planning a novel, was full of thoughts about it, but had not yet
started to write because 'I do not yet feel within me that lucidity,
that strength, without which it is impossible to say a *lasting* word.
The example of Grigorovich is enough to frighten anyone – and it
is not talent which he lacks. It is difficult for the present-day writer,
especially if he is Russian, to be at peace – either outwardly or

inwardly.' This is from a letter of 16 October 1852 to Konstantin Aksakov.[39] Later, prompted by reading Harriet Beecher Stowe's famous book, he repeated the same fear of becoming what would now be called a 'propagandist': 'As regards *Uncle Tom* which I read the other day' – he wrote in reply to Annenkov who had written that Uncle Tom and Akim, the peasant hero of 'The Inn', were 'polemics' – 'the same thought had struck me, that perhaps Akim and Uncle Tom were of the same calibre. *Your* letter confirmed this impression – in consequence of which I promised myself never to write things like that again.'[40] On 28 October 1852, Turgenev had explained his new thoughts in greater detail to Annenkov, who had for some years past been a constant, severe, and frank critic of almost everything he wrote:

> I must go by a different way – I must find it – and say goodbye once and for all to the old manner. I have tried for long enough to extract from human characters diluted essences – triples extraits – in order to pour them off into little phials – there you are, respected readers, sniff them, uncork them and sniff them, is it not the true smell of the Russian spirit? Enough, enough! But the question is: am I capable of something great, something calm? Will I succeed in drawing simple, clear lines? That I don't know and shall not discover until I try.[41]

In his enforced winter seclusion (normally Turgenev would have spent winter in the capital, from which he was now exiled), he began in the late autumn of 1852 to work feverishly on the novel, *Two Generations*, which he would eventually abandon and destroy, uncompleted. By 25 May 1853 the first of the projected three parts of the novel had been finished and the manuscript was despatched to Annenkov for criticism.[42]

On 21 February 1852 Gogol died in Moscow, at the early age of forty-three. Rumours about the circumstances of his death immediately began to course through the literary circles of Moscow and of St. Petersburg. They were as fantastic as much of Gogol's fiction. Though he had been, intermittently, a sick man for some time, his physical illness had not been expected by anyone to carry him off so prematurely. He had also been in a state of spiritual anguish and perplexity for several years before his death, much perturbed by the generally hostile reception accorded to the *Select Passages* and in an agonizing state of uncertainty over Part II of *Dead Souls* and over his duty as a writer and as a Christian to point out the path of redemption for Chichikov from the moral depravity in which he wallows in Part I. Some significant part in Gogol's extraordinary end seems to have been played by a fanatical priest, Father Matvei, who urged him to abandon the frivolity of literature and to prepare for eternal salvation. According to one account (which Pogodin, the historian and editor of *Moskvitianin*, claimed to have heard from Gogol's servant), some ten days before he died he sent for his manuscripts and threw them on the fire, and in the process mistakenly burned the chapters of Part II of *Dead Souls* which he intended to preserve.[43]

The possibility of error thus cannot be excluded: but radical legend-makers, faithfully followed by Soviet critics, who felt uncomfortable over the religious undertones surrounding Gogol's death, have ever since enshrined in history the theory that the burning of Part II of *Dead Souls* and the subsequent death were the result either of a fit of religious mania, or of ultimate recognition of his artistic and moral defeat. Actually, several chapters of Part II have survived and while some of the characters are indeed of an ethical level not attained by any single character in Part I, there is certainly no trace of the moral regeneration of Chichikov in the chapters which escaped the fire. After the burning, Gogol had refused to take any food, and persisted in what looked like either suicide by self-starvation, in spite of the urgent appeals of friends and doctors, or a decision that the time of his death had come and that he wished to welcome and accept it.[44] So far as Turgenev was concerned, Gogol had died 'because he was determined, wished, to die, and this suicide began with the destruction of *Dead Souls*'.[45]

Whatever story one chose to believe in 1852, there was enough drama about the end of this tortured genius, whose writing had effected a revolution in Russian literature, to throw the liberal intellectual public into despair. The great majority of them had for some time regarded Gogol as the greatest satirist of the regime of Nicholas I, and dismissed his preoccupation with religious and moral problems as an aberration. Russian officialdom, even more obtusely, treated Gogol with hatred and contempt as the man who had unpatriotically slandered his country, and was anxious that his death should not be marked by any kind of public tribute. It could not stop the vast assembly of leading literary and intellectual figures which attended his funeral in Moscow. Turgenev, when he heard in St. Petersburg of the death of Gogol and of some of the strange circumstances surrounding it, was shattered. According to his own account he got the news from I. I. Panaev (one of the editors of the *Contemporary*) on 24 February. Further details reached him in letters from E. M. Feoktistov and V. P. Botkin.[46] Turgenev had met Gogol twice fleetingly in 1841, but had his first, and only, long encounter with him some six months before his death, when M. S. Shchepkin, the actor, brought them together.

A few days later Turgenev was present when Gogol gave a reading of *The Government Inspector*. He was deeply impressed on both occasions – though slightly shocked when Gogol got very near to defending censorship as something which developed cunning in a writer. On 21 February, before he knew of Gogol's death, he had started on a long letter to Pauline. On the 27th, when the news had reached him, he writes that he finds it impossible to continue the letter in view of the great grief which Gogol's death and the burning of his manuscripts means for every Russian. 'He revealed us to ourselves – he was in more than one sense the continuator of Peter the Great for us. ... One has to be a Russian to understand everything that we have lost.' Five days later he completes it with an account of the funeral in Moscow and adds 'Just imagine: the censorship here already forbids all mention of his name!!!'[47]

This was indeed the case, as Turgenev discovered when he tried to place a short article on Gogol in a St. Petersburg newspaper, which was designed to appear on the day of the funeral in Moscow. A few days later he inquired of the editor why the obituary had not appeared and was informed that the chairman of the St. Petersburg Censorship Committee, M. N. Musin-Pushkin (the highest local instance of censorship), had already issued a pronouncement that there was to be no public reference to 'that lackey' Gogol, and had rejected Turgenev's essay out of hand, though without issuing any official statement. This, according to the chief censor of St. Petersburg, Nikitenko, was not in formal terms a valid rejection, and entitled Turgenev to submit the article again.[48] But the Russian censorship was not in 1852 particularly concerned with legal niceties. The authorities had in any case for some time regarded Turgenev with suspicion, and the Emperor was probably looking for a pretext to teach him a lesson.

This soon occurred. Through the agency of his Moscow friends, Botkin and Feoktistov, stung by their reproach that the St. Petersburg literary world had passed over Gogol's death in silence, Turgenev submitted his article to *Moskovskiia vedomosti* and received permission to publish it from the Chairman of the Moscow Censorship Committee, who knew nothing of what had happened in the capital. Certainly, Turgenev did not think that in submitting it to the Moscow censorship he was doing anything illegal.[49] It was published on 13 March 1852. It was in substance little more than a simple lament over the death of a man 'whom we now have the right, the bitter right, to call great; a man whose name signified an epoch in the history of our literature, a man of whom we are proud as one of our glories.'[50] But the mere reference to Gogol as 'great' was enough to stimulate the Emperor to action. On receipt of Musin-Pushkin's report he personally ordered Turgenev's detention in a police station for a month, followed by indefinite exile to Spasskoe. For their part in ensuring publication Feoktistov and Botkin were called in for interrogation, much to their alarm, but were released with a warning and ordered to be kept under police supervision.[51] S. T. Aksakov, who published an obituary notice on Gogol in the same issue of *Moskovskiia vedomosti*, even on the same page, suffered no consequences from imperial displeasure.

Turgenev was arrested and confined in one of the central St. Petersburg police offices on 16 April and spent a month there, until 16 May; after two days spent in Moscow on his way, he travelled on to Spasskoe to begin his long exile. On 1 May a letter addressed to Pauline and Louis Viardot, which he had arranged to be posted outside the frontiers of Russia, informed them of his imprisonment for which he maintained that what he had written about Gogol had only been an excuse: 'I have been regarded with disfavour for a long time past. . . .' He did not blame the Emperor, who had been basely misled. He told them that he had a comfortable room to live in and was allowed books and visitors – at least he had been allowed visitors for the first few days, but so many had come to call on him that these were now forbidden. He added that he was in good health, but had 'aged laughably' and his hair was going white. He did not dread his exile; on the contrary. He looked forward to much shooting, to working on his novel, and to devoting himself to the study of the Russian people. He begged them to keep the letter and its contents secret since 'the slightest reference to my situation in any periodical would be enough to finish me'.[52] So far as is known there was no reference to Turgenev's arrest in the foreign press – or in the Russian press either.

It was not until 23 November 1853, after at least three vain applications to the highest authorities, including the Grand Duke Alexander (the future Alexander II), that Turgenev was granted permission once again to enter the capital cities. Apart from a secret visit to Moscow with a false passport, he spent all this time, so far as is known, in Spasskoe, on visits to Orel and to his uncle's estate near Orel, and on frequent short expeditions to call on neighbours or to shoot. He was closely followed on these journeys by very conspicuous police spies.

*   *   *   *   *

Life in Spasskoe during the many months of enforced residence there did not prove too irksome. Indeed Turgenev's correspondence gives the impression that there were many compensations for enforced absence from St. Petersburg during the winter of 1852-3, except – a big exception – that it meant missing the Viardots on the occasion of Pauline's reappearance in the capital. It is also not difficult to imagine how much the gregarious Turgenev missed the familiar arguments and badinage with his many friends in the capital cities – the Countess Sailhas de Tournemire, Botkin, Feoktistov, and Granovsky in Moscow, and Annenkov, Nekrasov, and the literary coterie which gathered around the *Contemporary* in St. Petersburg. There were the usual health troubles. At the turn of the year 1851-2, in St. Petersburg, he had been incapacitated by a prolonged illness, the nature of which is undisclosed. The following year, in Spasskoe, he complains of his health to Pauline in frightening terms, which proved unfounded. He strongly suspects, he writes on 17 April, that his continuous trouble with his stomach is what is known medically as 'cancer au pylore', and indeed, he has named one of Diana's recent pups Pylore.[53] There was a great deal of shooting, as always when Turgenev was in the country, and there are several descriptions in letters to like-minded friends of the size of his considerable bags – 304 various game birds in the 1852 season, for example. His favourite Diana was getting rather old, but she had had several litters, and one of her pups was shaping well as a gun dog.

Turgenev has left a number of descriptions of the house at Spasskoe. In 1876 in a letter to Flaubert he described it (or, rather the small part of it which had survived the fire of 1840) as distempered in mauve, with a green roof. The attic floor was disused and boarded up, the verandah overgrown with ivy.[54] A visitor to the house shortly before the second fire in 1903, found the trees in the park, the alley of limes, the abundance of birds, and the rookery all still much as pictured by Turgenev. 'Faust' contains a description of some of the interior furnishing – the articles made on the estate – the pot-bellied chests of drawers with brass fittings, and white armchairs with oval backs, the faded paintings and the portraits of the Lutovinov ancestors. These are now in the Turgenev Museum in Orel.*

The household in Spasskoe consisted of a one-time member of Belinsky's circle, N. N. Tiutchev, who acted as Turgenev's estate

---

* The Museum also houses the famous vast and extremely comfortable divan which stood in Turgenev's study-bedroom, and to which there are frequent references in memoirs and correspondence. It went by the name of 'autosleeper' (*samoson*).

manager, his wife, who seems to have been a very attractive and civilized lady, and the wife's sister. From the beginning of 1853 onwards the number of inhabitants was considerably increased by the arrival of Turgenev's uncle, his wife, and sister-in-law, Tiutchev's mother-in-law and several other unspecified local ladies who seem to have settled at Spasskoe.[55] Tiutchev, though no doubt an agreeable companion, was not much good as a manager and the arrangement had to be brought to an end if Turgenev was not to be completely ruined. He gave full details of Tiutchev's disastrous administration in a letter to Pauline.[56] According to Panaeva, Tiutchev for his part complained that he had been ruined by Turgenev. But even Panaeva, for all her notorious dislike of Turgenev, was unable to decide which of the two was right.[57] Turgenev himself took over the affairs of his estates but his husbandry for the few months during which he acted as his own manager was not a great success, and by November 1853 he had decided to hand over the management of his affairs to his uncle, N. N. Turgenev, an arrangement which in the course of years proved to be even less successful.

With his mother's death Turgenev somewhat optimistically believed his financial worries to be at an end. He now estimated that after the division of the property with his brother, his annual income would never fall below 25,000 francs – quite a substantial sum at that date. He also behaved with generosity towards his serfs. He gave all domestic servants their freedom, and transferred all other peasants who wished to do so to the service payment system, which meant both the freest condition possible for a serf, and the least profitable to a landlord in a fertile province like Orel. He also made it possible for all his peasants to buy their freedom with a remission of one fifth of the current rate, and without making any redemptive payments for the land tilled by them.[58]

When not writing or shooting, or forced to manage his estates, or listening to music, Turgenev spent much of his time on chess, playing with neighbours or following games in notation from the *Chessplayer's Chronicle*.[59] Music could fortunately be provided by Madame Tiutchev or her sister, or occasionally both, playing four-handed on the piano. This was not entirely satisfactory; Madame Tiutchev needed a great deal of persuasion and preferred the company of her husband, who was totally unmusical, and her sister was sentimental and affected. 'There is no one here who has a hunger for music, and this distresses me', he wrote to Pauline. There was, it is true, some prospect of hearing music at the estate of a neighbour some thirty-five miles away, who had purchased a whole orchestra, presumably of serfs, and equipped it with a German conductor.[60] Turgenev visited this neighbour on 24 November 1852 and was very well impressed with the orchestra. It played the slow movement of Beethoven's Ninth Symphony; and, to his especial delight, his favourite Mozart C Minor Piano Fantasia in an orchestral arrangement.[61] Whatever the limitations of the Tiutchev ladies as musicians, he missed them very much after they had gone, and wrote more warmly of their musical talents in retrospect than he had done while they were still performing for him. His musical preferences remained very much unchanged – Mozart, Rossini, Gluck, Haydn, Weber, Mendelssohn, and Beethoven are all mentioned in his correspondence as favourite composers – with expressions of special enthusiasm for Gluck's operas.[62]

Turgenev's possibly exaggerated description of his life at Spasskoe suggests extreme monotony. 'I have found', he wrote to Pauline on 12 November 1852, 'that there is only one way of contending with boredom, and that is – would you believe it? – by uniformity. Let me explain. I have divided my day into separate portions, devoted to certain preoccupations, always the same, and I do not ever deviate from this fixed timetable.' He goes on to say that he has achieved a great deal of work, especially reading, and then appends his daily timetable.

I rise at 8. I breakfast etc. till 9. Then I walk for an hour. From 10 to 2 I read, or I write letters etc. At 2 I eat a snack, followed by another walk. Then I work until 4.30. Dinner is at 5 in the house with the Tiutchev family (I inhabit a small wing of the house which leads into the garden). I stay with them until 10. I read until 11 and go to bed – and so day after day, one day like another.[63]

But Turgenev's solitude at Spasskoe was frequently relieved or enlivened by visits, which he obviously very much welcomed. Two guests who gave Turgenev particular pleasure were, on separate occasions, Ivan Kireevsky and Ivan Aksakov, the leading Slavophiles. Kireevsky was a neighbour or at least within reasonable range of the carriage and horses.* Turgenev had paid a call and Kireevsky returned the visit, to Turgenev's great delight – he was a man of 'crystal purity and transparency – it is impossible not to love him'. Ivan Aksakov's visit was a 'real holiday' and there were endless conversations and discussions.[65]

* Or *tarantas* rather, a rough contraption without springs, which Turgenev was obliged to use because the more comfortable carriage which he ordered for the sum of £95 from a coachmaker turned out to be so incompetently made that he rejected it.[64]

Among other visitors there was the poet Fet, with whom Turgenev later became friendly, in spite of initial reservations. 'A poetic nature, but a German, a system-monger and not very clever – that is why he venerates Goethe's *Faust* Part II. He is surprised that all humanity, if you please, is portrayed here – that is a bit simpler than to occupy oneself with one human being, I suppose.' He admired Fet's renderings of Horace, but sent him an 'enormous' letter pointing out mistakes. Fet did not accept most of the suggestions; nevertheless Turgenev offered to have the translations printed at his own expense. They were in fact published in 1856, though whether Turgenev paid for them is unknown.[66]

Another visitor was Konstantin Leontiev, then still a young medical student, but destined to become an important philosopher and historian. At that time he was beginning his career as a writer with a play and some stories. Turgenev took an immediate interest in the young author whose talent for fiction he seems at first to have somewhat overestimated. He spent much time and effort trying to help him to get his work published, and even advanced him money. There are no fewer than thirteen letters from Turgenev to Leontiev in the space of two and a half years. Turgenev's interest in him was purely professional; he rather disliked him as a person, and indeed Leontiev, to judge by his own account of his encounters with Turgenev, seems at that time to have been inordinately self-centred, and pretentious. Having started off with a veneration for Turgenev, he turned against him in later years, probably after developing his strongly nationalistic and anti-Western views.[67] Turgenev was scathing about him in a letter to Annenkov: 'He has talent, but he is a worthless urchin, vain and all mixed up. So far as his voluptuous intoxication with himself is concerned – his veneration for his "God-given gift" – to use his own expression – he has long out-smarted the semi-late-lamented Fedor Mikhailovich [Dostoevsky] who used to make your eyes start from your head.'[68] (Dostoevsky was still serving his sentence.) Turgenev's enthusiasm for Leontiev as a novelist did not last very long. By July 1855 he agreed with Panaev's verdict on Leontiev's *Life on the Farm* that it 'had no single character truly and skilfully delineated' and was 'artificial and false'.[69]

There seems also to have been a succession of humbler callers at Spasskoe – local inhabitants – and Turgenev certainly went visiting a good deal himself. 'I can say that I try to miss no opportunity of extracting every kind of benefit from provincial life. I have made the acquaintance of a great multitude of new people, and have come closer to the contemporary way of life, to the people,' he wrote to

S. T. Aksakov on 6 and 7 October 1853. At that date he had still
not received permission to live in St. Petersburg and had therefore
decided to spend part of the winter in Orel, and to take part in the
elections to the local assembly of the nobility.[70] On one occasion
he was pressed into acting as best man at a local wedding which he
found very entertaining, and which, from his description, seems to
have been conducted in the best manner of Russian provincial life.
'I hope you and I will never marry,' he wrote to Annenkov, 'at least,
I give you my word not to marry like that.'[71] On another occasion
there were festivities at Spasskoe. The household serfs put on a mas-
querade; while the workers from his brother's paper factory at Turgenevo produced a drama about robbers, with a chorus, and 'in a
language which represented a mixture of popular songs, phrases à
la Marlinsky and [Ozerov's] *Dmitry Donskoy*'.[72]

We can form a fair idea of Turgenev's literary and intellectual
interests during his stay at Spasskoe. He devoted much time to his
favourite reading, history, concentrating especially on ancient
Russia, and on Russian folk and traditional literature. His preference
for history over philosophy (which seldom figured in his reading
after his student days) is very marked, as well as his frequently
expressed hostility to 'systems' and indeed to all abstract speculation.
He constantly re-read the classics such as Homer, Molière, and above
all *Don Quixote*, which in the summer he intended to translate into
Russian, if he should eventually decide not to go on writing his
novel.*[73] In the spring of 1853 he was much absorbed with the correspondence of Goethe's friend J. H. Merck (generally supposed to
have been the model for Mephistopheles), whose trenchant criticism
of contemporary literature ('a talented critic directs the writer's gifts,
elucidates his task for him') Turgenev admired.[74] There is a
characteristic outburst against Rousseau, occasioned by an article in
the *Revue des Deux Mondes*, to which Turgenev subscribed, and which
he read diligently:

His self-indulgent sufferings were well suited to his self-indulgent pos-
terity – but enough is enough. He is a wonderful writer so far as style goes –
in that respect he is really creative – but what sort of a martyr, damn it all,
is he, when all is said and done? After all he was persecuted just exactly
enough to give him the occasion for exhibitionism and for pouring out
his bile.[75]

Contemporary Russian literature – with the exception of Gogol,
whose works he read and re-read, and Pushkin – aroused his interest

*He abandoned the novel, but unfortunately never translated *Don Quixote*.

very little. He commented on all the issues of the *Contemporary* as
they appeared, and thus kept abreast of the new fiction, for which
he showed little enthusiasm – with the striking exception of Leo Tolstoy's *Childhood*, which aroused his warm praise when it appeared
in the *Contemporary* in September 1852.*[76] In the course of his exile
Turgenev eventually obtained and read the few chapters of the
second part of *Dead Souls* which had survived the burning. His
comments on these are a mixture of praise and disappointment – on
one occasion he goes so far as to suggest that if the rest of Part II
was as bad as the surviving Chapter 5 'then was it not perhaps because
of revulsion of artistic feeling that Gogol burned his novel?'[77] This
chapter describes how Chichikov is rescued from well-deserved
imprisonment through the intervention of a skilful intermediary
who bribes the necessary officials with complete cynicism.

Turgenev's library at Spasskoe, which is now rehoused in the
Museum in Orel, reflects the various stages in the development of
his intellectual interests up to 1858, after which he ceased to pay more
than occasional short visits to Spasskoe. His time at the university
in Berlin is marked by a large collection of Greek and Latin authors
(always his favourite reading), edited with commentaries by the German classicists. The German romantics (along with Goethe and
Schiller) are well represented, as are also the philosophers such as
Schlegel, Schelling, and Hegel, and the historians, like Ranke and
Zumpt. The works of other professors whose lectures he attended
also figure in the library. One item of this period is particularly notable: the works of Shakespeare, in English, but published in Leipzig.
This volume was presented to him by Granovsky in 1838 with an
inscription 'Approach this with fear and with faith'. The interests
of the years which he spent in France are evident in a large collection
of works on the French Revolution and on the modern history of
France. His love of the culture of Spain, aroused by his friendship
with Pauline Viardot, and his study of the language after 1847, is
marked by such collections as the works of Cervantes and Calderón,
of *romances* and *canciones*, as well as Spanish grammars. There are also
some items of Italian literature, and books on chess.[78]

In the course of 1851 Turgenev had provided himself with sexual
companionship in the form of a serf girl called Feoktista. She
remained at Spasskoe until 1853, although by December 1851 she
was already 'beginning to bore me stiff – but there is nothing to be
done about it', as he wrote to a friend. 'Even immorality is no cure

---

* Tolstoy was as yet unknown, and Turgenev only met him some years later.

for boredom.'[79] According to one doubtful account, he had taken a strong fancy to the girl, who belonged to his cousin Elizabeth, and had purchased her for the enormous sum of 700 roubles – the market price for girl serfs at the time was at most 50 roubles.[80] Feoktista bore a son who she claimed was Turgenev's, though he maintained in later years that he 'had sufficiently good reasons to suppose that the son is not mine' but could not be certain. Since she only became pregnant in 1855, some time after she had left Spasskoe, he may well have been right. In 1865 he wrote to a friend asking him to help Feoktista to find this boy, who had apparently been taken in to be looked after by some local lady.*[81]

It was ironical that the author of the *Sketches from a Sportsman's Notebook* should have taken up with a serf girl in this manner, and possibly fathered another bastard, especially after his experience of the disastrous effects of her birth and early background on Paulinette. Even more astonishing is to find Turgenev, whose friendship with Pauline Viardot was, to put it mildly, unconventional, behaving as a stern moralist. The story which follows comes mainly from the memoirs of E. M. Feoktistov, a literary friend of Turgenev's which, no doubt, exaggerated the dramatic details. But it is confirmed in its essentials by a letter which Turgenev wrote to him. In 1851, when Turgenev was living in Moscow with his brother and sister-in-law, the susceptible Botkin was much enamoured of a cousin of the Turgenev brothers, Elizabeth Turgeneva, who was also living in the household, recovering from the effects of a broken marriage. Botkin had an affair with her which he kept very secret. By some chance a compromising letter from Botkin to Elizabeth Turgeneva fell into the hands of her chambermaid, who in a fit of moral righteousness passed it on to the head of the family, Uncle Peter Turgenev. The scandal now broke in a grand manner, and Elizabeth was ignominiously banished from the household by the virtuous German wife of brother Nikolai (who had, incidentally, lived out of wedlock with him for some years before marrying him). Feoktistov was certainly embellishing when in later years in his memoirs he relates that Ivan Turgenev characterized Elizabeth as ready to sell herself to anyone with the money to spend. But the indisputable facts remain: that Elizabeth was driven from the household; and that Turgenev unreservedly took the side of his sister-in-law in this affair. The incident

---

* We do not know whether Feoktista ever found her son, or what became of him. Turgenev continued to pay her a pension for some years. When she married in 1856 he paid her off with 600 roubles (about £95) but renewed her allowance after her husband died.[82]

caused some cooling off between Turgenev on the one hand and Feoktistov and Botkin (who were close friends) on the other – but not for long.[83] There is no denying that it is redolent with most distasteful cant and inhumanity. One can only surmise that in common with most of his male contemporaries Turgenev believed that in matters of sexual morality there was one law for a man and another for a woman.*

After returning to Russia, Turgenev wrote regularly, or fairly regularly, to Pauline: eighteen letters to her, for example, dated between 9 July 1850 and 17–22 January 1851 have been published. Only four letters from Pauline are known, three (and, since one of those breaks off in the middle, possibly all four) with long postscripts by Louis Viardot, dated between June 1850 and April 1851. It is, however, clear from Turgenev's letters to her that she wrote more than four during the period. Those that are available to us are no more than friendly, dealing largely with musical news and with news of Paulinette, whose relations with her adoptive mother remained for the time being harmonious; he, for his part, sends messages to the child and enquires after her tenderly. In writing to Pauline he often includes the familiar, somewhat embarrassing, endearments in German, sometimes scored out but still decipherable in the manuscript. There is nothing to suggest any change in his feelings for her. 'My God, I wish I could spend my whole life as a carpet under your dear feet, which I kiss a thousand times ... you know that I belong utterly and entirely to you.' Or again, 'I kiss your feet for hours on end. A thousand thanks for the dear fingernails.'

In a letter which has not been published, to which Turgenev replied on 11 January 1852, Pauline and Louis (jointly apparently, since Turgenev's reply is addressed to them both), informed him that Pauline was expecting another child in the spring. Turgenev's reaction, hoping that the baby would be a boy, is full of excited anticipation of the event. A daughter, Claudie, was safely delivered on 21 May 1852. Did the child symbolize Pauline's complete reconciliation with her husband, after the disturbance of marital harmony caused by Turgenev, and perhaps by Gounod? This seems the most probable hypothesis. It would also explain Turgenev's remark to her in his letter of 8 December 1850 – 'even if I could come [to see you in 1851],

---

* Nikolai and his wife seem to have made something of a habit of driving destitute young women from their door. The same fate as that which befell Elizabeth was suffered by Anna Yakovlevna's sister in 1865, when she was seriously ill with consumption and quite without means. We do not know the reason for this inhuman act. Ivan Turgenev found out about it, and took steps through Annenkov to help the girl with money and medical assistance.[84]

I shall only come if you summon me'[85] – as showing her decision that they must remain apart for a certain time. Further evidence in support of this view is the fact that Pauline eventually pressed Turgenev in April 1852 (when she would have been safely eight months gone with child) to visit them in Paris – by that date Turgenev, although she did not yet know this, was under arrest.[86] However, the possibility of a secret meeting between Turgenev and Pauline in August 1851, which would have been the time Claudie was conceived, cannot be completely excluded, and Turgenev may have been her father. This conjecture is supported by the extraordinary circumstance that there is a complete blank in Turgenev's otherwise fully and meticulously documented Soviet biographical chronology for the period from 27 July to 4 October 1851. Not a single letter to anyone at all has so far become known for this period; and researches into the vast literature of reminiscences and memoirs dealing with Turgenev's life have failed to discover a visit by anyone during these relevant months to Spasskoe where Turgenev would have been living, had he remained all the time in Russia. (In contrast, for 1852 we know of the existence of one letter for July, two for August, and two for September. For 1853 there are three letters in July, four in August, and four in September.) Since it was impossible in 1851 to leave Russia without a special passport issued for the particular journey, and since no application for one by Turgenev has survived in the official archives, it follows that if he did leave Russia it must have been on false papers. We know that in 1853 he did, in fact, travel secretly to Moscow on a false internal passport to see Pauline, so he had some means of procuring fake documents. It is, however, very unlikely that someone so physically conspicuous as Turgenev, and with friends in so many parts of the world, could have travelled unnoticed to Europe – unlikely, though not impossible. Until further correspondence between the two of them is published, if ever, the suggestion that Turgenev fathered Claudie must remain no more than simple conjecture.

At the end of 1852 Pauline and Louis arrived for the season in St. Petersburg. Turgenev's distress at being unable to join her there can well be imagined. She was later reproached by some of his Russian friends for not making the journey to Spasskoe. But she could not possibly have travelled without Louis, and a joint visit for the first reunion with Turgenev after nearly three years (assuming that they had not met in 1851), might well have been more painful than continued separation. Turgenev bombarded his friends, particularly Annenkov, for details of Pauline's performances, and obviously resented even the very slight criticism which came from Annenkov – her high notes were not so good as her low notes, and she tended to overact. Nothing less than reiterated proclamation of Pauline's complete perfection would do for Turgenev.

Before the end of the year Louis fell ill – a victim of the Russian winter – and had to return to France. Meanwhile Pauline decided to travel to Moscow alone, to give some concerts. Turgenev heard all this news from Princess Meshcherskaia: 'I must admit,' he wrote to Pauline on 20 February 1853, 'without wishing to reproach you in the very slightest, that I should have preferred to learn all this from you.' No further letter from Turgenev to Pauline has been published until one dated 17 April. Meanwhile, with the aid of his false internal passport, he paid a secret visit to Moscow and met Pauline. He left about 22 March and returned on 1 April. Since the journey from Spasskoe took several days, the meeting must have been very short. We know nothing of what passed between them, where they met, or how the arrangements for the meeting were made. Certainly, everything must have been done in the greatest secrecy, since had he been discovered breaking the imperial order, Turgenev risked a term of imprisonment and indefinite exile. Pauline did not refer to his visit in her letters from Russia[87] – very properly, since they may well have been censored. She made no secret of it, however, on her return to London direct from St. Petersburg, and told Herzen, among others.[88]

By 23 November Turgenev had received the welcome news that he was free to travel and to live in either capital if he pleased. He remained under police supervision. The lifting of the ban had apparently been accomplished with the help of his friend Count A. K. Tolstoy, who intervened with the Grand Duke Alexander (the future emperor).[89] Turgenev abandoned his plan of spending part of the winter in Orel, and decided to move to St. Petersburg. To Annenkov he wrote that he would have to economize, that he would be travelling with one servant only who would also do the cooking, and he asked him to find two furnished rooms.[90] He arrived in the capital on 9 December 1853.

CHAPTER SEVEN

The Search for a Style

The move to St. Petersburg meant for Turgenev a return to the literary circle around which his life in the capital was now to be centred until his departure for Paris in July 1856. This was the group of the *Contemporary* – the journal to which Turgenev had, from the time of its revival in 1847, been a regular contributor, and the progress of which he had followed closely during his exile in Spasskoe. Of its two editors, N. A. Nekrasov, a few years younger than Turgenev, had already acquired some reputation as a lyric poet, and was later to acquire a great – if, from the literary point of view, undeserved – reputation as the author of poetry depicting the sufferings of the peasants, and thus become the darling of the populists. Apart from some of his lyrics, his verse never aroused much enthusiasm from Turgenev who disliked its 'energetic, but often dry and rigid passion', as he wrote in 1854.[1] Nekrasov was a flamboyant character, an inveterate gambler for high stakes, and devoted to good wine and food. He was, however, an excellent editor and critic who raised the *Contemporary* to a high literary level, at any rate until such time as he allowed it to become the political mouthpiece of the revolutionaries Chernyshevsky and Dobroliubov, and thereby lost his best contributors. But in 1854 this still lay some years ahead.

Nekrasov and Turgenev were on terms of close intimacy, as their correspondence shows. They spent time in one another's country houses, and went shooting together. Nekrasov's reputation in Russian intellectual circles suffered severely from two accusations which were levelled against him. The first, that he had failed to give Belinsky full scope on the *Contemporary* – a charge which he hotly denied, and which was probably untrue. The second related to some shady transactions over money in the course of which Ogarev was financially damaged. The truth of this sordid affair seems to have been that the real culprit was Nekrasov's mistress, Panaeva, whom he tried to shield.

The other editor, I. I. Panaev, was rather a sad, pathetic character. He was a minor writer of fiction of a fairly radical nature. Probably his main contribution to literature had been raising the capital to buy the *Contemporary* from Pletnev by mortgaging his serfs. Panaev was married to Avdotia Yakovlevna, a vivacious and most attractive woman, and herself an author of fictional works, some jointly with Nekrasov. Being interested only in male company, she played an independent part in the literary circle of the *Contemporary*. For many years, from 1848 onwards, she maintained an open liaison with Nekrasov, who over a long period shared a large flat on the Fontanka with the Panaevs. The weak Panaev seems to have tolerated this situation. He was treated kindly and affectionately by his friends and colleagues, and Turgenev's letters to him are invariably warm and full of sympathy. Madame Panaeva was as little acquainted with truth as she was with the social conventions, and late in life published her memoirs, which have already been referred to. Lively and amusing, they have become a frequently exploited source of anecdotes for Turgenev's biographers. However, whenever the facts can be checked they prove to be wrong, and the long verbatim conversations written down many years after they are supposed to have taken place do not add much conviction to what is basically a work of fiction. Panaev died in 1862, at the early age of fifty. A year later his widow parted from Nekrasov, and shortly afterwards remarried. Turgenev detested her: 'this coarse and beastly woman' who was certain to drive Nekrasov 'out of his mind', was his verdict on her in 1857.[2]

Among other regular members of the 'circle' were P. V. Annenkov, V. P. Botkin, D. V. Grigorovich, A. V. Druzhinin, and I. A. Goncharov. Count L. N. Tolstoy, whose early works were published by the *Contemporary*, can also be reckoned a member of it after his return from military service at the end of 1855, though he was never so intimately connected with it as the others. Except for Tolstoy and the much younger Druzhinin, all these men of letters were drawn together by a common bond – the friendship, respect, and affection which had drawn them to Belinsky. It was not regard for Belinsky's opinions that attracted them; Belinsky's socialism in his later years, for example, was alien to all the members of the 'circle', except Nekrasov. It was the fact that Belinsky had stood for the integrity of the critic, for opposition to the regime, the bureaucracy, and the censorship – in short for what would now be known as 'liberal principles', which all these men shared.

Annenkov, possibly the outstanding memoirist of the century, was in 1854 engaged in preparing an edition of the works of Pushkin and writing the first life of the poet. V. P. Botkin, a minor but significant literary figure, had been Belinsky's intimate friend and his regular correspondent. Like Goncharov, he originated not from the nobility, but from a family of merchants, but this in no way inhibited the closest friendship between him and the others. Turgenev, in particular, had great affection for Botkin and especially valued his critical opinion of his own writings.[3] Grigorovich, still in his early thirties, was fast building up a reputation as a novelist who graphically depicted the sufferings of the serfs. Turgenev had doubts about his merits as a writer – indeed, at times looked on his work as a warning that he, as author of the *Sketches from a Sportsman's Notebook*, had to take to heart if he was not to become the Russian Harriet Beecher Stowe. For some years, in spite of surface cordiality, he despised him.[4] But he changed his opinion both of the man and of his work later in life.

A. V. Druzhinin had made his debut in literature in 1847 when the *Contemporary* published his novel *Polin'ka Saks*, devoted, in the manner of George Sand, to the theme of the emancipation of women. By this time, however, he was established as an outstanding literary critic. He wrote a good deal, incidentally, on English literature and helped to introduce much of it to Russian readers. His writings were later to help to polarize opinion on the function of literature – was it, as Druzhinin maintained, a form of art, without any social purpose? Or, as Chernyshevsky and Dobroliubov, the two leading radicals argued, a tool of social protest? This controversy belongs to the years 1855–6 and centred, somewhat artificially, around the evaluation of Pushkin and Gogol – with Pushkin cast by Chernyshevsky in the role of the adherent of art for art's sake, and Gogol in that of the realist and merciless satirist – thus attributing to each writer exaggerated attitudes which neither ever adopted. Druzhinin became the defender of Pushkin in this controversy, in which Turgenev, as was to be expected, refused to adopt either extreme position.

I. A. Goncharov had won literary fame in 1847 with his first novel *An Ordinary Story*. In 1852 the future author of *Oblomov* had sailed around the world in the naval frigate *Pallada* as secretary to Admiral Putiatin, but in 1854 he was back in St. Petersburg, a frequenter of the *Contemporary* 'circle', and, for the time being, a friend of Turgenev, who much admired him as a writer.

When not in the country in the summer, Turgenev spent much

of his time in the company of these authors. Always an early riser, he was at one time in the habit of visiting the office of the *Contemporary* every morning. Evenings which were not spent at the theatre or at the houses of the socially eminent where he was welcome, were frequently devoted to hilarious gatherings of the *Contemporary* litterateurs at the flat of one of their number, (most frequently that of Turgenev, or of Panaev and Nekrasov), or at a restaurant. These were very different gatherings from the ascetic and intellectually serious 'circles' of the thirties and forties, of Stankevich or Belinsky, for example, where the most stimulating diet consisted of tea and dry rusks, and the topic of argument such subjects as the existence of God or the philosophy of Schelling or Hegel. At the *Contemporary* gatherings the drink was champagne, and the food plentiful and often luxurious.* The usual subjects of conversation were personal gossip and literary argument. A favourite amusement was the improvisation of verse epigrams, a pastime at which Turgenev excelled. Five of these were written down and have been published. Another effort written in 1856 by Turgenev in the same manner was a wildly indecent satire on Nicholas I and on Russia's role in the Crimean War, which incidentally includes a dig at Konstantin Aksakov.[6]

Turgenev occupied a fairly spacious apartment near the Anichkov bridge, on the Fontanka. He now had two servants – Zakhar and his cook Stepan. The cook was a great artist – Turgenev had bought him for 1,000 roubles.† Stepan was devoted to Turgenev and always abandoned whatever engagements as chef he had undertaken during Turgenev's absences from St. Petersburg in order to cook for him whenever he returned to the capital. The apartment cost 450 roubles (about £85) a year. The share of the estate which Turgenev had inherited from his mother – around 5,500 *desiatins* (14,850 acres) of land and 1,925 male 'souls' – should, especially in the black earth region, have been yielding an income of between 20,000 and 27,000 roubles. Owing to his Uncle Nicholas's mismanagement it was producing no more than 5,500 roubles, of which Turgenev could only extract 3,600 roubles a year from his reluctant uncle, and he complained to Pauline of lack of money.[7] But another reason for his fairly chronic lack of funds is likely to have been his extravagance, or rather indifference to money. He lived with the aristocratic self-assurance that his needs would somehow be met. His lack of interest

---

* These dinners were not inexpensive. When, in 1858, one of them was planned for a special occasion, it was reckoned that the cost a head would be the equivalent in roubles of between five and six pounds.[5]
† He gave him his freedom a few years later.

revealed itself particularly in his failure to look after his literary income – this was in the days before the advent of agents. To take one example, he sold to Nekrasov the rights to the second edition of the *Sketches from a Sportsman's Notebook* for 1,000 roubles, which Nekrasov promptly resold for 2,500 roubles. So far from resenting this, Turgenev, as he wrote to Herzen, was 'very pleased, because I have sold him the rights to the *Sketches* with the very intention that he should make a profit' – apparently even a profit of 150 per cent! This was not the end of the story, however, as will be seen later.[8]

Turgenev's literary earnings at this date were not very high. Moreover, since his financial relations both with the *Contemporary* and with the *Annals of the Fatherland* were always in a state of chaos because of frequent editorial advances, the sums he earned were not necessarily equivalent to the sums he received. For example, in the one period for which detailed accounts of his transactions with the *Contemporary* are available, 1856–8, his drawings and advances exceeded his earnings by nearly 380 roubles.[9]

During these years in St. Petersburg, Turgenev was publishing both in the *Annals* and in the *Contemporary*, though more frequently in the latter. His letters to Kraevsky, the editor of the *Annals*, contain frequent expressions of guilt at having failed to write for his journal. In July 1855 he offered him his novel (which, in the event, he never completed) for 500 roubles. This was to represent the advance 'together with what I still owe you'.[10] Kraevsky seems only to have advanced a further 250 roubles, since this was the amount which Turgenev returned to him a few months later, after he had abandoned all intentions of completing the book.[11] In the course of 1856 Nekrasov concluded an agreement with Grigorovich, Ostrovsky (the playwright), Tolstoy, and Turgenev not to publish anywhere other than in the *Contemporary*, and in return to be entitled to a percentage of the profits of the journal in addition to their normal fees.[12] This was an attempt by Nekrasov to restore the fortunes of the *Contemporary* which was suffering sadly from competition: M. N. Katkov had started a serious rival in the form of *Russkii vestnik* (the *Russian Herald*) while Druzhinin had left the *Contemporary* to become editor of the *Biblioteka dlia chtenia* (the *Reader's Library*) and had given that moribund periodical a new lease of life. So far as Turgenev was concerned, the agreement, which was not observed by any of the authors concerned, led to long drawn out and unpleasant public conflict with Katkov, which was, however, based on a misundersanding.[13] Eventually they made up their quarrel – if only temporarily – and after

1859 Katkov's journal became for a time Turgenev's principal forum.

Turgenev was not fortunate with the first translation of his *Sketches from a Sportsman's Notebook*, which appeared in French in 1854. The translator, M. E. Charrière, apart from perpetrating the inaccuracies which beset virtually all translations from the Russian, took the liberty of altering the text more or less as he pleased – the very title, *Mémoires d'un Seigneur Russe*, was misleading. Moreover the changes to the stories, where not due to ignorance of the Russian language, were inspired by the anti-Russian prejudice which was fashionable in France during the Crimean War. Turgenev published a long and detailed letter of protest in the *Journal de St. Pétersbourg*.[14]

In part, Turgenev's chronic lack of means was also due to his generosity to those in need – an aspect both of his weakness of character and of his genuine indifference to money. It did not need his enemies to point out this weakness and lack of determination and courage, since these were defects to which Turgenev repeatedly referred himself throughout his life. Those who were not susceptible to his charm, or, like the legal philosopher and historian B. N. Chicherin, totally lacked any sense of humour, saw little but debility and lack of principle in Turgenev as a man, while having regard for the writer.[15] But in one sense Turgenev's easy-going and mild nature, which sometimes led him to do things which his friends found reprehensible, was also the cause of some of his most endearing qualities, like his complete lack of vanity, indeed at times even of dignity; or the almost inexhaustible willingness to help the young with advice and support, which his correspondence shows again and again. It is difficult to imagine a less pompous celebrity.

During the summer of 1854, Turgenev embarked on another of his romances, this time with a distant cousin, Olga Turgeneva. He became particularly friendly with her that summer, when he was living near Peterhof. Olga, then aged eighteen, was the only daughter of Aleksandr Mikhailovich Turgenev, a typical educated liberal of the eighteenth century. She had lost her mother at an early age and was brought up by her father with the aid of a clever and civilized woman called Nadezhda Mikhailovna Eropkina. The girl was given an excellent education, and became a very accomplished musician. (She played Turgenev's favourite Beethoven beautifully.) Turgenev was undoubtedly much fascinated by her. Many of his friends believed that he was contemplating marriage, and warmly approved of the prospect. Although Turgenev on a number of occasions strenuously denied the rumours,[16] there is little doubt that his romance with Olga, failing as it did to lead to marriage and domestic bliss, represented for him one of those situations, often portrayed in his fiction, where the hero is deprived of the quiet happiness of family life either through his own indecision or through his inability to overcome a wild infatuation for a more dominant woman, or both. This is the theme of *A Correspondence*, finished around this time, in December 1854, though in fact begun many years before. It was also the subject of *Spring Torrents* and of *Smoke*, written many years later – in spite of the unconvincing 'happy ending' of the latter.[17]

But apart from the evidence of his fiction, Turgenev's correspondence reveals how much his affection for Olga had meant to him, and leaves no doubt that marriage had been in his mind at some time. Shortly before he left for abroad in 1856, Turgenev wrote to Countess Lambert, with whom, largely by correspondence, he was embarking on what the French call *une amitié amoureuse*:

At my age, to leave for abroad means to doom oneself finally to a gypsy life and to abandon all thoughts of family life. What is to be done? Evidently, such is my fate. Incidentally, I may as well add: people who have no strength of character like to invent a 'fate' for themselves: this relieves them of the necessity of having a will of their own – and of responsibility to themselves.[18]

To Olga herself, with whom he remained friendly after their closer intimacy had come to an end at the beginning of 1855, he wrote on the eve of his departure from Russia, that 'the permission to go abroad has given me no particular joy – and that I am even now in a melancholy frame of mind'.[19] (He wrote in very different terms to Pauline Viardot about his impending departure.)[20] In 1872, when Olga died, having married and borne four children, he wrote to Annenkov, who had been his confidant in the affair: 'One beautiful, pure creature the fewer in the world. I remembered a lot ... and the memory was bitter. Shadows keep on falling on life, falling not only on the present and the future, but on the past.'[21]

Mild and innocent as Turgenev's romance with Olga had been, Pauline Viardot evidently sensed the importance of it for Turgenev, and seems to have displayed signs of jealousy when he himself told her about Olga. He wrote to her a long letter justifying himself and assuring her, twice, in Spanish, that 'ya se acabó' ('it is all over').[22] Evidently Pauline was not satisfied with his assurances, because a few months later he wrote to her: 'Your last letter was very short, and, forgive the expression, very dry. Why do you tease me on the subject of Mademoiselle T.?'[23] It would seem that the dominating Pauline regarded it as her privilege to decide when and to what extent Turgenev should remain attached to her, and resented any attempt, however hesitant and tentative, by him to decide his own destiny.

Apart from the ties which bound him to Pauline, Turgenev may have had other reasons for hesitating to plunge into marriage. 'It is not good for an artist to marry ...', he once told Leontiev. 'Perhaps an unhappy marriage can help talent to develop, but a happy marriage is no use at all. ... Generally, I have never understood passion felt for a young girl: I prefer the married woman who is experienced and *free* and is better able to manage herself and her passions.'[24]

To complete this account of Turgenev's love life, mention should be made of a Polish lady of easy virtue ('lorette' as he describes her) with whom he seems to have had a short, passionate affair in the winter of 1855 – 'giving her silver table sets and spending the nights with her until eight in the morning', as he wrote to Botkin.[25] Six months later he informed Botkin and Druzhinin, from Spasskoe, that he was leading a 'very chaste' life, and was very glad of it after 'the excesses of the winter'.[26]

While living in Spasskoe in 1854, Turgenev made the acquaintance of his close neighbours, Countess M. N. Tolstaia, the sister of the novelist Count L. N. Tolstoy, and her husband, also a Count Tolstoy, another member of that vast family. As he wrote to Nekrasov, the Countess was 'an enchanting woman, clever, kind and very attractive'.[27] During his time in Spasskoe, that autumn and in the following summer, Turgenev became a very frequent visitor at the Tolstoys' estate, Pokrovskoe, read his stories to the Countess and went shooting with her husband. It seems clear that his susceptible heart was smitten by the charming Countess; and, from what she told her daughter many years later, when she had become a nun, she had not been indifferent to him.

There is some evidence that Countess Tolstaia served Turgenev as the prototype of Vera in his story 'Faust', which was written in the course of a few days in the summer of 1856, in between visits to Pokrovskoe, and published in the *Contemporary* in October.[28] The story, which is told in a series of letters, is remarkable both for its descriptions of Spasskoe and for the evidence which it provides of Turgenev's continuing preoccupation with Goethe, and particularly with Part I of *Faust*. The resemblance of Vera to Tolstaia seems limited to the one circumstance that Vera, now married, has been brought up by her dominating mother completely isolated from all poetry, and that Tolstaia also had no feeling for poetry. However, the physical description of Vera is very like that of the Countess. The impact in the story on Vera of Goethe's *Faust*, when read to her by the narrator, is dramatic. She falls in love with him, as he does with her, and they exchange a single kiss. But the ghost of Vera's mother appears to her, as if to reclaim her both from poetry and from illicit passion. Vera falls ill with a mysterious sickness and, within a few days, dies. 'Faust' is a work of great beauty and artistry, and succeeds superbly in conveying the kind of unspoken, unacknowledged love of a man for a married woman and its shattering consequence which to Turgenev's imagination may well at the time have appeared as the literary sublimation of his own feelings for Countess Tolstaia.

The epigraph of the story, taken from Part I of Goethe's *Faust*, underlines the moral – that duty is all ('Entbehren sollst du, sollst entbehren'). The concluding paragraph of the last of the letters which make up the story expands on this theme:

I have derived one conviction from the experience of the past years: life is neither a jest nor a pastime, it is not even a source of delight ... life is hard toil. Its secret meaning, the solution to its riddle, is self-denial, constant self-denial. Not the fulfilment of our favourite thoughts and dreams, however exalted these may be: what a man has to worry about is fulfilling his duty. Without putting on himself the heavy iron chains of duty man cannot reach, without falling down, the end of his life's aim – and when we are young we think that the freer the better, the further one will go. It is permissible for the young to think like that. But it is shameful to comfort oneself with deceit when the stern countenance of truth has at last looked you in the eyes.[29]

Meanwhile, in 1854 and 1855, Turgenev was eager to meet Tolstoy the young writer, whose *Childhood* and *Youth*, and other early works, he much admired. Tolstoy in turn had the highest opinion of the older author, and had dedicated a story to him. Turgenev heard much about him from his sister, and in October 1855 he wrote to Tolstoy, then still on military service in the Crimea, in terms of admiration and friendship, and expressing the hope that they might meet.[30] On 19 November 1855 Tolstoy arrived in St. Petersburg and went straight to Turgenev's apartment, where he stayed for some weeks. Turgenev spoke of him with enthusiasm, though from the start their different temperaments foreshadowed the future break. 'You cannot imagine', he wrote to Annenkov three weeks after their meeting, 'what a charming and remarkable man he is – though on account of his wild jealousy and obstinacy like that of a buffalo he has been nicknamed by me the Troglodite. I have come to love him with a strange kind of feeling, rather like a paternal feeling.'[31] The seeds of future discord were evident from the start. As we know from his diary, the more forthright Tolstoy really disliked Turgenev from the very first. He also despised the frivolity of the whole *Contemporary* circle. He preferred for his diversion spending his evenings until the small hours with the gypsies, or at high society parties, returning late and sleeping late. There were frequent, almost emotional, clashes between the two writers; one such conflict, which nearly resulted in a break, arose over a moralistic diatribe uttered by Tolstoy against the heroines of George Sand's novels:[32] these, of course, included Consuelo, modelled on Pauline Viardot who was a close friend of the French writer, although Tolstoy may not have known this. Similar petty incidents were witnessed by the poet Fet.[33] This was the unhappy beginning of a relationship which a few years later was to culminate in the dramatic quarrel which separated the two men for so long.[34] In a conversation many years later, in which he discussed the whole *Contemporary* circle, Tolstoy said that he had soon come to despise its members for what he regarded as their immorality, their pettiness, and their lack of character.[35]

Literary activities apart, Turgenev devoted much of the year to shooting expeditions, spending several months at Spasskoe for this purpose. Diana was getting old. She died on 6 September 1858, and Turgenev shed tears at her burial.[36] Her place had been taken by one of her pups – Bubulka – endowed with this ridiculous name by Pauline Viardot. (Tolstoy, with his uncanny gift for saying the wrong thing to Turgenev, used to mock at his great devotion to the dog and at its name – though again he was probably unaware of the link with Pauline.) The summer of 1855 was severely disturbed by an epidemic of cholera. This disease always threw Turgenev into a frenzy of fear. On this occasion the alarm was very well founded. Shooting was out of the question. There were deaths almost daily in the village, and from his window Turgenev could hear the wailing of the peasant women rising from the neighbouring cemetery.[37] The news from the Crimea was also very disturbing – Sebastopol fell on 10 September 1855. Turgenev followed Russia's fortunes in this ill-conceived war with intense emotional interest, and his correspondence contains repeated references to the varying fortunes of the Russian army in the Crimea, in the course of 1854 and 1855. The rupture of diplomatic relations declared by Russia against Great Britain and France on 21 February 1854 provoked a patriotic outburst by Turgenev in a letter to Pauline of a kind in which he rarely indulged.

Our country is preparing itself with determination and energy for the struggle which is about to erupt. The entire people, from the highest classes down to the humblest peasant, is behind the government. Our sixty-five millions are as one at this moment – you can be quite certain of this – and this is what Europe does not realize. This unity of deed and feeling, and of will, is something very impressive, and very strong. It would suffice to make us defy the whole world. I say this with certainty – whatever may happen we shall not retreat by as much as a hair's breadth – you will see. No one knows our strength – we do not know it ourselves until we are challenged. Russia is rising at this moment as it did in 1812.[38]

Indeed, an extraordinary and quite uncharacteristic tirade. On the other hand, the death of Nicholas I in March 1855 which was to mark the end of an era in Russia produced no recorded comment from him beyond one indirect reference to the 'shattering event'.[39]

In the summer of 1855, life at Spasskoe was enlivened by the arrival of Botkin, Grigorovich, and Druzhinin, who stayed from 13 May until 1 June. In the course of this visit the four friends, with some help from neighbouring residents, put on two farcical plays which they composed themselves. One was a parody on a play by the 'pseudo-majestical' Ozerov, a comic scene between Oedipus and Antigone. The other was about a landowner who has imprudently invited dozens of guests to his estate, which he has not visited for years. He arrives to find it decrepit and desolate, just as the guests are beginning to assemble. A fire adds to the confusion. Turgenev, who acted the role of the landlord, agreed to rush on to the stage when the fire broke out and to pronounce the words 'Save me, save me, I am my mother's only son'.[40] The allusion would have been obvious to all present. The phrase was widely supposed to have been used by the panic-stricken young Turgenev in 1838, when the fire broke out on the ship in which he was sailing to Germany. He frequently denied that he ever spoke these words. The fact that Turgenev should have consented to utter these lines merely to amuse his guests is a typical example of his lack of vanity – some could, and did, say lack of dignity.

The varied social life which has been described left little time for literary activity, and indeed Turgenev did not write much during these three years – apart from *Rudin*. He did, however, expend much energy in promoting the work of others, notably the poetry of Fet and Tiutchev. He somewhat annoyed Fet by editing his translations from the classics and insisting on numerous alterations.[41] His dealings with Tiutchev were more serious in their consequences. Tiutchev, as Turgenev rightly pointed out in an article published in 1854, was the greatest living Russian lyricist, comparable only to Pushkin. Turgenev persuaded the poet to let him edit a volume of his collected lyrics. Tiutchev agreed, and then, characteristically, took no further interest. The result was that Turgenev corrected what he thought were Tiutchev's faulty rhythms and produced a text of the poems which was for long accepted as authentic, but which in many instances contained serious distortions.[42]

It will be recalled that by 25 May 1853 the first of three parts of a projected novel, entitled *Two Generations*, had been sent off to Annenkov for his comments. Turgenev's friends, notably Feoktistov and Annenkov, had for some time past been urging him to produce a full scale work of fiction. The first part of *Two Generations* was completed in a short burst of intensive work of about six months. But he had been thinking of its contents for a long time – probably since the end of the forties.[43] From the correspondence which was quoted in the last chapter it is evident that he attached great importance to this new venture in literary style as a test of his ability to produce something which would be quite different in scope and manner from the *Sketches from a Sportsman's Notebook* on which his fame as a writer as yet mainly rested. Part I of *Two Generations* was read not only by Annenkov, but by Sergei and Konstantin Aksakov, Botkin, and Ketcher (a Moscow friend, who had been close to Belinsky, Stankevich, Granovsky, and Herzen, and was the translator of Shakespeare). Although Annenkov's opinion was slightly more favourable than that of the others, there was a fair degree of unanimity among the critics that most of the persons portrayed lacked colour and definition. Botkin went so far as to say that the work did not absorb 'because none of its characters evokes either great sympathy or great curiosity'. All the critics were agreed that the descriptions of nature were excellent, but this is unlikely to have brought much comfort to Turgenev, who was searching for a quite different literary objective.[44] His expressed intention was to rework the novel, but the task of revision was repeatedly postponed and he never succeeded in rewriting or completing it. Eventually he destroyed the manuscript. As he later wrote to Botkin from Paris, on 17 February 1857: 'The day before yesterday I did not burn (since I was afraid of behaving as if I were Gogol) but tore up and threw into the W.C. all my unfinished efforts, plans and so forth.'[45] But one chapter and an early plan of the novel survived.

The chapter, which he published in 1859 under the title 'The Privy Office' (in Katkov's journal the *Russian Herald*), was very much in the style of one of the *Sketches from a Sportsman's Notebook*. It portrayed, on the basis of personal observation in Spasskoe (as a number of details conclusively prove), his mother at her most tyrannical and capricious, spending the morning persecuting her domestic staff – all of whom are clearly identifiable as Spasskoe characters. The description of Varvara Petrovna (named Gagina in the novel) is brilliant, but shows nothing new in the manner of composition or writing.[46] The plan which escaped the ignominious fate of the manuscript appears to have been an early one, as comparison with the comments of some of Turgenev's friends on the finished Part One shows. The scene is set on an estate owned by the tyrannous Gagina, and managed (as was Spasskoe) by her late husband's brother. The arrival of a young girl Elizaveta Mikhailovna (originally assigned a German surname, Baum, and based on Turgenev's brother Nikolai's wife, Anna Yakovlevna Shvarts) to act as Gagina's companion, causes all manner of complications. Both the uncle-in-law and Gagina's son Dmitri fall in love with her: she, in a manner, keeps the two men on a string. Chermak, a neighbouring landlord – apparently a complex and very devious character – interferes between the men and Elizaveta Mikhailovna, and is eventually thrown out of the house. Elizaveta leaves for Moscow, where she is wooed both by young Gagin and by his uncle – and refuses them both. Apart from portraying his mother's estate and her habits, the main purpose of the novel seems to have been to show the effect on this quiet household of the sudden injection into it of an attractive girl, with the consequent reactions of young and not so young men – Chermak is forty and Gagin twenty-six. Possibly it was because of this difference in the ages of the men involved with Elizaveta Mikhailovna that the novel was given its title.[47]

After the departure of the boisterous trio of Botkin, Druzhinin, and Grigorovich from Spasskoe, Turgenev immediately, on 5 June 1855, settled down to concentrated work on a new novel (which he described as a *povest'*, or 'short novel') and which he finished on 24 July. This was *Rudin*. Turgenev himself attributed the intensity with which he worked on *Rudin* to boredom induced by the fact that the prevalence of cholera prevented him from going shooting. It is unlikely that this was the whole explanation. During the years he remained in Russia after his exile – was indeed forced to remain in Russia because of the Crimean War – Turgenev's literary activity was very slight, and confined to a few stories and articles. Having abandoned *Two Generations*, he was searching for what was to become his real medium, the novel, in which social analysis is always subordinate to human relations, and the delineation of the charac-

ters assumes dominant importance. In *Rudin*, to some extent accidentally, he found the form which he had long been searching for.

Some of the pursuit of his true style is revealed in the stories
published in 1854 and in 1855–6. The longest of these was 'A Quiet
Spot', published in 1854. Part of the symbolism in the story lies in
the title – the quiet country spot in which nothing seems to happen,
but which in fact is the scene of a passionate human conflict, culmi-
nating in tragedy. A young landowner, on a rare visit to a much
neglected estate, is persuaded to pay a call on a rather dull neighbour –
an extended Russian visit lasting for days. Vladimir Sergeevich, the
young landowner, is a rather priggish young man. At the 'quiet spot'
he becomes involved in a smouldering conflict: the intense young
sister-in-law of the widowed neighbour, Maria, is in love with the
hero of the story, Veretiev, and it is clear when we meet Veretiev
that there is very little seriousness on his side. He is a pleasure-loving,
easy-going, immensely attractive young man, with a predilection
for wine and female company, and without any fixed purpose in
life. He is destined for a bad end, which he achieves, and indeed,
after an interval of time and a second visit, Vladimir Sergeevich witnesses the suicide of Maria, in despair at Veretiev's desertion and at
her own failure to redeem his character. There is a slight suggestion
that Maria's impulsive suicide (regretted at the last moment, as Turgenev with great subtlety suggests) was not unconnected with the
awakening which Vladimir Sergeevich evokes in her by reading to
her Pushkin's 'Anchar' on his first visit.★ The awakening of wild
passion by a poem would be more fully developed in 'Faust', which
was written two and a half years later.

Veretiev, who is heir to a whole line of Russian literary heroes –
Pushkin's Eugene Onegin and Lermontov's Pechorin are the leading
examples – is in the tradition of the 'superfluous men' of the forties
whom Turgenev had already begun to depict – the 'Swashbuckler'
for example, or Chulkaturin in the 'The Diary of a Superfluous
Man'. But the duelling maniac in the former story is hardly a serious
character, and the consumptive Chulkaturin never really had a
chance in life. Veretiev is, in one sense, the victim of his own temperament. But Turgenev leaves no doubt where his sympathies lie –
not with the priggish and successful Vladimir Sergeevich, but with
the failure Veretiev, who (like Faust) at any rate has the courage to

---

★ This poem tells the story of a slave sent by a prince to gather venom from
a poisonous tree for his arrows. The slave succeeds in his mission, but expires
overcome by the toxic fumes, at the feet of his master on his return. 'Anchar
is the upas tree, *antiaris toxicaria*, which yields a poisonous juice.

taste life to the full. In a sense, Veretiev's flippancy and lack of responsibility must be seen as the direct consequence of social and political conditions. In the forties there were many idealistic young Russians anxious to lead useful lives of service, yet denied the opportunity to do so unless they were prepared to accept the *poshlost'*, the hypocrisy and prevarication, of official society under Nicholas I. It was this which drove many of them to lives of cynical disillusion. The banality of Vladimir Sergeevich's chosen conventional way of life is further underlined by the suggestion in the story that, owing to his lack of initiative, he fails to secure the hand of Veretiev's enchanting sister, with whom, indeed, he is half in love.

Of the remaining stories of this period, 'A Correspondence', written in the form of an exchange of letters, was started as far back as 1844 and deals with a favourite theme of Turgenev's fiction – the man who loses the quiet happiness which could be his with a simple, gentle woman because of a physical passion he cannot control for an inferior woman. The last letter, in which Aleksei explains his sudden disappearance and writes about his infatuation for a dancer, contains reflections on love which are typical of Turgenev. It is not 'the free union of souls and other ideal things thought up by German professors when they have nothing better to do' (what would Bettina von Arnim have said!). 'Love is a heavy chain, in love the one is the slave and the other is the master.' But there is also a suggestion (which is to be found in the part of the story that was written last) that Aleksei too is a victim of the Russian forties, a 'superfluous man':

When you come to think of it, what a fate mine has been! In my first youth I was quite determined to conquer the sky ... then I began to dream about the well-being of all mankind, of the well-being of my country. Then all that passed. I only thought of arranging a domestic family life for myself – and then I tripped on an anthill and bang! flat on my face, and into my grave. ... What past masters we Russians are at finishing up in this manner![48]

'The Two Friends', written during his exile in Spasskoe and published early in 1854, contains several sketches which reflect some of Turgenev's experiences of meetings with the local minor gentry on his travels. The two friends of the story are neighbouring small landowners; Krupitsin is a traditional Russian figure, the other, Viazovnin, has a certain veneer of Western European culture, and hankering after it. Against Krupitsin's advice, Viazovnin woos and marries a gentle, domesticated, and unsophisticated girl, daughter of another minor landowner for whom she keeps house. Krupitsin is afraid that with his 'Western ways' Viazovnin will soon tire of a simple, uneducated Russian country girl. But the two men remain friends after the marriage, and Krupitsin looks after the young wife in a fatherly manner. Eventually Viazovnin's longing for the flesh-pots of Europe gets the better of him, and he escapes to Paris for a holiday, intending to return. Very soon after his arrival an officer (always one of Turgenev's special *bêtes noires*) picks a quarrel with him over a grisette, and kills him in a duel. Another pointless death – but Viazovnin is scarcely to be classed as a 'superfluous man'. A year later Krupitsin marries Viazovnin's young widow, and they live in the greatest contentment, 'peacefully and quietly. They enjoy their happiness because there is no other form of happiness on earth.'[49] The story thus has a certain almost Slavophile undercurrent in its glorification of the simple, Russian way of life as contrasted with the bizarre futility of Paris, with its grisettes and its officers.

The most remarkable of the stories of these three years, and the one which is most indicative of the development of Turgenev's out-look is beyond doubt 'Yakov Pasynkov'. The plot is complicated, and too involved to summarize here, nor is it particularly relevant. The real importance of 'Pasynkov' lies in the love and devotion with which Turgenev delineated the character of the narrator's friend, who dies in the course of the story. It is easy to recognize Belinsky as the prototype of Pasynkov, though there are certainly also elements of Stankevich in him. Pasynkov is poor and ungainly. His character is near to saintliness – 'in his lips the words "the good", "the true", "life", "learning", "love", however exultantly they were pronounced, never sounded like a falsehood'. In the presence of Pasynkov it is impossible to lie – he is too transparently sincere, he is kind and upright in all his actions. An interesting point is the hint that Pasynkov is a believer, contained in a passage which was curi-ously enough added only at proof stage.[50] Turgenev was not at that date a believer, though he may have begun to feel the hankering for a faith which he would later frequently express. (Perhaps his atti-tude to religion was best summed up in the words of Faust: 'Die Botschaft hör ich wohl, allein mir fehlt der Glaube' – 'Indeed I hear the message, but I lack the faith'.)

Pasynkov is modest and retiring; it is only on his friend's deathbed that the narrator discovers that Pasynkov loved, without revealing his passion because she was loved by another, the very girl with whom, he, the narrator, had also been in love. Of course, it is possible to dismiss (as did many contemporary critics) 'Yakov Pasynkov' as an idealization of the German romanticism in the midst of which Turgenev spent his student days. That is, however, beside the point. It was not for their enthusiasm for the German romantics that Turgenev venerated the memory of Stankevich and Belinsky, but, as he has recorded, for their sincerity, their purity of moral purpose, and their enthusiasm for truth and beauty – the qualities which before long were to be singled out as characteristic of the 'Don Quixotes' in what is probably Turgenev's most significant work for the understanding of his outlook – 'Hamlet and Don Quixote'. But something of the lesson of 'Yakov Pasynkov' – that what matters is not what you achieve, but what you are and how you live – was to enter, if only belatedly, and almost accidentally, into the fabric of *Rudin*.

The plot of *Rudin* must be sufficiently familiar not to require a long summary. As originally conceived, and in essence completed, it was a story of a human failure – a man of brilliant capacities, who captivates the household into which he is by chance introduced, by his eloquence and his talent, but who is basically empty, vain, and incapable of achieving anything in life. The culmination of Rudin's spinelessness comes when he declares his love for the daughter of the household, Natalia, and discovers that he is loved in return. Yet no sooner is he informed of the opposition to the marriage by Natalia's mother, Lasunskaia, than he accepts the impossibility of their future happiness and departs – leaving the girl deeply hurt and disillusioned. But, since she is much the stronger character, one feels that she will not remain broken-hearted for long. If the novel had ended there, Rudin would almost have remained a singularly unattractive person – not so much a 'superfluous man', but a weak, vain, and boastful idler. Almost – but not quite. In his farewell letter to Natalia (and this is part of the novel in the original first version), Rudin strikes a note of sincerity and tragedy, which of itself transforms him into a 'superfluous man' of the forties. 'Strange, almost comic is my fate. I give myself entirely, greedily – and I cannot give myself. I will end by sacrificing myself for some nonsense in which I don't believe. Dear God! At thirty-five to be still preparing to do something!'[51]

There is no doubt, because Turgenev said so, that Rudin was to a great extent based on Bakunin. In a letter to a close friend in 1862 he wrote that he had painted a 'fairly accurate portrait' of Bakunin, who has now become a 'Rudin who was not killed on the barricades', and who, 'between ourselves, is a ruin' and 'a spent agitator'. True, at the time of publication in February 1856, he wrote to S. T. Aksakov expressing pleasure that 'You do not seek in Rudin a portrait of some well-known figure.'[52] But the similarities speak for themselves – the infatuation with Hegel, the brilliance in argument, a tendency to borrow money from all and sundry, and an irresistible passion for meddling in other peoples' love affairs, for example. That the intention was to satirize Bakunin, or contemporaries similar to him, is also suggested by the original, derisory title – 'The Genius'.

Between the completion of the novel in its original form in July 1855 and its appearance in 1856 several things happened which led Turgenev to make some changes. First was the arrest of Bakunin, the handing over of him to the Russian authorities, and his imprisonment in the Schluesselburg Fortress in the autumn of 1855. It would have been unthinkable for any liberal-minded Russian to publish a bare satire on Bakunin at that date. The second event was the death of Granovsky, whose funeral in Moscow on 7 October 1855 Turgenev attended. His death was sudden and untimely, and came as a shock to Turgenev who had always entertained the highest regard, veneration indeed, for the historian whom he had first known in Berlin when he was there as a student. He wrote a most heartfelt and moving tribute to Granovsky.[53] It is hardly fanciful to suppose that thoughts of Granovsky and of his own youth, and of his former great love for Bakunin, would have inclined him to more charitable thoughts on his one-time closest friend.

And thirdly, there was the urgent advice of his friend Botkin that the novel could not be left as it stood; Nekrasov was enthusiastic that Turgenev had taken Botkin's advice to heart,[54] but it is likely that it fell on very willing ears. So there came into existence the Epilogue of the present text, but without its last paragraph in which Rudin dies in 1848 on the Paris barricades. The addition of this paragraph in 1860, when a collected volume of Turgenev's stories including *Rudin* appeared, coincided with a new ideological climate in Russia and raised a storm of protest from the radicals – but this belongs to the later story of Turgenev's break with the *Contemporary*. The Epilogue of 1855–6 supplied the charity and humanity which the original version lacked: from an, on the whole, unsympathetic *poseur*, Rudin is transformed beyond question into a tragic figure, a real 'superfluous man' of the forties, a victim of the Russia of Nicholas I much more than of his own lack of character. In the Epilogue, Rudin, a few years after his ignominious departure from Lasunskaia's estate, meets by chance her neighbour Lezhnev, who figures in the novel as a one-time companion of Rudin in Stankevich's 'circle', but is now a well-to-do landlord with few intellectual preoccupations. Lezhnev is critical of Rudin in the early part of the book, but now, seeing him old and broken after some years of desperate effort to establish himself, ending in the exile for which he is now bound, the old affection of student days returns. The two men recover their lost intimacy; and the reader is left with the impression that Lezhnev has genuinely succeeded in restoring Rudin's self-respect, and in making him see that what matters is not what you achieve, but the effort you make. *Rudin* marked the beginning of a new phase in Turgenev's work.

It was not accidental that *A Nest of the Landed Gentry*, which was to be characteristic of this phase, was first conceived early in 1856. It was the first statement of one of Turgenev's messages which he was frequently to offer in his art: that it is the noble endeavour alone that redeems one's life, whatever the consequences or the actual attainment. This was a part of Granovsky's faith, and of Goethe's.

Only six letters from Turgenev to Pauline Viardot for the period 1854–6 have been published – all very recently – though no doubt there were more which have been lost, or which remain in private possession. Her letters for these years are not known. But even the few from him which are available suggest that their friendship was suffering from some strain. On Pauline's side there was displeasure over Turgenev's affair with his cousin Olga. So far as he was concerned, his love and devotion remained unaltered, and are expressed in the usual terms. There is also much concern in his letters for Paulinette; there seem to have been some difficulties over the child's continued residence with the Viardots, and she had been placed in a *pension* with a governess, an arrangement of which Turgenev approved. Two letters from him to Paulinette for this period exist, and both show affection and fatherly concern for her progress.[55] His correspondence with Pauline also discloses that he was in the process of making capital provision for Paulinette in the event of his death: apparently there were difficulties in French law which prevented him from making dispositions in her favour in his will which would be accepted as valid by the courts.

With the end of the Crimean War in sight, Turgenev's thoughts turned to France, for which he must certainly have longed during the years of separation from Pauline. On 21 May 1856 he heard that his application for a passport for foreign travel had been successful.[56] He wrote to Madame Garcia, and then later to Pauline herself, announcing the news. Naturally enough he did not share with Pauline the ambivalent feelings about leaving behind him the possibility of settling down to domestic bliss in Russia which he had hinted at in his letters to Countess Lambert and Olga Turgeneva. He had some time before taken the precaution of reserving a berth on the St. Petersburg – Stettin vessel due to sail on 21 July, as the sailings were very heavily booked. After writing farewell letters to Druzhinin, Countess Lambert, and Botkin, among others, he set sail on his journey to London and Paris. He was given a festive dinner before his departure.[57] We cannot know with certainty his state of mind as he set out on his journey. He had evidently confided something of his mood to Nekrasov, whom he often entrusted with details of his feelings for Pauline. 'And what is it going to be like for you to set off for abroad?' Nekrasov wrote a few weeks before his departure. 'Well, it is after all no business of mine. And I dare not say anything because if I were in your place I would do the same.'[58] We can be sure of one thing: Turgenev must have felt in his heart that relations with Pauline were not going to be the same as they had been in the past.

CHAPTER EIGHT

Return to Literature

The discomfort of travel in the mid-nineteenth century notwith-standing (there was as yet no railway connection between St. Peters-burg and Berlin, for example), Turgenev seems to have had a restless and insatiable appetite for moving around Europe. His itinerary between 2 August 1856 when he left St. Petersburg and his third return to Russia on 12 May 1861 may serve as an illustration. He travelled to London, with a short stop in Berlin, and stayed there until 8 September. He then returned to France, first to Courtavenel and then to Paris, where he remained from about 26 October until 12 May 1857. After a second visit to London of about a month's duration, he came back to Paris, where he lived until 17 October, with interruptions for trips to Dijon, Baden-Baden, and Courtavenel. The next six months found him in Italy, mainly in Rome. After short stays in Vienna and London, he spent a week in Paris before leaving for Russia in early June 1858. He lived for nearly a year in 'Russia, until 11 May 1859, distributing his time as usual between Spasskoe and St. Petersburg. Then back to Paris (with a very short visit to London) where he remained, save for extended visits to Vichy and Courtavenel, until 17 September, when he once again left for Russia. On 6 May 1860 he made the long journey to Paris and settled for about twelve months, until 3 May 1861, before travelling back to Russia. The year, however, was interrupted by several visits to Ger-many in the early summer (including a health cure lasting for some weeks in Soden, near Frankfurt), and about a month's stay in London and Ventnor. He arrived in Russia on 12 May after short stops in Munich and in Berlin, where he was made 'heartily welcome' by the German sage, Varnhagen von Ense.

Turgenev had been in London before, but it was mainly during his repeated visits in the course of the next few years that he got to know England and the English, who took the Russian author to

their hearts. His visit in 1856 was very short – from 31 August until
8 September.[1] He saw the Viardots, who were staying with friends
in Highgate,[2] and, of course, Herzen, who was avid to hear news
of the mood in Russia in the new reign of Alexander II. He did not,
so far as we know, make any English friends on this occasion. But
in the following year he paid a more extended visit – from 24 May
until mid-June, staying at the Sablonnière Hotel in Leicester Square.
This time he was supplied with influential letters of introduction –
including one to Richard Monckton Milnes (later Lord Houghton)
who had abandoned politics for a life of wide cultural contacts and
pursuits, and one to the Speaker of the House of Commons, Charles
Shaw Lefevre, who that year was created Viscount Eversly on his
retirement from the office. Turgenev seems to have been warmly
welcomed in English intellectual and political circles. He spent an
evening with Carlyle on 3 June, and was somewhat put out by
Carlyle's insistence on the virtues of Nicholas I, and admiration for
what he regarded as the Russian talent for obedience, and Carlyle
was displeased when Turgenev pointed out to him that this talent
'was not as perfect as he imagined'. Turgenev liked the old man –
'but I should like to see Carlyle inside a Russian skin just for one
week'.[3] Jane Carlyle, who much admired Turgenev's writings, *
liked Turgenev much better than Botkin, whose English she could
not understand. Botkin had translated *Heroes and Hero Worship* and
on the occasion when he visited Carlyle in 1858, found only Jane
at home. Botkin, she wrote, lacked the restrained manners of his
compatriot – 'He does not possess himself like Tourgeneff, but bends
and gesticulates like a Frenchman.' † [5] Turgenev also met Thackeray
('whom I did not like much'),[7] Macaulay, the historian Grote, and
many other distinguished people. There were plans to introduce him
to Lord Palmerston and to the Prince Consort, but Turgenev was
in too much of a hurry to get back to Germany for a cure to prolong
his visit.

His stay in England in 1857 was not just a matter of meeting eminent people. He had the opportunity of learning something of
English social and cultural life. He saw the actor Robson in a stage
adaptation of Balzac's *Eugénie Grandet*, and was well impressed. He
heard Rubinstein play a late Beethoven Sonata (opus 101) 'which

* These she presumably got to know when French translations began to appear
in 1858 – the first serious study of Turgenev's work in English did not appear
until 1869.[4]
† Botkin was armed with warm letters of introduction from Turgenev to Carlyle,
Monckton Milnes, and to Lord Eversly's nephew but does not seem to have made
use of the last two, and only met Monckton Milnes in 1859.[6]

I was unable to understand', and he went to the Derby. He was proposed by Monckton Milnes for the Athenaeum Club, and duly
elected a member.[8] He also took a trip to Manchester to visit the
magnificent Fine Art Exhibition, at which – in a building specially
constructed in Old Trafford – there were assembled over a thousand
first-class paintings, mostly Italian and Dutch, from the great private
collections, as well as much else of note. It was opened by the Prince
Consort, and attended by large numbers of visitors.[9]

He spent a weekend at Embly Park in Hampshire, on the edge
of the New Forest, the beautiful estate of the parents of Florence
Nightingale, who was not herself present. The Nightingales were old
friends of Monckton Milnes. The house party included Sir Charles
Trevelyan, the distinguished Civil Servant, and Lady Trevelyan, the
sister of Macaulay. Turgenev much admired the beauty of the estate,
and its magnificent trees. Mr. Nightingale he found to be 'a country
gentleman in the full strength [*sic*] of that term'. There were similar
comments on the other guests, who included the commodore of the
Queen's yacht, Captain Denman, and his wife, and Colonel Cure,
said to be the model for Rawdon Crawley in *Vanity Fair*. On Sunday
there was a visit to Salisbury Cathedral, which Turgenev found very
beautiful. He thought that Sunday family prayers that evening were
most impressive; he did not share the religious sentiments of the
English, he wrote to Pauline, but they are none the less powerful
for all their convention and respectability; because something is
ridiculous, 'this is no proof that it is neither useful nor even magnificent'. On return to London, he spent the morning at the House of
Commons where, like many a foreign visitor before and since, he
was struck by the lack of formality, which did not however preclude
an impression of grandeur: 'one senses that this is the heart of a great
Empire and that it will endure'. He lunched with Monckton Milnes
and the banker Lord Ashburton, a patron of literature and a friend
of Thackeray and Carlyle.[10] The afternoon was spent in the House
of Lords, with Viscount Eversly's nephew, George John Shaw
Lefevre. He met Disraeli briefly – 'very vain, with the mannerisms
of a leading tenor or fashionable author'.[11] He also saw old friends:
Herzen, Manuel Garcia, and the exiled German socialist, a friend of
the Viardots, Müller-Strübing. He complained of the English summer and was somewhat scathing on the toilettes of some ladies. He
makes no mention of the food.[12]

On his visit to London in the following year, 1858, he stayed in
furnished chambers at 11 Hollis Street, Cavendish Square, which he
found much more comfortable and cheaper than an hotel.[13] The

highlight of this visit was the annual dinner of the Royal Literary Fund, attended by some three hundred guests. He had been invited by Monckton Milnes. The editor of *Biblioteka dlia chtenia*, Druzhinin, who was planning to found a charitable literary fund in Russia, heard that Turgenev had attended this dinner, and invited him to describe it for his journal. Turgenev was enormously impressed with Lord Palmerston, who presided; he had the manner of a man of birth, used to command, unlike Disraeli 'who looks like a fop and an actor'. He went on to describe in some detail the speeches and some of the guests.* He left the dinner with 'the feeling which never departed from me in England every time when I happened to come face to face with some aspect of English public life. . . . Here, as everywhere, where this people, full of shortcomings but a great people, has left the trail of its lion's claw – here too there is strength, durability, and efficiency.'[15] A few days later he called on Thackeray who, having apparently forgotten that he had already met Turgenev the previous year, was very pleased that the Russian author had called on him without an introduction, and had not even referred in conversation to his own writing.†[16]

Turgenev's attitude to the English (like so many foreigners he did not distinguish the Scots or Welsh) remained throughout his life one of critical admiration. 'One must not forget', he wrote to Tolstoy in 1861, 'that they are as shy as they are haughty, and are unable either to express or to display themselves.'[18] A few years later they were 'in spite of everything the best people on earth'.[19] Unlike so many Russians, Turgenev particularly admired British tolerance. His friend and translator, Ralston, later recalled a debate at Cambridge on the subject of the Paris Commune at which Turgenev was present. After the proposer's speech in support of the Commune had been listened to without interruption, and the motion in the end heavily outvoted, Turgenev remarked: 'Now I understand why you English are not afraid of revolution.'[20]

From his first short visit to London in 1856 Turgenev returned to Courtavenel, where he had already moved on arrival in Paris from Russia. He stayed there for nearly two months, until about 26 October.[21] Whatever difficulties with Pauline lay ahead, it was a

---

*He was placed next to Thackeray, but Thackeray was not present owing to an 'indisposition', about which Monckton Milnes was extremely sceptical.[14]

† According to one account, not corroborated by any other evidence, he called on Dickens during this visit. But since the story comes in the memoirs of one E. Ya. Kolbasin (a Russian journalist living in Paris who accompanied Turgenev to England) which in other respects bristle with inaccuracies, it is open to considerable doubt.[17]

very happy time for Turgenev, as he wrote to Botkin: 'I feel at home here. I don't wish to go anywhere and I am light and quiet in spirit.' There was much reading aloud, and even more music and amateur theatricals (including a performance of a play by Molière) – 'The days pass wonderfully.' All the symphonies and all the sonatas of Beethoven were played. 'We were as happy as trout in a clear stream when the sun strikes it. . . .' Many years later, near the end of his life, he wrote to Pauline's daughter Claudie, that the times he spent in Courtavenel had been 'the happiest days' in his life.[22] It was on the occasion of this visit that the game of portraits was inaugurated. Turgenev, Pauline, or one of the other participants would draw a few profiles and everyone would then write under each what he or she thought was a fitting description of the character delineated. 'Naturally Madame Viardot was always cleverer, subtler and more apt than the others.'[23] Turgenev carefully preserved these sheets, both in 1856 and in later years when the game was resumed in Baden and elsewhere, and they have been studied in detail by the French scholar André Mazon and by Soviet scholars.[24] Mazon identified the drawings which he believed were done by Turgenev. (Turgenev was devoted to comic drawing and had some talent for it. His letters, particularly those which were addressed to children, are often adorned with little sketches or caricatures.) Turgenev's stay in Courtavenel was also enlivened by a short visit from his friend Fet, who described the incident in detail in his memoirs.[25] Turgenev had made some muddle over the arrangements. The result was that Fet arrived unexpectedly, but was graciously welcomed by Pauline. According to Turgenev's account of the visit in a letter to Tolstoy, he made an 'unpleasant impression'. There was also an excited argument in Turgenev's room between the two Russians, which alarmed the quiet French household as it became filled with the 'wild sounds of Slav speech'.[26]

These happy months apart, for much of the time during these years Turgenev was in the depths of despair. In part this was due to doubts about his calling, and gifts, as a writer and to the inability to achieve what he felt to be his true style – evidently *Rudin* had not satisfied him. Except for a short sketch, he wrote nothing between 'Faust', written in the course of about two weeks in Spasskoe in June and July 1856, and the long story 'Asia', begun in the summer of 1857 and finished in Rome in November of that year. (As he noted on the manuscript it was 'written with many interruptions by the kind favour of my illness'.) Even before he left Russia, and before completing 'Faust', he had complained to Botkin of his inability to write.

'I did indeed begin a chapter with the following (so original) words "One fine day" – then I crossed out "fine", then I crossed out "one" and then I wrote in large letters "—your mother!" and that was that. But I doubt if the *Russian Herald* will be satisfied with it.'[27] In his correspondence of 1856 and 1857 there are numerous laments about being unable to put pen to paper owing to the effects of his illness. His bad health was no doubt a serious handicap, but it was not the sole reason for his inability to write. In the letter to Botkin in which he told him of the destruction of all plans and drafts, he said: 'All this is nonsense. I have no talent of a character and integrity of its own. There were some little poetic strings, but they have sounded off, and have now ceased to sound. I don't want to repeat myself, and so – into retirement!'[28] This was in February 1857. Two months later he wrote in slightly more hopeful vein to Annenkov: 'I am living through, or perhaps getting over, a moral and physical crisis out of which I shall emerge either shattered to bits or renovated! No, what is this about renovation – I mean propped up, as a shed which has collapsed is propped up with logs.'[29]

His illness, a disease of the bladder with very painful and unpleasant symptoms, was serious enough, even allowing for his hypochondria and his tendency to seek refuge in illness whenever he was unhappy. It lasted, with varying intensity, from the end of 1856 throughout 1857 and until his return to Russia in June 1858. He described the symptoms of his illness in a letter to Botkin, but the squeamish Soviet editors of his letters have omitted the relevant lines.[30] But there is no doubt that the main reason for his depression was a change in Pauline's attitude towards him. She did not put an end to the friendship, but seems to have kept their meetings to a minimum after the idyllic months in Courtavenel in 1856. She hardly wrote to him when he was absent from Paris and his letters to his daughter abound in urgent requests for news of the Viardot family, of whom he says he has had none. To his friends he complained of melancholy, of depression, of life having come to an end, and the like. At the same time his letters to Pauline show exactly the same devotion as ever and he proclaimed his love for her in writing to friends – to Tolstoy, of all people, and to Annenkov, to whom he described Pauline as 'the only woman whom I have loved and shall always love'.[31]

Nekrasov, who saw Turgenev in Paris in the spring of 1857, related to Tolstoy a conversation on the subject of love. (Nekrasov's affair with Panaeva was going through a crisis at the time.) 'Even now, after fifteen years,' Turgenev had said to him, 'I love this woman so much that I am prepared to dance on the roof, stark naked and painted yellow all over, if she orders me to do so.'[32] As he wrote at the end of 1859 to Countess Lambert, to whom he confided his most intimate thoughts: 'I knew before my trip abroad, this trip which has been so unhappy for me, that it would have been better for me to stay at home – and nevertheless I embarked on the journey. The fact is that fate always punishes us both in the way we expect, and also a little in the way we did not expect – and this "little" is a real lesson for us.'[33] So far as Pauline was concerned, the rupture may have been due to the fact that in November 1856 she had conceived her son Paul to whom she gave birth on 20 July 1857 – indeed, the conception, which must have taken place soon after they had all returned to Paris from Courtavenel, could have marked her reconciliation with Louis. The suggestion sometimes advanced that Turgenev was Paul's father is extremely implausible in the light of what is known of the subsequent course of his friendship with Pauline – as Mrs. FitzLyon convincingly argues.[34] But it would have been physically possible for him to have fathered Paul, since both he and Pauline were in Paris at the time of the child's conception.

Turgenev spent most of 1857 in Paris, apart from the memorable visit to London. And the month of July he spent in Sinzig (on the advice of his Dresden physician, Dr. Hedenus), in an effort to improve his health. The waters of Sinzig did him no good,[35] but the little watering place on the Rhine gave him inspiration to start writing again on what was to prove to be one of his most beautiful stories, 'Asia'. He did not enjoy his life in Paris. As he wrote to Annenkov, he had never met so many people as on this occasion, but the acquaintance gave him no pleasure, and he had met 'not one remarkable, attractive individual'.[36] He was scathing about the leading French literary figures,[37] and he wrote to Countess Lambert that he had not 'learned to love a single Frenchman in the course of the whole winter' and that the French seemed to him 'cold, petty and banal'.[38] As he informed Tolstoy at the beginning of 1857, 'I have only met one attractive girl – and she is Russian – and only one intelligent man – and he is a Yid.' The girl was Princess Meshcherskaia, the 'Yid' was Professor H. B. Oppenheim of Heidelberg, at that time in exile in Paris for his radical political views.[39] Three years later Turgenev had not changed his views on the French.[40] He frequently expressed in his letters his longing to return to Russia, giving as the excuse for staying in Paris (which certainly did not suit his health) the need to look after his daughter, or his literary obligations. But the irresistible attraction of Pauline's presence was, to say the least, also a factor in keeping him there, as he admitted to Tolstoy.

The French apart, there were always Russian friends to be with in Paris, if not resident there, then passing through on their periodic visits to the city which had now replaced Berlin as the Mecca of the young Russian intellectual. Druzhinin visited Turgenev during his stay in Sinzig. Nekrasov, who had been on holiday in Rome with Panaeva (much to Turgenev's dismay, since he detested the lady and thought she had a bad influence over Nekrasov), met Turgenev in London. They travelled to Paris together, and Turgenev then accompanied the poet, together with Madame Panaeva, to Berlin. On 28 August, Goncharov arrived in Paris and during the next few days read *Oblomov*, which he had recently completed, to Turgenev, Fet, and Botkin. Fet at this time was living in Paris; Turgenev saw him frequently and had acted as best man at his wedding on 28 August. (Turgenev was in high spirits and, according to Fet, drank more than was good for him.) Botkin, then on a visit to the French capital, successfully persuaded Turgenev to spend the coming winter in his company in Rome.

Among the Russian residents in Paris with whom Turgenev was on friendly terms were the liberal Prince N. I. Trubetskoy, the writer and music critic N. A. Melgunov, and Prince Nikolai Orlov. It was during this period of his life in Paris that he first became friendly with his namesake and perhaps distant relative, the Decembrist N. I. Turgenev and his wife Klara. This Turgenev, though actively involved in the conspiracy, had emigrated before the actual rising of 1825 and escaped execution, but was forced to remain an exile. Ivan Turgenev had met him briefly in 1845. The old émigré was a fervent advocate of the emancipation of the serfs, and may well have influenced the young writer (who, it will be recalled, in 1842 still believed in reform of serfdom rather than in its abolition). The close friendship between Ivan Turgenev and the older Turgenevs lasted for the rest of their lives.[41] They took a warm interest in Paulinette whenever her father was absent from Paris.

Turgenev's love–hate relationship with Tolstoy continued intermittently. Until Turgenev's return to Russia in June 1858, they kept up a fairly regular correspondence (few of Tolstoy's letters of this period have been preserved). Literary and, occasionally, political matters apart, both men were concerned with what seems to have been an attempt to analyse, and overcome, the cause of the innate antagonism of temperament which inevitably led to collisions. Tolstoy started the correspondence by trying to discover the reasons for the 'ravine' which had formed between them. In reply Turgenev, at great length, tried to do the same – without great success. By

December 1856 Turgenev was optimistic enough about the future course of their friendship to write that 'the ravine had become a scarcely noticeable crack' which was not worth mentioning,[42] and a little later he told Annenkov that Tolstoy had 'evidently become wiser and kinder'.[43] When shortly afterwards Tolstoy arrived in Paris, Turgenev found in him a very significant change for the better. The two men spent a week together in Dijon, apparently without quarrelling, to judge from letters to friends describing the visit. Tolstoy could not stand France for long – especially 'Sodom and Gomorrah', as he called Paris. 'A mixture of a poet, a Calvinist, a fanatic, and a lordling – something that reminds one of Rousseau, but more honest than Rousseau – a highly moral and at the same time unsympathetic creature' was Turgenev's description of Tolstoy after his departure.[44]

The two men next met in Baden in August 1857. Turgenev (who had spent most of July in Sinzig) had planned to call for Tolstoy in Baden and accompany him to Fécamp, in order to join Botkin. He found Tolstoy in a bad state having lost a lot of money gambling. To add to Tolstoy's troubles, a letter arrived from Russia with the news that his sister had finally left her husband, who was systematically and flagrantly unfaithful to her. (This was the Countess Tolstaia, with whom Turgenev still maintained a fairly intimate correspondence.) Tolstoy decided to return home immediately, on money that Turgenev had borrowed for the purpose.*

The two authors did not meet again until Turgenev's return to Russia the following year, after his six months' visit to Italy with Botkin. Friendly correspondence between them continued, though with occasional undertones of the mutual irritation which had by now become habitual. Turgenev's advice to Tolstoy to become a professional writer and cease being a dilettante was, in particular, not very welcome. The two met only fleetingly for some time after Turgenev's return to Russia, though they did correspond occasionally, and Turgenev urged Tolstoy to visit him in Spasskoe. The visit eventually took place, and was not a success. The actual cause of what amounted to a breach on this occasion can only be surmised – but in two men of such different temperament, where each was convinced that the other was a poseur, there is little need to look for specific reasons. Turgenev wrote to Botkin from Spasskoe on 12 April 1859:

* Incidentally, and much to Botkin's disapproval, from the husband of a Russian *grande dame* A. O. Smirnova, whom Turgenev detested, the prototype of Natalia's mother Lasunskaia in *Rudin*.[45]

I have finished all dealings with Tolstoy. As a human being he no longer exists for me. God grant him and his talent everything of the best. But as for me, when I have said 'Good morning' to him I have the insuperable desire to say 'Goodbye', and without 'till we meet again'. We are created at opposite poles. If I eat a soup and like it I know from *that very fact* for certain that Tolstoy finds it repulsive – and vice versa.[46]

While the final break was still two years ahead, they did not meet frequently thereafter, though Tolstoy did in fact visit Turgenev again in October 1859.

Tolstoy's diary shows the same fluctuation of feelings, the same love–hate relationship:

7 February 1856: Quarrelled with Turgenev.
25 April 1856: I visited Turgenev with great pleasure.
31 May 1856: The relations of Masha [his sister] with Turgenev are agreeable to me.
19 March 1857 [in Paris]: Turgenev came at 5. He seemed to feel guilty. What am I to do? I respect and value him, even love him perhaps. .... But I do not feel sympathetic towards him, and this is mutual.
8 April 1857: I love him very much. He has made of me and continues to make of me another person.
4 September 1858: He is unbearably heavy. ...
13 April 1861: Paris. Turgenev and I have come closer together.

– to be followed only seven weeks later by a reference to the dramatic quarrel.

Turgenev rediscovered a daughter in Paris. She had been about eight years old when he had sent her there in 1850, to be brought up in the Viardot household. Her relations both with Pauline and with Pauline's children had undergone a certain strain at times, and she had for some years past been placed in a boarding-school – at first in a *pension* owned by a Mademoiselle Renard, and after 1855 in another *pension* presided over by its *Directrice*, Madame Harend (or Hareng). By the time of Turgenev's arrival in Paris in 1856 Paulinette was over fourteen years of age: during the following four or five years, which he spent intermittently in Paris, she grew into an adolescent, and then into a young woman. Pauline and Louis Viardot acted as her guardians in her father's absence. Turgenev's correspondence makes it abundantly clear that he provided her with ample, indeed over-generous (as Pauline occasionally remarked) financial means. He had written to her from Russia a few very affectionate letters containing fatherly advice, (though Paulinette had complained, with justice, that he did not write frequently enough), and had received news of her progress from Pauline. But it was really only now that he had his first chance of getting to know her.

Paulinette could certainly no longer fairly assert that her father neglected her. Whenever he was in Paris he regularly visited her in her *pension*, or took her out. On his frequent absences from the capital he wrote to her; forty-eight letters have survived for the period between his arrival in Paris in 1856 and his third departure for Russia in 1861. (The letters are all in French – Paulinette did not remember a word of Russian.) She was, it would seem, devoted to her father. But it would have been surprising, considering her background, if her character had been perfect. She was egocentric, and rather vain, not very proficient at her studies, and, as she grew older, more interested in clothes and parties than in the more serious matters that Pauline Viardot and Turgenev considered important. The fact that she occasionally expressed resentment at what she regarded as Pauline's neglect of her did not help to endear her to her father. For his part, as his letters show, he took his paternal responsibilities very seriously, and never failed to write in terms of affection and regard. He respected her religious beliefs, and her desire to be brought up in the Orthodox faith, which was somewhat surprising in a child educated in French boarding-schools. It may be that she was influenced in this by the Russian residents in Paris, like the Turgenevs, who must certainly have taken her to Russian Orthodox services. 'What makes you think', he wrote to Countess Lambert from Paris in 1862, 'that Paulinette (who sends you her fondest love) does not go to church? Not only have I not "taken God away from her", but I go to church with her. I would never permit myself such an assault on her liberty, and if I am not a Christian – that is my private affair, my private misfortune. Paulinette, on the contrary, is very religious.'[47]

Turgenev's affection (if that is what it was) for his daughter did not, as one would expect in a nineteenth-century parent, prevent him from expressing at times fairly severe criticism – not just on the subject of her spelling, but also of what he regarded as the defects of her character. It is true that he did also praise her occasionally. A long, critical letter (over which he had hesitated for some time) which he wrote to her from Spasskoe in November 1859 pointed out firmly, if kindly, what he regarded as her faults. She was touchy, conceited, self-opinionated, and secretive: 'You do not like being told the truth and you readily turn away from people whom you ought to love all the more, as soon as these people cease to make a fuss of you.' (This was a reference to Paulinette's complaint that Pauline Viardot did not pay sufficient attention to her.) 'You are jealous – do you think that I was not able to understand why you made pretence to avoid me during the last days of my stay at Courtavenel?' This, again, was a reference to Paulinette's resentment of the attention which her father paid to Pauline Viardot – though there may well have been some emotion other than petty jealousy in question. There was much more on the same lines for the poor girl to read. But the letter was also full of affectionate expressions; and it was followed within ten days by a second letter, almost apologizing for the sermon: 'Take what is of use in my advice – and as for the rest, you know that there is no one in the world who loves you more than I do.'[48] The affection was probably genuine on his side, but there was as much duty as love in his feelings for his daughter. There is also little doubt that at times the girl was very unhappy.

A passage in a letter to his confidante Countess Lambert, written about a year after the 'sermon', probably gives as true a picture of what he felt about his daughter as we shall ever have:

I want to explain to you precisely why there is little in common between me and my daughter. She does not like music, poetry, nature – or dogs – and that is all that I like. From this point of view it is hard for me to live in France – where poetry is petty and miserable, natural scenery is positively ugly, music is reduced to vaudeville or a joke – and the shooting is disgusting. Actually all of this is quite all right for my daughter – and she replaces the qualities which she lacks by other, more positive and more useful qualities. But for me – between ourselves – she is Insarov★ all over again. I respect her, and that is not enough.

Somewhat later he wrote rather more warmly of her, again to the Countess: 'She has no trace of artistic inclination – but much character, calmness, and common sense: she would make a good mother and excellent housekeeper. She loves me passionately – but she will not love many.'[49] It is noteworthy that Countess Lambert, who was less devoted to music, nature, poetry, and dogs than Turgenev, had a very great affection for Paulinette.

On 17 October 1857, after a short visit to Courtavenel, (as he wrote to Nekrasov, 'I have committed the precise folly against which you warned me'),[50] Turgenev and Botkin left Paris for Marseilles, Nice, and Genoa on their way to Rome, where they planned to spend the winter. Turgenev had often expressed a firm determination to return to Russia in the spring of 1857, and apparently for good: 'I am too old', he wrote to Tolstoy at the end of 1856, 'to have no nest of my own. . . . I will without fail return to Russia in the spring,

---

★ A reference to the strange Bulgarian hero of *On the Eve*.

although by so doing I shall be forced to say good-bye to my last
dream of so-called happiness. ...'[51] But he had delayed his return,
and given various reasons for yielding to Botkin's persuasion, such
as the prospect that Rome would be good for work, or his reluctance
to face the Russian winter. As far as work was concerned, he did
finish 'Asia' shortly after his arrival in Rome, but wrote little else,
apart from starting *A Nest of the Landed Gentry*, of which the theme
had been in his mind for over a year.

Turgenev was overjoyed to be in Italy again. In company with
Botkin, and frequently with the painter A. A. Ivanov,★ they looked
at pictures and ruins. One such expedition was later described for
publication in 'A Trip to Albano and Frascati', which appeared in
1861.[52] Turgenev's love of Italian painting is a constant theme in
his letters, and is also evident in some of his fiction – in *On the Eve*,
for example, and in *Spring Torrents*. His taste seems to have been
mainly for the painters of the High Renaissance – Raphael above all,
Titian, Correggio, Cima da Conegliano. He described his impressions of Italy in detail to Pauline. His letters to her of this period
contain several complaints about the poor music available – Verdi,
and even worse than that!

After a speech on 30 March 1856 by the new Emperor, Alexander
II, in which he said that 'it is better to abolish serfdom from above
than to wait until the serfs begin to liberate themselves from below',
the emancipation of the serfs seemed imminent. This was of course
a question which excited the interest of Turgenev and indeed of
every Russian landowner, both the few liberals who welcomed the
prospect, and the reactionaries who feared it. The Emperor's determination to put through the reform in spite of much opposition,
was in large measure due to the enlightened influences of those very
close to him and in particular of his brother Constantine and his aunt,
the Grand Duchess Elena Pavlovna, whose palace became a centre
for the discussion and propagation of views favourable to the liberty
of the serfs. The first step taken was the appointment of a secret committee, of mainly conservative members. It included General Y. I.
Rostovtsev, under suspicion at first by reformers on the grounds that
he had in 1825 betrayed the Decembrists' plans to the government.
He proved to be one of the most liberal members of the committee,
and his death in February 1860 was a blow to all who supported
reform. The committee's deliberations proceeded very slowly, and

★ An eccentric recluse, who spent virtually the whole of his active life on one
painting of Christ and died in 1858 soon after completing it.

in August it was decided to speed matters by entrusting the Ministry of the Interior with the task of collecting information and drafting proposals. The difficulty lay in the failure of the nobility to put forward their suggestions. In the course of November 1857 the tsar forced their hand by issuing several rescripts to governors and governors-general adumbrating the course which emancipation should take, and calling for concrete drafts. The publication of these rescripts created a public stir, and at last compelled the nobility to face the issue. During 1858 committees composed of two members elected by the nobility and two chosen by the governors were set up in most provinces.

The mass of material which came in from these committees was, on Rostovtsev's suggestion, submitted in 1858 for working up into concrete proposals to three Editorial Commissions (which in fact sat as one body) composed of both official and non-official experts. It was a body on which reformers predominated: the most influential of the non-official experts were the prominent Slavophiles Iurii Samarin and Prince Cherkassky. The Editorial Commissions worked for over two years before producing drafts which eventually became the Emancipation Statute of 19 February 1861. The main problems – neither of which was in the end solved satisfactorily – were: how much land were the peasants to get, and on what terms? And what kind of administrative authority was to replace that which the landlords exercised over their serfs?[53]

As Tocqueville so wisely pointed out, the most dangerous moment for a bad government arises when it begins to reform: expectations are aroused for change which hitherto seemed beyond hope. So it was after the death of Nicholas I. The radicals, notably Herzen and Chernyshevsky, were at first enthusiastic supporters of the reform from above initiated by Alexander II. But, as time went on, while its implementation was apparently being delayed, discussion of the many problems involved generated impatience among the radicals. This grew rapidly, and was not helped by government attempts to restrict debate. And so there took place a polarization of opinion among the extreme critics of serfdom. Herzen remained suspiciously dubious about the projected emancipation, but basically still opposed to violent revolt. Chernyshevsky and Dobroliubov called for revolution as openly as conditions of censorship permitted, and did it on the pages of the *Contemporary*, where their fire was directed against the liberal supporters of reform as much as it was against its reactionary opponents.

News of the publication of the rescripts, which was the real starting point for public discussion of the emancipation, reached Turgenev when he was in Rome. In the course of the winter of 1857–8 he participated actively in the debates on the problems connected with the liberation of the serfs in which the Russian colony in Rome engaged. This included at the time the Slavophile members of the Editorial Commissions, Samarin and Prince Cherkassky, as well as General Rostovtsev and the Grand Duchess Elena Pavlovna, both of whom visited Rome in the course of the winter. Turgenev had several long conversations with the Grand Duchess,[54] and was enchanted by Rostovtsev. His close involvement in the discussions in Rome is shown by the fact that he was entrusted by the group of Russian liberals in that city with the drafting of a project for a new journal to be devoted to the analysis of questions connected with the reform. A copy of the memorandum which he drew up was sent to the liberally inclined Grand Duke Constantine (in whose archive it remained),[55] and no doubt to others.

Nothing in the end came of the project, but Turgenev's proposals throw light on his views on the emancipation. The main contention which he advanced placed Turgenev squarely on the side of the tsar and his liberal advisers. He argued that the aims of the Emperor were genuine and honest, and that the opposition to them by many of the landed nobility was founded on misapprehension or ignorance. The purpose of the new journal would be to provide a platform for discussion which would help to dispel this lack of information and analyse the way in which the reform should be achieved. The new journal would also act as a central point for co-ordinating the vast mass of information emerging from the provincial Committees.[56] It was around this time, at the beginning of 1858, that Turgenev wrote a letter for publication in the Russian government newspaper published in Paris, *Le Nord*, protesting against a report, emanating from Moscow, which had suggested that the Slavophiles were not supporters of the emancipation of the peasants.[57] The absurdity of this accusation must have been particularly evident to one who was actively engaged in working for the freedom of the serfs in close co-operation with several of the leading Slavophiles.[58]

When the Emancipation Statute was eventually enacted in 1861, one of its main provisions was that the serfs freed from the power of their landlords were to receive land, in quantity and on terms to be agreed within two years, with the aid of specially appointed 'arbitrators of the peace'. When the terms had been agreed, the former serf would pay an annual sum in lieu of service on the landlord's land, or *obrok*, at a later stage to be replaced by a redemption payment.[59] Actually the system of *obrok* had been in existence for a long time before the emancipation. It was usually much preferred by the peasants to the alternative *barshchina*, or fixed service on the landlord's land, since under *obrok* the peasants could earn a living by whatever skills or labour they could market, and avoid all obligations to the landlord apart from the annual payment. Many serfs under *obrok* lived comparatively well, often working in the towns, and were in practice, if not in law, free men. The landlord of an estate of which the soil yielded a rich grain harvest stood to lose by the *obrok* system, since he was deprived of the unpaid labour of his serfs. But the more liberal landlords, especially when the emancipation was under active discussion, were willing as a matter of principle to make the financial sacrifice which transfer of their peasants to *obrok* involved.

After the death of his mother in 1850 and the division of the inheritance with his brother, Turgenev had inherited some two thousand serfs, at Spasskoe and on the minor estates. He had freed the domestic serfs, but they were a small minority. He continued to use the majority of his peasants as unpaid labour for the exploitation of his estates, which were in the black earth area and produced grain for export. When emancipation was in prospect, Turgenev decided that the time had come to rid himself of some of the stigma of being a slave-owner by transferring those of his serfs who desired it to the *obrok* system. As he wrote to Countess Lambert on 15 November 1857, and shortly afterwards to Tolstoy, he had firmly decided to settle all arrangements with his peasants in the course of 1858, after his return to Russia in the spring, and looked forward to being a landowner, 'but no longer a *pomeshchik* or a *barin*' – the two terms used to designate the patriarchal relations between landlord and peasants.[60] He carried out his intention. In a letter of 10 February 1860 addressed to N. I. Turgenev, he describes the arrangements he had completed with his peasants. He had transferred all of them to *obrok* at a rate of 3 roubles a *desiatina* (2.7 acres), allotting to each man as his property the land which he had tilled. He also offered to supply all necessary building materials to all peasants who wished to move away from their villages; to his surprise almost all of them took up the offer. He planned partly to work his estates with hired labour, and partly to lease them. He calculated that he had lost a little over a quarter of his total income,[61] but even so, in Annenkov's view the *obrok* which he had fixed was too high.[62] This settlement, however, only applied to Spasskoe. Several letters in 1861 and 1862 refer to difficulties in reaching agreement with his peasants, in spite of repeated concessions. The main obstacle seems to have been the reluctance of some of them to transfer to *obrok*, even after the emancipation, though this was the first essential step towards their ultimate freedom. Evidently some of them preferred to get by with a minimum of work on *barshchina*, rather than to fend for themselves on *obrok*.[63]

In the spring of 1858, after a fortnight's trip to Naples, Turgenev set out on his leisurely journey back to Paris. He stopped for varying periods in Sienna, Florence, ('ten of the most delightful days', as he recalled many years later), Pisa, Lucca, Genoa, Milan, and Venice. There is, curiously enough, no account of Venice in his correspondence though it is evident from the beautiful description of that city in *On the Eve* that Turgenev had been much impressed by it. He also stopped some time in Vienna, where he consulted Dr. Sigmund about his bladder complaint which had troubled him throughout his stay in Rome and was still causing him much pain and discomfort. Dr. Sigmund's prognosis was far from comforting, though in the end it proved unduly pessimistic.[64] Turgenev spent a few days with Annenkov in Dresden and about a week in London, where he attended the Royal Literary Fund dinner. He returned to Paris on 21 May 1858, in time to act as best man at the wedding of Prince Orlov.

CHAPTER NINE

Break with the Radicals

Turgenev stayed only a short time in Paris after his return from London before leaving for Russia by sea, probably on 8 June 1858. On 22 May he dined at the Russian Embassy. All the guests were Russian except one, Baron Haeckeren, a contemptible character who enjoyed the distinction of having first dishonoured Pushkin, and then killed him. It can be argued that Turgenev should immediately have walked out – but it was not in his temperament to make bold gestures of this nature. He interpreted the presence of this man as a mark of contempt by Russian officialdom for culture – as did also Herzen.[1] It was more probably designed to show displeasure at the liberalism with which many reactionaries associated Pushkin – so much so that Haeckeren met with approval in certain Russian circles.

On arrival in Russia, Turgenev stopped for a day or two in St. Petersburg, where he dined on 7 June with some literary friends, and then set off for Spasskoe. The ten months which he spent in Russia on this occasion was a period of intense literary activity: he was getting over his difficulty in writing. He had finished 'Asia' in Rome and despatched it to the *Contemporary*: it appeared on 11 January 1858. While in Rome, at Annenkov's persuasion, he also wrote an article entitled 'From Abroad. First Letter' for a newly founded journal, *Atenei*. It was not a particularly remarkable effort, and, although intended to be followed up, proved to be the only one of the projected series.[2] 'Asia', although it aroused much hostile criticism when it first appeared (Tolstoy, for example, disliked the story intensely), must now be regarded as a literary masterpiece. It marked Turgenev's return to literature, which he had decided earlier in the year, whether seriously or not, to abandon. There is no doubt, as a study of the manuscript with its multiple alterations, additions, and excisions reveals, that he devoted unusual care to the composition of this story.³ It is a work virtually devoid of any social or moral message, a light tale of unhappy love.

The scene is set in a small town on the Rhine, of which the prototype was Sinzig, where Turgenev in the course of 1857 had spent some weeks taking the waters, and where the idea for 'Asia' first occurred to him. The plot is simple. A young Russian, on holiday on the Rhine, runs into a compatriot, Gagin, an aspiring painter who is travelling with a girl, whom he introduces as his sister, Asia. The two men quickly become intimate, in the manner of Russians of similar tastes and social background meeting abroad. In so far as this story contains any serious comment at all it appears in a remark made by the painter: 'If I have enough patience, something will come of me. . . . If not, I shall remain a half-educated scion of the gentry.'⁴ This fear that members of the Russian nobility had a tendency to remain amateurs in everything that they did echoes what Turgenev wrote to Countess Lambert around the time when he was completing 'Asia': 'I can be nothing but a writer – but up till now I have been more of a dilettante. This will not be so in the future.'⁵ The story centres on the girl – a strange, wild creature, alternating between moods of reticence and exuberance, of shyness and forwardness. The narrator at first suspects that Asia is not Gagin's sister but his mistress, but learns from him her true story. She is his illegitimate sister, whom he has to a large extent brought up himself since the death of her mother (when Asia was nine – the age at which Paulinette was sent off to Paris) and their father. Asia adores her brother – but falls passionately in love with the narrator. He is more than half in love with her, but when he learns of her infatuation from Gagin, is overwhelmed by the thought of the responsibility of marrying her. At a meeting, appointed by her, when she declares her love, he hesitates. By the following morning, when he realizes that he loves her, it is too late: the pair have departed the town and have vanished forever. Asia leaves a note for him: 'If you had said one word, only one word, I would have stayed', and he realizes too late that his indecision has cost him his happiness – though, truth to tell, he does not grieve for her very long.

The theme of happiness in love missed through indecisiveness of character is frequent in Turgenev's fiction. In the case of Asia, the facts of her birth – reminiscent of Paulinette's – give a special poignancy to the story. There may also have been in the name Asia a recollection of his uncle's illegitimate daughter, Asia, whom Turgenev knew well since she lived in Spasskoe. She later married his cook Stepan.⁶ It was not indeed so very reprehensible in a young man to have hesitated before taking on the responsibility of a wife with such a difficult psychological background. The subtle delineation of the three characters is, however, the main purpose of the story. This was not the view of Chernyshevsky, who devoted an article to 'Asia', destined to become a landmark in the development of Russian radical thought, and much admired by future revolutionaries, including Lenin.

As literary criticism the essay was fatuous: it purported to discern in the indecisiveness of the narrator the basic vice of the generation of the 'superfluous men', who were incapable of action because of their social background, whereas Turgenev had plainly intended the story as no more than a highly professional tale. But Chernyshevsky's review entered into the mythology of Russian radical thought of the sixties and seventies both as a supposedly penetrating analysis of a generation, and, more significantly, as the first radical manifesto which had raised what in the next few years was to become the battle-cry: the call for 'new men', men of action, determined revolutionaries, who would replace the irresolute 'Hamlets' of the forties and fifties.[7] Side by side with the call for revolutionary deeds went withering contempt for liberalism, for any attempt to co-operate with measures of reform initiated from above, contempt which Chernyshevsky and Dobroliubov were henceforth to pour out in their articles in the *Contemporary*.

Turgenev stayed in Spasskoe until the beginning of November. He was delighted to be back there; his health was good, the house had been refurbished, and there was, at last, plentiful game for shooting. He renewed his former friendship with his neighbours. One of these was Fet, with whom he frequently went on shooting expeditions and to pay visits, all of which have been described in detail by the poet in his memoirs, and no doubt much embellished in the process. He describes Turgenev's glowing tributes to the skill of Bubulka as a gun-dog, whom he rewarded with special care and privileges. She always slept in his bedroom covered with a blanket. If the blanket happened to slip off in the night, she would prod him in order to wake him up so that he could get out of bed and cover her up again, which he invariably did (according to Fet). Turgenev occasionally saw Countess Tolstaia. The Countess was now separated, shortly to be divorced from her husband, and living with her brothers at the Tolstoy family estate, Yasnaia Poliana, soon to become famous as the home of Leo Tolstoy. Turgenev's feelings for Tolstoy's sister were no longer what they had been. As he wrote to Botkin, on 29 March 1859, 'She has changed very much in my eyes, and, on top of that, *je n'ai rien à lui dire*.'[8] Leo Tolstoy was not usually present when Turgenev visited Yasnaia Poliana, so it was presumably on the basis of what his sister told him that he recorded in his diary on 4 September 1858: 'Turgenev is behaving badly to Mashenka. The rotter.'

His closest woman friend during the next few years was Countess Elizaveta Egorovna Lambert. The Countess, who was three years younger than Turgenev, was the daughter of Count Kankrin, Nicholas I's Finance Minister, and the wife of the aide-de-camp of Alexander II. She belonged to the highest sphere of the Court nobility in St. Petersburg and was deeply religious and devoted to works of charity. Their correspondence continued, with long interruptions, until 1867. But it was in the winter of 1858–9, during the three months which Turgenev spent in St. Petersburg, and the many evenings of conversation with Countess Lambert, that their friendship really ripened. In April 1859, on leaving Russia, he wrote to her: 'I know of few places in the world where I felt so much at ease as in your little room. The thought of it is linked to so many memories of quiet evenings and good talks, and do you remember how once you wept?'[9] He confided his most intimate thoughts to her, and discussed with her his feelings for Pauline.

Turgenev's friendship with Countess Lambert was referred to earlier as *une amitié amoureuse*. But in truth, in so far as it had erotic undertones, these seem to have occurred on her side: 'Why do you say such sweet things to me, dear Countess? I, after all, do not say sweet things to you.' And later she reproached him: 'You have too often observed that many are fascinated by you and are *afraid* that this could unfortunately happen even with a person with whom you would not wish to find any feelings other than sincere friendship.' And a little after that: 'If you could think of me as not being kind you would be more attached to me. You would, perhaps, love me less, but it is certain that I should be a little more of a woman in your eyes.' There was also an occasional hint of jealousy of Pauline Viardot as, for example, when the Countess, at his importunate request, lent him a copy of a review which contained a glowing account of Madame Viardot's performance in *Orphée*.[10] In the summer of 1859, back in France, he wrote to her how much he was looking forward to spending the evenings in her room again. 'You will see how well we shall behave – quietly and peacefully like children in Holy Week. I can answer for myself. Perhaps you may think this an impertinent phrase – but I only meant to say that you are younger than I.'[11] These very slight indications of something more than friendship on the Countess's side should not be taken too seriously, since there is no doubt whatever that she was at all times a virtuous and faithful wife and (until the death in childhood of her only son) a devoted mother.[12] The bond between the two was precisely the fact that they found they could discuss their most heartfelt problems without serious intrusion of any erotic element.

The writing of *A Nest of the Landed Gentry*, with its strong religious undertones, belongs to the period of Turgenev's friendship with Countess Lambert, which began in 1856 (his first letter to her is dated 9 May that year). By 25 October the plan of the novel was already 'fully formed' in his head, and he had sketched the opening scenes.[13] But then came the year when Turgenev was unable to write, and the literary impasse was broken only by the writing of 'Asia'. Intensive work on his new novel began on his return to Russia and to Spasskoe in the summer and autumn of 1858. On 15 November Turgenev arrived in St. Petersburg with the finished manuscript of *A Nest of the Landed Gentry*, and before three days had passed, the novel was read to a literary 'jury' assembled in his apartment and, subject to some critical comment, approved.[14] The 'jury' consisted of Annenkov (who read the manuscript aloud, since Turgenev was suffering from acute laryngitis and was unable to utter a word), Goncharov, Nekrasov, Botkin, Panaev, Druzhinin, and five other friends or writers – Dudyshkin, N. N. Tiutchev, I. I. Maslov, M. A. Yazykov, and A. F. Pisemsky.*[15]

As is evident from Turgenev's letter to her in early December, Countess Lambert had not yet read the manuscript, since he promised to bring the proofs for her comment as soon as they were ready.[16] In view of the fact that he had not seen her since he left Russia in 1856, he cannot have discussed the novel with her before the proof stage, though there may well have been discussions after that, because at the end of 1858 and the beginning of 1859 they were both in St. Petersburg and meeting frequently while the work was printing. It is extremely probable that Turgenev looked to the Countess as a model for a type of which he had had little experience – a deeply religious, young Russian Orthodox Christian girl. The Countess, whose taste in literature was of a very simple nature, strongly approved the new novel. Its religious content seems to have raised her hopes that Turgenev was on the verge of conversion to

---

* It is often stated that Nikitenko, the censor friend of Turgenev, was present, but this is an error, since Nikitenko in his diary entry for 28 December (which was many weeks after the reading) does not suggest that he had heard the novel read, but merely records Turgenev's statement about it.

Christianity. '*A Nest of the Landed Gentry*', she wrote to him, 'is the visionary work of the pagan who has not renounced the worship of Venus, but who already understands a stricter form of worship towards which the strivings of his sick and relenting soul are bearing him a little against his will.'[17] She was being over-optimistic. It was, however, true that Turgenev, who had shown little interest in, and indeed occasionally revulsion against, religion was thinking increasingly about it – most probably under the Countess's influence. At Easter 1859 at Spasskoe, he went to the midnight celebration – the pinnacle of the Orthodox year – and was deeply moved.[18] Apart from weddings and christenings, and accompanying Paulinette, this was the first reference in his correspondence to attendance at a church service – if the visit to Salisbury Cathedral from Embly Park is excluded. His hesitant attitude towards religion, almost a longing for something he could not sincerely feel, persisted for some years, perhaps to the end of his life. 'Yes, everything earthly is dust and decay, and happy is he who has thrown his anchor into something other than these bottomless waters,' he wrote to Countess Lambert on 27 November 1861. 'He who has faith has everything and can never suffer any loss. But he who has it not, has nothing, and I feel this all the more deeply since I belong to the company of those who have no faith. But I still do not lose hope.' And a few weeks later he wrote: 'The natural character of death is far more frightening than its suddenness or unusual form. Only religion can conquer this fear. But religion itself must become a natural necessity in a human being, and he who has it not has nothing left but to avert his eyes frivolously or stoically (and in essence it doesn't matter which).'★[19] A year later, in defending himself against Herzen's charge that he had embraced 'mysticism', he described his attitude to God in Goethe's words from *Faust*: 'Who dare name Him, and who acknowledge: I believe in Him! Who can sense Him, and presume to say: I believe not in Him!'[20]

Turgenev's approach to the question of religious faith – something much to be desired as a natural blessing, but not to be achieved either by the force of reason or by intimidation – becomes very evident in his comment on Pascal. When he first read the *Provincial Letters* in 1848 he was repelled by what appeared to him to be the work of a 'slave of Catholicism', part of which made him 'burst into laughter'.[21] Some years later in June 1859 he read the *Pensées* which made an enormous impression on him, as

★ These reflections were prompted by the death of the Countess's only son.

the most frightening, the most disheartening book which was ever printed. This man tramples on everything which is most dear to you, throws you down in the mud, and then, for your comfort, offers you a religion which is bitter and violent and which brutalizes you (the word is his) – a religion which the intellect (that of P. himself) cannot fail to reject, but which the heart *must* accept by *contrition*. . . . Human character is the opposite of this. And I would dare add, Christianity is the opposite too – so soon as it has been reduced to the narrow and craven doctrine of personal salvation, of selfishness.[22]

It is perhaps hard to reconcile this indictment with what Pascal says. Nevertheless, the impression made on Turgenev by Pascal seems to have lasted for some time. In Chapter 21 of *Fathers and Children* he puts into the mouth of the atheist Bazarov a paraphrase of Pascal, yet clearly recognizable: 'The narrow little spot which I occupy is so tiny in comparison with the rest of space . . . and the portion of time which I succeed in living is so insignificant in the light of eternity where I have never been and never shall be. . . . And inside this atom, this mathematical point the blood is circulating, the brain is working, and seems to want something too. . . . How disgraceful! What nonsense!'[23] Pascal's moral (and, who knows, perhaps at this time Turgenev's as well) was to point to the barrenness and uselessness of this kind of reflection, compared with the consolation of faith.

There is also somewhat earlier evidence of his attitude to religion. Two prayers written by him during a severe and prolonged illness – most probably the painful bladder complaint which disabled him for considerable periods between 1856 and 1858 – have survived. One is a desperate appeal to God for relief. The other expresses thanks for recovery. The prayers were found in the archive of the poet and painter, Ya. P. Polonsky, who was a close friend of Turgenev for many years, with a note to the effect that Turgenev had wished to destroy them. These prayers may well suggest the desperate mood of a sceptic, rather than offer proof of any acceptance of religious faith.[24]

Nikitenko recorded in his diary on the basis of what Turgenev told him, that *A Nest of the Landed Gentry* was 'purely artistic' in its aim. In the sense that the novel lacks a clear social message this was true, but it was also the case that, together with *On the Eve* and 'Hamlet and Don Quixote' which followed it in quick succession, it revealed Turgenev's innermost beliefs. This faith was taking shape in his mind under the influence of the transformation which was happening in Russian life with the prospective emancipation of the serfs, and the beginning of the polarization of intellectual life into radicals and revolutionaries on the one hand, and moderate supporters of the new policy of reform promoted by the tsar and his liberal advisers on the other.

The ideas expressed in the two works which followed *A Nest of the Landed Gentry* had been germinating for years in their author's mind. The image of Elena, the committed and self-sacrificing heroine of *On the Eve*, had occurred to him, he later recalled, during his exile in Spasskoe and confinement in Russia as the result of the Crimean War – from 1853–5. He could not write the novel at the time for lack of a hero. The solution came when a neighbour, Karataev, before leaving for the front with a premonition that he would not return alive, left him a notebook in which was sketched, if somewhat roughly, the story of the love of a Russian girl for a Bulgarian patriot and how she followed him to Bulgaria, where he shortly afterwards died. The Bulgarian, Katranov, was a real and quite well-known figure, and Turgenev immediately recognized that here was the hero he was looking for: '. . . at that time', he reflected in 1880, 'among the Russians such a figure did not yet exist'.[25] However, being occupied with *Rudin* he put the idea of *On the Eve* aside, and did not take it up again until the beginning of 1858 when a short list of characters was prepared. Actual work on the writing of the novel did not begin until after Turgenev had left Russia for France – in Vichy on 28 June 1859. It was finished in Spasskoe on 25 October 1859, and published in January 1860.[26]

'Hamlet and Don Quixote', a lecture delivered on 10 January, was published about the same time as *On the Eve* but had been revolving in Turgenev's mind for much longer than the novel – possibly, even, as has been suggested,[27] as far back as 1848, inspired by the events in Paris that year, when he was able to observe revolutionaries in action and to discern the consequences of their actions. He was certainly discussing the projected essay with friends by 1851.[28] In spite of repeated assurances to Panaev that the article would be ready for the *Contemporary* by 1857, when he was spending a week in Dijon with Leo Tolstoy,★ it was not completed until 28 December 1859 in Russia. Since the thoughts underlying this lecture may be said to dominate the main ideas of the two novels, it forms a suitable starting point for a discussion of Turgenev's work of the period 1858–60.

The audience at the lecture, which was enthusiastically received, had, for the most part, a very simple interpretation of 'Don Quixote'

★ Tolstoy recorded approval in his diary of Turgenev's plan for the essay – 'very intelligent' he wrote.

and 'Hamlet': Don Quixote, they believed, stood for the brave revolutionaries, while Hamlet represented the useless 'superfluous men' of the forties and fifties. Turgenev's meaning was rather more subtle. Hamlet and Don Quixote represent, according to him, the two basic human types. By this he does not mean that everyone is exactly the one or the other – indeed, the pure type is rarely found. But the contrast between the two provides an approximation for the understanding of mankind. Don Quixote expresses faith in truth, in something outside or beyond man. He is completely devoted to his ideal, for which he is prepared to sacrifice everything, including his life. It is true that this ideal is sometimes based on fantasy or illusion, so much so that Don Quixote may appear to be a madman. But this does not in any way diminish its purity or sincerity, or Don Quixote's determination and strength of will. Hamlet, in contrast, is the complete egocentric: 'He is constantly preoccupied with his situation, not with his duty.' He doubts everything, including himself, and he inflicts merciless suffering on himself. Unlike Don Quixote, who naturally arouses laughter – 'we are ready to love someone whom we have laughed at' – no one laughs at Hamlet, and only exceptional people, like Horatio, can love him. Hamlet is charged by his father's spirit to exact revenge. But he hesitates, deceives himself, consoles himself for his inaction by the fact that he is so critical of himself – and then kills his usurping uncle by accident. Don Quixote tilts at windmills which he takes for giants, and rescues the boy from a beating, only to expose him to a much worse one as soon as his rescuer departs. In both cases the knight acts on impulse, without reflection, spurred on by indignation. Nothing of the kind could happen to Hamlet: 'He who, in preparing to sacrifice himself, thinks first to calculate and weigh all the consequences, all the probability of the utility of his action, is scarcely capable of self-sacrifice.' And a little further on Turgenev asks the question: we may laugh at Don Quixote, but who can truthfully claim that he can always distinguish the reality from illusion? 'For this reason it seems to me that the main things are the sincerity and strength of the conviction, and the results are – in the hands of the Fates. They alone can show us whether we struggled against visions, or against real enemies. . . . Our duty is to arm and struggle.'*

---

* The main moral of *Rudin* – that what matters in life is not what you achieve, but how you live – may well have been impressed on Turgenev's mind by Granovsky, whom he much admired, even if he could not aspire to call him friend. In a lecture on Louis IX delivered in 1851 Granovsky had said:

The great actors in history and the small . . . are alike bound by the duty to

Turgenev continues the contrast between the Don Quixotes and the Hamlets. The first are deep respecters of the established order, religion, and monarchs, but are at the same time free, and respect the freedom of others. The Hamlets berate kings and courtiers, but are at the same time oppressive and intolerant. Unlike Hamlet, who easily loses hope, Don Quixote never doubts his ultimate success. It is the comic Don Quixotes who move humanity forward: without them there would be nothing for the Hamlets to think about. At this point it should be clear where Turgenev's sympathies lie. It is not surprising that they should be wholly on the side of the Don Quixotes – the committed, unreflecting enthusiasm of a kind of person he could never be. And so towards the end (perhaps with himself in mind) he redeems Hamlet somewhat from the disdain with which he has hitherto been treated. Hamlet, he says, gains much from the devotion of Horatio, his faithful disciple and follower: 'One of the most important merits of the Hamlets consists in their ability to educate and develop people like Horatio, people who receive from them the seeds of thought, allow them to germinate in their hearts and then spread them all over the world.'

At the very end, he brings Don Quixote and Hamlet together by comparing the death of each, each noble in its way, each humble and submissive, recalling those very qualities of the Russian peasant which he had depicted in his early stories. Don Quixote asks forgiveness, and in one of the finest scenes in all literature refers to himself for the first time by the name by which he was commonly known before he became a knight errant: Alonso el Bueno, Alonso the Good. Hamlet, the sceptic, gives his dying voice in favour of young Fortinbras, and dies with the word 'Silence' on his lips. Both are redeemed and ennobled in the end by goodness, by kindness. Only

---

labour in the sweat of their brow. But they bear responsibility only for the purity of their intentions and for the zeal in carrying them into effect, and not for the remote consequences of the labour which they perform. Their actions enter history as mysteriously as a seed falls in the soil. The ripening of the harvest, the time of harvesting and its yield all belong to God.

It is unlikely that Turgenev was present at this lecture, but Granovsky, no doubt, expressed similar views in his conversation. That Rudin was elevated to the rank of the Don Quixotes for the purity of his intentions, not for his achievements, is proved by the Second Epilogue to the novel which Turgenev added when it was republished in a collected edition of his fiction in 1860. In this Second Epilogue, Rudin, red flag in hand, and armed with a crooked and blunt sword, is killed on the barricades in Paris in 1848, but at a time when the rising had already been almost crushed. In Turgenev's eyes, the very futility of his death ennobles him. Thus did Turgenev, in his own view, atone for the severity with which in the original version, he had criticized Rudin/Bakunin.

good deeds, says Turgenev, are 'more eternally enduring than the most resplendent beauty'.

The lecture ends with a somewhat garbled quotation from I Corinthians 13: 'Everything will fail, said the Apostle – Love alone will remain.'* The moral is that both the harm that Don Quixote has done by action and that which Hamlet has brought about by inaction are redeemed by love, kindness, and submission. A comparable idea (i.e. the contrast between 'agape' and 'eros', unselfish and sensual love) is voiced by one of the characters in *On the Eve*, in a conversation with his friend on 'altruistic' and 'egotistic' words, on words which unite people rather than divide them. Among 'uniting' words are art, fatherland, science, learning, justice. 'And love?' asks the friend; 'Love too is a uniting word, but not the kind of love that you are now longing for: not love which is a delight, but love which is a sacrifice.'[29]

In 'Faust' Turgenev had laid the main stress on the duty of renunciation, and on the disastrous consequence of the narrator's failure to suppress his love for a married woman whose imagination has been stimulated by her first contact with poetry. *A Nest of the Landed Gentry* takes renunciation and duty as its central themes. The hero, Lavretsky (whose family background bears resemblances to Turgenev's) has contracted an imprudent union with a light-hearted young woman who is beguiled and swept off her feet by the delights of social life in Paris, and shortly after the marriage is unfaithful to him. Shattered by the discovery, he parts from her, as he thinks for ever, makes her a generous allowance and after years of wandering abroad returns to his estate in Russia, with the intention of 'ploughing the earth, and ploughing it as well as I can'. He discovers a distant cousin, Liza Kalitina, whom he knew as a child, living with her widowed mother in a house in the district town (which is clearly Orel). She is deeply religious and serious. Lavretsky falls in love with her, and she, to her horror because he is a married man, finds that she is in love with him. For a time there appears to be a solution – an item in a Paris gossip column reports that Lavretsky's wife has died. But Liza's main concern is that he should pray for his wife's soul and for forgiveness for his failure as a husband – probably in her heart she does not believe the newspaper story. And, true enough, the wife arrives one day in Lavretsky's house, complete with an affected French maid and a small, spoilt daughter. Lavretsky is formally reconciled to his wife, in the sense that he establishes her

---

* The greek 'agape' is more correctly translated in Church Slavonic as 'love' than in the English version of the gospels, by 'charity'.

on his estate, and moves to one of his smaller properties. But his wife hankers after city life, does not stay long in the country, and moves to St. Petersburg, where she soon acquires a lover. Liza retires to a convent. Lavretsky in time becomes a model landlord, not only to his own advantage but to the benefit of his peasants.

Such is the simple outline of a story rich in detail and in subtle characterization. The subsidiary personages play a significant part in pointing up aspects of Turgenev's faith. There is Lemm, Liza's old German music master, stranded against his will in Russia. Lemm is completely unsuccessful and unrecognized – but he is in fact a magnificent composer, redeemed in his misery by the sublime music which occasionally pours from his piano. Then there is Panshin, a St. Petersburg official, one of those successful careerists with trite views and a paucity of human values whom Turgenev depicted with particular distaste. The young husband in *Alien Bread* and the narrator in 'A Quiet Spot' are other examples. Panshin is Liza's suitor and he is introduced as a foil to Lavretsky; the shallow, pseudo-westernized townsman, with an intellectual veneer, and the sturdy, solid Russian, rooted in the soil, the false contrasted with the true, the glib with the sincere. What with the corrupting effect of Paris on Lavretsky's wife and the unpleasant pro-Western Panshin, this is probably Turgenev's most anti-Western work. And lastly there is Mikhalevich, a university friend who visits Lavretsky for a night of interminable talk, in the course of which he shouts at him, without pausing to draw breath, about the idleness of Russian landlords, and the duty of the landed gentry to work for the good of the country. Mikhalevich is the complete idealist, poor as a church mouse, in love with a mysterious Ukrainian lady (who is rumoured to be a Jewish prostitute), always deeply concerned for the fate of mankind. The parallel with Don Quixote is further hinted at in his dress: a faded Spanish-type cloak.

A Nest of the Landed Gentry thus provides the first answer that Turgenev supplied to the question of the role of the 'superfluous man' of the forties and fifties – work for the good of Russia to the best of your strength and ability. It was not accidental that the novel was being thought about and written at a time when Turgenev was deeply involved in preparations for the emancipation of the serfs. There are other indications around this time that Turgenev was coming to the conclusion that the era of the 'superfluous man' was over, and that the future opened up prospects for all to play a part in the great transformation of the country that was taking place. For example, in a letter to an eighteen-year-old young man who was suffering from Russian *Weltschmerz* Turgenev wrote stern advice on 29 September 1858:

You say the surrounding atmosphere oppresses you. But ... if now, in 1858, you despair and are sad, what would you have done if you had been eighteen in 1838, when everything ahead was so dark – and stayed dark? You have no reason now, or time, for sorrowing: you are faced with a big responsibility to yourself. ... Remember that many young men, like you, are labouring and struggling on the face of Russia: you are not alone – what more do you want? ... You are under a moral duty to your comrades (whom you often do not know) not to fold your hands.[30]

A Nest of the Landed Gentry proved to be the most universally acclaimed work that Turgenev ever wrote, and provoked an enormous quantity of literature, both at the time and later. The image of Liza, as typifying Russian woman at her best, entered into Russian consciousness almost as deeply as Pushkin's Tatiana. The novel appealed to a greater variety of outlooks than anything he wrote before or since. It satisfied those who sought pure art as much as those who demanded a social message. It pleased those (like Countess Lambert) for whom the strong religious element was the most important aspect. There was even a sop to the radicals in the work – though it is improbable that this was Turgenev's intention: the model landlord, Lavretsky, who is so deeply concerned for the welfare of his peasants, is the son of a peasant woman. Assuming that it is correct to see certain aspects of Turgenev himself in Lavretsky, the peasant mother may well have been a, possibly unconscious, recognition of the traumatic effect on the young Turgenev of his own mother, the power-hungry serf-owner, and intended to point the contrast between himself and Lavretsky. Those with Slavophile inclinations were delighted with what they could discern as the truly Russian aspects of the novel, such as Lavretsky's roots in the soil, Liza's faith, self-sacrifice, and determination, and above all her submission to and acceptance of suffering.[31] The novel was a particular success among women readers. Invitations from the foremost houses of St. Petersburg poured in, and Turgenev was soon involved in a life of social gaiety.[32] The reaction to *On the Eve* was very different and in some respects may be said to have brought to a head Turgenev's growing rift with the *Contemporary*, and the new trends which were becoming evident in it.

From Turgenev's point of view, *On the Eve* provided in the person of its heroine, Elena, the secular counterpart to Liza. The plot of the book is simple, like the story on which the novel was based, given to Turgenev by his neighbour Karataev before he left for the Crimea. A young Russian girl Elena falls deeply in love with a Bulgarian patriot, Insarov, exiled in Russia. He returns her love. From the moment that they acknowledge their feelings, Elena gives herself to Insarov unquestioningly, without hesitation. His cause, the liberation of Bulgaria from the Turks, becomes her cause – she forsakes parents and her Russian life, knowing that it will be forever. Her relations with Insarov, secret at first, come into the open when she marries him, but not before she has had to live through the agony of watching him hover between life and death when he falls ill. After he has recovered a little, the two leave for Venice, where they spend some happy days in spite of premonitions of Insarov's death; he is still in the grip of his disease. Insarov dies before the call to take part in the insurrection against the Turks (with whom Russia is now at war) arrives from Bulgaria, where they are awaiting him. Elena leaves Venice for Bulgaria with Insarov in his coffin, never to return to Russia: his fatherland has become hers, she will take part in the national insurrection as a nurse, and thereafter – who knows? She is never heard of again.

Although the immediate reaction to the title of the novel was that Russia was 'on the eve' of having her own Insarovs, scilicet revolutionaries, this was not Turgenev's intention, as he pointed out to a correspondent in 1871. The title was chosen more because of the date of the novel's publication – 1860, the last year before the emancipation of the peasants. A new world was dawning in Russia, and such figures as Insarov and Elena appear as 'harbingers of what was later to happen'.[33] The choice of the Bulgarian hero was, moreover, determined by the original Karataev manuscript. Turgenev had indeed known some of the young Bulgarian nationalists, including Katranov, the prototype of Insarov in Karataev's copy.[34] It is therefore quite erroneous to see in Insarov a forerunner of the Russian revolutionary of the future. Turgenev's attitude to the revolutionaries in Russia was quite clear: he admired their courage and their commitment, but regarded their aim to set class against class as utterly wrong. As Insarov tells Elena: 'The last peasant, the last beggar in Bulgaria and I – we wish for one and the same thing. All of us have one aim. Just imagine, what strength and determination this gives us.' Turgenev's purpose at that time, as his activity in promoting the emancipation shows, was to bring about the co-operation of all sections of Russian society in the struggle for the interests of the nation as a whole.

If Insarov is not to be confused with the Russian revolutionary man, Elena is certainly not to be mistaken for the Russian revolutionary woman. In presenting Elena, Turgenev is concerned to show her complete devotion to a cause, her self-sacrifice and indifference to hardship in the name of an ideal. In a review of *On the Eve* shortly after its appearance, the novelist Evgeniia Tur (Countess Sailhas de Tournemire) pointed, very plausibly, to Anita Garibaldi, the devoted wife of the Italian leader, as the model for Elena. (Anita died from privation in 1849.) Numerous accounts of her were available to Turgenev, both at the time of her death and later,[35] and his correspondence includes frequent admiring references to Garibaldi. It is in this sense of selfless devotion to a principle or a cause that Elena and Liza are, in Turgenev's way of thinking, virtually identical.

This was not the opinion of Countess Lambert who regarded Elena as a 'forward hussy' lacking in femininity.[36] She called on Turgenev with her husband and attacked *On the Eve* to such effect that the poor author wrote to Annenkov that he had been minded to destroy it, and only refrained out of deference to Annenkov's opinion, since he had not yet seen the manuscript. He urgently begged Annenkov to come and read it: 'I expect you, and will keep the fire going in the grate.'[37] (Turgenev did not require very much persuasion by Annenkov to spare the manuscript from the flames.)[38] It was particularly ironic that Turgenev had intended to dedicate *On the Eve* to Countess Lambert.

It is significant that Elena and Liza, probably the two most serious and convincing Don Quixote figures in Turgenev's fiction, should have been women. Turgenev's male Don Quixotes always, or nearly always, seem to be slightly ridiculous – like Mikhalevich in *A Nest of the Landed Gentry*. Insarov is at best a rather wooden figure, and falls short of the heroic, if only because of his ill health. Bazarov in *Fathers and Children* is something of a caricature, and even Turgenev's own father in the autobiographical story 'First Love' (discussed in Chapter 1) which was published around the same time – in the spring of 1860 – is little more than a somewhat undignified philanderer. It was only women whom Turgenev could ever bring himself to put on a pedestal.

On the Eve was given a very mixed reception by contemporary critics. Tolstoy found it full of banality, and expressed the view that sad people who do not know what they want in life should not write novels. Botkin was enthusiastic: for him the poetic detail of the book made up for its lack of profound ideas. In general, the negative criticisms tended either to denounce the incomplete and ill-defined characterization of Insarov, or to condemn Elena for immorality;

this accusation, in turn, evoking passionate defence from the emancipated women whom she supposedly typified. Apollon Grigoriev probably got nearest to understanding Turgenev's own purpose when he wrote that while the author had faultlessly solved the general psychological and poetical problems, he had been less successful in dealing with the social problems with which the novel (and the overwhelming majority of its critics) was concerned. In a striking passage he described Turgenev's poetical aim as having been 'to represent two passionate existences, who had collided in a fateful and tragic manner, gliding over the precipice of their destination in the exceptional surroundings of Venice'. (He was referring here to the description of the last days of Insarov's life.) 'Their thirst for life, their intoxication with life on the edge of death and disaster, amidst the wonders of a poetic and obsolete world – the description of this is the aim which is brilliantly achieved, and which has created within the novel some kind of a feverishly Byronic episode, a magnificent and entrancing poem.'[39] The most influential, and most hostile, review of the novel came from the young radical Dobroliubov in his article 'But when will the real day come?', published in the *Contemporary*. But since this article was a contributory cause of Turgenev's break with that journal, we must first turn back a few years and examine the impact of the two radical critics, Chernyshevsky and Dobroliubov, on Turgenev's relations with the *Contemporary*.

It has been pointed out that the great bond between the members of the board of the *Contemporary* was the fact that they shared not only the same outlook and social background, but memories of friendship with Belinsky. This situation changed, or began to change, in 1855 when Chernyshevsky joined the journal, and more particularly after 1857, when Chernyshevsky's friend and protégé, Dobroliubov, became its chief critic. Although both were (within the limits possible under conditions of censorship) advocates of revolution and scourges of the liberal reformers who supported Alexander II's attempts to put through the emancipation of the peasants, the two men were different in temperament. Chernyshevsky retained some of the graces and interests of a genuine literary critic: Dobroliubov, in contrast, was a fanatical, hostile, sullen, committed revolutionary, and little else. Turgenev, who retained a tolerant respect for Chernyshevsky, hated Dobroliubov, and the feeling was warmly reciprocated. If Chernyshevsky's far from objective account is to be believed, the enmity actually began on Dobroliubov's side.[40] There was, beyond doubt, an element of class resentment by the humble seminarist against the rich landowner in

Dobroliubov's attitude to Turgenev, and possibly some element of snobbery on Turgenev's side as well.

Nekrasov's attempt in 1856 to secure the sole rights to the literary services of his most talented contributors ended in failure, and the abortive agreement which tried to achieve his aim was formally disavowed in February 1858.[41] But even its short existence, together with Nekrasov's importunate urging of his contributors to provide material for the journal, helped to precipitate Turgenev's ultimate break with the *Contemporary*.[42] He had published 'Asia' in Nekrasov's paper in January 1858. So far as *A Nest of the Landed Gentry* was concerned, he had a much more lucrative offer from Katkov had he been willing to publish it in the *Russian Herald*. but he agreed in the end to let Nekrasov have it. In return Nekrasov agreed to rescind the deal which he had made some time before for the republication rights of *Sketches from a Sportsman's Notebook* which was very unprofitable for Turgenev. 'Hamlet and Don Quixote', a year later, was the last work published by Turgenev in the *Contemporary*. That essay had been promised to Panaev for years past and had been much delayed in the writing. But by 1860 Turgenev and the editors were already on bad terms.

Panaeva, with her usual imaginative inaccuracy, attributed the break between Turgenev and the *Contemporary* to Turgenev taking offence at one single article by Dobroliubov attacking *On the Eve*, and forcing Nekrasov to choose between himself and Dobroliubov as contributors.[43] But the estrangement of Turgenev from the journal, and ultimately from Nekrasov, goes back much further than the offending review. The basic reason for it was clear: Turgenev's growing lack of sympathy for Chernyshevsky and Dobroliubov's political line. This was fully supported by Nekrasov, partly because of his own quasi-revolutionary sentiments and partly because he hoped to attract the young subscribers. Turgenev's unease at the new trend did not at first extend to Chernyshevsky – even the latter's own, very prejudiced, account of Turgenev's relations with himself and Dobroliubov admits that. He had admired Chernyshevsky's series of articles on the 'Gogol period' in Russian literature (published in 1855–6) and – more surprisingly – some of Chernyshevsky's political diatribes in which he lambasted the Russian liberals under the guise of discussing political events in Western Europe. When, after the accession of Alexander II, the change of climate had made possible the public mention of Belinsky, Chernyshevsky had been the first to recall his great reputation and influence, and for this, in particular, Turgenev respected him. When Tolstoy accused Cherny-

shevsky of making a fetish of Belinsky, Turgenev warmly defended
him. He was glad, he wrote, that someone had at last told the truth
about Belinsky who had been 'showered from all sides with dirt,
stones, epigrams and denunciations for expressing the very same
thoughts which have now become commonplace'.[44] Druzhinin and
Grigorovich, and particularly the latter, (who invented the rude
name of 'he who stinks of bed-bugs' for Chernyshevsky) were much
less tolerant of him than Turgenev. In the spring of 1856, in the interests of restoring harmony on the *Contemporary*, Turgenev, on behalf
of Botkin and himself, tried without success to persuade Nekrasov
to replace Chernyshevsky with Apollon Grigoriev.[45] Turgenev had,
it is true, reacted with unusual violence to Chernyshevsky's essay
on aesthetics – 'this vile stuff', 'this repulsive book'. 'In his eyes', he
wrote in July 1855, 'art is only . . . a surrogate for reality in life, and
only fit for the immature. . . . And this, in my view, is rubbish.'[46]
But this early disagreement was not, it would seem, of lasting effect.

The first real conflict with Nekrasov came over Dobroliubov, in
December 1858. The journal *Illiustratsiia* had published a strongly
anti-semitic article which drew objections on a wide scale in the
public press, signed by many liberals. Turgenev signed two such –
in one of them he was joined by Chernyshevsky. Dobroliubov's
article, in which he attacked the signatories of the protest, was an
intemperate effort typical of this young man, intended not as a
defence of anti-semitism, but to pour scorn on the liberals. Nekrasov
showed Dobroliubov's article to Turgenev, and notwithstanding the
latter's strong objection, published it, though he may have made
some minor alterations.[47] In March of the following year, 1859, Turgenev was incensed by Dobroliubov's scathing review in the *Contemporary* of the memoirs of S. T. Aksakov. (Aksakov, who was, of
course, a close friend of Turgenev, was mortally ill when the review
appeared, and died on 30 April.) As Turgenev wrote to Aksakov's
son, Konstantin, he had expressed his strong disapproval to the editors, and he assured Aksakov that he would never publish a line in
the *Contemporary* again.[48] The vulgar and abusive style of the review
of an old and respected author's work certainly struck a novel note
in the *Contemporary*.[49] On the other hand, Chernyshevsky's famous
article on 'Asia' seems to have evoked no comment, let alone protest,
from Turgenev.

In the course of 1859 and 1860 a number of contributions by
Dobroliubov, of which only one directly related to Turgenev's
work, clearly revealed the wide gulf in outlook which was opening
up between Turgenev and the leading radical critics who were in-

creasingly making the liberals their main target. This ran counter to Turgenev's belief at the time, shared by the supporters of reform with whom he remained on close terms, that the emancipation must be given full backing in the hope that it would succeed. He certainly did not, as did the radicals, write it off as little more than a land-owners' fraud as soon as it became evident, in 1858-9, that it was running into opposition, let alone call for bloody revolution – like Chernyshevsky and Dobroliubov. His constant argument (which was reiterated in *On the Eve*) was for the need to avoid bloodshed and for progress to take place by the union of 'all those thinking people who love their country' – as he had first expressed it in a letter to Aksakov as far back as October 1855.[50] He remained firmly opposed to revolution at the beginning of the sixties: 'It has been said and remains true: God forfend that we should live to see a Russian revolt, pitiless and senseless,' he said to a friend in conversation, quoting Pushkin.[51] Soviet authors often take the view that such an attitude was an expression of cowardice and of a landlord's selfish interest: experience of Russian history suggests that this judgement is somewhat over-simplified.

Unlike Turgenev, Herzen from his distance in London was less unequivocal on the subject of a peasant revolution. He did not want it, indeed probably feared it. But he was prepared to take the view that, however unwelcome, it might be necessary if the reform were sabotaged, or in the end proved to be a fraud. On 1 November 1858 Herzen published an article in the *Bell*, in which he stated that his paper would support a revolution whether it should come from above or from below.[52] The constitutional lawyer, the liberal-conservative Chicherin, sent Herzen a long letter, accusing him of fomenting revolution, which Herzen published. To this letter the liberal historian Kavelin sent a reply, in effect accusing Chicherin of playing into the hands of the reactionaries, who were constantly accusing Herzen of being a revolutionary. Turgenev joined with a number of others in sending a letter to Kavelin expressing support for his attitude.[53] This action is sometimes cited as evidence that Turgenev sympathized with revolution. But it was nothing of the kind. At that date no subversive organization was known to exist in Russia and Kavelin's argument that Chicherin was in effect giving aid and support to the extreme reactionaries may have appeared not unreasonable. Besides, loyalty to his friends was always a powerful motive with Turgenev. It was also the case, as his correspondence repeatedly shows, that he was a regular reader of the *Bell*, occasionally supplied it with materials emanating from Russia, and frequently expressed support for and approval of Herzen's strictures on the slow progress of the peasant reform in general and on the 'planters' (Turgenev's word for the reactionary landlords) in particular. It was only very occasionally that Turgenev urged restraint on Herzen – over criticism of Alexander II or the Grand Duke Constantine, for example. In an open letter to Turgenev, published in the *Bell* in February 1857, Herzen had concluded with the following words: 'Let us not quarrel about ways, our aim is one and the same. .... To work, to labour – labour for the good of the Russian people, which has in its time laboured so much for us.'[54]

Whatever Herzen's views on revolution may have been, he found himself on Turgenev's side in the discussion which proved the final straw in the latter's growing alienation from the *Contemporary* – the debate about the 'superfluous men'. For Dobroliubov (he naturally expressed himself in more guarded language, but the meaning was clear to his readers) they were synonymous with the contemporary liberals – spineless, passive, incapable of resolute action, the product of the feudal system. He developed this argument in a long article devoted to a study of Goncharov's novel *Oblomov*, of which the hero has become the byword in Russia for extreme idleness. For Dobroliubov, Oblomov was in the direct line of the classical 'superfluous men' – Onegin, Pechorin (in Lermontov's *A Hero of Our Time*), Herzen's hero of *Who is to Blame?* Beltov, Rudin, and 'The Hamlet of Shchigrov District'. Dobroliubov's implication was that their day was now over and that they must yield to 'new men' of energy and action. He did not say so outright, but he clearly meant men coming from a new class.[55] This article provoked a heated reply from Herzen in the *Bell* – 'Very Dangerous!!!' (the title was in English). Herzen angrily accused Dobroliubov of failing to see the significance and importance of the 'superfluous men' in their day: they quite sincerely recognized their duty to play their part in public life, but in the conditions of life under Nicholas I could find nothing to do. Now their time was over, because it was now possible to act. 'He who now can find no work to do, has no one to blame but himself, he is indeed an empty man, a good for nothing, or an idler' – like Oblomov. There was all the difference in the world between today's 'superfluous men' and the tragic 'superfluous men' of the past generation.[56] It was a somewhat unusual position for Herzen to adopt, perhaps, though he returned to the charge a little later in a second article which evoked warm approval from Turgenev. Possibly the Soviet historian Kozmin is right to discern other motives for Herzen's attack on the *Contemporary* than a desire to defend the 'superfluous men'.[57] Cer-

tainly Herzen had a particular dislike for Chernyshevsky: Dobroliubov he did not know. After the appearance of Herzen's article Chernyshevsky paid a secret visit to London to see Herzen, but failed to
win him over, and the gulf between them remained.

The climax of Dobroliubov's campaign against the liberals in
general, and against Turgenev in particular, came with the publication of his article 'But when will the real day come?', in which he
discussed the newly published *On the Eve*.[58] The main burden of
the article was a return to the attack on the reformers, in the guise
of an attack on the 'superfluous men': they must be replaced by 'new
men', not Bulgarians but Russians, who, unlike Insarov, will carry
on the fight against the inner enemy in the way that the Bulgarians
tried to fight against the alien occupier. The reason why 'new men'
are needed is because 'the Russian hero, usually emerging from educated society, is bound by blood ties to that very thing against which
he should revolt'.* So far as Turgenev the writer was concerned,
the article was mildly patronizing rather than derogatory – not that
Dobroliubov's opinion on literary questions was of much interest:
it is clear that what shocked Turgenev was the political implication
attributed to the novel by Dobroliubov, which was far from that intended by its author.

Nekrasov sent the article to Turgenev in proof – the original version. (It was toned down by the censor before he authorized publication.) Turgenev was appalled, and begged Nekrasov not to publish
it. 'I earnestly urge you, dear Nekrasov, not to publish this article',
he wrote on 19 February 1860 (underlining in the original). 'It can
cause me nothing but unpleasantness, it is unjust and sharp – I shall
not know where to hide myself if it is printed. Please respect my
request. I will call on you.'[59] Since the article was in fact published,
with excisions made by the censor, not by the editor, one must
assume that Panaeva is right when she says that Nekrasov printed
it knowing that he risked losing Turgenev as a contributor. An
additional irritant for Turgenev around this time was an attack by
Chernyshevsky, who had seen the proofs of the new version of *Rudin*
prepared by Turgenev for the collected edition of his tales in 1860.
This version contained the Second Epilogue in which Rudin is shot
dead on the Paris barricades. Chernyshevsky, irritated, no doubt, by
the Don Quixote-like figure of Rudin, dying needlessly for a lost
cause, crooked sword in hand (all of which, in Turgenev's terms,
was meant to be complimentary), decided to join the attackers. In

---

*It is an ironic reflection that the overwhelming majority of Russian revolu-
tionary leaders, including the Bolsheviks, in fact emerged from the landed gentry.

a review of a recent translation of one of Nathaniel Hawthorne's books he dragged in, completely irrelevantly, a fierce attack on *Rudin*. Instead of the intended tragedy, it had turned into 'a salad of sweet and sour, derisory and exalted pages', owing to the fact that the author had at first intended to portray the hero sympathetically and had then, in order to please his literary friends, turned him into a caricature[60] – the exact reverse of what had happened during the writing of the novel.

The cumulative effect of these events decided Turgenev finally to break with the *Contemporary*. According to what he wrote to Annenkov, it was the remarks on *Rudin* included in the review of the Nathaniel Hawthorne translation (which Turgenev mistakenly attributed to Dobroliubov) which finally swayed him. He forwarded, through Annenkov, a letter to this effect to Panaev, but did not write to Nekrasov.[61] Annenkov did not in fact pass the letter on to Panaev,[62] but when Nekrasov wrote to Turgenev in conciliatory terms, on 15 January 1861, stressing in his own defence that it was impossible for him, as editor, to refuse Chernyshevsky and Dobroliubov freedom to express themselves as they pleased,[63] he replied that he had 'firmly decided to take no further part in the *Contemporary*'.[64] When the editors of the *Contemporary* subsequently assured subscribers that they had rejected Turgenev as a contributor because his views were unwelcome, he sent a letter to the press denying this and stating, as was indeed the case, that it was he who had refused to contribute any longer. This raised a storm of protest from the young against Turgenev for daring to attack their idols. 'What did it matter if I was right?', was Turgenev's comment.[65] Personal friendship with Nekrasov also came to an end, though a year later the two men travelled by chance together from St. Petersburg to Moscow. 'We talked and laughed – but the abyss between us remained as it was.'[66] It did indeed. Turgenev's letters abound in contemptuous references to Nekrasov – the man and the poet. However, there was to be something in the nature of a reconciliation when Nekrasov lay dying in 1878.[67]

CHAPTER TEN

Friendships and Quarrels

The period of Turgenev's life described in the last two chapters was one of extraordinary literary energy. Having successfully overcome the depression and inability to write which beset him in the autumn of 1856, he produced three major and three minor works in the space of five years. 'Asia' was started in June 1857 and completed in November, and work was begun almost immediately on *A Nest of the Landed Gentry*, the plan of which had been revolving in his head for some time before. It was finished within a year. *On the Eve* was written in the course of 1859; in the same year Turgenev did most of the writing of his lecture 'Hamlet and Don Quixote', first conceived some years before. 'First Love' was composed in the course of the early months of 1860 and by the summer of that year, as his correspondence shows, he was deep in the planning of *Fathers and Children*. The writing and rewriting of this novel coincided with rapid political changes inside Russia, which were inevitably reflected in it. *Fathers and Children* was not finished until the summer of 1861 and was then subjected to substantial reworking later in the year. All this was by any standards a remarkable volume of literary output, which Turgenev never equalled.

Since the depression which had gripped him in the autumn of 1856 was the result of estrangement from Pauline Viardot – estrangement on her side, that is – it seems evident that this great burst of literary energy was his way of reconciling himself to the personal misery to which he now saw himself condemned. Throughout his life Turgenev was in the habit of pouring out laments, sometimes to the most unlikely recipients. This practice, seen in conjunction with his gaiety, and his enjoyment of the things which gave him pleasure, such as natural beauty, music, shooting, or good food, abundantly evident from his letters, must raise the suspicion that the complaints were in reality largely a pose. But his confidants included Botkin,

Annenkov, and Countess Lambert – close friends who knew him too well not to recognize the truth. There is a particular ring of sincerity in his letters to the Countess, who seems to have been in his complete confidence about his feelings for Pauline. He spent long evenings at her flat, in intimate conversation in her 'little green room' of which he often writes affectionately; presumably her husband was absent on these occasions. They met in Paris from time to time, and certainly once in Germany, in 1860, when Turgenev was taking the waters in Soden, and Countess Lambert was undergoing a cure at a neighbouring watering place.

The Countess was an unhappy woman, especially after the death of her only son at the end of 1861, and she found relief in confiding in Turgenev. Apart from seeking spiritual comfort, she was always willing to carry out numerous errands for him in St. Petersburg, mainly in connection with his travel arrangements, which he had to make from Spasskoe with the aid of an unreliable postal service. She also willingly responded to his appeals to her considerable influence in Russian society on the frequent occasions when he was trying to help someone find employment, or the like.

His letters to her over the years reflect the decline of intimacy in his life with Pauline, which came very sharply after his departure from Courtavenel in the autumn of 1856, and Pauline's conception of her son Paul soon afterwards. He continued to spend some time at Courtavenel every year, though it seems he now had to wait for an invitation. ('I shall go to Courtavenel – I hope I shall be invited there', he wrote to Paulinette on 22 June 1859.) Pauline Viardot was not always there. When she was, there was music, private theatricals, and games as in earlier years. Much of Turgenev's time was spent in the company of Louis – shooting, or collaborating on the translation of Russian authors. There is no evidence of any kind of friction or strain between the two men. Pauline's little girls (a second daughter Marianne had been born on 15 March 1854) were growing up and were a source of delight to Turgenev – especially Claudie.

It is hard to believe that life at Courtavenel was quite so painful for Turgenev to endure as he sometimes made out. There is no doubt that he learned to content himself with being the family friend in circumstances where he knew that he would never again be the lover. But the melancholy which the realization of his predicament induced is reflected in his letters. 'All the passion left in me has gone into my gifts as a writer. Everything else is cold and motionless,' he wrote to Countess Lambert from Vichy on 24 June 1859.[1] And a few weeks later, from Courtavenel: 'My health is good, but my spirit is sad.

Around me there is regular family life. .... What am I here for, and why ... should I be turning my gaze backwards? You will easily understand both what I want to say, and my position.'² The following year, again writing from Courtavenel, he refers to the 'sad mist' which has settled on the 'relations which you know about'.³ And a few months later, back in Paris, he wrote to her that a few days ago '... my heart died. .... The past finally broke away from me but, having parted with it, I realized that there was nothing left for me, that my whole life had separated off from me, together with my past.'⁴ The message in his letters is always the same: the need for resignation and acceptance. At the end of 1860 he offers the Countess advice which clearly reflects his own mood: 'Be approximately satisfied with approximate happiness ... the only thing on earth which is beyond doubt and clear is unhappiness.'⁵

We possess little evidence beyond these confidences to Countess Lambert of the course of relations between Turgenev and Pauline during these years. We do not even know if they were meeting apart from the Courtavenel visits, although there are occasional references in his letters to musical evenings at the Viardot household in Paris. No correspondence between them is available to us for 1860 or 1861 – we know from his frequent complaints to Paulinette that Pauline very seldom wrote to him. On his side the devotion remained unchanged – humble, undemanding, submissive, much as it had been from the first. On her side the demands of old friendship were, it would seem, quite compatible with long periods of neglect. Turgenev immediately obeyed any summons from her when it came. As he wrote to Annenkov, in July 1860, informing him of his plans to go to Courtavenel, 'Madame Viardot wishes me to go, and her wishes for me are law. Her son almost died and she suffered a great deal. She longs to recover in peaceful, friendly company.'⁶

Apart from a few mild and unimportant flirtations, and the intimate friendship with Countess Lambert, there seems to have been no woman in his life who could have aroused even the kind of jealousy which Pauline had manifested over his infatuation with Olga Turgeneva some years before. No doubt he had casual sexual encounters, especially when he was in Russia. A letter to Botkin, written from St. Petersburg in February 1859, refers to an otherwise unidentified Alexandra Petrovna who 'exhausted me to the marrow. No, my friend, at our years once in three months is enough.'⁷ (Turgenev was all of forty-one at this date!)

Paulinette was growing up. When the time came for her to leave her *pension* in the autumn of 1859 her father engaged an English companion for her, Mrs. Mary Innes, who seems to have been an admirable and sensible woman.* In October 1860 he took an apartment at 210 rue de Rivoli where he settled for a time with the two women, and built up the semblance of a home for which he had always longed, and had never been able to attain. There was still little in common between father and daughter, although Paulinette seems to have tried to fit herself for her father's world – by studying music and learning Italian, for example. She was very Slav in appearance and in manner, with a good share of the charm which characterizes so many Russian women. She still knew not a word of the language but remained Orthodox in faith and received religious instruction from a priest, in accordance with arrangements made by her father. There was a time when, probably under the influence of Countess Lambert, who befriended her when on a visit to Paris, Paulinette was taken with the idea of returning to Russia and of reassuming her lost personality. Turgenev always resolutely resisted any such thoughts on her part, on the plausible grounds that her illegitimate status would have caused difficulties in Russian society. However, it is not improbable that he also did not want to deprive himself of the convenient excuse which Paulinette provided for his long stays abroad; however much he complained about France and the French, to be near Pauline Viardot had become a necessity. His daughter was only too well aware of this, and this it was that accounted for her frequent outbursts of jealousy against Pauline. These in turn caused the reproaches which figure in Turgenev's letters to his daughter. As he informed all and sundry in his correspondence, he was much preoccupied with finding a husband for his daughter. The first efforts were unsuccessful. A certain Monsieur Honsez, who sought her hand in 1862, was rejected by her (her father showed little enthusiasm for him either),[8] and Paulinette had to wait until 1865 before embarking on marriage – which in the end was to prove disastrous.

Turgenev wrote several descriptions to his friends of his life in Paris during those years, which certainly do not suggest undue gaiety. He does not seem to have made or sought to make much contact with French literary figures (with the exception of Prosper Mérimée, whom he had met in 1857) as he would do in later years – indeed in his correspondence there are frequent expressions of contempt for the French literary scene. He remained on friendly terms with his namesake, the Decembrist N. I. Turgenev and his wife (who con-

*He kept in touch with Mrs. Innes, long after she had left Paulinette in 1865, indeed until her death in 1879.

tinued to show much attention to Paulinette), and with other prominent members of Russian society then living in Paris. But Paris did
not suit his health, and he stresses in his letters that nothing but the
anxiety to find a husband for his daughter could keep him there –
even if this was not the whole truth. The French capital did not prove
conducive to writing. His most intensive work on the enormous
literary output during these years of unusual creativity mainly took
place in Spasskoe, during his annual extended return to Russia.
There is much nostalgia in his letters, especially in those written to
his neighbour and shooting companion Fet, for the Russian spring
and landscape. Whatever the truth of Turgenev's assertion that but
for his responsibilities as a father he would return to Russia to settle
there permanently, there is no doubt about his fierce, almost visceral
love for the Russian countryside and the free and easy life of a Russian
country gentleman: '... nightingales, the smell of straw and of birch-
tree buds, the sun and the puddles in the roads – that is what my soul
is thirsting for!' It was this almost physical passion for his country
which was reflected in his close friendship, in spite of political differences, with the Aksakovs, and in his love for the poetry of the
Slavophile idol, Tiutchev.

Life in Paris must, indeed, have seemed somewhat grey when
compared with Russia; he writes on 20 January 1861:

You wish to know how I spend my time in Paris? ... I occasionally see
a few Frenchmen and a few Russians; from time to time I hear good music
at M. Viardot's; I am working pretty lazily; on Thursdays I give very
modest soirées. And that is all. My health is respectable. I see Maria Aleksan-
drovna Markovich nearly every day. I have been out shooting a few times,
and shot reasonably well. Before dinner I go to play chess at the Café de
la Régence and am frequently defeated. ... I am tired of the theatres and
don't go to them. I read the Russian journals with which Prince Trubetskoy,
that kindest of men, supplies me.[9]

Madame Markovich, to whom he refers, was a young Ukrainian
author who wrote under the pseudonym Marko Vovchok. Born in
1833, she was fifteen years younger than Turgenev. He met her early
in 1859 and the two became close friends for the next few years.
Around the same time, he was on good terms with the St. Petersburg Little Russian (Ukrainian) colony, in whose company he used
to spend a good deal of his time whenever he found himself in
that city. This Little Russian circle included the national poet Taras
Shevchenko, about whom Turgenev was later to publish a short
memoir. The circle usually met either at the house of Madame V.

Ya. Kartashevskaia, with whom Turgenev maintained a friendly correspondence for many years; or at the home of her brother N. Ya. Makarov, who occupied a floor in the house of a scion of one of the noblest Little Russian families, P. A. Kochubei.★

The Ukrainians seem to have been strongly nationalist in outlook and politically active. But Turgenev's interest in them was entirely literary. He was in full sympathy with their aim of establishing Little Russian culture in its own right, and not as an appendage of Great Russian culture. But he is scornful in his letters of some of the more extreme nationalist sentiments expressed in the periodical published by members of the group, he never visited the Ukraine, and never, so far as is known, expressed any views on political issues connected with that part of Russia. The Little Russian characters who appear in his fiction are often portrayed as mildly ridiculous.

Madame Markovich, who was then twenty-six, plainly fascinated him, though there is no suggestion in their very sizeable correspondence of any erotic element in the friendship.[10] A photograph taken in Paris in 1860 or 1861[11] suggests a humorous and intelligent gamine rather than a beautiful woman. His letters to her, when he is not giving her literary advice ('read Pushkin!'), are full of banter, teasing her for her scatterbrained and bohemian behaviour, her extravagance and the like. There is one letter which amounts to a disapproving sermon about a trip which she undertook to Rome with a young man who was her lover (and who was one of the causes of the break-up of her marriage). But then Turgenev always held strong views on any irregularity of sexual behaviour so far as women were concerned. But though there was no romantic side to their friendship, they enjoyed each other's company and sought as much of it as possible when circumstances threw them together, in Germany, or more usually in Paris. It was probably Turgenev who persuaded her to undertake her first journey abroad, in 1859, and who travelled with her, her husband and son, to Germany and France. There were also two short trips *à deux* in Germany a year or two later.

What first attracted Turgenev to Madame Markovich was undoubtedly her writing. Not only did he express the greatest enthusiasm for her early works, but he translated them into Russian – presumably learning Ukrainian for the purpose (the two languages are very similar, but far from identical). This early fiction consists of a volume of sketches, which portrayed the life of the Little Russian

★ Annenkov and the novelist Pisemsky also formed part of this company – Annenkov soon after married a relation of Kartashevskaia, much to the delight of his friends, who had written him off as a confirmed bachelor.

peasant in conditions of serfdom, and which appeared in Turgenev's translation in the *Contemporary* in 1859, and a novel, *The Boarding-schoolgirl*, of which his version was published in 1860. He showed less enthusiasm for her later works, which were highly coloured by her increasingly radical views. It was indeed Madame Markovich's growing radicalism that spelt the end of their intimacy. The fact that she fell under the influence of Herzen and Ogarev (whom she met through Turgenev) and of Chernyshevsky at the time when the mounting revolutionary situation in Russia was alienating Turgenev from his former connections with the more extreme trend in Russian politics contributed to the estrangement between the two. There was no quarrel, but the friendship was virtually at an end by 1862.*

The early sixties was a time of major quarrels. The break with Nekrasov, which was a political one, has already been described; the parting of the ways with Herzen will be dealt with later. There were no political undertones to the conflict either with Goncharov or with Tolstoy.† Goncharov, the older man by six years, had won some literary fame with his *Ordinary Story*, published in 1847, and highly praised by Belinsky. Until around 1858, he and Turgenev were on perfectly good terms, and admired each other's work. But Goncharov was a suspicious, highly neurotic, and very jealous man, with a strong sense of what he considered was due to his position as a writer. These traits were much exacerbated both by the difficulties which he had to face during the first half of his life and by his somewhat ambiguous standing among the liberal-minded *Contemporary* coterie because of his government appointment as censor after 1855. He had much admired *Sketches from a Sportsman's Notebook*. His attitude changed markedly when Turgenev began to emerge as a writer of full-sized novels (and hence a competitor), and there was a noticeable change in his behaviour towards him after he had heard Annenkov read *A Nest of the Landed Gentry* in November 1858. Turgenev's novel was published in January 1859, and although *Oblomov*, Gon-

---

* Recently discovered evidence suggests that Madame Markovich was also the cause of an estrangement between Turgenev and his French publisher Pierre Jules Hetzel – see an article by Patrick Waddington in the *Slavonic and East European Review* Vol. 55, No. 3 July 1977, pp. 328–47.

† The breach with Dostoevsky was not to happen until the end of the sixties. For the time being, as their correspondence, though infrequent, shows, they were on excellent terms: 'You cannot doubt', Turgenev wrote to Dostoevsky on 11 November 1861 from Paris, 'the sincere regard I feel for you and for your journal [*Vremia*] – and for everything that concerns you.'[12] Dostoevsky, in two anonymous articles in his journal, had warmly espoused Turgenev's side in his conflict with the *Contemporary*.[13]

charov's greatest work, began to appear in instalments around the same time, it took rather longer for it to achieve success.

It was around this time that Goncharov first accused Turgenev of plagiarism. He alleged that in *A Nest of the Landed Gentry* Turgenev had copied characters and situations from *The Precipice*. This was a novel on which Goncharov was working, but parts of which had in the past been read to many literary friends, including Turgenev. It is also very probable that the two of them discussed the plan of *The Precipice*, since this was the common practice among writers at the time. Turgenev rather weakly agreed to remove one scene from his book, thereby, of course, feeding Goncharov's paranoid suspicions. A long, querulous letter in March 1859 repeating the accusation of plagiarism and belittling Turgenev's talents, drew a fairly tart, but still conciliatory, reply. But the appearance in the following year of *On the Eve*, convinced this unbalanced man that Turgenev's work was nothing but a bad copy of his own (a suggestion which to anyone who has read both authors is ridiculous). He began to spread rumours to this effect in St. Petersburg literary circles, with the result that Turgenev sent him a letter (now lost) demanding either arbitration, or a duel. On 29 March 1860 the arbitration took place before Annenkov, Druzhinin, the literary critic Dudyshkin, and Nikitenko. The four of them, anxious to avoid a breach between the quarrelling writers, made a compromise pronouncement that since both drew their themes from the same Russian background, certain similarities of incidents and thoughts were inevitable; and added that this fact excused both parties. According to Annenkov (Nikitenko's account, though shorter, is substantially similar) Turgenev at this point turned deathly pale and, in a state of excitement of a kind which he, Annenkov, had never observed in him before, informed Goncharov that, while he would continue to admire his talent, 'friendly relations between us are at an end from this moment'.

Turgenev's anger was justified by subsequent events. The two men were reconciled in 1864, although Goncharov's letters over the next few years, while ostensibly friendly, are peppered with hurtful remarks and innuendos, and his hatred of Turgenev led to an end of friendly intercourse between them, though there was no further open quarrel. In the mid-seventies Goncharov wrote down, although not for publication (it did not see the light of day until 1924), what purported to be an account of what he had suffered in the way of plagiarism not only from Turgenev, but also from a number of French authors with whom Turgenev was known to be friendly. He also levelled this accusation against him in 1874, when

the two met by chance in the streets of St. Petersburg.[14] The seeds
of a psychopathic disorder already present in 1859 and 1860 had by
now grown to maturity.[15]

★   ★   ★   ★   ★

In spite of the history of constant friction between Tolstoy and
Turgenev, their quarrel was as sudden and unexpected as a mountain
tempest. Although their meetings in Spasskoe in April and October
1859 ended in the now usual conflict and antagonism, it was Tolstoy
who made a move towards reconciliation, when he sought out Turgenev in Paris in February 1861. Tolstoy's motive may in part have
been the wish to hear about the last days of his brother: Nikolai Tolstoy had recently died in France, but had spent his last weeks with
Turgenev in Soden, in a vain attempt to cure the consumption with
which he was mortally smitten. Turgenev found Leo Tolstoy
changed very much for the better. After the two had parted, he wrote
to Tolstoy expressing joy at a letter (now lost) from him which
showed that the old hostility was at an end, and expressed confidence
that they would meet as good friends in Russia.[16] Tolstoy, for his
part, recorded in his diary for 13 April that 'Turgenev and I have
come closer together'.

Things turned out rather differently. After a few days' stay in St.
Petersburg Turgenev returned to Spasskoe, about 10 May 1861. He
had invited Tolstoy to join him there. They met on good terms and
there was no sign of impending disaster when shortly afterwards they
set off for the neighbouring Stepanovka, to visit their friend Fet and
his wife. A day of unclouded delight followed. Good food, much
champagne (Turgenev's favourite Roederer served with ice, a rare
commodity in those days), and animated conversation. The storm
broke on the following day, 27 May, at breakfast. The only witness
who left a record of what happened (apart from a second-hand version of Turgenev's account years later) was Fet, who had a tendency
to embroider.[17] Making polite conversation, Madame Fet inquired
if Turgenev was satisfied with the English governess whom he had
installed to look after his daughter. Turgenev was warm in his
praise of Mrs. Innes. She had even insisted, he added, that he should
allocate a sum of money which Paulinette could spend on charity.

'And now', he continued, 'this Englishwoman insists that my
daughter should take away the poor clothing of the paupers, mend
it with her own hands, and then return it to its owners.'

'And you consider this a good thing?' inquired Tolstoy.

'Of course. It brings the purveyor of charity close to the actual need.'

'And I think, that a dressed-up young woman, holding dirty, stinking rags on her knees is acting an insincere theatrical scene.' This remark infuriated Turgenev, who clearly lost his self-control.

'I must ask you not to say such things.'

'Why should I not say something of which I am convinced?'

Turgenev, pale with rage, exclaimed, 'Then I will force you to be silent with an insult,' rushed from the room, came back in order to apologize to Madame Fet, and then left the room again. (Fet does not record what the insult was. One of Turgenev's later letters of apology to Tolstoy suggests that it was a rude word.) The incident is more remarkable for the unspoken undertones than for what actually happened: on Tolstoy's side, the old charge that Turgenev was an empty poseur and, no doubt, moral disapproval of Paulinette's origins;* on Turgenev's side, there was the nagging sense of guilt about Paulinette which was never far below the surface. In the numerous letters which he wrote subsequently to Fet and others about the incident, Turgenev invariably took full blame for what had happened – except for one hint in a letter to Countess Lambert that there were 'reasons at the basis [of the quarrel] which justify me'.[19]

A series of misunderstandings and of postal miscarriages now combined to blow up a relatively insignificant occurrence to the brink of a duel. Fet immediately arranged for the departure of his two turbulent guests to their respective estates. But Tolstoy could not wait to return to Yasnaia Poliana to give vent to his rage, and sent Turgenev a stern demand for an apology from a posting-station on the way. Turgenev replied with a stiff and formal, but nevertheless complete, apology. However, he failed to notice the address from which Tolstoy had written, and sent his answer to Fet's house, Stepanovka. Meanwhile Tolstoy, believing that Turgenev had ignored his letter, sent him a challenge to a duel. The misunderstanding was patched up after much agitated activity by Fet and hurried posting by messengers between the various estates. Tolstoy's letters to Turgenev of this period are lost, but those which he wrote to Fet reveal his rage and contempt, and his determination to break finally with his fellow-author. This was not the end of the matter. A few months after the incident Tolstoy, smitten with one of his occasional onslaughts of Christian humility, wrote to Turgenev, taking upon himself the blame for the incident and expressing regret for his insulting

* According to the second-hand account of Turgenev's version of the quarrel, Tolstoy actually referred to Paulinette's illegitimacy.[18]

remarks. To make sure that his letter would reach Turgenev, who by then had returned to Paris, he entrusted it for transmission to a St. Petersburg bookseller – with the result that the conciliatory missive took several months to reach its destination. Meanwhile, Turgenev, having heard rumours that Tolstoy was accusing him of cowardice, and allegedly spreading copies of one of his letters in an effort to discredit him, sent him a challenge to a duel. However, he accepted Tolstoy's assurance in reply that there was no truth in the gossip – as the letter expressing regret clearly confirmed when it eventually reached Turgenev after the long delay. Their friendship was not renewed for seventeen years.[20] Turgenev, however, always retained his admiration for Tolstoy's writing. Fet, who was much involved in the affair, blamed Turgenev squarely for it.[21] But he was not a very balanced judge of human conduct, and was moreover much exasperated by Turgenev's constant criticism of his verses.

Turgenev's estates should have brought him a substantial income, but such was not the case, because of the mismanagement by his uncle, Nicholas, who was both incompetent and grasping. The extent of Uncle Nicholas's failings may be gauged from the following: while Turgenev's brother Nikolai, whose estates were approximately of the same size and value as his own, extracted 20,000 roubles a year, Ivan Turgenev was still not succeeding in squeezing more than 5,500 roubles out of his. His brother managed his property himself, no doubt with the able assistance of his parsimonious German wife.[22] Turgenev's literary earnings, however, were, for the time, quite substantial – 4,000 roubles, for example, was paid to him by Katkov for *On the Eve*. For the rights to publish his collected works which appeared in 1860 and 1861 in five volumes, the fee agreed was 8,000 roubles, although there was a certain amount of trouble in recovering the sum in full from the publisher. His writings were by now also being published in French, English, and German translations, and his reputation, especially in France and Germany, was growing. His appearances at public readings in aid of the Literary Benevolent Fund, of which he was a founder member, drew enormous, enthusiastic audiences. His literary fame was crowned on 29 December 1860 by his election as a corresponding member of the Imperial Academy of Sciences.[23]

So far as public affairs were concerned, his main preoccupation was always the question of the emancipation of the serfs, a subject debated anxiously with, among others, N. I. Turgenev in Paris and Prince Cherkassky and other liberal friends in Russia. Nothing had come of his project for the publication of a new journal devoted to discussion of the problems of emancipation. Another scheme, designed to further the spread of elementary education in Russia which in the end proved equally fruitless, was the result of lengthy deliberation among a group of Russians, including Turgenev, who spent some weeks in August 1860 at Ventnor on the Isle of Wight. A draft 'Programme' which embodied Turgenev's idea, was composed by him in co-operation with Annenkov, but others, including the son of General Rostovtsev, took part in the discussions. The plan was to co-ordinate the numerous, but scattered, attempts which were being made in Russia to spread literacy among the peasants. This was to be achieved by founding a 'Society for the Spread of Literacy and Primary Education'. The aims of the Society would be to set up schools and reading rooms, to produce text books, and to co-ordinate the efforts already being made by others to teach reading and writing. The Society was to be financed by members' contributions. Turgenev and Annenkov certainly attached a great deal of importance to the scheme. It was circulated by the two of them to a number of prominent figures and, according to Annenkov, was fairly widely copied and read, at any rate in St. Petersburg, and won sympathy from many moderates. The radicals on the *Contemporary* treated it as a liberal pleasantry, and Herzen, who did not reply to Turgenev's request for comments on the draft, referred to it with irony some years later. Whatever chance of success the project may have had was killed in 1862 after government measures, such as the closing of St. Petersburg University and of Sunday schools, had been taken in reaction against the spread of revolutionary proclamations and other radical activities in 1861 and 1862.[24]

By the end of 1860 the issue of emancipation was already decided. Although the Manifesto was not publicly proclaimed until 19 February 1861, the draft was already in existence and in unofficial circulation at the end of 1860, and Turgenev was acquainted with it. His attitude to the reform was characteristic of the small group of Russian liberals: warm support for the Emperor for his achievement, and, while not ignoring the shortcomings of the terms of the Statute, anxiety to co-operate fully with government institutions and with organizations of the landed gentry in making the momentous change in Russian life a success. At the end of 1860 he composed a draft address to the Emperor which, in guarded terms, urged the adoption of certain political changes to accompany the social transformation which emancipation would achieve. (It was written in anticipation of the Manifesto.) After assurances that the signatories fully supported the Emperor, the address urged six reforms: complete abolition of corporal punishment; public hearings in the courts; annual accounting of government expenditure and (unspecified) 'participation' in checking it; enlargement of the sphere of activities of provincial assemblies; shortened terms of service for soldiers, and the assimilation of the status of religious dissenters with that of other subjects. It ended with an invocation to the Emperor not to believe those who would try to persuade him that acceptance of these proposals would plunge the country into violent upheavals.[25]

Turgenev's intention was to collect signatures to the draft inside Russia – an enterprise which was fraught with considerable risks, since events were soon to show that Alexander, while intent on putting through social reforms of a far-reaching nature, would every time stop short at any kind of move to involve the landed gentry in political decisions. Turgenev entrusted the draft to one Arthur Benni, a Russian radical journalist who had become a British subject, and who called on him at the end of 1860 with an introduction from Herzen. Benni did indeed make an effort to muster some signatures, without naming Turgenev as the author of the address, but was unsuccessful in enlisting any prominent supporters. Herzen, whom Benni tried to persuade to sign at the end of 1861, was very unenthusiastic, but this was probably because, by that date, without a trace of factual evidence, he suspected Benni of being a Russian police agent. It is not known if Turgenev arranged with Benni that his authorship should be kept secret; if he did, then Benni scrupulously observed his undertaking. He destroyed the draft in 1861, when he suspected that he might be arrested and, when interrogated along with many others at the end of 1862, made no mention either of the address or of Turgenev.[26] Turgenev seems to have entertained some idea of proceeding with this, or possibly a different memorandum, which would include a request for the summoning of an all-Russian assembly.[27] But nothing came of the plan. Bakunin may have been right in his view that as a politician Turgenev was a 'nitwit'; but it was also true that by that date political conditions in Russia had changed so much for the worse that any attempt to urge peaceful reforms, however moderate and loyal, was doomed to failure.

CHAPTER ELEVEN

Fathers and Children

News of the publication of the Manifesto on 19 February 1861 reached Turgenev in Paris in a telegram from Annenkov on 6 March. The excitement caused by the momentous event among the few liberal *émigrés* was intense. Those whose incomes depended on their serfs were less delighted. 'The Russians here are mad with anger – fine representatives of our people they are!' Nevertheless, there was a service of thanksgiving in the Russian Church with many tears of joy, and a moving address by the priest. The Decembrists N. I. Turgenev and Prince Volkonsky were present, at what one can imagine was the emotional climax of their lives. 'We prayed with all our hearts for the Emperor. God grant health to the Emperor,' Turgenev wrote to Annenkov.[1]

The serfs were emancipated from the personal power of the landlords. They were to receive land on the basis of inventories prepared on all estates, and submitted for final decision to arbitrators of the peace. When the terms had been agreed, the peasants would become 'temporarily obliged' to their former owners, either to pay dues or to give service. At a later stage they would begin annual redemption payments which would eventually give them ownership of the land. The settlement was a compromise and created many difficulties in the years to come, which were to be fully exploited by the nascent revolutionary movement. But, as Hugh Seton-Watson has aptly pointed out, 'serfdom was peacefully abolished in the same year in which failure to abolish slavery in another great country was a principal cause of one of the most bloody wars of the nineteenth century'.[2] It would soon become the common charge of Herzen and Ogarev in London and of the radicals inside Russia that the liberation was not real, that the peasants remained serfs in all but name, and that the allocation of land was derisory. On his return to Spasskoe in the spring of 1861 Turgenev, who, after all, knew something

Turgenev's parents

St. Petersburg – the Nevsky Prospect around 1840

Pauline Viardot, by Ary Scheffer. Painted about 1841.

I. S. Turgenev. From a daguerreotype of the late 1840s.

V. G. Belinsky

A. I. Herzen with his daughter Tata. From a daguerreotype of the early 1850s

N. A. Nekrasov

Michael Bakunin

A. A. Fet

I. S. Turgenev in 1856. From a photograph.

I. S. Turgenev in 1868. From a photograph.

Turgenev's daughter, Pelageia Turgeneva-Bruère,
known as Paulinette

Claudie Viardot. From a drawing by
Pauline Viardot.

I. S. Turgenev. A drawing by
Ludwig Pietsch, 1866–8.

Pauline Viardot in 1868.
From a photograph.

The theatre in the grounds of the Viardot villa in Thiergartenstrasse, Baden–Baden (since demolished). From a water-colour by Heinrich Adriano.

Frau Anstett's house in Schillerstrasse, Baden-Baden, where Turgenev lived on the first floor from 1863 to 1868 (since demolished)

A musical party at the Viardot villa in Baden-Baden, from an engraving from a drawing by Ludwig Pietsch. Among those shown are Anton Rubinstein (at the piano); Pauline Viardot; Turgenev; Louis Viardot (seated); Theodor Storm and Manuel Garcia (standing); King William I and Queen Augusta of Prussia; Bismarck; and Gustave Doré (seated on the right).

Pauline Viardot in the role of Orpheus, by Aimé Millet

Louis Viardot. A portrait by A. A. Kharlamov.

Turgenev (standing behind the last table) among chess players in the Café de la Régence in 1874. Engraved from a drawing.

I. S. Turgenev. A portrait by A. A. Kharlamov painted in 1875,
and said by Turgenev to be a good likeness.

Savina in 1874. From a photograph.

Savina in the role of Verochka in
A Month in the Country

Madame M. A. Markovich (Marko
Vovchok). From a photograph taken
in the 1860s.

Tatiana Bakunina. A water–colour of
the 1830s.

about peasants, observed the momentous change in them that had taken place: 'Neither the former "Lords" nor the former "muzhiks", nor indeed the former relations remain. The peasants have discovered their rights and are insisting on them,' he wrote to Botkin on 22 May 1861. But there were difficulties. As we have already seen, the peasants did not wish to change from service (*barshchina*) to the system of payment in lieu of service (*obrok*) in spite of the fact that the latter was much more profitable to them. Their reluctance was in part due to the fact that, with discipline reduced, they could get by on *barshchina* with very little work, and partly to a widespread belief that they would eventually get all the land which they worked free – an idea which in some cases was inculcated by self-appointed 'advisers'.[3] There were other difficulties too; centuries of habits of lawlessness were not going to be wiped out overnight. But Turgenev remained optimistic that things would right themselves in the end.[4]

The compromises which had been necessary in putting through the reform were seen as a betrayal and a fraud by the impatient radicals. The gradual liberation of the peasant from the effects of serfdom and the often inadequate allocation of land, designed both to secure the co-operation of the landlords and to cause the minimum of disruption to the economy, were interpreted as proof of malevolent insincerity on the part of the government. The hostility which the regime had deservedly bred in the past under Nicholas I was now recoiling upon it at a time when it genuinely sought to improve. This inimical attitude was aggravated by the severe repression of peasant disturbances (caused, as usual, by rumours that the 'real' emancipation was being frustrated by the landlords) in which the familiar floggings and other violent means were used. And so, in the summer of 1861, 'Land and Liberty', the first revolutionary organization since the abortive Decembrist movement of 1825, came into existence.

The title derived from an article by Herzen's friend and collaborator in London, N. P. Ogarev, and had been written by him in consultation with several of the founders of the new conspiratorial centre. It was published in the *Bell* on 1 July 1861, some four to five months after the Emancipation Manifesto. 'What do the people need?' was its title, and the opening sentence read: 'Very simple. The people need land and liberty.' The article contained a full revolutionary programme.[5] There had, apparently, been some earlier plans for organizing a peasant rising to coincide with the publication of the Manifesto, which some Soviet historians suggest (unconvincingly) emerged from the meeting between Herzen and

Chernyshevsky in London in 1859.[6] When these plans failed, the
organization which called itself 'Land and Liberty' set 1863 as the
new target date for an uprising. Their conspiracies were secret, and
indeed very little is known about them even today. But in the course
of the eighteen months which followed upon the Act of Emancipation there was enough revolutionary activity to cause the government to panic, to alarm its moderate, liberal supporters and to exhi-
larate the less temperate radicals.

In July 1861, the first of a series of pamphlets, entitled 'The Great
Russian', was secretly but widely circulated. It purported to emanate
from a committee (as indeed it did), and in the course of the series
of three issues laid down in detail a plan for the future transformation
of Russia on democratic lines, after a successful peasant uprising
planned for 1863. Its programme included a demand for a constitutional monarchy or a republic, radical agrarian reforms, basic
civil freedoms, responsible government, religious tolerance, and the
right of self-determination for the non-Russian components of the
Empire, including Poland and the Ukraine. There is ample evidence
of the close influence of Chernyshevsky on the policy advocated by
'The Great Russian'.[7]

The pamphlet's first issue was followed by other proclamations,
notably one entitled 'To the Young Generation', circulated in September 1861, and another called 'Young Russia' in the summer of
1862. The co-author of the former, M. I. Mikhailov, was sentenced
to six years' penal servitude. This, together with his courageous conduct at his trial, evoked a good deal of sympathy in liberal circles,
who strongly disapproved of the revolutionary methods advocated
by the pamphlet, but believed in the need for freedom to express
all views. Turgenev, who had been on quite friendly terms with
Mikhailov, was distressed by the outcome of the trial and among
others, subscribed some money for him.[8] 'Young Russia' was the
most violent in tone of all the proclamations, calling for open battle,
axe in hand, in the streets and in the villages.[9] All this must be seen
against the growing background of unrest, not only in Russia proper,
but in Poland (then, of course, part of Russia), where preparations
were being made for what would culminate in the rising of 1863.
There was growing student unrest in several Russian universities, and
St. Petersburg University was closed by decree on 21 December,
though, as Nikitenko recorded in his diary, it had already been shut
down by the students themselves who had refused to attend lectures.

On 24 May 1862 four fires broke out simultaneously in several
parts of St. Petersburg. The general public was convinced that these

fires were the work of the 'nihilists'. (The word, revived by Turgenev in *Fathers and Children*, had rapidly gained popular currency. In later years Turgenev regretted that he had provided the 'reactionary bastards' with this label for the radicals.)[10] To this day the origin of the fires is unknown; Soviet historians quite plausibly, though without evidence, attribute them to police provocation, but they might well have been accidental. The government reacted promptly and sternly although the Emperor refused to accede to a popular clamour for capital punishment. In June the Sunday schools were closed down and the *Contemporary* suspended for eight months – 'the proper reaction to the senseless and vile deeds committed by our reds' was the not untypical comment of a liberal observer, Nikitenko.[11] In July 1862, the Third Department, on the basis of a denunciation, arrested P. A. Vetoshnikov on his arrival in Russia bearing letters from Herzen, Ogarev, Bakunin, and others. This was to form the beginning of a vast and lengthy inquiry by a Senate Commission, of which the evidence in eight volumes fills over three thousand pages. The inquiry was directed at uncovering links between the Russian revolutionaries and the London radicals, headed by Herzen.* The inquiry was concluded in December 1864, and ended with sentences of varying severity.[12]

Chernyshevsky, also implicated in the Third Department's 'windfall', was arrested in July 1862 and a long investigation began into his connections with revolutionaries both in Russia and in London, which ended in a heavy sentence of imprisonment and exile. While it was the case that some of the evidence adduced against him by the Third Department was forged,[13] the widespread view that Chernyshevsky was a publicist and not a revolutionary is only partly true: he advocated (within the limits of censorship) revolution in the *Contemporary* after 1861 and was a constant influence on the nascent movement. It is a curious fact of history that his greatest mark on the future of Russia was made by his novel *What is to be Done?*, written while in prison and published in the *Contemporary* early in 1863. But this novel was intended as a retort to *Fathers and Children*, and will therefore be discussed later.

The Russian security authorities saw the key to the whole of their problem of dealing with the rising tide of violence as lying in the persons of the most prominent London exiles, Herzen and Ogarev. This was only true in part, although there is no doubt that their influence, through the *Bell* and through personal contacts, was enormous.

* It also involved, as will be seen later, Turgenev, who figured in the correspondence found on Vetoshnikov.

Unlike Herzen, Ogarev was not inhibited by any apprehension that revolution might lead to excesses which would nullify its achievements. As the publication of his papers many years after his death revealed, he had in some respects anticipated the very forms of the organizational underpinning of revolutionary activity for which Lenin was later to become famous. Herzen was rather more ambivalent in his attitude: his hesitation in the pages of the *Bell* on the extent of welcome to be accorded to the more violent manifestations in St. Petersburg brought about a decline in his popularity among the 'progressive' youth of Russia, and earned him the pejorative epithet of 'liberal.★ But Herzen's 'liberalism' should not be exaggerated. Many of the blood-thirsty proclamations of 1861 and 1862 were, in fact, printed in London on the presses controlled by him; and the appearance of the appeal to Young Russia, which called for streets running with blood, was defended by him in the *Bell*, albeit critically.[14] On the other hand, as a populist Herzen believed in a revolution made by the people in its own time, when it had grown to sufficient maturity. But he was very sceptical about any revolution accomplished by an élite of intellectual leaders purporting to act in the name of the people. As he wrote to Bakunin towards the end of his life: 'One cannot liberate a people externally more than they have liberated themselves *internally*.'[15]

The wholly intransigent determination of the government to refuse to allow any kind of modification of the autocratic system of rule also did little to moderate the conviction of the radicals, and of Herzen, that liberal support of the Emperor in his reform policies was doomed to failure. For example, shortly after the Emancipation Act, in 1861, a group of thirteen members of the Tver nobility petitioned the Emperor to set up an assembly of elected deputies in order to deal fairly with the complex problems involved in putting the Act into practice. They were seized and imprisoned for some months in the fortress of St. Peter and St. Paul.

Turgenev, who had never supported revolution, was faced with no such dilemma as Herzen. But the growing divergence between his views on the Russian situation and those of Herzen did not, at this stage, affect their friendship. Turgenev's letters to Herzen are warm and sympathetic, as often as he found he could support the vigorous assaults on the many dark sides of Russian government: Herzen's letters to Turgenev are friendly, although often tinged with

★ Chernyshevsky, after visiting him in London in 1859, had already then described him to Dobroliubov as 'Kavelin squared' – no greater opprobrium from Chernyshevsky was conceivable.

a certain patronizing irony. The breach between them would only come about both as the result of a long-drawn dispute on historical and sociological questions and of Herzen's attack on Turgenev for what he believed to be his cowardice in giving evidence before the Senate Commission of Inquiry in 1863. (See Chapter 12.) Turgenev's hostility to Ogarev was a different matter, and already in April 1861 Herzen asked Turgenev to reveal what had happened to upset their relations.[16] Turgenev, who always shunned explanations of this nature, and in any case probably did not wish to hurt Herzen, did not at the time reply.

This, then, was the political background against which *Fathers and Children* was conceived and completed. The first mention that a scheme for a new novel was forming in his head came in a letter to Countess Lambert, of 6 August 1860, from Ventnor on the Isle of Wight,[17] where Turgenev and Annenkov were deeply engaged in drafting the Programme about public education. By 30 September the plan of *Fathers and Children* had been worked out 'down to the smallest detail' and had been approved by Botkin.[18] But work on the new book did not proceed very fast and advanced in short rapid spurts, with long interruptions. About half was finished during the winter of 1860–1, in Paris. Then, after an interval, he wrote the second half in Spasskoe between May and July 1861; the date of completion was variously stated by the author himself to have been 20 July, 30 July, and 'August'.[19] Soon after, there began the familiar subjection of the manuscript to the verdict of friends and acquaintances. It was delivered to Katkov in Moscow for publication in his journal, *Russian Herald*, at the end of August 1861, with the injunction that it should be given to Annenkov for comment before publication; Annenkov only sent his detailed analysis (which considerably influenced the subsequent revision of the text) to Turgenev in Paris on 26 September 1861. There were also other comments. Katkov saw the novel as a panegyric in favour of the revolutionaries. Countess Lambert found the hero, Bazarov, very antipathetic. On the other hand, a group of friends which included Botkin, to whom the novel was read after Turgenev's return to Paris from Russia, were warmly in favour of it.

The story opens with the arrival of two students – Arkadii Kirsanov and his friend Bazarov – on a visit at the country estate of Kirsanov's widowed father. The father is a kindly, affectionate, and ineffectual member of the landed gentry, who mismanages his modest estate. There is a clear echo of Turgenev's own difficulties with his peasants in the description in Chapter 22 of Kirsanov's tribulations in running his patrimony. Since his wife's death he has formed an attachment with a peasant girl, who has borne him a son. The girl is yet another of those Russian women, so deeply moving in their simplicity and charm, whom only Turgenev knew how to depict. The household is completed by Arkadii's uncle – a foppish Anglophile, whose life has been pointless and frustrated, and who is irritable, ironical, and intolerant. Bazarov, a medical student, was intended to represent the 'new men and women' who, under the influence of the *Contemporary* and especially of Dobroliubov, were becoming the idols of the thinking younger generation. Bazarov and Arkadii are, in their own words 'nihilists', which means that they accept nothing on authority, and subject every proposition to the test of practical reason.★ A considerable number of the conversations recorded in the book are devoted to expounding Bazarov's views.

The first part of the novel illuminates the conflict between Bazarov (and the 'new men and women' generally) and the brothers Kirsanov and what they stand for – hence the title. The next part of the story introduces what is probably the main moral – that in the conflict between extreme theoretical radical views and human nature, it is nature that wins. This is brought out by the author in two ways. First, when Bazarov falls in love with a widow, Odintsova, in spite of his anti-romantic and materialistic theories on relations between the sexes. Secondly, in the final parting between Arkadii and Bazarov which comes about with Arkadii's realization that his infatuation for Bazarov and his beliefs was a passing phase which did not reflect the things which he really valued in life – love, marriage, children, and family. The third part of the novel is concerned mainly with Bazarov's attitude to his simple, lovable, slightly ridiculous parents, and with his death. Bazarov's father is a retired army doctor, owner of a minuscule estate: his mother, an uneducated, superstitious daughter of the minor Russian nobility of the turn of the century, completely devoted to her son, her husband, and her household. Bazarov's death symbolizes much of Russian life as Turgenev saw it; it is caused by an infection contracted through a cut sustained in performing an autopsy at a country doctor's. This proves fatal only because this primitive practitioner was not equipped with the elementary means of dealing immediately with the wound.

The book ends with one of the most touching passages ever

★ Turgenev did not invent the term, as sometimes asserted, but revived a dormant word which served as a condemnatory label for all crude materialism. The first use of the word in the sense of someone who no longer believes in anything seems to have been by M. N. Katkov in an article written in 1840.

written by Turgenev, and one of his most religious. It describes the old parents praying and weeping at the grave of their only son.

Can it be that their prayers and tears are fruitless? Can it be that love, holy, devoted love is not all-powerful? Oh, no! Whatever the passionate, sinful, and rebellious heart that has been covered by the grave, the flowers that grow on it look on at us serenely with their innocent eyes. They do not speak to us only of eternal peace, of that great peace of 'indifferent' nature: they speak also of eternal reconciliation and of the life everlasting. ...*

Turgenev was well aware at the outset that in painting what he believed to be a fair picture of the young radicals and their parents, he would offend both the conservative and the revolutionary camps: the former demanding a portrayal in black and white of the old order as perfect, and the revolutionaries (everyone knew that Bazarov was a revolutionary, though it is nowhere even hinted at) as villains, the latter expecting the exact opposite. Awareness of these attitudes, together with the rapidly increasing political excitement inside Russia which followed the emancipation, explains the meticulous working to which the author subjected his novel. There were, in the main, three such processes of revision – two of the fair copy of the manuscript completed in the summer of 1861 for its publication in Katkov's journal, and a third for its first appearance in volume form in September 1862.

Comparison between the fair copy of the 1861 manuscript and as it was later altered and added to for publication shows that Annenkov's detailed criticism had resulted in several modifications. Two of the additions reveal considerable political subtlety, which Turgenev, no doubt, appreciated. In one of the arguments between Uncle Paul Kirsanov and Bazarov, in which the radical, if somewhat ironically and contemptuously, expounds his views, Paul retorts: 'Strength! The wild Kalmuk and the Mongol have strength – but what is that to us? It is civilization which is dear to us'[20] – words which epitomize the conflict between the Russia of the landed gentry, and the coming reign of the masses. Another passage which was added shows Bazarov cynically welcoming the services of an intellectually contemptible follower: 'I need oafs like him. It is not for the Gods, surely, to fire the pots!'[21] Here again, Annenkov had correctly discerned the élitism of the 'nihilist' radicals of the sixties, which was in marked contrast to the humility before the wisdom of the peasants which was to characterize most of the populists of

---

* 'Indifferent' nature is an echo of Pushkin: 'eternal reconciliation' and 'the life everlasting' are reminiscences of the Orthodox service for the dead.

the next decade, whom Turgenev described in his last novel, *Virgin Soil*. The remaining alterations made in response to Annenkov's comments were designed to improve the characterization of Odintsova, (such as the long paragraph analysing her character in Chapter 16), and of Bazarov's feelings for her. It was also on Annenkov's advice that an epigraph which originally figured in the manuscript was omitted: 'Young man to middle-aged man: "You had contents without strength." Middle-aged man: "And you have strength without contents."' It is not clear what Annenkov's reasons were.[22]

It was also from Annenkov that Turgenev heard that Katkov was appalled by the work, which he regarded (with singular lack of perspicacity) as the 'apotheosis of the *Contemporary*'. All the evidence suggests that the political views of Turgenev and Katkov had completely diverged by 1861: for all his detestation of revolutionary activity, Turgenev the artist refused to see the two sides of the dispute, the radicals and the government, in stark black and white contrast, while as a liberal he could sympathize with the motives of the radicals even while disapproving of their methods. ('The news from Russia distresses me,' he wrote to Countess Lambert from Paris at the height of the political unrest, on 10 December 1861. 'It is impossible for me in many respects not to blame my friends, but I cannot exonerate the government either.')[23]

Since Katkov's letters to Turgenev covering the relevant months have disappeared, we cannot know which alterations introduced between the manuscript stage and the published text were the result of Katkov's criticisms.[24] Besides, Turgenev was well aware that the political climate, and particularly the attitude of the censors in the last months of the year, coloured by the growing unrest and radical activity, made it inauspicious to publish the novel in 1861, and it was at his request that publication was delayed by Katkov for a few months, until March 1862.[25] Some of the alterations which appear on the original manuscript may well have been due, therefore, to apprehension about the reaction of the censorship rather than to Katkov's suggestions. Many of the minor alterations which tend to make Bazarov less human, grimmer, in some respects even occasionally slightly ridiculous (as, for example, in the scene in Chapter 27 where he totally fails to reach any common ground in his conversations with some peasants), can be interpreted as wishing to mollify the censor; but they could also have been the result of Katkov's comments. Again, in preparing the first edition of the novel in book form, Turgenev inserted several details which tended to underline Bazarov's humanity, tender-heartedness almost – as, for example, in the deathbed scene with Odintsova when he says to her, 'And be gentle to my mother. You won't find people like them [i.e. his parents] in broad daylight with a lamp.' Other alterations seem on the contrary to be designed to remove all traces of sentimentality from Bazarov: as Turgenev wrote to Herzen, 'It would have been easy to portray him as ideal; to portray him as a wolf and yet to justify him was difficult.'[26]

Turgenev's primary motive for the numerous alterations was, as always, his meticulous concern to make his characters convincing as human beings. Apart from suggesting changes, there is no doubt that Katkov actually made some in the published text without consulting the author. His public denial of this, in 1874, threw Turgenev into a fury.[27] However, comparison between the text as published in the *Russian Herald* and the reworked fair copy of the manuscript in the Bibliothèque Nationale in Paris, does not suggest that the alterations made were very extensive.[28]

Turgenev was so much absorbed in the character he had created that, while engaged in writing *Fathers and Children*, he kept a diary in the name of Bazarov, in which he recorded day by day his hero's reactions to literary, political, and social events. The 'very substantial notebook' which resulted was lent to a friend – and, predictably, lost.[29] Of his deep sympathy for Bazarov no fair-minded reader could be in doubt. ('My favourite offspring, over whom I finally quarrelled with Katkov', he wrote in 1874.)[30] If further proof were required of Turgenev's admiration for Bazarov (of which he wrote and spoke repeatedly) it is surely to be found in his dedication of the novel on its first publication in volume form to the memory of Belinsky. But the young radicals were not fair-minded, and saw nothing but a vicious caricature, variously interpreted as intended to lampoon Chernyshevsky or Dobroliubov. The *Contemporary*, aware of the contents of the novel even before publication, came out with a vulgar, intemperate and, from a literary point of view, grotesque attack by its critic M. A. Antonovich, entitled 'The Asmodeus of our Time'. (The article even hinted at Turgenev's relations with Pauline Viardot.) This was published in its March issue – that is to say, within only a week or two of the appearance of the second number of the *Russian Herald*. Asmodeus, a super-demon in Jewish tradition, was meant to be Bazarov, as the author of the article explains, most unconvincingly. The general views of Antonovich were fairly representative of the young radicals who, with one notable exception, had no good word for *Fathers and Children*, and, for full measure, believed the wild rumours that Turgenev had plotted with Katkov to besmirch the fair name of their idols, Chernyshevsky and Dobroliubov.[31] The exception was D. I. Pisarev, writing in *Russkoe slovo*, and, as he later wrote to Turgenev, expressing his own views with which none of his colleagues agreed.[32]

Pisarev was no revolutionary: he believed that Russia could only be transformed by the emergence of an intellectual élite, and he saw in Bazarov the prototype of this élite, which he believed would emerge from the midst of the common people. Above all, he discovered that Turgenev's sympathies lay wholly with the uncouth, but intellectually honest and devoted nihilist, rather than with the more polished, but completely ineffectual, brothers Kirsanov. In his summary of the moral of the novel, he says: 'The young people of today become enthusiastic and fall into extremes, but in their very enthusiasms are to be discovered fresh strength and incorruptible spirit. This strength and this spirit ... will lead these young people on to the right path.'[33] Pisarev, who despised art for its lack of practical value, was careful to point out that his interest in Turgenev's novel was purely utilitarian. Bazarov was a useful model for the young, none of Pushkin's heroes was, therefore Turgenev was good, and Pushkin bad, so far as Pisarev was concerned.[34]

Subsequently, in 1867, Pisarev and Turgenev met and, as Turgenev's letters show, the young man made a very good impression on him. Pisarev was a member of the gentry, which no doubt helped![35] There was a further reason for the sympathy between the two men: Pisarev was a fellow Westerner. He was also a strong opponent both of the idealization of the peasants by the populists, and of what Turgenev later described as 'the romanticism of realism', in other words the search for 'something great and significant in reality ... which is nonsense: real life is prosaic and must be such'. Bazarov, he continued, has something of this kind of romanticism in him – as Pisarev alone discerned.[36] The novel did not fare much better at the hands of critics from the 'right' who usually felt that Bazarov, as a 'nihilist', had not been shown up sufficiently as a monster. It was not easy in 1862 for Russians to judge their literature objectively. Debates on the character of Bazarov have continued ever since.

While no serious attention need be paid to scurrilous attacks of the kind produced by Antonovich, there is no doubt that the general outlook of Bazarov recalls in many respects the views of Chernyshevsky and Dobroliubov. Like Chernyshevsky, Bazarov is a materialist: like Dobroliubov, he judges the value of works of art solely by their practical utility. As a 'nihilist' he regards his function as purely destructive, to clear the ground from fetishes and prejudices which have had their day; as to what will be built on the levelled ground, that is the concern of those who come after him. Like Chernyshevsky (and Bazarov's utterances can be matched by exactly parallel quotations from Chernyshevsky's writings), he denies the need to study individuals as distinct from society: 'People are like trees in a wood: no botanist will spend his time studying each individual birch tree.' Or again: 'Ill health is simply the result of bad education or of social conditions: improve society and there will be no more disease.' These examples could be multiplied. Bazarov's preoccupation with scientific study, usually exemplified in his insatiable pursuit of frogs in the course of the novel for the purpose of dissection, accurately reflects, as memoirs of the period show, the absorption of the young generation of the sixties with the natural sciences,[37] and a number of distinguished scientists of the 1860s believed Bazarov to be a 'paragon of a new realism built upon science'.[38]

Whatever Turgenev may have borrowed from the writings of Chernyshevsky or Dobroliubov, Bazarov is neither of these men. On several occasions Turgenev himself referred to a young provincial doctor, whom he met on a train and with whom he had a long discussion, as the prototype of Bazarov.[39] But this search for models is likely to prove fruitless because Turgenev, although he invariably composed his characters from life, made them a synthesis of many observations. It is, above all, Bazarov the man who dominates the story, and shines through the rough, cynical, almost brutal exterior to give artistic life to a novel which could so easily have become a dull tract for the times. Turgenev is really absorbed with the human predicament of Bazarov – his views are only incidental. For if one thing emerges clearly from the novel it is that politics and political views are transient – only life and its true values persist for all time. Bazarov's pointless and untimely death fits in with this; it underlines the ephemeral, unimportant nature of Bazarov's philosophy: what matters are the eternal values – love and death. Readers of 'Hamlet and Don Quixote' will find this view of Bazarov self-evident. It will also be obvious to them that Turgenev loved and admired Bazarov for his Don Quixote-like qualities – his integrity, his will, his courage, his relentless pursuit of truth. Compared with these, errors of view were to Turgenev of minor concern. In contrast, the gentry portrayed in the novel are, though kindly, completely ineffectual. But if Bazarov too was wrong, where then did the future of Russia lie? Perhaps the lady who once commented to Turgenev that the novel should have been entitled *Neither Fathers nor Children* was right.

According to Turgenev, only two people understood the intended message of Bazarov: Botkin and Dostoevsky.[40] We know that Botkin admired the work, but do not know the reasons for his admiration. In Dostoevsky's case, the letter containing his comments is lost, but we can guess something of his views of Bazarov from a later article in which he wrote disparagingly of the attacks on Turgenev's character, 'that unquiet and wistful Bazarov (the sign of a great heart), in spite of all his nihilism'. Something of his views can also be gleaned from Turgenev's letter thanking him for his comments.[41] Herzen missed the point of the book, notwithstanding his admiration for it, by accusing Turgenev of having been too obsessed with Chernyshevsky when he wrote it. He also found the last paragraph 'dangerous' – on the verge of 'mysticism'.[42] Turgenev in reply denied the charge of 'mysticism', which in Herzen's terminology meant any kind of religious feeling. Yet the paragraph quoted earlier speaks for itself.

Kropotkin in his *Memoirs* probably gives the real reason why Bazarov failed to please the young generation: they could not be satisfied 'with the merely negative attitude of Turgenev's hero. Nihilism ... was but a first step toward a higher type of men and women who ... live for a great cause. In the nihilists of Chernyshevsky, as they are depicted in his far less artistic novel *What is to be Done?*, they saw better portraits of themselves.'[43]

The young generation, which felt alienated from the landed gentry, probably also sensed something of Turgenev's attitude as a writer, and deplored it: 'I never wrote for the people', he asserted in 1863. 'I wrote for that class of the public to which I belong, beginning with *Sketches from a Sportsman's Notebook* and ending with *Fathers and Children.*'[44]

Chernyshevsky's dreadful book, with its wooden and at times almost ludicrous depiction of the 'new men and women', was written in prison, and published in the *Contemporary* in 1863. (Turgenev's comment on *What is to be Done?* was quite immoderately scathing – but apt.)[45] There is no doubt that it influenced and inspired young radicals for the next twenty or thirty years: the young Ulianov (Lenin), for example, read it in 1887, under the impact of the execution of his elder brother, and it 'ploughed him over', in his own words, as recorded by a friend.[46] Unlike Bazarov, Rakhmetov the hero of *What is to be Done?* is a kind of comic-strip superman, with no weaknesses or waverings. The heroine abandons her bourgeois background to embrace free love and to found a sewing commune. Her like-minded noble male companions are similarly selfless and self-denying, with but one aim – socialism. They can only, like Vera with her sewing commune, achieve the first steps: the real transformation, it is understood, will be the work of supermen, like Rakhmetov, when the time comes. They are the new men and women, the harbingers of that Utopia on earth the dream of which was now to absorb so many of the younger generation of Russians. For them the age of Onegin, Pechorin, Rudin was over: the time now called for Rakhmetovs who would accomplish the great transformation, instead of just talking or dreaming about it – with consequences that no one in the sixties foresaw. They had little use for Bazarov who, for all his fine talk, still remained a victim of such outmoded vanities as falling in love – or, for that matter, dying of a trivial infection.

Above all, they could not forgive Turgenev for making Bazarov less than perfect in every respect. We find in memoirs of the sixties some typical comments of the younger generation on *Fathers and Children* and its author: 'Of course, he stays abroad, entranced by the singing of his Viardot, and has ceased to understand what is happening in Russia.' Or, 'It would be difficult to make up a more vicious slander. Bazarov, this representative of the younger generation is a glutton, a drunkard, a gambler who is even proud of his vile character. . . .' Or, 'He is represented as a vulgar male animal, who cannot keep his hands off any presentable woman' – and much more on the same lines.[47] Such were the reactions of the generation of radicals, of whom Chernyshevsky's characters in his novel were typical, who believed with unparalleled priggishness not only in the rightness of their radical ideas, but in the necessary and indisputable purity and asceticism of those who professed them.

However, there were also more moderate critics of Turgenev's Bazarov, and it is possible that he missed in his novel one dimension of the conflict between fathers and children in the early sixties. This was the rejection by the children of the moral and ethical standards of the fathers; Turgenev's fathers were ineffectual, but much too nice for this question to arise between them and their sons. But centuries of corruption and absence of legal standards had left a heavy mark on many members of the Russian nobility which the Emancipation Act was not going to remove at a stroke. The younger generation, apart from their nihilism and hankering after revolution, were often impelled to their revolt by a longing for such new standards as marriage for love and without regard for questions of social status or family fortune, equality of sexes, or human relations based on honesty and not on calculation. This aspect of the generational conflict is well brought out in a play called *Out of the Past*, written in prison, probably in 1864, by N. A. Serno-Solovievich, but only very recently published. This remarkable young man, although one of the founders of the Land and Liberty movement in 1861, was in fact, as his surviving writings show, probably more an advocate of far-reaching constitutional and social reforms within the framework of monarchy than an all-or-nothing revolutionary.

The play is concerned with an ugly family intrigue aimed at preventing the younger son from marrying the girl of his choice, who is illegitimate and penniless. In the end the young man is outwitted and falls a victim to his own weakness; but his sister, Olga, vindicates the honour of the 'children' by renouncing her family and going off – presumably to join a revolutionary group. The play includes a radical, Basov, whose views (and name) are very similar to Bazarov's, but Basov is more moderate and less inflexible in his views than Turgenev's hero. There is a very revealing discussion in the play between Basov and Olga, which shows that what the younger generation resented in *Fathers and Children* was Turgenev's lack of faith in the 'new men and women', though incidentally, Basov does not suggest that the 'new men and women' had much confidence in themselves:

After all, Turgenev is among our best people, but he christened as 'nihilist' a man who scarcely reached twenty years of age, and found death in his science. Those are the kind of surroundings in which we live. ... Either thought will devour us or prison rot us. ... If you want to live, go and crawl, commit all kinds of baseness, lie, become a slave and a cheat. Our fathers dreamed their whole lives away without once hearing the question: what is the difference between a slave and a free man?[48]

Perhaps, after all, Turgenev was out of touch with the 'children'.

CHAPTER TWELVE

Happiness in Baden

In 1863 the Viardots decided to leave France and to make their permanent home in Baden-Baden, a fashionable German watering place, in the midst of the Black Forest country. Pauline's voice was beginning to deteriorate (although she was only forty), and this persuaded her to break with the Paris Opera and the other great musical centres, and to confine her appearances for the next ten years to the smaller German theatres, and to concerts. Louis's increasing dislike for the political regime in France was another reason for the move. The Viardots built themselves a villa on the outskirts of Baden, and before long Pauline's house became one of the important social centres which attracted visitors of great distinction from many parts of Europe. There was much music performed in the concert hall built in the grounds of the villa, while the carriages of the eminent guests lined the street outside – including, at different times, the King and Queen of Prussia, Bismarck, the Empress Eugénie, the Grand Duke of Baden, the Queen of Holland, the Duchess of Hamilton, along with numerous Russians, both aristocratic and more humble. Clara Schumann when she settled in Baden, and Brahms, who established himself there in order to be near her, were frequent visitors, along with many other musicians. The brilliant musical occasions were depicted in numerous sketches and described in his memoirs by the German artist and littérateur, Ludwig Pietsch, a close friend of the Viardots and of Turgenev. Turgenev had first met him in Berlin in 1846 and saw him frequently thereafter at the Viardots', but the two men only became close friends after the move to Baden.[1] The rising star in music, Wagner, was also received at the Viardot household.[2] Pauline eventually became a 'Wagnerite to my fingertips ... the only music which interests me'. Turgenev was rather reticent on the subject: Wagner's music, he wrote to her, called for an effort in order to understand it – he was the founder of the 'school of groaning' in art.[3] It was a polite way of saying that he loathed it. He frequently said so more openly to others – 'The music and the text are equally unbearable' was his comment on the first performance of *Das Rheingold* in Munich. But he had to be cautious with Pauline who regarded herself as the sole arbiter on musical taste, even to the extent of excising some of Turgenev's judgements on composers when eventually she edited a selection of his letters to her for publication.

The previous year, 1862, had been marked by a change in Pauline's attitude towards Turgenev. Perhaps as she grew older she felt more need for the support of a friend of nearly twenty years' standing, whose devotion had never faltered. Turgenev readily accepted the limited role of family intimate that was now accorded him. Three letters (out of at least four) which he wrote from Russia in the early summer of 1862 reveal all the epistolary characteristics of the period when their love affair was at its height; the German phrases of endearment, the easy conversational style and detailed description of his life, and his love for her children, especially Claudie, or Didie as she was called. The one letter which Pauline wrote to him during this period which has been published shows that on her side as well many of the old feelings had revived; she reproaches him petulantly with having written to Madame Markovich ('Your fat Little Russian') before writing to her and Louis. These recently published letters[4] are probably only a fraction of their total correspondence at this period.

In the summer of 1862 the Viardots were in Baden-Baden, arranging for the building of their villa and planning the details of their removal. Turgenev travelled direct from Spasskoe to Baden, where he arrived on 21 August and stayed until 26 October. It was a very happy time, for he loved the countryside, he was constantly in the company of the Viardot family, and his health was better than it had been for a very long time.

It was, one presumes, during this trial visit that Turgenev decided to follow the Viardots, and to settle in Baden. He moved there on 3 May 1863, together with Paulinette and Mrs. Innes, and found quarters which were to be his home for the next few years. This was the upper storey of a two-floored house in 277 (later 17, now numbered 7) Schillerstrasse, within a few minutes' walk of the Viardot villa in Thiergartenstrasse (now Fremersburgstrasse). The house (recently demolished), which recalled a Russian summer-house in style, stood in a courtyard off the road, and was modest in character. It was owned by an oven-maker called Anstett, who inhabited the ground floor with his wife. Frau Anstett looked after Turgenev with motherly care, and he retained great affection for her long after he had left her house to move into his grand villa in 1868.

Everything suggests that the years which he spent in Baden were indeed the happiest in his life. The shooting was good, the country-side lovely, and there was a profusion of brilliant social and musical occasions and also a great deal of private music at the Viardot household. There were regular concerts on Sunday mornings, which Turgenev helped to organize. Several programmes for these Sunday occasions in the spring of 1866 have survived, written in Turgenev's hand. Each included songs by Pauline, occasionally one of her own settings of a Russian poem.[5] On 10 March a 'Petite Suite pour piano, violon, tambourin et triangle', composed by Pauline was performed by her at the piano with her young son Paul at the violin and her two little girls, then aged about fourteen and twelve, in charge of the percussion.[6] The Viardot children, particularly Didie, were an unending delight to Turgenev. Friendship both with Pauline and with Louis was close and affectionate. Turgenev also acquired a dog, Pegasus, whose retrieving talents became legendary, and who was well-known in Baden.*

Baden very much suited Turgenev's health and apart from occasional references to bouts of minor indisposition, there are few complaints about illness in his letters. No doubt the fact that he was happy had a good deal to do with this. His only ailment was the reappearance in 1863, of his old bladder trouble in the form of an inflamed prostate, which disabled him for a number of weeks – 'no good thinking of shooting or champagne or crumpet – but as far as this last is concerned, the devil can take it'.[9]

Paulinette's presence in Baden was not a success. The antipathy between her and Pauline Viardot resulted in painful scenes, in which Turgenev, invariably, took Pauline's side. Many years later, he blamed the 'stupid and hidebound' Mrs. Innes for Paulinette's beha-viour towards Pauline – how justly is another matter.[10] So Paulinette and Mrs. Innes returned to Paris – first to their old address at 210 rue

* He must indeed have been an exceptionally talented gun dog, if one considers the great variety of game he was called upon to deal with – for example, on one occasion, '1 wild goat, 1 hare, 1 wild cat, 1 pheasant, 1 woodcock and 1 partridge.'[7] He was a cross between an English setter and a German Schaefer. In 1871, when Pegasus was already 'pensioned off', his master wrote a glowing account of his prowess, which was published as a pamphlet a few years later.[8] Pegasus, however, had an unfortunate trait. In general he showed great favour to women and invari-ably growled at men, but he made one very tactless exception: he detested Pauline Viardot, and did not conceal this fact. Strange to say this does not seem to have diminished his master's regard for him.

de Rivoli, and thereafter to a smaller apartment in Passy, at 10 rue Basse, where they remained until Paulinette's marriage in 1865. The match was brought about by the efforts of an old friend, Madame Valentine Delessert, who had taken a kindly interest in Paulinette. The man who won her heart when they met at the end of 1864, was twenty-nine-year-old Gaston Bruère, of French bourgeois stock, who was manager of a large glass factory owned by Madame Delessert's son-in-law. The young man was 'very calm and simple, not talkative, a little cold and in appearance like the late Prince Albert'.[11] The engagement delighted Turgenev, but added to his financial difficulties. He had spent the money put by for Paulinette's dowry. He had also bought some land in Baden in June 1864 – between seven and eight acres adjoining the Viardots' villa. He intended to begin building the following spring, and had already started to have the garden laid out.[12] The Viardots, ever generous, came to his rescue with a substantial loan.[13] Turgenev's financial position was aggravated by his uncle's mismanagement of his estate and his dilatoriness in realizing the compensation to which, as a former serf owner, he was entitled under the Emancipation Act. Turgenev's habitual extravagance did not help. The dowry agreed for his daughter consisted of 100,000 francs to be paid on marriage, and a further 50,000 francs within a few years.[14] The 50,000 was paid over, in instalments, by the autumn of 1873.[15] He paid interest on the capital which remained owing. By one means and another the harassed father succeeded in raising the money, though he was to remain in difficulties for years afterwards, and very often in debt. In addition to the dowry, he gave his daughter a piano,[16] so he cannot be said to have acted ungenerously.

Because of Paulinette's illegitimacy, for some months before the marriage Turgenev was much occupied with the problem of obtaining the elaborate documentation which was required by French law. Shortly before the wedding the bride was received into the Catholic Church. Turgenev insisted that this ceremony should be kept as secret as possible, though it is not clear why.[17] The civil marriage took place on 23 February 1865 at the Mairie in Passy; the religious solemnization followed two days later in the Church of Notre Dame de Grâce, also in Passy. Turgenev was convinced of his daughter's future happiness: 'I have never seen a face so radiantly happy as hers in church during the ceremony,' he wrote to Annenkov.[18] Alas, things were to turn out very differently; but early reports of the marriage were encouraging, in spite of Paulinette's miscarriage in October.

Life in Baden and Paulinette's marriage were the happy sides of the years which followed the publication of *Fathers and Children* in the spring of 1862. But there was enough to harass Turgenev – the worsening of relations with Herzen and Ogarev, a senatorial inquiry into his political contacts, and finally the breach with Herzen. He had left unanswered, it will be recalled, Herzen's request in April 1861 for the cause of his estrangement from Ogarev, and his friendship with Herzen, as suggested by their voluminous correspondence, remained for the time being unimpaired. Around the middle of May Turgenev went to London for three days to talk to Herzen before leaving for Russia. While there he also met his close friend of student days, Michael Bakunin, for whom by now he had an affectionate contempt. Bakunin, who had recently escaped from imprisonment in Siberia was, as usual, penniless and in debt, and Turgenev had organized a fund for his support and contributed 500 francs to it.[19] Bakunin's wife was in Irkutsk, and he was very anxious that she should come to England to join him. When Turgenev met Bakunin briefly in London in May, he agreed to help by arranging for Madame Bakunin to move from Irkutsk to the Bakunin estate in Tver province – an undertaking which required the consent of the Russian authorities, the co-operation of the Bakunin family, and money. On his visit to Russia in the summer of 1862 Turgenev successfully overcame all these difficulties, though it called for considerable effort – not least in persuading the Bakunin relatives to co-operate (two of the Bakunin brothers were locked up in the fortress of St. Peter and St. Paul for their participation in the appeal of the Tver nobility to the Emperor in 1861, and Turgenev had to obtain permission to visit them there). Two letters from Bakunin to Turgenev have survived, warm in their thanks and assuring him that despite political differences the old feelings still survived on Bakunin's side, the only political opponent of whom he was prepared to say this.[20] Turgenev for his part assured Bakunin that he could rely on the ties of old friendship between them, 'which, thank God, are independent of all political outlooks'.[21] Madame Bakunin did reach London eventually. But gratitude did not deter Bakunin from blackening Turgenev's character to all and sundry.

On his short visit to London, Turgenev had engaged in lengthy argument with Herzen on the nature and future of Russian society. The result of this debate was a series of eight articles by Herzen, entitled 'Ends and Beginnings', cast in the form of open letters to a friend, published in the *Bell* in the second half of 1862.[22] Turgenev originally intended to print his reply in the same journal, but in

consequence of a general warning from the Russian authorities not to
write for that paper, thought better of it. Turgenev's views in the
debate therefore appear in his private letters to Herzen of the period,
and in summaries of his arguments incorporated in Herzen's articles.
Herzen's open letters, written with the brilliance and exuberance
which characterized his style at its best, expound a theme which is
familiar enough in his writings – that Western civilization has
reached the end of its creative potential and is destined to sink into
the slough of vulgar, bourgeois self-satisfaction. In return for a 'mess
of potage', well served, it is true, 'we yield up … our measure of
human dignity, our measure of compassion for our fellows' and support, if only negatively, an order 'which has become repellent to
us'. Where is the new art? 'In the future music of Wagner?' In Italy
the ideals of Mazzini are overtaken by the bourgeois society of
Cavour. While an honest union of religion and science is impossible,
the union exists: 'You can form your own conclusion on the
morality which results from such a union.' There is only one rule:
'*think* as you please, but *lie* like the others'. The terrible days of June
1848 were 'a protest of despair'. They did not create, but destroy,
but that which was being demolished proved the stronger, and the
'Utopia of a democratic republic disappeared into thin air much like
the Utopia of the Kingdom of Heaven on earth'. Where was the
hope in the West? Not in liberalism, which had learnt to combine
'constant protest against the government with constant obedience
to it'. The only ground for optimism lay in Russia, in the Russian
people: 'The Russian people … as a kind of cousin to the general
European family, had played practically no part in the family
chronicle of the West. … This people must either contribute its complete incapacity for development, or develop something of its own
under the influence of … its neighbours and its own angle of reflection.' Why should such a people have to live through the same experience as Europe '*knowing quite well where it leads to*'?

Turgenev's rejoinders were evidently inspired by Herzen's style,
because they are of a light-hearted brilliance which he rarely displayed when engaged in serious debate. Perhaps he did not take the
argument very seriously; if so, he is unlikely to have endeared himself
to Herzen. The only hope for progress in Russia lies, he says, in its
educated class. As for the people

… whom you worship, it is conservative *par excellence*. It even bears within
it in embryonic form such bourgeois habits – inside its tanned sheepskin
jacket, its warm and filthy hut, its stomach always stuffed full to the point

of indigestion, together with its revulsion from all civic responsibility or self-reliance – this people, I say, will far outstrip all the characteristics which you have so rightly and aptly depicted in your letters as belonging to the Western bourgeoisie.[23]

'I am beginning to think', he writes a month later, 'that the so oft repeated antithesis between the West, beautiful on the outside and hideous within, and the East, hideous externally and beautiful within, is false.' Even Herzen's eloquence, he adds, will not save this out-moded view from the kind of grave which it is destined to share with the philosophy of Hegel and Schelling, and 'dare I add, with the articles of that great socialist Nikolai Platonovich [Ogarev]. . . .' 'Russia is no Venus of Milo . . . she is the same kind of young woman as her elder sisters, only a bit broader in the backside. . . .'[24] And a little later he tells Herzen that he ignores the undoubted fact that

. . . we Russians belong in language and in nature to the European family, '*genus Europeum*', and consequently, in accordance with the unalterable laws of physiology, must travel the same road. . . . By reason of your spiritual pain, your weariness, your thirst to place a fresh snowflake on a parched tongue, you hit out at everything which should be dear to every European, and therefore to us – civilization, legality, the revolution itself, when all is said and done. Having filled young heads with your not fully fermented social-Slavophile brew, you send them intoxicatd and befuddled into the world where they are destined to stumble at the first step they take.

Herzen and Ogarev, he says, should either continue to serve revolu-tion (by which he clearly meant not a bloody peasant revolution in Russia, but the liberal ideas which we should today describe as 'democracy') or else admit their errors of the past, but certainly not make exceptions for some kind of Russian Messiah 'in whom, when all is said and done, you believe as little as you do in the Jewish Mes-siah'.[25]

The banter notwithstanding, the correspondence between the two friends in 1862 and 1863 began to show signs of bitterness, even hos-tility. The first symptom came with Turgenev's reaction to a pro-jected address to the Emperor which Ogarev, with the support of Herzen and Bakunin, planned in the autumn of 1862 and for which they sought Turgenev's signature. Nothing in the end came of the scheme. The gist of the address was to call on the Emperor to sum-mon a 'Meeting of the Lands' (*Zemskii sobor*) in order to put right the injustices of the Emancipation Act. Since it was inconceivable that the Emperor would agree to this, the true aim of the address was to expose the reactionary policy of the Emperor and thereby to stimulate revolutionary activity. Turgenev's main objections to the address were twofold. First, that it was grossly inaccurate in its description of the effects of emancipation. And second, that by including some of the grievances of the landlords, it dishonestly sought to enlist as allies people who were in no sense the friends of liberal progress – the more reactionary gentry. In his letter to the intermediary who had delivered the draft address to him from London, Turgenev adds that his main disagreement with Ogarev, Herzen, and Bakunin lies in the fact that whereas they despise the educated class in Russia and suppose that reforms can come from the people, he, Turgenev, saw the hope for 'revolution' (again meaning liberal democracy) in Russia solely in the educated minority. In this letter Turgenev discloses that he himself had in mind the preparation of an address (clearly different from the one prepared by him for Benni in 1860) which would urge the Emperor to crown the peasant reform with reform of the government on liberal lines.*[26] He followed up this letter with similar criticism in writing to Herzen.[27]

Herzen did not reply for some time. When he did, he once again asked Turgenev to explain his hostility to Ogarev, if he was not to 'regard this stone-throwing at people who do the work as the caprice of a pregnant woman'.[28] Turgenev at long last complied with the request and gave three reasons. First, that he disagreed with Ogarev's 'antiquated socialist theories'. Second, that in his articles on the peasant question he showed a lack of understanding of the basic facts. And third, that his style was turgid and without talent and was responsible for the decline in popularity of the *Bell*.[29] Herzen in reply did not refer to the subject. Turgenev did not write until some months later, when he told Herzen of a summons which he had received ('me, your antagonist') to appear before a senatorial inquiry into revolutionary activities.[30] Herzen replied, with little sympathy, that this was 'a lesson for your grey hairs. Don't publish works in journals which are suckled by the Third Department.' (A reference to *Fathers and Children* published in Katkov's journal.) 'God saw it and punished you.'[31] As will be seen, it was Herzen's reaction to Turgenev's appearance before the Senate which led to the breach between them. But months before that Herzen published in the *Bell* an anecdote attributed to Turgenev, though accompanied by the statement that he (Herzen) did not believe the attribution. It was during the Polish rising: the miserable anecdote recounted a supposed quarrel between two Russian officers who could not agree whether roast Polish babies were better eaten with French or with English

* Nothing came of this idea either.

mustard. It was preposterous, even accompanied by a denial, to associate Turgenev's name with this scurrilous tale. Turgenev insisted on the publication of a statement in the *Bell* that the whole story was an invention,[32] and Herzen complied.

It will be recalled (see Chapter 11) that when the Russian police arrested one Vetoshnikov in 1862 and confiscated his papers they stumbled on enough information about contacts between Russian radicals and the London *émigrés* grouped around the *Bell* to launch an investigation by the Senate which lasted for the better part of two years. Turgenev was mentioned in several of the letters seized, almost entirely in connection with his efforts to arrange for the travel of Madame Bakunin to London. The Russian police worked slowly but thoroughly, and in January 1863, to his utter amazement, Turgenev heard from Annenkov that rumours were current in Russia that he would be sent for to St. Petersburg to give evidence in the Senate inquiry. He refused to believe it – why should he be summoned now, after the row over *Fathers and Children* and 'after I have finally – almost publicly – broken with the London exiles?' Neither the outgoing nor the new Russian ambassador in Paris, both of whom he had recently seen, had said anything about it.[33] However, the summons duly arrived on 3 February 1863. With the approval of the Russian ambassador, Turgenev wrote a letter to the Emperor in which he expressed surprise that any suspicion could fall on him, since he had never concealed his views, which he claimed were moderate and conscientious. Since his poor health and family business which could not be postponed (he meant efforts connected with an abortive marriage project for Paulinette) made it impossible for him to return to Russia at the time, he begged the Emperor to arrange for a series of questions in writing to be addressed to him, all of which he promised to answer 'with full sincerity'.[34]

Nine questions were delivered to Turgenev through the Paris Embassy. His answers, running to ten and a half printed pages, were despatched on 22 March.[35] Four recent letters, two each from Bakunin and Herzen, were included with the replies.* The purpose of appending the letters was to show how far apart politically Turgenev was from the London exiles. The Senate was interested mainly in three matters: first, in Turgenev's relations with Bakunin, about which the Senate had taken evidence from an arrested intermediary, one Nabaldanov. This referred exclusively to Turgenev's efforts regarding Madame Bakunin, and Turgenev confirmed Nabaldanov's

* One of Bakunin's letters referred, incidentally, to a 'military operation' in Russia towards which 'we are striving' – a typical Bakunin cock and bull story.

evidence and added some further detail. Second, in Turgenev's contacts with N. A. Serno-Solovievich, one of the leading St. Petersburg radicals. (He was eventually exiled for life to Siberia, but died shortly afterwards.) Turgenev quite truthfully claimed that he had only seen him twice, in his bookshop, in connection with a manuscript which he was trying to get published for a friend.

But the Senate's main interest centred on Turgenev's dealings with the London exiles, and it was this question, question number three, which he answered in the greatest detail. He had first met Ogarev, he said, around 1842, but they had never been intimate. He had made the acquaintance of Bakunin in Berlin in 1840, and they had lived for about a year in the same house. But after that he had lost sight of him, and had never shared his political views nor participated in political action with him. Herzen had been an intimate friend, and he had not broken with him even when he began to act against the government. 'It is unnecessary to add that I took no part in such action.' (This last statement was not strictly true: Turgenev's correspondence over the years shows that on a number of occasions he supplied the *Bell* with information which had reached him from Russia, and which Herzen used in his paper.) He then set out the course of his contacts with Herzen with fair accuracy. They had met in the forties in Russia: he had been, along with Herzen, one of that generation which had many aims and aspirations in common – such as the emancipation of the peasants. Some of their number, among them Herzen, went forward so impatiently that 'they lost sight of Russia itself'. After Herzen's departure abroad, the two of them had met in Paris in 1848 but he, Turgenev, was a mere spectator of the rising storm, while Herzen at that time exercised no influence over the Russian public. (This again was something of an understatement: in 1848 and 1849 in Paris he was seeing Herzen almost daily.) Turgenev had then returned to Russia for six years and become an author: in 1856 when he returned to Europe Herzen was editing the *Bell*;[36] he had not yet abandoned all faith in the peaceful evolution of events in Russia, in spite of his severe criticism of the government. 'I saw him in London – and although I already then felt what a deep gulf lay between us, nevertheless I did not think it necessary or even useful to break off relations with him, in spite of the fact that these frequently took the form of quarrels.' This was overstating the case. It was probably more true to say that Turgenev deliberately avoided the kind of questions on which he knew he would clash with Herzen. But all this changed – Herzen ceased to be merely negative and began to preach, 'with the noisy exaggeration which characterizes sceptics when they become fanatics. I saw him ever more rarely, and felt more estranged from him every time.' Like many of his old friends, he (Turgenev) did not abandon his old convictions; but 'Herzen, having become a republican and a socialist' under the influence of Ogarev, no longer had anything in common 'with any right thinking Russian, who did not separate the tsar from the people, or honest love of sensible freedom from the conviction of the necessity for the monarchical principle'. The first breach came over the debate around 'Ends and Beginnings'.

The worst that can be said against this account of the years 1856–62 is that Turgenev had underemphasized the extent of his friendship for Herzen, which so often overrode political differences, and had therefore distorted the picture. One important omission in his evidence has already been noted, to which may be added his failure to mention the draft address to Alexander II, which he had entrusted to Benni for the collection of signatures. But Benni, who was among those arrested in the wake of the Vetoshnikov débâcle, had mentioned neither the address nor Turgenev in his evidence, and the Russian authorities presumably knew nothing about it.*

The Senate was not satisfied with some minor details of Turgenev's replies, and on 26 September he received a second summons to attend the Senate inquiry in person. With the help of the ambassador and medical certificates he managed to postpone his return to Russia, and finally arrived in St. Petersburg on 4 January 1864. He saw the President of the Senate the same day, and felt optimistic about the outcome.[39] Three days later he called at the Senate, and was received by 'six old gentlemen in uniform decorated with gongs' (*crachats*), asked if he had anything to add, and told to come again in six days' time.[40] A few days later he felt completely reassured when the chief of the police spoke to him amicably at a grand party given by the Italian ambassador.[41] His second visit to the Senate on 13 January turned out to be little more than a formality,[42] and by 16 January he knew that he had been completely exonerated and was at liberty to leave Russia,[43] although the formal decision of the Senate was only declared on 1 June.[44] He returned to Baden on 11 March.

On 15 January 1864 Herzen had published the following note in the *Bell*: 'Our correspondent tells us about a certain grey-haired Mag-

---

* Benni was eventually, as a foreigner, banished from Russia. Turgenev later met him and tried, without success, to get the order reversed.[37] He died at the end of 1867 as the result of an accidental wounding. Turgenev published a letter to the press in defence of his reputation.[38]

dalen (of the male sex) who wrote to the Emperor that she had lost
sleep and appetite, her rest, her white hairs and her teeth, tortured
by the thought that the Emperor does not yet know of the repentance
which has overtaken her, on the strength of which "she has broken
all connections with the friends of her youth".' Turgenev saw this
copy of the *Bell* in St. Petersburg, but hesitated until 2 April before
taking it up with Herzen. He was distressed, he wrote, by the remark.
He was not at all surprised by the abuse that Bakunin was spreading
about him – this was to be expected. But he was hurt that Herzen
should sling mud at a friend of twenty years' standing 'for the sole
reason that he no longer shares your opinions'. He then claimed that
his written answers to the Senate had neither insulted his former
friends nor repudiated them – perhaps a little less than accurate. He
enclosed a copy of his letter to the Emperor and begged Herzen,
for whom his 'old feelings had not yet completely vanished', to insult
him no more.[45] Herzen's reply was somewhat evasive. He wrote,
inter alia, that he had been appalled to find Turgenev's name in a
list of subscribers for the benefit of Russian soldiers wounded in
action while putting down the Polish rising. Besides, he had reliable
evidence that Turgenev in fact *had* repudiated his former friends.
'The time will come', he ended his letter, 'when, if not the "fathers",
then the "children" will appreciate these sober, honest Russians, who
alone protested, and will continue to protest, against base appease-
ment. Our task is, perhaps, over. But the memory of the fact that
not all Russia belonged to Katkov's "ill-assorted herd" will remain.
... We saved the honour of Russia's name – and suffered for this from
the slavish majority.'[46] There was to be no further contact between
the two men for several years.

The reference to Poland is characteristic of Herzen, who had
enthusiastically supported the Polish insurrection of 1863 from the
first; had indeed lost much of his following among his radical readers
in Russia for doing so. Turgenev, who was in no sense a blind Russian
nationalist, deplored the horrors and cruelties which were taking
place on both the Russian and Polish sides. He considered the revolt
futile from the start, and incapable of leading to greater freedom for
the Poles. The sooner the carnage ended the better, was the view
which he expressed more than once in his correspondence. Already
in 1861, rumours of a rebellion in Warsaw had prompted him to
comment to Countess Lambert: 'God preserve us from such a disaster! A revolt in the Kingdom can only do harm to Poland and
to Russia, like every revolt and every conspiracy.'[47] When the rising
broke out in 1863 and news of it reached Paris, Turgenev wrote to

Annenkov in terms of horror at the news of the bloodshed: 'It is impossible not to wish for the speediest suppression of this senseless rebellion.' Nor was it inconsistent (as has been alleged) with this essentially humanitarian and non-political outlook, for him to have praised Herzen a few days later for an article calling for fraternization between Russian and Polish troops.[48]

This incident between Herzen and Turgenev has been dealt with at length because, more than any other event in Turgenev's life, it illustrates the nature of political alignment in Russia in the years which followed the emancipation. This quarrel between two upright men, each of whom sincerely worked for the welfare of his country, enables us to discern the unbridgeable gulf between the intelligentsia and the Russian government which was to grow ever wider as the years wore on. Of course Herzen did not believe that Turgenev sided in all respects with the repressive and arbitrary Russian regime. But at the same time he was unable to understand how one who had fought, as had Turgenev, for the emancipation of the serfs, could ever find himself at the same table as the government without having sold his soul. He could not understand that, without accepting the emancipation as perfect, an upright patriot could in the sixties support any attempt to make the reform work. In exactly the same way, future generations of radicals would fail to perceive that a Russian could be both a loyal monarchist and honest. The whole question arose with particular force after Russia became a semi-constitutional state in 1906. Forty-five years after the quarrel which has just been described, a group of leading Russian intellectuals published a slim volume entitled *Vekhi* (*Signposts*) in which the intelligentsia was severely taken to task for what Peter Struve, one of the contributors, called its 'apostasy' – deliberate fostering of a gulf which could never be bridged, between the government, even when it was making efforts to reform, and the intellectuals who formed the conscience of Russia. *Vekhi* called for a reaffirmation of religious values, and an acceptance by the intelligentsia of the primacy of civic virtues like law and order. *Vekhi* aroused a storm of protest from the entire Russian radical movement, from the recently formed liberal parties to Lenin.[49] Herzen would have understood and sympathized with this attitude because he too felt that the only decent position which any self-respecting critic of the Russian regime could occupy was on the barricades; and that any co-operation with it, even with the best of motives, was a defilement of the ideals for which he stood.

★　　★　　★　　★　　★

Although he was pining for Baden and was still, no doubt, slightly apprehensive about the outcome of the Senate inquiry, Turgenev's life in St. Petersburg in the winter of 1864 was full of pleasant activity. We know about it in detail from the long letters which he wrote to Pauline at intervals of a few days.* Pauline also wrote regularly and frequently; her letters for this period are unknown, but judging from his replies they were most friendly and concerned. On Turgenev's side, his correspondence is very loving, with the familiar endearments in German. It abounds in nostalgia for Baden: 'Oh my dear friend,' he writes under the impact of the funeral of the critic Druzhinin, 'live for a long time and allow me to live near to all of you.'[50] He was still in love with the whole family.

He listened to a good deal of music, and reported in detail on the singers' and instrumentalists' performances. He met the critic and composer Alexander Serov and heard a performance of his opera *Judith*. It proved to be too much under the influence of Wagner for his taste. He liked much better the second opera, *Rogneda*, which he heard in instalments, as performed by the composer, and which showed much more the influence of Glinka and of the Russian nationalist school in music generally. A great deal of time was spent in overseeing the engraving of a collection of Pauline's songs, in which he succeeded in interesting Anton Rubinstein, the composer, whose works Pauline, but not Turgenev, much admired. This first volume of songs was published in St. Petersburg in 1864, and consisted of six poems by Pushkin, five by Fet, and one by Turgenev all with German translations), set to music by Pauline. A second volume of Pauline's songs appeared in the following year. Both also came out in Leipzig. (The German versions were by Friedrich Bodenstedt, a poet who had spent some years in Russia, and who translated a number of Turgenev's long short stories, which were published in 1864 and 1865.)[51] Pauline was not a novice as a composer for a collection of her songs had been published as tar back as 1843, and she had also some instrumental works to her credit.[52] She had more time for this creative activity after her semi-retirement, and was much encouraged in this by Turgenev. He took infinite trouble on her behalf. He went over Bodenstedt's translations meticulously and made many suggestions for improving them where the rhythm of the Russian originals demanded it. He also actively tried to promote the success of Pauline's songs by bombarding critics with whom he was on good terms with requests for reviews, probably

* Fifteen in all have been published, numbered somewhat erratically, and including some letters despatched in the course of the journey to Russia, nos. 1 to 18.

somewhat to the embarrassment of his Russian friends who were inclined to be put out by Turgenev's demonstrative adoration of Pauline.

His stay in St. Petersburg provided an opportunity for seeing old companions such as Annenkov (now happily married) and Botkin. He was also, as usual, lionized by St. Petersburg high society. He was received by the Grand Duchess Elena Pavlovna and attended at least one grand and luxurious ball, at which the Emperor was present. Some quieter evenings were spent with Countess Lambert, but they were no longer as intimate as they had once been. It would seem that the Countess felt isolated and excluded by Turgenev's ecstatic happiness in Baden, so different from the time when the course of love between Turgenev and Pauline had been far from smooth. She reproached Turgenev for living in Baden (especially after she learned of his purchase of land and of his intentions to build himself a house), and indeed for staying abroad for such lengthy periods of time. In her letters she attributed this to his love of comfort and pleasure (she knew, of course, the real reason and obviously resented it). Turgenev in his defence claimed that the only way in which he could serve his country was as a writer. 'There is no necessity for a writer to live in his own country ... at least, there is no need to do this continually. ... In a word, I see no reason why I should not settle in Baden. I do this not out of any desire for material delights ... but simply so as to weave a little nest for myself in which to await the onslaught of the inevitable end.'[53]

Turgenev stayed for some time in Paris, on his way back to Baden. The fourteen letters to Pauline Viardot which have come down to us chronicle in detail Turgenev's time in the French capital, and especially at the opera (Gounod's *Mireille* was the main new musical event, and did not impress him). There was much anxiety about the course of Louise Héritte's (Pauline's eldest daughter's) first confinement, which was retarded by complications – but happily all was well in the end. Turgenev also saw Prosper Mérimée, with whom he had become friendly in 1857. Mérimée, who knew Russian, had commented critically on the French translations of Turgenev's stories 'The Jew' and 'Petushkov' and himself translated 'Ghosts', and 'The Dog'.[54] Mérimée's knowledge of Russian, to judge from his correspondence with Turgenev, was far from perfect. His version of 'Ghosts' had to be substantially revised by the author before it could be published in a volume of collected stories.[55]

The other French writer who was to become an intimate, Gustave Flaubert, was not then in Paris. The two men had met on 28 February

1863 at the famous literary *dîner Magny*. Turgenev sent the French master his works (in French), which evoked enthusiastic praise. There were further exchanges of translations and eulogies. But Flaubert had left Paris soon after their meeting, and their close friendship did not begin until 1868.[56]

According to one, very detailed and circumstantial, but quite uncorroborated, account, Turgenev made the acquaintance of Ferdinand Lassalle at the end of the summer of 1864. (This would have been shortly before Lassalle's death in a duel on 31 August 1864.) The meeting is said to have taken place at a hotel or *pension* in Geneva. Lassalle recognized Turgenev, and asked to be introduced. Their conversation was cordial and animated, but had lasted only for about ten minutes when Lasalle was called away on urgent business.[57] While there is no reference in Turgenev's correspondence to this meeting, or to any visit to Geneva in August 1864, such a journey could have taken place: there is a gap in the evidence of Turgenev's presence at home in Baden between 4 August, when he wrote a letter to his brother, and 19 or 20 August, when he was visited in Baden by the composer Serov.[58]

The period bounded by the completion of *Fathers and Children* in August 1861 and the start of work on his next important novel *Smoke*, in November 1865, was very unproductive. Only three quite minor fictional works were accomplished: 'Ghosts', 'Enough', and 'The Dog', as well as a short lecture on Shakespeare. 'Ghosts' (subtitled 'A fantasy') consists mainly of a series of scenes which the narrator witnesses while borne aloft by a mysterious female ghost clad in white, who answers to the name of Ellis. (The ghost in the end turns out to be a vampire and the narrator breaks off his night expeditions with her only just in time to survive the repeated bloodsucking to which he has been exposed.) 'Ghosts' was first thought of by Turgenev in 1855, and indeed he started work on it in that year, and promised it to Katkov as a first contribution to his new journal *Moscow Herald*. In the end he put it on one side and produced 'Faust' instead – and had a very acrimonious correspondence with Katkov when it was published in the *Contemporary*, since Katkov refused to believe that 'Faust' and 'Ghosts' were not one and the same. Turgenev did not return to 'Ghosts' until 1861, after he had finished *Fathers and Children*. He promised the story to Dostoevsky's journal *Vremia* by the end of the year. But he worked very intermittently on it, and it was only completed, finally revised, and sent to Annenkov for his opinion on 27 September 1863.[59] Further alterations to the text were made on the advice of Annenkov and of another friend,

N. V. Shcherban. 'Ghosts' was finally published at the end of February 1864 in the Dostoevsky brothers' journal *Epokha*, which by this time had replaced *Vremia* after the latter had been closed down.

The series of nocturnal excursions with Ellis are superbly described, and are both contemporary and historical, since Ellis can fly not only through space, but also backwards in time.* Certainly some, if not all, of the episodes are reminiscences of Turgenev's own experiences at, for example, Blackgang Rock on the south coast of the Isle of Wight (where Turgenev spent some time in 1860), Isola Bella on Lago Maggiore, Paris, and the Schwarzwald. There is an historic scene set in first-century Rome where Caesar appears to his troops, and a brutal episode in the Camp of Stenka Razin, the robber-rebel, re-enacting what was traditionally supposed to have happened to one of Turgenev's ancestors. In spite of its beauty, the work leaves one unsatisfied and bewildered – such indeed was the reaction of Turgenev's friends (among them Botkin) and of the majority of the literary critics. Dostoevsky, though full of enthusiasm in his comments to Turgenev, was not really impressed: 'I think there is a lot of rubbish in it,' he wrote on 23 December 1863: 'something nasty about it, something sick and senile, with a lack of faith due to weakness, in a word the whole of Turgenev with his convictions. But poetry will redeem a lot.'[61] Turgenev, some years later, maintained that he had had no interest in 'mysticism' when writing 'Ghosts': his sole object had been to present a 'series of pictures'.[62]

'Ghosts' is a work of profound pessimism and of lack of faith in or hope for the future of mankind. Turgenev was much depressed at the time of writing the work by the rejection of *Fathers and Children* by the younger generation, which he had not expected. He was probably also much influenced by Schopenhauer, whose *World as Will and Idea* he was reading around this time. There is indeed a direct reminiscence of Schopenhauer in the description which he gave in 'Ghosts' of the earth as seen from above, when the humans look small and unimportant and are locked in eternal struggle with blind forces which they cannot control – creatures who have emerged from the slime that covers the earth's surface. This recalls the first paragraph of the second volume of *The World as Will and Idea*,[63] and in the draft of the story there appears an entry 'View of the earth (Schopenhauer)' which shows that the borrowing was conscious.[64]

* The idea of flying may have been suggested to Turgenev by the recollection of a very vivid dream in which he soared like a bird above the surface of the earth, and which he described with great detail in a letter to Pauline Viardot.[60]

Statements are sometimes made that Schopenhauer is repeatedly mentioned in Turgenev's letters. But there are only two references, one in 1862, and a second, much later, which is merely an enquiry of Fet about how he is getting on with his translation of Schopenhauer. Nevertheless, it is clear from a number of his works that Turgenev was much influenced by this philosopher's sombre pessimism. The most striking influence of Schopenhauer's view of the nature of sexual passion occurs in two later works, *Spring Torrents* and *Song of Triumphant Love* (see Chapters 14 and 16). But Schopenhauer's themes abound in Turgenev's writings. For example, the illusion that man can attain happiness, which is in essence nothing but deliverance from pain; this deliverance once achieved, boredom sets in, and the striving after satisfaction reasserts itself. Or again, that temporary escape from the driving of the cosmic will is to be found in aesthetic contemplation; or that in the hierarchy of art the pride of place belongs to music, which exhibits no ideas, only the will itself, so that in listening to it one obtains a direct revelation (in non-conceptual form) of the reality, the will, which underlies all phenomena. Above all, the insignificance of man in the scheme of nature which pursues its own course, its will, with total disregard for his existence.

Most of these ideas are to be found in 'Enough', which is even less of a story than 'Ghosts'. 'Enough' was written at intervals between 1862 and 1864, and was first published not in the usual periodical form, but as a new item in the collected edition of the works which appeared in 1865; nor was it submitted before publication to the judgement of friends. 'Enough' is sub-titled 'Fragments from the Notes of a Deceased Painter' and consists of fourteen paragraphs of recollections and reflections on a very unhappy life. Several of them refer to a love affair long past, but we are not told why what appears to have been a reciprocated passion ended in despair. The underlying thought is the impotence of man in the path of all-devouring, indifferent nature – the cosmic will of Schopenhauer. Art is a temporary consolation since art is not an imitation of nature – where in nature are the symphonies of Beethoven or the poems of Goethe? But art too cannot resist the ineluctable, blind march of nature, which knows neither art nor freedom nor the good. Nature 'creates, even as she destroys, and is quite indifferent to what she creates or what she destroys – she is concerned only that life should go on, and that death should not lose its rights'. The only dignity left to man is to turn away from it all and say 'enough'. At this point Turgenev paraphrases Pascal's reflection that man, who is as insignificant as a reed when crushed by the force of the universe, is nevertheless superior to the universe because he knows that he is being crushed, and the universe does not.[65]

'Enough' was received with even more hostility than 'Ghosts' – and it is true that it cannot be classed with any of Turgenev's major works. It is of interest as a gloss on a period of his life when he was afflicted with moods of intense unhappiness, and he later expressed regret that he had ever published so intimate a reflection of his private thoughts.[66] But depth of despair is easy to parody – as Dostoevsky would show in his merciless satire on Turgenev in *The Possessed* (after the two had quarrelled) in the person of the famous writer Karmazinov, and his public reading of 'Merci'.

'The Dog', a tale of the supernatural, was written in a sudden burst of inspiration, in Paris, between 3 and 5 April 1864. According to one account Turgenev had heard the story told at an inn in 1859.[67] Having completed the story in 1864 Turgenev had considerable doubts whether it was worth publishing and resolutely refused two insistent requests from Dostoevsky, who had heard rumours of the existence of 'The Dog' and wanted to print it in *Epokha*. However, Turgenev eventually yielded to the persuasion of the editor of a daily newspaper to publish it on his literary pages, and it appeared in 1866. It was not well received at the time, though highly praised in the *Illustrated London News* in 1870 after the appearance of an English translation in *Temple Bar*, and much later by Chekhov, in 1893.[68] The plot is simple. A minor landowner is troubled by the ghost of a dog under his bed; night after night he can hear it grunt and scratch, but there is nothing to be seen. He is eventually advised to consult a holy man, who tells him to buy a puppy and keep it beside him day and night. This he does. The upshot is that the puppy, Tresor, to whom he becomes devoted, when it grows up twice saves him from the assaults of a mad dog, losing its own life the second time. But the ghost under the bed is heard no more, and the narrator is no longer pursued by the mad beast.

It was probably in 1862, under the impact of his controversy with Herzen over 'Ends and Beginnings', that the idea for a new novel occurred to Turgenev. As so often happened with him, an idea had to germinate for some time before he was ready to start writing. He began work on *Smoke* in Baden on 12 November 1864.

CHAPTER THIRTEEN

Emigration

The idea for a new novel, *Smoke*, which marked a significant stage in Turgenev's intellectual development, probably first occurred to him in 1862. The original intention seems to have been to write a pure love story. But two political trends in Russia after 1861 decided him, by the end of the following year, to expand the projected story into a social analysis of post-reform Russia. These were the obstruction of the implementation of the emancipation by many of the landlords, and the growing radicalism – both of which he had closely followed, as his correspondence shows. The three years which elapsed before he sat down to write *Smoke* (after discussing his plan with one of his favourite critics, Botkin), also gave him the chance to incorporate in it the reflections which had first been prompted by his argument with Herzen over 'Ends and Beginnings'. The result was a hybrid work, in which the original love story, satirical exposure of the foibles both of the Russian revolutionaries and of high society, and discourse on Russia's place in Europe and on the old controversy between 'Slavophiles' and 'Westerners' are intermingled in what is not always a happy amalgam.[1]

The plot is simple. A penniless student, Litvinov, is in love with, and is loved by, Irina, the very beautiful daughter of an impoverished Moscow aristocratic family. But Irina is oppressed by her degraded domestic circumstances and, when opportunity offers, after a dazzling success at her first grand ball, she moves with an elderly distant relative to the capital, breaks with Litvinov, and eventually contracts a society marriage. (The frailty of Irina is treated with a compassion which recalls Shakespeare's portrayal of the weak Cressida.) Years later Litvinov, now engaged to marry the gentle, domesticated Tatiana, is awaiting in Baden the arrival from their travels of his fiancée and her aunt. He unexpectedly meets Irina there, now surrounded by the *haut monde* in which she and her rather repulsive husband, General Ratmirov, move. His old love for her, which has never really died, revives, and he discovers that she still loves him. They arrange to fly from Baden together, and Litvinov breaks the news to Tatiana. At the last moment Irina's courage deserts her, and Litvinov departs, alone and desolate. There is a very unconvincing 'happy ending' some years later when Litvinov is reconciled with Tatiana. There were very few happy endings in Turgenev's other stories – for that matter there were few, if any, in his own love affairs, which his fiction almost invariably reflected. There is good evidence for the view that Tatiana's prototype was his cousin, Olga Turgeneva,[2] with whom he had consoled himself many years before, after his traumatic parting from Pauline Viardot in 1850, and whom he nearly married. Nearly – but not quite. It is as little possible to imagine Litvinov liberated from Irina as it is to picture Turgenev free of his subjection to Pauline. Litvinov is designated 'X' in the conspectus of the novel which Turgenev drew up in 1862, in which most of the other characters are given recognizable initials, which leads one to suppose that, to some extent, 'X' was a self-portrait.

Much of the novel is taken up with satirical and rather bitter descriptions of Irina's husband and their friends – a narrow-minded, empty-headed band of former serf-owners who have learned nothing, and still pursue the old ways as best they can. But the irony directed at these 'planters' is fully equalled by the contempt with which the members of a group of radicals which happens to find itself in Baden is depicted – self-seeking, hypocritical charlatans, whose advanced views are essentially a pose. Since Turgenev nearly always based his stories on fact, some of the characters and incidents can be identified. The worst of the radical company, Gubarev, (designated 'O' in the conspectus) was generally believed to be Ogarev, whom Turgenev certainly did not like. But, physical description apart, the facts in the novel do not fit Herzen's friend. Turgenev's diatribes hit their mark, and both sides were offended. Even Pisarev, who, almost alone among the radicals, had greatly admired *Fathers and Children*, reproached Turgenev with the fact that no noble type comparable to Bazarov figured in *Smoke*.[3]

But the main storm provoked by *Smoke* arose over the long monologues of a character called Potugin, whose presence in Baden is only loosely connected with the main story, and whose principal function seems to be to expound the nature of Russia from the point of view of a confirmed and uncompromising Westerner. Potugin's discourses take up nearly a tenth of the whole book, they are of no direct relevance to the narrative, and, as Turgenev himself acknowledged, voice views which were close to his own.[4] They contain a devastating attack on the Slavophile notions of the distinctive nature of Russian national culture, denigrate in strong terms Russia's past or present achievements (with the exception of those, such as the reform of the legal system of 1864, which were directly borrowed from Western Europe), and advocate complete Westernization of Russia as the only way for the country to progress out of its native barbarism. It was an opinion not very different from that of Belinsky (of whose writings there are echoes in Potugin's speeches) or, for that matter, from the attack delivered by Chaadaev in his First Philosophical Letter in 1836, to which the arguments of the Slavophiles in the forties and fifties were in some measure a response. These Slavophile doctrines, usually in much cruder and more chauvinistic form, were being revived in the sixties. They were much disliked by Turgenev, who contemplated writing about them, but apparently never got beyond a few pages, despite the fact that as late as 1882 he referred to his essay as 'finished long ago'.[5]

The reactions to Potugin's words were for the most part inimical. (There were exceptions: Nikitenko, for example, saw nothing shocking in them, nor did Annenkov.) Some of the hostility was very crude, such as social boycotting of Turgenev by the more reactionary of the Russian families living in Baden;[6] or the Grand Duchess Maria's denunciation to Prosper Mérimée of Smoke, and of its author as 'a man who is execrable to women'.[7] There were many critical reviews which took issue with Potugin's opinions.[8] There were also considerable difficulties with Katkov, in whose journal Smoke was published in the spring of 1867, which very nearly caused Turgenev to withdraw his manuscript.[9] Katkov objected primarily to the satire on the 'planters', to the suggestions of immorality in Litvinov's relations with Irina, and to her supposed resemblance to an identifiable person.* For the most part the altered passages were restored to their original state when the novel was published in volume form in 1868. The incident contributed to the final rupture between Turgenev and Katkov shortly afterwards, although he still wrote two stories for the Russian Herald in 1868, and a further one in 1869.

Turgenev used the occasion of the publication of Smoke to make up his quarrel with Herzen. In the letter accompanying the offprint of the novel which Turgenev sent him he expressed apprehension

---

* It was in fact the case that Irina was modelled on Princess Alexandra Dolgorukaia, who was the wife of General P. P. Albedinsky.[10] She was the favourite of Alexander II and lady-in-waiting to the Empress Maria Alexandrovna.

that Herzen would not like it, but hoped that their old friendship could be resumed.[11] Herzen did not particularly admire *Smoke* – least of all Potugin's speeches[12] – but a full reconciliation did follow, which was to last until Herzen's death in January 1870. The old arguments between the two men continued, although with less acrimony than before. 'Europe is not so old, nor Russia so young as you make them out to be. We are sitting in one and the same sack, and there is no prospect of any "special new word" emanating from Russia', Turgenev wrote in December 1867. And a fortnight later he poured scorn on the supposedly 'democratically-social' tendencies discernible in Russia in the peasant commune and the work association (*artel'*) which were, in his experience, regarded as burdensome handicaps by peasants and workers.[13] Very shortly before Herzen's death, in 1870, Turgenev met him for lunch in Paris. He seemed in high spirits and well. It was the first time the two men had seen each other since their heated arguments in London in May 1862. Within a day Herzen was gravely ill: Turgenev was no longer allowed to see him, though he called daily to enquire. On 22 January he heard that he was dead. 'An old friend is gone,' he wrote to Annenkov within an hour of hearing the news, and sent a warm letter of sympathy to Herzen's son, Alexander.[14] Some months later he wrote enthusiastically to Annenkov about some posthumous works of Herzen which the family had sent him: 'How deeply he penetrated to the real truth of all our nonsense. But for that very reason he was least of all a politician. ... His language, ungrammatical to the point of lunacy, fills me with delight....' 'He was the only Russian who could write like that,' was his comment a few years later after reading some unpublished chapters from *My Past and Thoughts*. 'We have never had a wittier – or cleverer ... writer.'[15]

The most dramatic consequence of *Smoke* was the rupture which it indirectly provoked between Turgenev and Dostoevsky in Baden, on 28 June 1867. The enmity between the two may have dated from 1863 or earlier when they met several times in Baden. Dostoevsky (who was gambling heavily and probably borrowed some money from Turgenev) was not well impressed and, as he wrote to his brother, found Turgenev to be 'a bit of a fop'.[16] According to Dostoevsky's version of their meeting in 1867, described in a long letter of 16 August to the poet Maikov, he called on Turgenev at noon, and found him at lunch: 'To tell you the truth I never liked this man even before as a person. ... I also detest his aristocratic, pharisaical way ... of coming at you to embrace you, and then thrusting forward his own cheek for you to kiss.' (Kissing was a very usual form of greeting between Russian men.) Dostoevsky made three charges against Turgenev, allegedly as the result of this meeting. First, that he was an atheist: 'He declared to me that he was a definitive atheist.' Second, that he hated Russia: 'His book *Smoke* irritated me. He told me himself that the main thought, the fundamental point of his book, was contained in the phrase, "If Russia were to be sunk without trace there would be no loss or cause of excitement for mankind". He declared that this was his fundamental conviction about Russia.' Third, that he was a Germanophile. As Dostoevsky was leaving, so he says, he made some derogatory remark about the Germans, to which Turgenev retorted: 'In speaking like that you offend me personally. You must know that I have finally settled here, that I regard myself as a German and not as a Russian, and that I am proud of this.' In ending his letter Dostoevsky says that he promised himself never to see Turgenev again: 'He has offended me too much with his convictions.' On the following day Turgenev called on Dostoevsky at ten o'clock in the morning, which Dostoevsky interpreted as an insult, since he had told Turgenev that he and his wife always slept until eleven.[17]

At the end of the year Turgenev learned from Annenkov that a copy of this letter had been deposited in the documentary library which also produced the journal called *Russian Archive*, with a stop on its publication until 1890. (It had not been forwarded by Dostoevsky, as was widely believed, but by a third party to whom Maikov had shown it.)[18] He wrote to the editor giving his version of the encounter, denying that he had confided any of his innermost convictions to Dostoevsky – if only because he considered him a sick man who was not in full possession of his mental faculties. Dostoevsky had 'relieved his spirits' with violent abuse of the Germans, but he, Turgenev, had had neither the time nor the inclination to retort.[19]

It is improbable that either of the two men was telling the whole truth about the conversation of 10 July. Turgenev was not a determined atheist; there is ample evidence (much of which has been cited in earlier pages) which shows that he was an agnostic who would have been happy to embrace the consolations of religion, but was, except perhaps on some rare occasions, unable to do so. Turgenev certainly did not hate Russia – a judgement of this kind about the author of *Sketches from a Sportsman's Notebook* or *A Nest of the Landed Gentry* is palpably absurd. He admired Germany, and was a convinced Westerner by taste and inclination. But it would have been inconsistent with everything we know of his outlook for him to have

declared that he now regarded himself as a German and not a Russian.
On the other hand, it is extremely improbable that one of Turgenev's
argumentative temperament would have sat silent in the face of the
diatribes levelled against him by Dostoevsky, whom he disliked, and
probably rather despised as well.

Whatever each of them may have said to the other on this unhappy
occasion, there is no doubt that the roots of the quarrel went much
deeper than any exchange of words could suggest. Dostoevsky's
spiritual development around this time was beginning to take on the
characteristics which dominate his great novel, *The Possessed*, which
he began to think about in 1869. These may be, somewhat baldly,
summarized as the primacy of Christianity; intense Russian national-
ism and belief in the special mission of Russia in Europe; and the
conviction that a direct line of paternity led from the 'liberals' of
the forties – especially Belinsky and Granovsky, but also Turgenev –
to terrorists like Karakozov (who made an attempt on the life of
the Emperor in 1866), and eventually Nechaev, the Peter Verkhovensky of *The Possessed*.*

Already in 1867 Turgenev personified for Dostoevsky, especially
after the appearance of *Fathers and Children* and then of *Smoke*, everything that he deplored in contemporary Russia, and especially 'nihilism'. Turgenev, in turn, could feel little enthusiasm for the religious
message of the second part of *Crime and Punishment* though he
approved of the first part. While retaining his admiration for Alexander II (he was horrified by the attempts on his life in 1866 and
1867) and his more enlightened advisers, he was becoming increasingly disillusioned at the slow pace of the transformation of Russia
which he had once so confidently expected to follow quickly on the
emancipation of the peasants.[20] He was also beginning to be obsessed
with the fear that his increasingly long absences from Russia were
affecting his writing. Dostoevsky's advice to him to procure himself
a telescope from which to observe distant Russia was like rubbing
salt in the wounds. However, in its essence, the quarrel was rooted
in the perennial dichotomy of outlook which divides thinking Russians to this day – is Russia an integral part of the family of European
peoples, or a nation apart, with a separate destiny of her own?

Dostoevsky brooded over his detestation of Turgenev (much
enhanced when Turgenev's laudatory memoir of Belinsky appeared
in 1869) and eventually gave full vent to it by satirizing him in *The*

---

* The gentle Granovsky, one of the noblest minds of the Russia of Nicholas I,
is satirized in the novel in the person of the father of Peter Verkhovensky – the
paternity is not accidental.

Possessed in the person of Karmazinov. The satire is extremely cruel, but some of the traits ridiculed correspond to the ones which those of Turgenev's contemporaries who were not overwhelmed by his charm used to dislike. Nor were the two works which Dostoevsky picked on for derision – 'Ghosts' and 'Enough' – among Turgenev's best, to put it mildly. Turgenev was deeply hurt by the parody, and especially by the absurd implication that he sympathized with the terrorist and charlatan Nechaev. As he wrote to a friend in Russia, Dostoevsky had praised 'Ghosts' to the skies when it was sent to him for publication in *Epokha*. (This was true; but Turgenev did not know that the praise was not sincere, since in the letter to his brother Dostoevsky was very critical of both 'Ghosts' and its author.) Turgenev added that before defaming him, Dostoevsky might have paid him the money which he had borrowed some years before.*[21]

Apart from *Smoke*, Turgenev published five stories between 1868 and 1870, six of the eleven essays which since 1874 have been collectively known as *Literary and Social Memoirs* (the canon since 1884 has also included as a 'supplement' a twelfth sketch entitled 'Un incendie en mer' devoted to the fire on board the *Nicholas I* which Turgenev had experienced in 1838), and two short articles. Two of the stories were written mainly in 1867 and published in the following year in Katkov's journal the *Russian Herald*. One of them, 'The Story of Lieutenant Ergunov' deals with the robbing and near murder of a susceptible young naval lieutenant by a ruffian who appears to be acting in co-operation with a household which includes two Jewish prostitutes – or so they seem. None of the detail in this poor story is at all clear. Unlike almost all the rest of Turgenev's work, it does not appear to have been based on any episode either in his experience or on any incident related to him; nor was Turgenev (so far as is known) ever in the port of Nikolaev where the action takes place in the early years of the century. 'The Brigadier' was inspired by a letter which Turgenev found among his mother's papers, and which is reproduced almost verbatim in the story. The brigadier's military career dates from the Napoleonic wars, and he is now living out the end of his life in penury in the country. The letter, which is a minor literary masterpiece, is a request for aid and shelter addressed to the niece of a rich woman landowner with whom

---

* The money was repaid in July 1875, through an intermediary. This led to further unpleasantness. Turgenev was under the mistaken impression that the debt was a hundred, not fifty thalers, and somewhat pettily pointed this out – until he found the original letter requesting the loan, and returned it to Dostoevsky with the receipt endorsed on it.[22]

the brigadier had been deeply in love, and to whom he had shown many years of utter devotion.

'An Unhappy Girl' was published in the following year, also in Katkov's journal. Like 'The Brigadier' it was based to some extent on real life, on an episode which Turgenev recalled from his days as a student in Moscow, though considerably enriched in the telling. It is much more powerful than 'Lieutenant Ergunov' or 'The Brigadier', the characters are delineated with the skill which Turgenev shows at his best, and the details of the plot are more thoroughly worked out than in either of the other two stories. Although completed in the course of a few months in the summer of 1868, it is, perhaps, significant that it was written in Spasskoe where (as Turgenev wrote to Pauline) he was overwhelmed by memories of his youth – and, it is possible, inspired by renewed contacts with Russia. It is the tale of a girl, Susanna, the illegitimate daughter of a minor member of the nobility, who never acknowledges her, and marries off his mistress to a German or Czech. The mother, who is a Jewess, dies and Susanna is left at the mercy of her stepfather – a particularly repulsive sadist whose vile nature is portrayed with loving care. This man, at the instigation of the brother of Susanna's real father, who has since died, succeeds in frustrating a love affair which has grown up between Susanna and this blood uncle's son. Susanna eventually dies very suddenly – whether of natural causes, by her own hand, or poisoned by her stepfather who stood to inherit her income, is left open.

Both the theme and the treatment recall in many respects Dostoevsky's writings, especially *The Humiliated and the Insulted* (published in 1861). 'An Unhappy Girl', like the other two stories, had scant success and attracted little attention; some critics, including Pauline Viardot, found it very distasteful. It was, incidentally, the first of Turgenev's works in which a Jewish character is portrayed sympathetically. Up to this time, both in his fiction and in occasional remarks in his correspondence, Jews had been treated by him as inferior and rather contemptible beings. We do not know what brought about the change in his outlook, if real change there was. Turgenev once admitted in conversation that prejudice against Jews was inculcated in Russians from childhood, but claimed that he himself so far from feeling any antipathy for them was, on the contrary, 'very well disposed towards them'.[23] There is no doubt from the evidence of the reworkings of the manuscript that Susanna's Jewish origin was scrupulously emphasized in the final version, and her name, originally intended to be Magdalena, was changed to Susanna, which in Russian ears has an unmistakably Jewish ring.

Of the two stories published in 1870, Turgenev wrote one, 'A Strange Story' in a fortnight in July 1869 in Baden, when he was forced to interrupt work on the considerably longer 'King Lear of the Steppes' while waiting for legal and technical information which he needed to arrive from Russia. In 'A Strange Story' the daughter of a rich money-lender, inspired by Christian devotion, throws up her life of luxury with her father in order to look after one of those simple-minded (and very verminous) holy men who used to wander around Russia, living on alms. 'King Lear of the Steppes' was also written in Germany (in Karlsruhe), but was thoroughly revised in Russia. It is in all respects a more serious and solid work than any of those referred to above, and was based on events which had taken place near Spasskoe. The scene is set in the Russian countryside, and the style and atmosphere recall the *Sketches from a Sportsman's Notebook*, of which 'King Lear of the Steppes', but for its length, could well be one. The tale is closely and deliberately modelled on Shakespeare's play, as becomes particularly evident when one looks at the revisions to the first version.* A neighbour of the narrator's rich mother lives in pre-reform Russia with his two daughters, one of whom is married, on a nearby estate. He is very eccentric, and physically a powerful giant. Acting on a premonition that he is going to die soon, he divides his property, with all due legal formalities and traditional ceremonial solemnity, between his two daughters – with predictable results. In the end he takes revenge on them and on his vile son-in-law by breaking up the roof of the house, falling to his death in the process.† 'King Lear' is written in Turgenev's best manner, but again had little success in Russia – the passions aroused by *Smoke* were possibly not yet stilled. It won acclaim, however, in translation.

Of the pieces which make up the *Literary and Social Memoirs*, three of the five published in 1869 dealt with Belinsky, Turgenev's professor at St. Petersburg University, the critic P. A. Pletnev, Gogol, and some other literary figures. The remaining two consisted of a general 'Introduction' and of a discourse on *Fathers and Children*. Turgenev also included the description of a visit to Albano and Frascati first published in 1861 when he spent some time in Italy with Botkin, and a delightful semi-technical study on 'Nightingales' written for

* The plays of Shakespeare were the objects of Turgenev's enthusiastic admiration from childhood, and he re-read and quoted them all his life.
† Turgenev spent much time obtaining authentic information on the legal technicalities involved in pre-emancipation Russia, in giving away land and serfs, and on the correct terms for the component parts of the roof which the old giant breaks to pieces.

inclusion in a volume of sporting memoirs published by his old friend S. T. Aksakov in 1855. The collection published in 1874 also contained an episode based on the author's experiences in Paris in the course of 1848 (a second story of revolutionary Paris was added when the *Memoirs* were republished in 1880), the panegyric on Pegasus, and, above all, the remarkable 'Execution of Troppmann', which first appeared in 1870. The twenty-one-year-old Troppmann was publicly guillotined in Paris on 19 January 1870 for the brutal murder of an entire family. Turgenev was invited by his writer friend Du Camp to spend the night before the execution in the prison, to witness the preparation of Troppmann for guillotining, and the final act. He accepted the invitation, immediately regretted his decision, but was afraid of appearing to be a coward. So he went along in trepidation. The description, which runs to over twenty pages in print, and which spares the reader no detail, is shattering. Turgenev was anxious to give his reportage as much publicity as he could in the hope, as he wrote, that his account would 'at any rate supply some arguments to the advocates of the abolition of capital punishment....'[24]

In the course of 1868 Turgenev was occupied with a plan for writing a long historical novel about which the normally very open author was strangely reticent. We only know of its existence from his sole confidant on the matter, Prosper Mérimée, who strongly encouraged him to proceed. Turgenev's letters to Mérimée were destroyed (after the latter's death) in a fire in 1871; no drafts or other papers relating to this work are known to have survived, and there is only one cryptic reference in his correspondence to 'a new and very strange novel indeed, in fact it is not a novel at all – but silence, silence'.[25]

So far as can be gathered from Mérimée's letters, the story was to be set in the seventeenth century and was to deal with a rebel Old Believer priest, Nikita of Suzdal, known by his enemies as 'Pustosviat' ('His Holynaught'). Turgenev had for years expressed considerable curiosity both about Russian dissenters and Old Believers, though more from the social than from the theological aspect. In 'Kasian' (in *Sketches from a Sportsman's Notebook*) and in 'The Inn', Turgenev had portrayed with great sympathy the humility of Russian dissenters. But that was in the fifties, when he was living in Russia.[26] Ten or more years later his preoccupation was different. His interest in Old Believers was now not to portray their moral qualities, but their close links in Russian history with the violence and revolt that he detested. All that can be gleaned from Mérimée's letters is that the work as planned was to deal with the rebellion of

Old Believers against the tsar led by Pustosviat in June and July of 1681. (Pustosviat was burnt at the stake on 11 July for insulting the tsar's honour.) The whole project was apparently abandoned by the end of 1869, if not before.[27]

Turgenev's literary earnings by this time must have been considerable. Between 1860 and 1869 three separate editions of his collected works were published, and although we do not know what royalty he was paid on the third and fullest of these in 1869, we know that Turgenev was very pleased with the amount.[28] For his stories and novels he earned 400 roubles for a printer's sheet in both the journals in which they appeared (the *Russian Herald* and the *European Herald*).[29] This was a substantial amount for the time (around £64). *Smoke* was also republished, like all the previous novels, in book form, for which there were additional royalties.

His writings sold readily in spite of – perhaps because of – the critical reception accorded to some of them. They were also being widely translated, especially into German and French. In a letter dated 23 June 1869 addressed to the author of a bibliographical article on the translations of his works, Turgenev summarized the position. Virtually everything that he had written had already appeared in French; German versions of the *Sketches*, *A Nest of the Landed Gentry*, and *Smoke* had been published, as well as of some ten long stories; *Fathers and Children* and some further tales were in process of appearing in an edition being prepared in Riga. In England there were available *Smoke*, *Fathers and Children*, and *A Nest of the Landed Gentry* – the latter in a particularly good recent translation by William Ralston, under the title of *Liza*.[30] There were also a few renderings into Dutch, Swedish, Czech, Serbian, and Hungarian.[31] Turgenev seems to have been well satisfied with most of the German versions of his works, but was severely critical of some of the French translations which had not been done in collaboration with Louis Viardot, or checked either by himself or by Prosper Mérimée. The first English rendering of *Smoke* was such a travesty of the original that it drew two very critical reviews from Ralston. One of them, published anonymously in the *Pall Mall Gazette*, was followed by an angry letter from Turgenev, which the editor duly published, protesting that the translation of *Smoke* was as bad as that of the *Sketches*, which had appeared in Edinburgh.[32] These publications in foreign languages, while they enhanced his international reputation, were not very lucrative. There was no copyright agreement in operation with Germany, and Turgenev frequently disclaimed all interest in any royalties on German versions of his works. There was some copyright agreement with France, but French editors and publishers were at that time not over-scrupulous in paying their foreign authors, and Turgenev claimed that he had never received a farthing in respect of French translations – although it was also true that they did not sell particularly well.

Turgenev badly needed all the money he could scrape together. Apart from his usual extravagance (such as building the grand house in Baden) there was the growing importunacy of Paulinette, whose husband's business affairs were not going well. The root cause of Turgenev's indigence, in spite of the fact that he was the owner of one of the largest properties in Orel Government, was the old problem of the mismanagement of his estates by his uncle, Nicholas Turgenev, who had never been very brilliant, and was now getting on in years. He had been associated with Spasskoe for a very long time. After the death of his brother Sergei, Turgenev's father, he had become manager to the dreaded Varvara Petrovna – Turgenev had depicted him as a rather timid and downtrodden character in the only extant fragment of his uncompleted novel *Two Generations* (see Chapter 7). In 1853, having been all but ruined by N. N. Tiutchev, who was then in charge of the properties, Turgenev had called on his uncle for help, and entrusted him with the management of Spasskoe and the other estates – in all about 5,500 *desiatins* or nearly 15,000 acres of excellent land. Uncle Nicholas settled in Spasskoe with his wife and two daughters, and a female relative. He received a salary of 2,000 roubles a year. In 1856, very unwisely as it turned out, Turgenev also gave him two bills of exchange for 10,500 roubles, to be presented only in the event of his predeceasing his uncle, but without recording this arrangement in writing.[33] The two were on very cordial terms at the time. As a boy Turgenev had been devoted to his uncle as his early letters show (see Chapter I), and after his father died he had to some degree found a substitute in his uncle, who, among other things, introduced him to the art of shooting game. All this explains why Turgenev seems to have tolerated for many years the mismanagement of his properties by a man whom Botkin described as running the estates 'badly and in a disorderly way because he is old, dilatory and idle'.[34] A further cause of friction between uncle and nephew was that the uncle, a man of old-fashioned outlook, tried in every way to frustrate the generous arrangements which his nephew made after the emancipation for his peasants in the matter of allocation of land, and ignored his directions regarding reductions in the redemption payments due from the former serfs.[35]

Matters came to a head in 1866 when Turgenev at last reached a decision to pension off his uncle (who by then was seventy-one years old) and replace him as estate manager with one N. A. Kishinsky, whom Annenkov helped him to find. In the numerous letters which he wrote to his friends, Turgenev maintained that he had never had more than 5,500 roubles as income from all his properties in any one year, which was certainly a very small amount.[36] There were other serious grounds for complaints; procrastination over the presentation of a claim for compensation under the terms of the Emancipation Act, for example, and all but allowing a sequestration order to be issued on Spasskoe for non-payment of some trifling debt.[37]

But the parting with Uncle Nicholas proved much more agonizing than could have been anticipated. The old man believed himself to have been abominably treated, and was determined to exact every penny he could from his nephew by fair means or foul. His temper was not improved by the fact that Turgenev, who arrived in Moscow at the beginning of March 1867 with the avowed object of going to Spasskoe in response to 'insane letters'[38] from his uncle, who was incensed by the arrival of Kishinsky, started off for his estate on 11 March, but returned to Moscow next day with a severe attack of bronchitis. It was the kind of affliction which, though apparently genuine enough, we should nowadays call 'psychosomatic'. He had dreaded the thought of going to Spasskoe, and was obviously much relieved when the providential illness and the appalling state of the Russian roads (there was as yet no rail connection with Orel) furnished him with an excuse to turn back; and he comforted himself with the remarkable impression that his uncle's letters were becoming 'reasonable'.[39] Botkin wrote to Fet that Turgenev's failure to go to Spasskoe was due to his 'empty character, cowardice and frivolity'.[40] The negotiations were left in the hands of Kishinsky, and the results were disastrous.

Uncle Nicholas was offered a pension of 800 roubles and a capital sum of 3,000 roubles and some other perquisites. At a later stage he was offered one of Turgenev's smaller estates, said to be worth 20,000 roubles. But the old man would not look at either of these proposals. He presented the two bills for payment, added another which Turgenev maintained had already been paid, put in a claim for interest in respect of the bills and a further demand for 6,200 roubles, alleged to be his children's capital spent on the estate – a total of 28,000 roubles. After lengthy and acrimonious negotiations, in which Turgenev's old friend and neighbour Borisov played a very helpful role, the matter was eventually settled by a payment of 20,000 roubles. Turgenev was left in debt as a result, and could see little prospect of any income from his estates until such time as the new manager had repaired the ravages left by Uncle Nicholas's years of neglect. He was also forced to sell his newly completed house in Baden to Louis Viardot, at a loss of 60,000 francs,[41] and become his tenant.*

*　　*　　*　　*　　*　　*

Life in Baden continued as idyllic as before. There was social and musical life at the Viardots' and absorption in the affairs of the family. There was the shooting. Occasionally Russian or German friends came to stay, at the Schillerstrasse flat under the care of Frau Anstett, or at the grand villa in the Thiergartenstrasse where Turgenev moved on 17 April 1868. ('There is a lot of comfort here. But I am not used to all this, and I keep on fancying that I am on a visit somewhere, and that any moment I shall be shown the door as the result of some unpleasantness.')[43] At the beginning of 1867 he suffered his first attack of gout, which lasted for some weeks.[44] This painful affliction was to recur at intervals for the rest of his life – medical science in the nineteenth century was not in a position to do very much to relieve it. In May 1869 he also suffered what appeared to be the symptoms of a heart attack. The local doctor duly confirmed some form of cardiac trouble and prescribed a strict regime, the prospect of which left Turgenev very depressed – no more shooting, no meat, no wine, no 'dallying with the fair sex'. The famous Heidelberg physician, Dr. Friedreich, agreed with the diagnosis and approved the regime which had been ordered.[45] Happily, things did not turn out as grimly as all that. By September he was out shooting again, and in April of the following year an eminent Paris specialist declared that there was nothing wrong with his heart, and that the alarming symptoms had been caused by gout.[46]

Turgenev and Pauline had already collaborated in the setting of Russian poems, including his own, to music. Several single songs, and a third volume of collected songs were published between 1866 and 1868: Annenkov was faced with the embarrassing request from Turgenev, which he fulfilled, of countering an attack on the music which had appeared in the Russian press,[47] probably occasioned by

---

* Uncle Nicholas came to a sad end. In 1872 he went blind. Two years after that his wife died, and he was left alone in his village – old, blind, solitary, and ill. A few years later Turgenev visited him. His uncle was overjoyed at the reconciliation, and still well enough to celebrate the occasion with 'immoderate' drafts of champagne.[42] He died in 1881.

the prejudice which many chauvinistic Russians felt against Pauline. The collaboration between Turgenev and Pauline was not, however, confined to songs. Between 1867 and 1869 they produced four operettas, for which Turgenev wrote the libretti and Pauline the music – *Trop de Femmes*, *Le Dernier Sorcier*, *Krakamiche*, and *Le Miroir*.[48] The first three were staged in Baden, mostly in the theatre attached to Turgenev's villa, and were very successful with the distinguished invited audiences, which on a number of occasions included the Grand Duchess of Baden, as well as the King and Queen of Prussia. There were also plans to stage *Le Miroir*,[49] but nothing seems to have come of them. Turgenev and Pauline were much occupied with the preparations, rehearsals, the ordering of costumes, and all the paraphernalia of amateur theatricals. Pauline and three of her children – Marianne, Claudie, and Paul – performed, as well as some of Pauline's pupils. Turgenev acted in the comic parts, without, however, venturing to sing. He was, he confessed in a letter to Pietsch (and later in conversation) embarrassed when, as he lay on the floor in the character of the Pacha in *Trop de Femmes*, he observed 'the Crown Princess of Prussia looking at me with an ironical, and by no means flattering, smile'.[50] Turgenev's libretti are amusing, with occasional hints of political irony directed against France (very popular with a German audience!) but amount to scarcely more than amateur frivolities.

At the suggestion of the Grand Duke of Weimar (brother of the Queen of Prussia) Pauline was invited to have *Le Dernier Sorcier* staged professionally in Weimar. The music had been highly praised by Liszt, who offered to orchestrate it, but had to leave it to the conductor of the theatre for lack of time.* The work was performed on 8 April 1869, and again on 11 April. It was mildly successful. In an unsuccessful endeavour to have the operetta staged in Russia, Turgenev wrote an account of the performance for publication in a Russian newspaper. Along with hyperbolical praise of Pauline's singing, he also included a warm recommendation to Russians to buy the volumes of songs which she had had published in Russia. This provoked acid comments, which infuriated Turgenev when they got back to him.[51]

The next professional staging in which Pauline sang one of the parts, in Karlsruhe on 28 January 1870, proved a disaster. In a long letter to Pietsch, Turgenev, probably rightly, attributed the lack of success to intrigue, jealousy, dislike of the French, and other im-

---

* The full score, the only one of the operetta scores to survive, is still in Weimar.

proper motives. He also blamed the director of the theatre, Devrient, on whom he delivered a savage attack a few years later in *Spring Torrents*. Happily he did not know that Devrient, in his diary (only recently published) attributed the operetta's failure to Pauline Viardot's 'cracked voice'.[52] 'Cracked voice' or no, Pauline sang in Gluck's *Orfeo* with enormous success in Weimar a few weeks later.[53]

There also seems to have been another form of literary collaboration between Turgenev and Pauline, possibly at this time. A notebook containing twelve poems, eleven by Turgenev and one by Pauline's brother, has survived. The poems are mildly scatological, and quite amusing. Since several of them are in Pauline's handwriting she may well have had some part in their composition.[54]

The serious troubles with Paulinette's affairs still lay well ahead. For the first few years after her marriage in 1865 she lived happily with her dull and philistine in-laws in Rougemont. As Turgenev wrote from there to Pauline, 'I am quite sure that no one ever reads anything whatever here. That is no disaster perhaps, but I am a little surprised that *my* daughter should be like that.'[55] Turgenev saw Paulinette at intervals in Paris or at her own house. On one occasion, in June, 1867, he arranged to take Paulinette to see the Paris Universal Exhibition. As he wrote to Pauline, he had 'the misfortune to fall into the hands of Grigorovich' who drove him frantic by his zeal in guiding the two of them for the whole of five hours through 'all the tohu-bohu of machines, furniture, diamonds, emeralds as large as melons' and all the rest. Turgenev was only interested in the paintings, which he returned to inspect, alone, a few days later.[56] He did not encourage Paulinette to come to Baden – unless she was prepared to mend her behaviour towards Pauline Viardot.[57] She suffered several miscarriages and was only successfully delivered of a daughter on 18 July 1872. Her father's letters to her are affectionate enough, but he never succeeded in shedding the rather nagging and censorious tone in which he had written to her for years. For example, when the first signs of her husband's lack of success with the glass factory became apparent, Turgenev blamed Paulinette for the fact that he lost customers, attributing this to her refusal to let him travel.[58] Paulinette, in turn, seems to have showered her father with reproaches for neglecting her, to judge from his letters in reply to hers (which are not available to us). She also kept on pressing him for financial help at a time when, owing to the troubles with his uncle, he was in no position to do very much for her and his son-in-law.

Turgenev's trips to Russia became more infrequent, and shorter. He spent just over three weeks in Spasskoe in 1865. His stay was cut short by a summons to return – presumably from Pauline.[59] His next journey to Russia was in 1867, for five weeks. His express intention in going there was to settle affairs at Spasskoe and attend to the installation of the new manager, but of course he never got there. There were further visits to Russia of about five weeks each in 1868 and 1870. Since he wrote almost daily to Pauline on the occasion of his visits of 1867 and 1868 we can gather a fair impression of his mood. More than ever before, there is constant reiteration of distress at his separation from Pauline and the family, and of longing to be in Baden again. As for Russia, his first reaction to being back in Spasskoe in 1865 was a sense of 'being in quarantine here'.[60] The fourteen letters available for 1867 are a long recital of misery, relieved only by such interludes as the success which he enjoyed when he read *Smoke* to a group of friends in St. Petersburg.[61] No doubt the contrast with Baden, separation from Pauline, and the dreadful cold all contributed. Attacks of gout could not have helped.

The seventeen letters extant which chronicle his visit to Russia in 1868 tell much the same story: 'Oh! How little I should like to live here!', he wrote from St. Petersburg.[62] But this time, in addition to going through the usual social and literary rounds in Moscow and St. Petersburg, he spent some three weeks in Spasskoe. 'The impression which Russia now makes on me is a very sad one. . . .', he wrote on 13 June. 'I have never seen dwellings so pitiable, so decrepit, or faces so emaciated or so sad. . . . What a difference from the villages of the Schwarzwald!'[63] 'Freedom has not made them any richer – on the contrary. All this first generation will have to disappear . . .', he wrote a few days later. He had promised to restore the school which had formerly existed in the village, and the cost of rebuilding together with numerous small pensions which he allotted to dependants amounted in all at this time to around 1,000 roubles a year.[64] The soft-hearted Turgenev was besieged daily by a flood of poverty-stricken applicants, whom he found impossible to refuse.[65]

The friendship between Turgenev and Pauline during the years spent at Baden seems to have been intimate and unclouded. His letters abound in passionate declarations of adoration, usually in German: 'I think constantly of you, day and night – and with what unending love!' 'I fall at your feet, with my lips on your feet. God bless you.' But whatever these and similar expressions were meant to convey, it was not the pangs of unrequited physical passion. As he wrote to her at the end of 1870, just after the removal from Baden, during one of her short absences from London where they were then all installed,

... time goes slowly without you. ... To the deep and unchanging feeling that I have for you there has become added some kind of impossibility of being without you: your absence causes me physical disturbance, it is as if I lacked air. ... When you are there my joy is serene. ... I feel at ease, at home, and wish for nothing else. Ah, dear friend, I have all the past 27 years to treasure [they met in 1843] ... and it will be as it was for Burns's 'Joe Anderson my Joe' [*sic*], we will go down the hill together.[66]

The few of her letters to him that have been made accessible to us are warm and affectionate, but more soberly worded. She wrote to him frequently while he was in Russia (as we know from his letters) and was sufficiently worried in July 1868 about the state of his gout to send him two successive anxious telegrams.[67] Pauline's daughter Claudie (Didie), now growing up and showing considerable talent for painting, who had always been Turgenev's favourite, began almost to rival her mother for his love. His letters to her, after 1869, contain phrases similar to those which he addressed to her mother, often in German – 'mein kleiner Abgott' ('my little idol'), 'a thousand kisses on your dear hands', and the like.

As time went by they were to become even more loving, erotic at times, in the manner characteristic of Turgenev's style when writing to any woman with whom he felt an emotional bond – and there is no doubt at all about the affectionate intimacy which existed between him and Claudie. He often illustrated his letters to her with amusing drawings, and on a number of occasions composed for her very amusing (and highly improper) scatological fantasies, revolving around Mademoiselle Arnholt, the Viardot children's former governess.[68] He wrote enthusiastically about her beauty and talent to his Russian friends, sometimes enclosing her photograph. In 1870 he directed I. I. Maslov, who usually acted as his financial agent in Russia, to hand over all the shares which he had deposited with him to Pauline Viardot for her daughter Claudie, in the event of his death. The total dowry which he put aside for her amounted to 31,000 francs by 1870, and he planned to increase it to 50,000. By 1871 he had succeeded in allocating nearly 80,000 francs for her. (He rejected Louis's suggestion that part of the money should be invested in French bonds, as a 'patriotic sacrifice'.)[69]

Turgenev spent six weeks in Russia in May and June of 1870, much of the time in Spasskoe. He was engaged there on the thorough revision of 'King Lear of the Steppes', which was published in October. He also had staying with him for a time his English translator, William Ralston, with whom he had recently become friendly, and whom he had invited to Spasskoe in October of the previous year.[70] He showed him something of Russian country life. He took him to the meeting of the local justices of the peace, and laid on a festival of dance and song by the peasants of Spasskoe. He also invited his neighbours Borisov and Fet.[71] Ralston was delighted with what he observed of Turgenev's easy and warm relations with the peasants. Years later, as he recalls, a plan was discussed for the two to return to Spasskoe, Turgenev to write, and Ralston to translate, a new novel on which Turgenev then proposed to start. This was to be about a Russian girl radical who marries a French socialist, and was to describe the gulf that opens up between the two when she discovers how different the aims of Russian socialists are from those of their French counterparts.[72] Ralston, a librarian at the British Museum, had learnt Russian thoroughly and had made a name as a writer on Russian literature and folklore. Turgenev thought highly of his work and published, in England, a warm review of his book on Krylov. His reputation in Russia, a country he came to know well, was so high that he was elected a corresponding member of the Imperial Academy of Sciences.

On his way to Russia Turgenev used to stop in Berlin where he had many friends and admirers. His closest companion there, no doubt in part because he was a frequent and welcome guest at the Viardots, was Ludwig Pietsch. The critic Julian Schmidt had also paved the way for a lasting friendship with his enthusiastic articles on Turgenev's writing. The author Berthold Auerbach (for whose *Villa on the Rhine* Turgenev had written a preface when it appeared in a Russian translation) was also frequently in his company in Berlin, though Turgenev seems to have been a little bored by his importunacy. As always Turgenev particularly enjoyed himself among artists – the painter Adolphe Menzel, for example, or the sculptor Rheinhold Begas.[73]

These short visits apart, his contacts with Russia were becoming more tenuous. Old friends occasionally visited Baden, and he corresponded regularly with Annenkov, Borisov, Fet, the poet and painter Polonsky, and some others. So far as Fet was concerned, Turgenev's letters show an increasing acerbity towards his old shooting companion. He was evidently becoming less tolerant of Fet's growing antagonism to any form of 'progress, liberalism, emancipation etc.'[74] It would not be long before they quarrelled.

Turgenev's real interests now lay only with the life which centred around Pauline Viardot. After the antagonism aroused by *Smoke*, a work which had been intended as a defiant challenge to the two extremes that he detested in Russian life – pretentious radicalism and reactionary obscurantism – he seems for some years to have lost confidence in himself as a writer. The stories which he produced in the last years of the sixties were not among his best, and he knew it. Emigration, even if self-imposed, was beginning to show its normal effects. He did not much seek to maintain literary contacts with Russia; it was a world which for the time being had become too remote for him. He had little admiration for what was being written there. He was tired of the poetry of Fet, thought nothing of Maikov and A. Tolstoy, and detested Nekrasov. But he much admired the verse of his friend Polonsky, in whose defence against critics he wrote an open letter in 1870.[75] Leo Tolstoy's apart, the only Russian novels which Turgenev had much use for were those of the now forgotten Reshetnikov, Pisemsky's *A Thousand Souls* and Saltykov's *History of a Certain Town*, in praise of which he published an article in English. This was the first work of Saltykov (Shchedrin) which Turgenev is known to have liked: he had been critical of his earlier writings, but he much admired Saltykov's *chef-d'œuvre Gospoda Golovlevy*, when it appeared in 1875.[76] He found Goncharov's *The Precipice* (the plot of which he was once supposed by its paranoid author to have plagiarized for *A Nest of the Landed Gentry*) very long-winded, and false.[77]

There are numerous comments in Turgenev's correspondence, both enthusiastic and critical, about *War and Peace*, which was coming out in instalments towards the end of the decade.[78] He detested the philosophical disquisitions and what he regarded as Tolstoy's over-facile acceptance of 'systems' which purport to explain everything. He thought the psychology was crude, particularly where the women were concerned. The good women, he says, are mere females for breeding, even fools; while the clever ones are liars and phrasemongers. 'Natasha in particular is rather weak, and tends towards the type so beloved by Tolstoy (*excusez du mot*) ——' at this point the prudery of the Soviet editors leaves an intriguing blank.[79] Tolstoy, he says, displays some similarity with Wagner – not a compliment, coming from Turgenev. The historical detail is false and meretricious – it is dragged in to suggest a profound knowledge of history which the author in fact lacks. But – with all its faults – it is the most interesting book to have appeared in Russia for a long time, Tolstoy is unequalled as a writer, and his descriptions of action and incidents are truthful and superbly beautiful. He is a giant among the rest of the literary fraternity.

Turgenev did not become immersed in French literary life until he came to live in Paris in 1871. But he maintained, by correspondence

and on his occasional visits to the French capital, some contacts with
the writers. These were principally Du Camp, and, until his death
in 1870, his friend and translator Prosper Mérimée. The two men
were drawn together by Mérimée's interest in Russian language,
history, and literature. In an obituary on him published in a Russian
paper Turgenev described him as 'one of the subtlest and cleverest
writers of fiction', praised him for his love and understanding of
Pushkin's poetry, and emphasized his modesty and lack of vanity.[80]
His closest French friendship, with Gustave Flaubert, still lay ahead.
Among Russians, his most intimate association was probably that
with his namesake (or very remote relative) N. I. Turgenev, his wife,
and family. A recently published diary by Fanny, the daughter of
N. I. Turgenev, records both the frequency of Turgenev's visits to
her parents' Paris household and the warm respect and affection in
which he was held. It also vividly reproduces some of his much famed
conversation.[81]

But life in Baden came to an end. In November 1868 the Viardot
family moved to Karlsruhe. The main reason was the need to provide
their son Paul with a better education than Baden could offer, and
to enable Claudie to study painting, which was also not possible
there.[82] Turgenev, for whom the prospect of life in Baden without
the Viardots was 'frightening', soon followed them.[83] He did not,
however, give up his house, but took some rooms in an hotel for
the winter. He stayed in Karlsruhe until the end of March 1869, and,
after a visit to Paris, returned there and visited Weimar for the performance of *Le Dernier Sorcier*, before removing once again to Baden.
He stayed until February 1870. The Viardots also seem to have
returned to Baden, at any rate for part of the time, since on 8 June
1869 a musical party took place at their villa – 'after a long interruption' – in the presence of the Queen of Prussia.[84] In February 1870
the Viardots and Turgenev moved again, this time to Weimar for
a couple of months – once more, in order to provide Claudie with
a suitable painting master, though Pauline seems also to have given
'brilliant' musical matinées, in the hotel in which they all lived.[85]
In May Turgenev left for Russia, and the Viardots once again moved
back to Baden. But not for long.

On his return journey from Russia to Baden Turgenev found himself in Berlin on the very day that war between France and Prussia
was declared – 15 July 1870. He despised this 'hideous, disgusting
war', which had been expected for a long time, but decided to stay
in Baden, as did the Viardots. His sympathies were stoutly with Germany – not for love of Prussia so much as because of his detestation

of the regime of Napoleon III: 'Prussia is not much of a liberal state – but the victory of France would spell amen to all freedom in Europe.'[86] In a long letter to Annenkov of 8 August, which was to become the first of a series of reports on the war which Annenkov arranged for publication in the *St. Petersburg Chronicle*, Turgenev claimed that he had respect and affection for the French people. But he expressed the hope that military defeat would prove a salutary lesson for France – and above all, lead to the overthrow of Napoleon III.[87] There were five such reports in all, in the form of letters, the last dated 30 September, by which time French defeat was evident and Napoleon III in captivity. These accounts are balanced, and in the main accurate. They are highly critical of the French press but also of the Prussians, and in particular of their intention to annex Alsace-Lorraine. He expressed his fears that the Prussians would attempt to put Napoleon back on his throne as well as his hope that the Germans would not succeed in capturing Paris.[88] Similar sentiments are to be found in his private letters.

So far as his other literary activities were concerned, notwithstanding the apprehensions which he was now voicing with increasing frequency that his prolonged absence from Russia was damaging him as a writer, he was approaching a new period of literary effort, which was to include one of his masterpieces, *Spring Torrents*. But the pattern of his life was now rudely interrupted. In spite of the war, the Viardot family had attempted to carry on in Baden, 'making music, caring for the wounded, reading aloud in order to pass the time'.[89] But the hostilities had a very adverse effect on their income, and Pauline had decided by the beginning of October to move to London where she had good prospects of substantial earnings from concerts and from giving lessons. They left for London on 23 October. Turgenev accompanied them as far as Ostend, and made arrangements to follow them as soon as possible. He arrived in London on 13 November 1870.

CHAPTER FOURTEEN

Spring Torrents

On arrival in London in October 1870 Pauline and her two daughters settled at 8 Seymour Street, Portman Square, while Louis stayed on in Baden with Paul. She wrote impatiently to Turgenev asking him to join her.[1] By the time he reached London on 13 November, Pauline, now reunited with Louis and Paul, had moved to 30 Devonshire Place, a handsome, late-Georgian house which still stands. It was at this house, at the end of April, that Turgenev read a notice of Pauline's death, which appeared in a number of European newspapers, including the *Pall Mall Gazette*. One can imagine the shock that this item would have caused had it not been for the fact that he was sitting in the same room with her when he read it. He promptly wrote off to his Russian friends, denying the report. A few months later he saw the news of his own death in *Le Temps*, which had confused him with the Decembrist.[2] The press was doing well.

The first lodgings which Turgenev found in London were very uncomfortable, and before long he moved to 4 Bentinck Street, Manchester Square, where he stayed until he left for Russia in February of the following year. In fact, most of his time was spent at 30 Devonshire Place, his real home, and the taking of separate lodgings was for the sake of appearances. His visit to Russia in 1871 was short – a little over five weeks – and he was back in London[3] on 7 April. Pauline was away when he arrived, or left London soon after. But she wrote to him in such 'poetic' terms that she seems to have caused some offence to Louis – the letter to Turgenev is lost, but her reply to her husband explaining that 'it was only right that Turgenev who was alone and in pain should receive a more detailed letter than you' has survived.[4] On his return Turgenev took new lodgings at 16 Beaumont Street, Marylebone. At the end of July he accompanied the Viardot family to Boulogne, stayed with them there for a few days, and then returned to London on his way to

Scotland. On 21 August he rejoined the Viardots, temporarily back in Baden to wind up their property. The short London interlude was over.

Turgenev renewed his literary friendships in London: there were several visits to Carlyle, and at least one to Tennyson. It is difficult to imagine any common intellectual ground between Turgenev and Carlyle – and indeed some ten years later Turgenev told his friend Polonsky that the old man had 'talked a great deal of nonsense'. Carlyle thought Turgenev was 'by far the best [talker] I have ever heard who talks so much.'[5] He met Sir Charles Dilke, and it may be presumed that he renewed his long-standing friendship with Richard Monckton Milnes, later Lord Houghton. He met Swinburne and other literary figures at Ford Madox Brown's house, and again in Scotland, in August. He expressed admiration for his poetry on a number of occasions, especially for *Songs before Sunrise*, which showed 'sparks of undoubted talent', even if occasionally 'obscure' ('A genius', he described him to George Moore.) For the work of Rossetti ('decadent') and of other contemporary poets he had little use.[6] Swinburne was a protégé of Lord Houghton, who may well have brought the two men together on other occasions. Turgenev also became a frequent visitor at the house of George Lewes (whom he had known in his student days in Berlin many years before) and George Eliot, at Regent's Park. George Eliot much admired Turgenev's work, as he did hers; a cordial letter from him to the novelist, written in very good English some years later, expresses much gratification at her favourable judgement of his writings. He regarded *The Mill on the Floss* as her best novel[7] – the usual favourite of liberal-minded Russians was *Felix Holt*. It was at George Eliot's, too, that he met William Henry Bullock, who shortly afterwards inherited (along with the surname of Hall) what Turgenev described as the finest partridge shooting in England, at Six Mile Bottom, between Cambridge and Newmarket. In spite of frequent invitations from Hall, Turgenev did not succeed in visiting Six Mile Bottom until 1878, when G. H. Lewes and George Eliot were two fellow guests, much to his delight.[8]

His visit to Scotland was occasioned by an invitation (at Lord Houghton's insistence) to participate in the centenary celebrations of the birth of Sir Walter Scott at Edinburgh on 9 August 1871. There was also an invitation to take part after the ceremony in grouse shooting at Allean House, Pitlochry, from Mr. and Mrs. Benzon, who were musical friends of the Viardots. Turgenev's short speech at Edinburgh, translated and polished up by Ralston, was mercilessly garbled by the press; the author became variously Tourquenoff and Torguenoff, while Pushkin in one version became Tourhaine. As he wrote to Pauline, he felt like a completely unknown man, talking about a subject (Russian appreciation of Scott, which was, in fact, enormous) to which his audience was completely indifferent. He did not enjoy the grouse shooting very much and an accident to his leg on the moors on 13 August did not improve matters. Robert Browning, who lived nearby, called several times at Allean House while Turgenev was there. The poet did not impress him: he found him 'empty-headed', 'very vain, and not very amusing ... boring'. The company also included the Master of Balliol, Benjamin Jowett, as well as Swinburne.[9]

When the Franco-Prussian war came to an end and order had been restored in Paris after the fall of the Commune, the Viardots decided to return to the French capital. There was no question of resuming life in Baden; Louis, who had detested the French Second Empire, was both reconciled to France, now republican once again, and opposed to Germany, whose treatment of France outraged his patriotic sentiments. As for Turgenev, life without the Viardots was naturally unthinkable, and to return to Paris (much as he disliked that city) was the only possible course.

The properties in Baden were sold, including Turgenev's villa of which Louis Viardot had become the owner when Turgenev got into debt over the final settlement with his Uncle Nicholas. The villa was sold to a Moscow banker, Th. G. Akhenbach. The Viardots returned to their old house in Paris, 48 rue de Douai, and Turgenev moved into the third floor – quite modest quarters, small and crowded, of which several descriptions have survived.[10] Until his death in 1883 he was to remain with the Viardot family, spending the winters in Paris and the summers in Bougival, on the Seine, about an hour's journey from the capital.

The three, Pauline now aged fifty and Turgenev and Louis fifty-three and seventy respectively, no longer even kept up the little pretence that they had felt necessary to engage in while they were younger. Louis Viardot, who had never (or hardly ever) shown any jealousy or resentment, now completely accepted Turgenev's presence as part of daily life and the correspondence between the two men which has survived bears ample testimony to the genuine friendship between them. Many years later, in 1907, Pauline's eldest daughter, Louise Héritte, in two very unpleasant letters published in the *Frankfurter Zeitung*, accused Turgenev of having sponged on her parents for years. Louise was unbalanced and embittered, and her accusations were undoubtedly unjust. On the other hand, it is only fair that allowance should be made for the psychological disturbance which Turgenev's love affair with her mother must surely have caused. (She was only eight or nine when the infatuation was at its most intense on Pauline's side.) Apart from providing the dowry for Claudie, Turgenev left all his property to Pauline (see Appendix). This included his share in the villa at Bougival, 'Les Frênes', which Turgenev and the Viardots acquired jointly in 1874 as a permanent summer home, to replace the one of which they had been tenants. Turgenev's contribution to the price of 'Les Frênes' amounted to at least a third of the value of the property.[11] He raised the money by the sale of one of his smaller estates. We have no evidence about the arrangements regarding household expenses. But whatever faults Turgenev had, meanness was not one of them, and it is very probable that he contributed in the form of gifts, if not in the direct sharing of bills.

With Turgenev's removal to Paris began the period of his close contacts with most of the leading French writers of the day, which lasted for the rest of his life. Turgenev's regard for Flaubert was as much for the man as for the supreme craftsman. (There is a masterly description by Turgenev of Flaubert reworking, and in the process completely transforming, a translation into French of one of Pushkin's short stories made by Turgenev and Louis Viardot.)[12] Turgenev frequently spoke of Flaubert as so good-natured that he could hate one thing only: the kind of bourgeois self-satisfied pettiness which he had so vividly described in *Bouvard et Pécuchet*. Turgenev at one time suggested that the two of them should travel together in Russia – Flaubert did indeed hint in his correspondence that he would enjoy a visit to Spasskoe – but nothing ever came of it.[13] In his letters Flaubert repeatedly writes of Turgenev with genuine warmth, even if he shows occasional slight signs of irritation at the Russian's lack of character, about which he was perfectly frank: 'Ever since I wrote to him that he is a "soft pear" they call him nothing but "soft pear" at the Viardots!'[14] But of his affection there can be no doubt: 'Apart from you and Turgenev,' Flaubert wrote to George Sand on 2 July 1870, 'I know of no mortal with whom I can unburden myself of the things which are closest to my heart....'[15]

The close link between Flaubert and the Viardots was furnished, not only by Turgenev, but also by George Sand. Turgenev was friendly too with Zola, Daudet, and Edmond de Goncourt. There was, of course, more casual acquaintance with other writers, such as Théophile Gautier. The Frenchmen delighted in his company and have recorded scores of anecdotes based on their numerous conversations: the tendency to exaggerate and embellish on all sides, not least Turgenev's, makes the reliability of these stories at times open to doubt. (One also gets the impression that Turgenev, who, in spite of his occasional predilection for crude language and scatological jests, was rather prudish, sometimes showed embarrassment at the frank Gallic discussions of sexual experiences.) They met at each other's houses, and instituted the practice of foregathering regularly at a restaurant for luxurious and protracted meals. These occasions – mainly attended by Zola, Flaubert (when in Paris), Edmond de Goncourt, Daudet, and Turgenev – were jocularly known as the dinners of the 'failures' (Turgenev qualified because of the lack of the success of his plays). They started on 14 April 1874 and normally took place every month.[16] We get a fairly clear picture from these French littérateurs of their Russian companion, whom they all liked. He was massive in build, grey or white haired, and had a slight impediment in his speech. Soft and malleable, and without much firmness of character, he had all the marks of the Russian grand gentleman (*barin*) – extravagance, a natural consciousness of his own superiority and, above all, his unpunctuality. (Turgenev's collected correspondence bristles with apologies for forgotten appointments or for the postponement or alteration of social arrangements.) But at the same time all were agreed on his modesty, total lack of vanity, and his charm. He was always elegantly dressed and most carefully groomed when in company. In the privacy of his study he was usually found by visitors attired in old bedroom slippers and a shabby woollen jacket or jersey.

In general, one senses that (Flaubert apart) these French intellectuals treated Turgenev as a somewhat frivolous character. We have, however, a record of his own view of himself which is rather different, and is an aspect which the Frenchmen probably missed. It is contained in a letter to M. A. Miliutina, widow of the liberal-minded minister N. A. Miliutin: Turgenev had been on very friendly terms with both after the 1850s. The letter is dated 22 February 1875, and is a reply to a request for help for her son who had been set the task at school of writing an essay on Turgenev's outlook. 'To put the matter briefly,' he wrote, 'I am first and foremost a realist – and am, above all, interested in the living truth of the human physiognomy. I am indifferent to everything supernatural. I do not believe in any absolute, or in any systems, and I love freedom above everything else. As far as I can judge, I have an understanding of poetry. Everything human is dear to me.

The doctrines of the Slavophiles, like all orthodoxies, are alien to me.'[17]

Some years after Turgenev's death Daudet was appalled to read in a volume of memoirs that a man whom he had considered his friend had in conversation frequently disparaged him both as a writer and as a human being. The memoirs concerned were by one Isaac Pavlovsky, a young Russian radical whom Turgenev befriended during the last years of his life, in Paris. Turgenev was not incapable of occasional hypocrisy. But Pavlovsky's recollections of him bristle with every kind of inaccuracy. Moreover, there are at least four favourable references to Daudet's writing in Turgenev's correspondence and he was also instrumental in ensuring for him the post of regular French literary correspondent on *Novoe vremia*. The authenticity of the remarks quoted by Pavlovsky are therefore open to considerable doubt.[18] Several close friends of Turgenev, Polonsky for example, also confirmed after his death that he had referred to Daudet's writing approvingly.

In general it was true that Turgenev was not a great admirer of French literature, always excluding the work of Flaubert which (with the possible exception of *Un Cœur simple*) he could not praise highly enough. He liked some of Zola's novels, though with reservations about their outspoken realism: 'How on earth can it concern me to know whether she sweats in the middle of her back or beneath her arms?' he remarked to the young George Moore on the subject of Gervaise in *L'Assommoir*.[19] He had no time for Victor Hugo, and found Balzac's novels unreadable. He ranked Maupassant highest after Flaubert: 'undoubtedly the most talented of French writers'.

It was only after his return to Paris that he really got to know George Sand, rather surprisingly, in view of the intimacy between George and Pauline. He had met the formidable lady previously at Courtavenel in 1845.[20] At that date he was much impressed by her as a novelist. Her literary influence on his own early writings, notably some of the *Sketches from a Sportsman's Notebook*, can be clearly discerned, and he acknowledged it many years later. Twenty-five years were to elapse before he saw her again, during a visit to Paris in 1870, when he had not yet recovered from the shock of witnessing the guillotining of Troppmann.[21] After he settled in Paris, Turgenev paid a number of visits to George Sand's house in Nohant, during the last few years before her death in 1876. The 'advanced' views voiced in her novels no longer inspired the veneration which he had felt when he first read them as a young man, but he still much admired her descriptions of travel.[22] Above all, he was completely captivated by her as a person and repeatedly wrote of her and her household to his friends in terms of the warmest affection. To Ralston he praised her 'good humour, cordiality and benevolence'; to Flaubert her 'serenity', and 'goodness', for the sake of which one should tolerate a few eccentricities in her political views. To another friend he extolled the kindness and the complete lack of egoism of 'this wonderful woman'.[23] In the short obituary which he published when he heard of her death he described her as 'one of our saints'.[24]

An incident occurred in 1876 in Paris involving Turgenev to which he attached so much significance that it is recounted on the basis of his own words by no fewer than five memoirists – with variations, of course. But the basic facts are not in doubt. On 4 March 1876 Turgenev and Flaubert (and also possibly Daudet and Zola, or one of them), attended the performance of a play entitled *Madame Caverlet* by Emile Augier – apparently a tract for the times intended as criticism of the impossibility of obtaining a divorce in France.

The heroine, separated from her scoundrel husband, has been living in perfect happiness with her lover, to whom she has borne a son and a daughter who know nothing of the irregularity of the situation, and believe themselves to be legitimate. After many years the husband, with purely mercenary motives connected with the inheritance of some property, calls, reveals to the son the true situation, and departs. When the lover returns home and is about to kiss his daughter, the son, in an excess of Gallic virtue, forbids him to do so – to the loud applause of the Paris audience. Turgenev was incensed beyond control – according to one of the accounts he rose in his box and hissed. Later (in the presence of Edmond de Goncourt, who recorded the incident), he explained his indignation to Flaubert, claiming that every Russian would have felt the same. You Latins, he told Flaubert, are men of the law. Russians are, above all else, motivated by considerations of humanity, and the letter of the law takes second place in their attitude to problems of life.[25]

As his correspondence shows, while Turgenev lived in Paris he was able to promote the publication in Russia of translations of some French writers whose work he approved – Flaubert, above all, but also Zola, Daudet, and Taine's *Ancien Régime*. He was unsuccessful in persuading Stasiulevich, his new editor, to publish a translation of Flaubert's *La Tentation de Saint Antoine*, for which he had the highest admiration, while recognizing that it was the kind of work that would only appeal to a discriminating minority of readers.[26] But he mobilized a number of his German friends to write about Flaubert's latest novel in Germany. He was more successful in Russia with Taine and Zola, and the latter achieved quite wide popularity among his Russian readers. Turgenev endeavoured to popularize Edmond de Goncourt's novels in Russia, but with little result.[27] He was also active in publicizing Russian books among French readers, especially those of Tolstoy for whose writing, the personal quarrel notwithstanding, he retained great, if occasionally critical, admiration. He did not like *Anna Karenina* – the first part to be published he found 'pretentious, petty, with a preconceived prejudice – and, besides, dull'. In spite of occasional magnificent pages, it is 'sour, smells of Moscow, incense, old maids, Slav nonsense and the nobility, etc.'[28] Some time later, he described it as 'Orthodoxy, nobility, Slavophile ideas, gossip, the Arbat, Katkov, Antonina Bludova, ill manners, conceit, lordly habits, the officer caste, hostility to everything strange, sour cabbage soup, and an absence of soap – in a word, chaos!' – a splendid catalogue of everything that Turgenev disliked![29] In spite of the break in their personal relations, Tolstoy gave Turgenev authority for the translation of his works into French, at Turgenev's request and through Fet as intermediary, and Turgenev arranged for the French rendering of *The Two Hussars*, to which he wrote a preface in most laudatory terms, introducing Tolstoy to the French reader.[30] He also tried to promote the plays of Ostrovsky among the French public but did not succeed.[31]

Turgenev's very extensive correspondence, running to many thousands of letters, conveys the impression of a man who spent a fair proportion of his resources and his time in miscellaneous forms of help to others. He was, of course, rich and with plenty of time at his disposal – and could well have been even richer, but for his extravagance and lack of method in handling his income. He could, perhaps, have made better use of his time if he had been less subject to the natural idleness which beset most Russian landed gentlemen. He paid out a large number of small pensions to aged, destitute relatives, some of whom were also given food and shelter at Spasskoe, and to retired household servants. Altogether, the pensions and the Spasskoe school and old people's home cost him 1,200 roubles a year, which in 1878 amounted to around an eighth of his gross income.[32] He seems always to have been ready to lend money to his friends and even strangers, and responsive to charitable appeals, especially if they had a liberal political flavour, such as funds for students victimized by the repressive measures of the government. He made frequent efforts to help indigent Russian writers and singers to earn something by appealing to his influential friends in Russia.

Presumably most men and women in a position of influence spend some of their time in trying to help others. Even so, Turgenev's correspondence in later life leaves the impression that he spent more effort on the concerns of others than many do. Thus (to take a statistic), for the last two complete years of his life – 1881 and 1882 – the Soviet Academy of Sciences' edition of his letters reprints 740 items. (There are undoubtedly many more letters, either as yet undiscovered, or published since the completion of the Academy edition.) Of these 740 letters, 79 deal with help to strangers in one form or another – promoting publication of the works of young authors, efforts to secure employment for those in need, or simply financial help (support for Paulinette is not included in this calculation). One of his most lasting charitable efforts was co-operation in the setting up in Paris of a Russian Reading Room for the benefit of the Russian colony, mainly for political *émigrés* and for students. In order to raise funds Turgenev helped to organize a literary and musical afternoon at the Viardots' house, in which Pauline, as well as several Russian musicians then in Paris, participated. Turgenev read his sketch 'There's Knocking!' and a story by Gleb Uspensky, and in all 1,800 francs were realized. Turgenev also donated subscriptions to several Russian periodicals to the Reading Room, which survived until the German occupation of Paris in 1941,[33] and was active in establishing a society for help to Russian painters in need, of which for a time he was secretary.

His wide circle of friends in Paris was by no means confined to the French literary stars. There were frequent visitors from Russia – the novelist Pisemsky, Annenkov, and Prince Cherkassky (who had been prominent in active co-operation in the peasant emancipation) among them. Of the resident Russians, one of his most frequent companions for dinner parties was N. V. Khanykov (1822–78), a geographer and ethnographer, and specialist on eastern affairs. When Khanykov died in 1878, Turgenev spoke at his funeral and organized a subscription to pay for a monument on his grave at Père Lachaise cemetery, which the sculptor Antokolsky made. Another Russian friend in Paris was A. A. Kharlamov (1842–1922), an accomplished painter whose portraits Turgenev greatly admired ('There can be no doubt that there is no portrait painter comparable to him in the whole world.').[34] His paintings of Pauline and Louis Viardot (executed in 1874) were exhibited in the Paris Salon in 1875. He also did a portrait of Turgenev which was generally considered a good likeness.[35] I. Repin, (1844–1930) a young Russian painter, like Kharlamov of the rather rigidly realist school, whose work was also occasionally mildly praised by Turgenev, was sometimes invited to dinner. Among the other Russians whose company Turgenev enjoyed were P. V. Zhukovsky (1845–1912), a painter and architect, and son of the poet, and G. N. Vyriubov (1843–1913), a positivist philosopher, long resident in Paris, who was Herzen's literary executor and joint editor of *Revue de la philosophie positive*.

But his closest Russian friends in Paris were still the members of the family of N. I. Turgenev, the Decembrist. He spent many evenings with them and one of the events of the year, whenever possible, was a celebration on 19 February of the anniversary of the emancipation of the serfs, attended by other active promoters of the liberation of the peasants present in Paris. These occasions were marked by emotional speeches. In spite of the difference in their ages (the Decembrist was twenty-nine years older than the novelist) they had been close friends for many years, sharing a detestation of serfdom, and a determination to do what they could to bring about its abolition. The older man had been active in the preparatory stages of the Decembrist conspiracy, but left Russia in 1824 before its improvised implementation in 1825. He was condemned to death in his absence, and remained thereafter in exile, mainly in France, earning great respect among the liberal-minded members of the Russian emigration for his writings. Eventually he was granted an amnesty, and paid several visits to Russia. When N. I. Turgenev died in 1871, his namesake published a long obituary on him,[36] and maintained both the friendship with his widow and children and the customary commemorative dinner.[37]

Turgenev had always shown a great appetite for painting, first evoked by his travels in Italy as a student. Settled in Paris, with his finances for once more or less in order, he was able to indulge his interest by amassing a small collection of pictures, and of occasional *objets d'art*. His taste in pictures seems to have centred on the masters of the Barbizon School, who were beginning to achieve recognition. He particularly admired Rousseau, one of whose landscapes he acquired in 1875, along with a work by Dupré.[38] We have no direct record of his opinion of the impressionists, but he much admired Corot, who may be regarded as their forerunner; and, in later years, usually in argument with his friend Polonsky, vigorously defended the painter's duty to portray what is characteristic in nature rather than to indulge in lifeless photographic realism.[39] Turgenev also owned a Diaz, and a painting of a courtesan by the less well-known Blanchard (which he acquired in the Salon in 1872), which was admired by its owner (in spite of some embarrassment caused by the fact that the lady had no clothes on) but not by friends like

Théophile Gautier or Flaubert.[40] His other great enthusiasm was for the Dutch seventeenth-century masters, Rembrandt above all, but also the landscape painters, and the domestic painters like Ostade and Pieter de Hooch.[41] He was not much drawn to Rubens. His own small collection of Dutch painting included a Salomon van Ruysdael and a Van der Neer.[42] Except for the portrait painter Kharlamov, Russian artists did not arouse any particular interest in him.

He was much impressed by the work of a young sculptor, Antokolsky, to whose representation of Ivan the Terrible he devoted a laudatory article after a visit to his studio on his Russian trip in 1871, and whom he continued to extol in his correspondence.[43] Antokolsky was a Jew, and many of his sculptures were devoted to Jewish themes. He later settled in Paris, and Turgenev was often in his company. (Antokolsky modelled a bust of him, which was completed in 1880.) One of Antokolsky's most successful sculptures depicted Christ, and Turgenev was quite unable to persuade the outraged Russian ambassador, Prince Orlov, that a Jew could possibly have done such a thing with reverence.[44] While in St. Petersburg in the spring of 1871 Turgenev sat for his portrait for the painters N. N. Ge and K. E. Makevsky. He was very satisfied with both – the one by Ge, in particular, he considered a 'striking resemblance'.[45] In 1872 he was painted by V. G. Perov, and in 1875 by Kharlamov. Except for the portrait by Kharlamov, which is in the State Russian Museum in Leningrad, these portraits are either privately owned or lost.[46] In 1874 Repin painted what is probably the most frequently reproduced likeness of Turgenev, seated patriarchally, with a book in his hands. Repin had to alter the portrait several times before Pauline, who took a great interest in its progress, was satisfied.[47]

Music always remained an essential part of Turgenev's life. In Paris there were the regular musical days at the Viardots' house in the rue de Douai, and visits to the opera, especially on the very rare occasions when Pauline appeared. On his Russian trips he heard whatever was available – though as he wrote tactfully to Pauline on 21 February 1871 regarding a forthcoming visit to St. Petersburg of Adelina Patti who had caused a sensation in Moscow, 'I know someone who will not go to listen to her'.[48] His taste in music changed little over the years. He liked Gluck, Mozart, and Beethoven best. Of the moderns he approved of Bizet, Gounod, and Saint-Saëns – perhaps more because of associations with Pauline's performances in their operas than for the intrinsic quality of their music. He was delighted with Schumann's music when he first heard it[49] (though he expressed doubts about it later) and surprisingly had some praise for Wagner's

Meistersinger.[50] He was contemptuous of most of the modern school of Russian composers (Balakirev, Dargomyzhsky, even Glinka), but he admired Tchaikovsky. He attended, in February 1879, the general rehearsal of *Eugene Onegin*, staged for the first time by Nicholas Rubinstein. Turgenev already knew it from the piano score, which he had obtained for Pauline to play when it was published at the end of 1878, and was delighted with it. The music impressed him even more when he heard it performed by an orchestra. It was 'warm, passionate, youthful, very colourful and very lyrical' he wrote to Claudie. He was, however, most critical of the libretto, which he regarded as a travesty of Pushkin's poem.[51] He also spoke well of Rimsky-Korsakov (of whose compositions he knew little) and, on one occasion, was well impressed by the young Moussorgsky's *Boris Godunov*.[52]

Russian music was a favourite subject of heated argument between Turgenev and the critic V. V. Stasov when they met, or when they exchanged lengthy letters. There was a political undercurrent to the debate, for Stasov's promotion of Russian music had a nationalistic motive. Although he was in no sense a Slavophile, his immoderate praise (as it seemed to Turgenev) of contemporary Russian composers was sufficiently open to suspicion of Slavophile affinities. The two men were originally drawn together by dislike of Briullov's romantic and dramatic painting of the 'Last Days of Pompeii' (which acquired some fame outside Russia and was said to have inspired Bulwer-Lytton's novel). But it was almost the only thing they agreed on. The suspicion of Slavophile affinities was enough to raise the hackles of Turgenev. He had by now completely shed even the slight sympathy with the views of those Russian nationalist enthusiasts that he had shown in the far-off days of the early fifties when he was living in Russia, writing about the peasants, and was friendly with the Aksakovs. For years past, and especially since the writing of *Smoke*, he had never lost an occasion to express his dislike of Slavophile doctrine and everything connected in his mind with it – Moscow, for example, with its stifling 'smell of icon lamps'.[53] Russian music was singled out for special ridicule in one of Potugin's speeches in *Smoke*. And so Stasov's promotion of modern Russian composers, whom in any case Turgenev disliked, was a constant irritant, and provoked much heated argument, with much Slav excitement and much Turgenev exaggeration. His letters to Stasov are long diatribes, which the recipient enjoyed as much as the writer – mostly about music, although art and literature figured as well. Occasionally they agreed, much to Turgenev's dismay, real or feigned – Stasov recalled later with delight one such occasion when Turgenev pretended to open the window and shouted 'Take me, take me off to the madhouse, I agree with Stasov!'[54] He later caricatured Stasov, or aspects of him, somewhat cruelly in *Virgin Soil*, in the person of Skoropikhin.

There is a curiously personal note in one of the many exchanges between the two men. Stasov once enquired of Turgenev why he had never included a study of marriage in his fiction, to which Turgenev replied: 'You know, there are unofficial marriages as well as official: the unofficial form can indeed be more venomous than the more generally accepted one. The whole question is, indeed, very well known to me, and I have studied it thoroughly. If I have not hitherto touched on it in my literary efforts, that is simply because I have always avoided subjects which are too personal – they embarrass me. When all this has receded even farther from me, I will perhaps think about trying to put down something about it.'[55] This was a clear reference to his friendship with Pauline Viardot of which Stasov (like everyone else) was well aware. But Turgenev never wrote about the 'unofficial' kind of marriage – unless the lost novel in which he is reported to have described his personal life was in fact written.[56]

★   ★   ★   ★   ★

Whatever the mysteries of the relationship of Turgenev and Pauline Viardot, to the outward observer it was as plain as could be. He declared his utter devotion to her to all and sundry. There were few of the many hundreds who subsequently published recollections of Turgenev who did not witness some act of dedication by him to Pauline or her children, or who failed to observe how much the whole pattern of his life was determined by that of the Viardot family. Pauline's wishes, her comfort, her domestic, to say nothing of her professional needs, were for him the supreme law, which took precedence over everything else and it is only fair to add that there is no evidence (even from Pauline's many detractors and ill-wishers) to suggest that she ever abused this enormous power which she held over him. Repin, the painter, recalls one morning when Pauline was expected at his studio: 'The bell rang. And I did not recognize Ivan Sergeevich – he was radiant with rosy enthusiasm. How much younger he looked! He rushed to the door, greeted Madame Viardot, was all absorbed in excitement – where was she to sit?'[57] Another friend, the historian Kovalevsky, recalls how Turgenev frequently replied to importunate friends who urged him to return to

Russia that he could not live apart from his friends, the Viardots, and would follow them wherever they moved. He would often abandon a dinner party in order to escort 'his ladies' to the opera or theatre, and would refuse invitations in order not to miss an evening's reading or a game of cards at the Viardots'.[58] Another author of memoirs recalls how Turgenev's constant enthusiastic references to Pauline and her daughters caused embarrassment to his Russian friends, and even at times resentment that these foreign women should deprive Russia of her great writer.[59]

It is probable that this utter subjection to Pauline oppressed and overwhelmed him at times. Occasionally one can catch glimpses of extreme loneliness, of Turgenev's realization that there was something missing from his life, which Pauline could not supply. It would have been surprising if it had been otherwise in one so essentially Russian in temperament and tradition as was Turgenev. There is no reason to disbelieve what an acquaintance, whose identity has never been established, recalls him as saying more than once: 'I have close friends, people whom I love and who love me. But not everything that is close and dear to me is close in the same way and of the same interest to them.... It is understandable that there are quite long periods when I feel alienated and lonely.'[60] The same impression was formed by another memoirist, who knew him in her early youth and enjoyed his confidence.[61] Besides, the complaint that he had no 'nest' of his own and was compelled to perch on the edge of a 'strange nest' was a constant refrain both in his correspondence and his conversation. It may be that his occasional flirtations, or *amitiés amoureuses* (like the one with Baroness Vrevskaia which is described later), were attempts to escape, if only temporarily, illusorily, perhaps, from his state of enslavement.

No sooner had Pauline settled in Paris than the musical at-homes were resumed in the rue de Douai, on Thursdays. The fare was simple: tea and cake replaced the more customary Parisian refreshments – champagne and a cold buffet. But the talent and company (as recalled by Paul Viardot, an accomplished violinist from a very early age) were most distinguished: Renan, Flaubert, Augier, Jules Simon, Gounod, Saint-Saëns, and when in Paris, Rubinstein, Wieniawski, and Sarasate, among others. On Sundays more frivolous gatherings of equally distinguished company took place, devoted to improvised charades, and little humorous dramatic sketches in which, as usual, Turgenev excelled.[62] In summer, in Bougival, entertainment was of a more domestic nature, although there were frequent visitors and much music. Turgenev had built himself a chalet in the grounds, on a slight hillock, but he also had a study in the main house, which was large, luxuriously furnished, with red as the predominant colour, and with a magnificent view over the Seine. It was here that the company frequently gathered, often for reading aloud. Claudie had set up her easel there, and there was constant, animated conversation in which Turgenev took the leading part.[63]

Turgenev's affection for the Viardot children was, in the main, restricted to Claudie and Marianne, especially Claudie. He seldom referred to the youngest, Paul, in his correspondence, and did not like him. At the end of 1880, when Paul visited Russia to give some recitals, Turgenev and Pauline supplied him with introductions.[64] Paul seems to have behaved in a rude, vain, and aggressive manner,[65] and no doubt reports of this got back to his mother, and Turgenev. As he recorded in the fragment of his diary for 1882 which has survived, Paul was an 'ill-mannered boor and stinks of wine. . . . I have done with him'.[66] The eldest daughter, Louise Viardot-Héritte, born in 1841, inherited some of her mother's musical gifts, but not her character. She had an unhappy temperament and something of a grudge against her parents, her husband, from whom she was separated, and life in general; as has already been suggested, her mother's affair with Turgenev when she was a child could hardly have failed to have left a scar. Turgenev concealed his dislike for her, although he saw her regularly on his visits to St. Petersburg where, after 1868, Louise had an appointment as teacher of singing. He wrote fairly frankly about her to her mother: 'The impossible temperament, her odd and curt manner . . . her bitter and contemptuous loneliness. . . .'[67] To Annenkov (who became slightly involved in one of the many clashes between Louise and her parents) he described her as 'an unhappy and crazy woman'.[68] Claudie remained the undisputed favourite and he behaved towards her like an obsessively fond father. She married Georges Chamerot, whom Turgenev seems to have liked very much. Her first confinement gave cause for anxiety, and Turgenev's letters at the time are full first of his fears for the young mother-to-be, and then happy relief when all turns out well in the end. His devotion to Marianne, although rather less demonstrative than that which he showered on her sister, was also very warm. He often spoke of her to friends, affectionately and admiringly, and showed great interest in her progress, particularly in music, for which she too had inherited some of her mother's talent.[69]

There could be no greater contrast than that between Turgenev's letters to Claudie and those to his daughter. Although always affectionate and concerned, and less nagging in tone than they had been before Paulinette's marriage, they lacked the bubbling warmth, the gaiety and the boisterous love which characterized those he wrote to Claudie. He seems to have been genuinely delighted when Paulinette was at last safely delivered of a daughter in July 1872, although it was some time before he was able to get to Rougemont to see the baby; one cannot help suspecting that he was in a little less of a feverish hurry to see his granddaughter than he was to see Claudie's first born. (He showed even less interest in the son whom Paulinette bore in 1875.) His solemn promise to visit her on 24 September could not be kept because of an attack of gout. He was becoming increasingly subject to severe bouts of this disease and the illness which kept him from Rougemont was the tenth such affliction in four months. (Two months later the score had become twelve in six months.)[70] Whatever the reason, his visits to his daughter became less frequent, and were repeatedly postponed on grounds of ill health; the reproachful tone of Paulinette's letters (to be inferred from his replies) possibly reflects her scepticism about his excuses.

For a time Rougemont offered an additional attraction, and his visits became more regular. He acquired some modest shooting rights there through his son-in-law, Gaston Bruère, and was able to get some sport in the company of Louis Viardot, or of Chamerot senior. But Gaston apparently spoiled the shoot by taking excessive game, and there were constant troubles with the authorities over breaches of the laws, ending in fines, and the project was abandoned after some years.

The main subject in correspondence between father and daughter was money. Paulinette's husband had not prospered in his business and was increasingly in serious financial difficulties: by 1874, according to his father-in-law, he had gone through his wife's dowry of 150,000 francs.[71] For some years Paulinette was pressing (no doubt on Gaston's behalf) for discharge of the amount still owing on the dowry (50,000 francs), on which her father paid regular interest. Turgenev, as always short of capital which he could only raise by selling off parts of his property in Russia, and unable to borrow from his rich, but rather mean, brother, had difficulty in raising the sum. The debt was eventually repaid at the end of 1873. But since this meant that the regular interest on which Gaston and Paulinette relied for their income now that the business had foundered, was no longer coming in (the capital was, of course, soon swallowed up by debts), their financial situation did not improve. Worse unhappiness between father and daughter lay ahead. But for the rest of his life Turgenev was obliged to find money to support his daughter and grandchildren.[72]

★   ★   ★   ★   ★

Turgenev had grown to detest Katkov. He resented what he regarded as Katkov's improper behaviour as editor of his works in the *Russian Herald*. There was also a political reason. As reaction returned in Russia, extinguishing many of the high hopes raised by the years of reform, Katkov became a leading opponent of liberal changes, and a frequent target of abuse in Turgenev's letters. So when M. M. Stasiulevich invited him to publish in a new journal, *European Herald* (*Vestnik Evropy*), which he had founded in 1866, and also edited, Turgenev readily agreed. His first contribution, his 'Memories of Belinsky', appeared in 1869, to be followed a year later by 'The Execution of Troppmann'. He continued to write almost exclusively for the *European Herald* to the end of his life. This paper embraced not only literature but social and political questions as well, and it numbered among its contributors the leading liberal writers and scholars of the time, including the historians S. M. Soloviev, N. I. Kostomarov, A. N. Pypin, and K. D. Kavelin, the lawyer A. F. Koni, and Turgenev's sparring partner, the critic V. V. Stasov. The journal also attracted many of the leading literary figures of the day, both Russian and Western European.

It is interesting to observe the close coincidence of views on many political questions between Turgenev and the *European Herald* over the years – on such matters, for instance, as the Franco-Prussian war, on which both Turgenev and his new editor started off in a completely pro-German position, and gradually veered towards a pro-French attitude after the fall of the monarchy in France, as the imperialistic ambitions of Germany became increasingly evident. Their judgement on the illiberal educational reforms of Count D. A. Tolstoy, of which both Turgenev and the *European Herald* strongly disapproved, was also identical.[73]

Turgenev's literary output in the seventies, until he embarked on the writing of *Virgin Soil* in 1876, was very small. The only work of importance which he completed was *Spring Torrents*, written between mid-1870 and the end of 1871, and published in January 1872. This apart, he published three short stories in the *European Herald* – 'Knock, Knock, Knock' in January 1871, composed while he was engaged in writing *Spring Torrents*, 'Punin and Baburin', in

April 1874, and 'The Watch' in January 1876. At the end of 1872 he also produced for the *European Herald* the first addition to the *Sketches from a Sportsman's Notebook*, entitled 'The End of Chertopkhanov'. The new contributions to the collection of *Sketches* were three in all – of the other two, 'Living Relics' was written for a literary symposium (edited by Nikitenko, Kraevsky, Nekrasov, and Goncharov) published in 1874 in aid of the victims of the famine in Samara Government; and 'There's Knocking!' which first appeared in the collected edition of his works published in 1874. He also wrote several obituary notices for the *European Herald*, including the one on N. I. Turgenev in 1871 and one on A. K. Tolstoy in 1875. Although he did not admire this Tolstoy very much as a writer, he always remembered with gratitude his intercession with the authorities many years before which had helped to end his exile in Spasskoe.

Spring Torrents, in length between a short story and a novel, is mainly cast in the form of an incident in the past, recalled in middle years by a lonely and disappointed man. A chance encounter among his possessions takes his mind back some thirty years, when, like Turgenev then aged about twenty-two, he was travelling extensively through Italy and Germany. While wandering in Frankfurt, as he passes by a pastrycook's shop, a young girl of extraordinary beauty rushes out and appeals to him to help her brother whom she believes to be dying. Sanin (as the young man is called) successfully restores the boy from his faint, and is welcomed by the family as their saviour. He is taken to their hearts by the whole household which consists, apart from the brother and sister, Emilio and Gemma, of an Italian widow, Signora Roselli, an emotional lady of limited intelligence, an ex-singer Pantaleone, who combines the offices of family friend and servant, and a dog, Tartaglia. The weak-minded Sanin cancels his journey to St. Petersburg in order to stay on in Frankfurt, and before long is head over heels in love with the enchanting Gemma. Gemma, however, is engaged to be married, at her mother's insistence, in the hope of improving the family fortunes, to a particularly detestable ambitious young German shop assistant, Herr Klüber – the German characters in *Spring Torrents* are without exception very unlovable.

The climax of the story develops as the result of an expedition which the young people, including Herr Klüber, undertake to the country suburbs of Frankfurt, for lunch at an inn. Gemma attracts the attention of a group of army officers at a neighbouring table, one of whom behaves towards her in a manner which, in the conventions of the time, was undoubtedly insulting. While Herr Klüber vents his indignation on the waiter, Sanin quietly reprimands the officer in terms which inevitably provoke a challenge. The duel which follows, which is not treated very seriously by the officers, and the circumstances surrounding it including, notably, the terrified Pantaleone in the role of Sanin's second, are portrayed with consummate skill – there is nothing comparable to this description anywhere in Turgenev's work. Gemma realizes that she loves Sanin, breaks her engagement to Klüber and the two declare their love and intention to be married.

After an initial attack of hysteria, the decision is accepted by Signora Roselli, but on condition that Gemma should remain in Frankfurt. So Sanin determines that he will sell his modest estate in Russia and use the capital to improve the pastrycook business. He plans to return to Russia, but is deflected by a chance encounter with a schoolmate, Polozov, a fat, somnolent, and complacent glutton, recently married to a very rich woman of peasant origins, reputed to be a legendary beauty. Polozov persuades Sanin to come back with him to Wiesbaden, because he is convinced that his wife, Maria Nikolaevna, will buy Sanin's estate. The story moves, with the inevitability which is almost that of a Greek tragedy, to its end. Maria Nikolaevna has determined, for her amusement, to seduce Sanin from his pure love of Gemma, and succeeds only too well: the weak young man is drawn, to his horror and against his will, into the magnetic field of her physical attractions. Polozov treats the affair with phlegmatic indifference – it is part of the conditions of the marriage.

The whole course of the conquest of Sanin by Maria Nikolaevna, which extends over several days, is described in great detail. The story contains the most outspoken description of sexual infatuation to be found in all of Turgenev's writing. (As he himself commented to Pietsch, 'never have I been so immoral!')[74] The tale culminates in the ultimate degradation of a man enslaved by his passion for a woman, possibly the most forceful statement by Turgenev of this recurrent theme in all his fiction. Sanin dare not return to Gemma, but sends her a cowardly letter. Maria Nikolaevna for a time keeps him among her entourage of devoted slaves, and then discards him. His life thereafter is bitter and joyless. In an epilogue to the incidents recollected we are told of the middle-aged Sanin setting off for Frankfurt to trace Gemma. He eventually discovers her address in New York where she is married to the well-to-do Mr. Slocum. She replies in warm and friendly terms to Sanin's abject letter. The last we hear of Sanin is that he is selling up his estates in Russia and is planning to move to New York – no doubt in order to spend his declining years on the edge of a strange nest.

The length of time, around eighteen months, spent on writing, copying and re-copying alone goes to prove that Turgenev attached some special importance to *Spring Torrents*. Plainly, it was not for the message which it contained – it would not be liked, he wrote to his friend Polonsky; it had nothing social or political in it.[75] Nor was it basically autobiographical – although an incident such as Gemma's dramatic encounter with Sanin indeed happened to the young Turgenev when he was in Frankfurt in 1840;[76] and most of the characters were drawn from real life. There are, however, slight indications that the novel had some deep personal meaning for Turgenev. 'This she-devil [i.e. Maria Nikolaevna] seduced me as she seduced that nit-witted Sanin,' he wrote to Hetzel, his French publisher.[77] In a letter to Madame Commanville (Flaubert's niece) who had, it would seem, disapproved of the second part of *Spring Torrents*, he agreed that this part was 'not very necessary' and explained it by the fact that 'I allowed myself to be carried away by memories'.[78] What memories? Of a fleeting encounter with a pretty girl in Frankfurt in 1840? Moreover, *Spring Torrents* was one of the very few of his works which Turgenev sent off for publication without submitting it to the preliminary judgement of Pauline Viardot – again why?[79] Not certainly for lack of time or opportunity. He expressed considerable relief in his letters to Pauline that she, and more particularly Louis Viardot, apparently approved of the novel.[80] We have no direct record of either Pauline's or Louis's opinion of the story. It seems unlikely that Louis, who had strongly disapproved of 'First Love' for its immorality (and was many years later unjustly blamed by Turgenev for the moralistic ending which was added to the story in the French translation)[81] would have been enthusiastic about the more outspoken *Spring Torrents*. There is, of course, no suggestion that, even if Sanin is Turgenev (which he is only in respect of weakness of character), either the gross and fat Polozov stands for the civilized Viardot, or the peasant nymphomaniac Maria Nikolaevna for the self-controlled and aristocratic Pauline. But the theme of enslavement to passion was one to which Turgenev repeatedly returned; and, in one sense, Louis could be seen as a complaisant husband. It is therefore, perhaps, not too fanciful to discern some personal elements in *Spring Torrents*.

There is a further point of interest about this extraordinary novel – its interpretation of sex as an unconscious force, overwhelming in its power against reason. The notion of the unconscious, accepted.

as axiomatic by generations nurtured on Freud, was much less familiar in 1870–1. Von Hartmann's *Philosophie des Unbewussten* was published in 1869, but there is no evidence that Turgenev knew it. It is a possible inference that Turgenev's view of sex as a world energy operating outside man's conscious existence, strongly suggested in the description of Sanin's seduction even so far as Maria Nikolaevna is concerned – she behaves as one possessed by the forces which she herself has unleashed – was influenced by Schopenhauer. In *The World as Will and Idea*, in a supplement to Book Four, there is a chapter entitled 'The Metaphysics of the Love of the Sexes', which Turgenev certainly knew. In this chapter Schopenhauer argues that 'all love, however ethereally it may bear itself, is rooted in the sexual impulse alone'. Nature is concerned only with the preservation of the species, with the future generation. A human being in the pursuit of love may delude himself that he is following his individual ends: he is in fact in thrall to the world will. (There is much more in this remarkable chapter that Turgenev must have pondered – for example, the notion that weak men seek strong women as partners, or that great passions 'arise, as a rule, at the first glance'.)

Spring Torrents was almost immediately translated into French, German, and Italian. The first English translation appeared in 1874 in America, but was not very warmly received. Yet Turgenev's literary reputation in America was soon to be higher than in England. In April 1874 the young Henry James published strong praise of Turgenev's work, which evoked a long letter from Turgenev, followed by a second one soon after – both in excellent English. He expressed the hope (somewhat unrealistically) that he might be able to visit America.[82] He and James were to meet in Paris in the following year and to become friends.

In France, Flaubert was enthusiastic about the novel, while Edmond de Goncourt was scathing.[83] The German critics were deeply offended by what they considered (not without reason) as an attack on their countrymen. In a letter to one of his greatest admirers in Germany, Julian Schmidt, Turgenev admitted that he felt 'a certain grudge' against Germany when he wrote the book (meaning, no doubt, anger at victorious Germany's behaviour towards defeated France) but claimed justly that he had in the past been even more critical of Russians; and he was very hurt when his friend Pietsch accepted as truth the gossip that Turgenev had said in public that he did not know a single decent German.[84] In Russia critics of all political persuasions were agreed on damning *Spring Torrents* – the radicals were particularly severe.[85]

The three short stories written between 1870 and 1875 are all set in the past. 'Knock, Knock, Knock' is about the suicide of a young officer in the early part of the century who believes his death to be at the mysterious behest of his dead beloved, although there is in fact a rational explanation for the apparently ghostly signals. Turgenev frequently declared himself a confirmed rationalist. Nevertheless, he probably retained some traces of the superstitious beliefs which characterized many nineteenth-century Russians, and he certainly recounted several experiences of seeing ghosts to his friends.[86] Turgenev intended the story as a study of what he believed to be the Russian form of suicide, which 'nearly always occurs as the result of self-love ... with a mixture of fatalism and mysticism'.[87] 'Punin and Baburin' (which contains some glimpses of life in Spasskoe under the grim rule of his mother) is mainly about an early nineteenth-century radical, a member of the Petrashevsky group of 1847–8. 'The Watch' which takes place in the reigns of Paul I and Alexander I, is a picaresque account of the adventure of a watch, which two boys try to get rid of because it had been presented to one of them by a man whom they despised.

Of the three new *Sketches*, 'The End of Chertopkhanov', a magnificent story, very largely about a horse, was, like 'Knock, Knock, Knock' written while Turgenev was engaged on *Spring Torrents*, and seems to have been based on something that he had been told about in 1848 when he wrote the original *Sketch* entitled 'Chertopkhanov and Nedopiuskin'. 'The Living Relics' is a short account of a completely bed-ridden peasant girl, who finds happiness in her faith and in humble acceptance of her plight. The story was written many years before and was then rejected by Turgenev as too slight to be published with the other *Sketches from a Sportsman's Notebook*. In sending it to Polonsky for inclusion in a volume produced in aid of victims of a famine, he recalled a conversation which he had had many years before with an old man, which exemplified the piety and humility of the Russian peasant, and added that to help such a people when struck down by misfortune was everyone's sacred duty.[88] The incident described in the story was based entirely on fact, as he wrote to Pietsch; but there is a further poignant possibility that the seventeen-year-old Turgenev had been the lover of the girl described in the sketch, who had been a beauty before she was smitten with her fatal illness.[89] 'There's Knocking!', about a rather gruesome incident on a journey on the Russian roads, was also based on a rough draft, dating from around 1848, which he found among his papers, and completed in 1874 for the new edition of his collected works.

Turgenev's trips to Russia were becoming less frequent and in general he seems to have gone there either because business affairs required his attention, or because he felt that he needed the inspiration of his own country for his writing. He was also concerned to gather material for his contemplated new novel, *Virgin Soil*. There were short trips of six weeks in 1871 and 1872. On the first occasion he did not even visit Spasskoe, and was anxious to leave as soon as possible. He was, it seems, losing interest in Spasskoe, which at one time he even considered selling. It was eventually leased for twelve years in 1876, to a neighbour, A. M. Shchepkin.[90] Shchepkin did not live in the house, but his son moved in with his family, and soon after became Turgenev's estate manager. Turgenev spent two and a half months in Russia in 1874 and then two more in 1876, for the specific purpose of writing *Virgin Soil*. But his heart remained with the Viardots in Paris; he wrote continuously to Pauline, and to Claudie, and, although very few of Pauline's letters to him are available, it is evident from his replies that she too wrote very often.

There were the usual literary and social rounds in St. Petersburg and in Moscow, which he duly described. As on previous trips, he sought out friends who had known Pauline on her Russian visits, or in France or Germany, with whom he could talk about her. He also busied himself with promoting the songs which she had composed and for which he had either selected suitable Russian poems, or translated French or German ones. In 1871 he made arrangements for the publication of six poems set to music by her, but at his own expense – her songs, he wrote to Annenkov, 'are no longer in demand with our public'. He made sure, of course, that Pauline should not know that he had subsidized her compositions. A further volume, the sixth, containing translations of five German poems set to music by Pauline, appeared in 1874. The translations (although not so designated) were in all probability by Turgenev, who again, in a manner elaborately concealed from Pauline, financed the publication.[91]

While in Spasskoe he took a great interest in the progress of the school and the almshouse, which he had established in the village. The school had fallen into a decline in 1871, and the master was unsatisfactory. Turgenev issued instructions to his manager for the man to be replaced, and fixed the new teacher's salary at 200 roubles a year. 'It is impossible to tolerate', he wrote, 'that there should be an unsatisfactory school ... on the estate of one who owes all his significance to his pen.'[92] In the following year his brother donated 1,000 roubles towards the construction of an almshouse in Spasskoe, an unusual gesture for one who was not noted for his generosity.[93] It took some time for the school to improve; an article published in October 1872 had been severely critical, especially of the school's practice of using corporal punishment, which particularly distressed Turgenev.[94] But things had greatly improved when he visited it in June 1874. There were then seventeen pupils reduced from over sixty in the winter. The teacher was now the village deacon and the children, when Turgenev examined them, seemed well instructed, at any rate in the scriptures. ('What can one do? The only teachers available are from the village clergy!') In later years, a woman teacher was appointed. The almshouse provided shelter for five very old men and four very old women, and seemed clean and well run.[95] Both the school and the almshouse had to be closed down after Turgenev's death for lack of funds to maintain them.

Apart from severe attacks of gout, his trip to Russia in 1874 seems to have been particularly enjoyable. The visit in 1871 had delighted him with its 'native soil and native air', but had been marred by abject fear of cholera, which drove him from St. Petersburg, which he liked, to Moscow, which he did not. The success of the 1874 visit was, in part, due to the fact that he found Russia on this occasion changed in atmosphere. Above all, 'the young generation has now much more goodwill towards me than it showed on my last visit'.[96] No doubt the shock caused by *Smoke* was wearing off. But, as always with Turgenev, his life was ruled by personal matters, and it may also have been as the result of embarking on one of his *amitiés amoureuses* that Russia appeared to him in a more agreeable light than usual. The lady concerned was Baroness Julia Vrevskaia, widow of a general whom she had married when she was seventeen, and who was killed in the Caucasus almost immediately afterwards. She was thirty-two when Turgenev met her in 1873 and a woman of great charm and beauty, intelligence and spiritual depth.

The friendship lasted for four years until Vrevskaia's death early in 1878. Fifty letters to her from Turgenev have survived. The tone of the letters is usually one of flirtatious banter, with occasional hints of erotic feelings. There is nothing to suggest that Vrevskaia ever felt more than friendship and affection for him; he constantly complains to her of her mysteriousness, and of her secretive private life and of the feelings which she conceals from him. In June 1874 when Turgenev was in Spasskoe, Vrevskaia, whose estate was relatively near, visited him – after he had pointedly informed her that he was disabled by gout and unable to call on her. Pauline Viardot had met her, presumably in Paris. On the day of Vrevskaia's arrival, 21 June,

Turgenev wrote about it to Pauline, prevaricating a little – she was passing Mtsensk, he wrote, with her brother, had heard that Turgenev was ill and had made the detour in order to see him. They had chatted for a little, then Turgenev had told her he wished to be alone. In fact she stayed five days.[97] Evidently, as had happened in the case of earlier affairs Turgenev felt the need for reticence when telling Pauline about Vrevskaia. Obviously Vrevskaia knew about the relationship between Turgenev and Pauline – everyone did – but it does not appear from his letters that he discussed it with her, as he once had done with Countess Lambert.

In the spring of 1875 Turgenev and Vrevskaia spent some further time together in Karlsbad. He had been there the year before to take the waters for his gout, and since they had done him some good (or so he thought) he decided to try them once again. Baroness Vrevskaia was taking a cure at neighbouring Marienbad, so of course they met. The Karlsbad meeting seems to have stimulated him to bolder hints of the physical attraction which he felt for the Baroness. 'I feel I am growing old,' he wrote in October. 'I would terribly like to perpetrate some absurd thing. ... Won't you, perhaps, help?'[98] There are frequent indications in the letters that Vrevskaia was alarmed by his intimations of feelings which were something more than friendship: 'Be happy and gay,' he wrote on 11 October 1876. 'I kiss your little hands mentally to my heart's content. In reality you always take them away from me. Can it be that you are afraid of me? That would be as flattering to me – as it would be unjust.'[99] It was presumably with the intention of allaying her anxiety that he wrote to her in June 1876: 'In essence the relations between us are very good and simple. I am sincerely devoted to you, but sometimes I notice that you are a young and charming woman.'[100]

On 26 January 1877 he sent her his confession, which caused her some embarrassment:

You call me 'secretive' – very well, I will be so frank that you will perhaps regret your epithet. Since I first met you I loved you as a friend – and at the same time felt a persistent desire to possess you. However, it was not so unbridled a desire (in any case I was no longer young) to make me ask for your hand – besides there were other circumstances which prevented this. At the same time I knew very well that you would not agree to what the French call *une passade* ... there you have the explanation of my behaviour. You wish to assure me that you never nurtured any 'concealed feelings' for me – alas, I was unhappily only too certain of that. You write that your age *as a woman* is over; when my *male* age is past – and I have very little time to wait – then, I have no doubt, we shall be great friends – because nothing will trouble us. But now I still go hot and somewhat frightened at the thought: what if she pressed me to her heart *not as a brother?* – and I want to ask, like my Maria Nikolaevna in *Spring Torrents*, 'Sanin, do you know how to forget?'[101]

It was characteristic of Turgenev, as of Sanin, that he should have visualized the woman as making the first move. There are several other similar hints of erotic feelings on his part – not on hers – in subsequent letters. With the outbreak of the Russo-Turkish war Vrevskaia went to the front as a nurse. They met briefly in June 1877 before her departure. She died soon after on 24 January 1878 in Bulgaria, of typhus fever. According to an account by a neighbour who was in a position to know, Vrevskaia's departure for Bulgaria was in part motivated by an unhappy love affair with a young man. But it is improbable that Turgenev knew of this. In a prose poem dedicated to her memory he wrote, 'Two or three men loved her secretly and deeply. ... To help those in need of her help was for her the only happiness – it was in truth the only happiness that life vouchsafed her.'[102] 'She gained the martyr's crown for which her soul yearned. ... Her life was one of the saddest that I ever knew,' he wrote to Annenkov.[103]

His quasi-love affairs apart, Turgenev seems to have had natural inclination and talent for intellectual relationships with young girls, who adored him in return. Such, for example, was his friendship with the brilliant daughter of the historian K. D. Kavelin, Sofia. Herself an historian of considerable promise, her career was ended by her early death at the age of twenty-six. Turgenev, who met her in St. Petersburg in 1871, corresponded with her, mainly on literary matters, until she died. Another such young friend was Elena Blaramberg, an intimate of Louise Viardot-Héritte, whom Turgenev advised and helped in her literary ambitions. He met her in St. Petersburg in 1871, at the house of the composer A. N. Serov, and remained friendly with her until his death. Under the pseudonym E. Ardov, she later published some attractive memoirs about Turgenev, especially valuable for the fact that they provide one of the very few available sources on life at Bougival in the Turgenev–Viardot household.

★   ★   ★   ★   ★

Virgin Soil, which Turgenev began to write early in 1876, was the result of several years of study of, and reflection on, political developments in Russia after the emancipation, and especially of the revolutionary movement. The first ideas for the novel were jotted down in 1870, and fuller conspectuses were prepared in 1872 and early in 1875. The long preparatory work before he started to write included the three trips to Russia between 1871 and 1874, in the course of which he paid visits to the law courts and to such institutions as penal colonies for juvenile offenders; study of materials obtained from Russia; and numerous conversations both in Russia and in France. *Virgin Soil* was from the first conceived as a kind of intellectual sequel to *Fathers and Children*, an analysis of the young generation in the light of the changes which had come over it in the years which had passed since the heyday of nihilism. This preliminary research was not the only reason for the long delay between the conception and the execution of the new novel. Throughout these years Turgenev's correspondence shows that he suffered from recurrent bouts of depression and of obsessive fear of death. He knew well that he could only write a novel about Russia inside Russia. Yet he was constantly reluctant to undertake the long journey and to interrupt the only life which he believed could give him some happiness – one shared with the Viardots. He was, after all, by nineteenth-century standards no longer young – by the time he embarked on *Virgin Soil* he was over fifty-seven.

The Russian revolutionary movement in the early seventies was quite different from what it had been in the years immediately following the emancipation, when the 'nihilists' dominated the stage – hard materialists and atheists, dedicated to the overthrow of the political system and of the whole order of society as soon as possible. It is true that this form of revolution never really died out in Russian society. Much of it was to reappear in the 'People's Will' movement at the end of the decade, and later in Bolshevism. All moderate, as well as anti-revolutionary Russians were horror-struck when the trial of Nechaev started in July 1871. Nechaev's fanatical dedication to the aim of revolution justified in his own view the use of all means without any exception, even against fellow revolutionaries – an attitude which in the end caused Bakunin, who had been his devoted supporter, to break with him. The case of Nechaev, the inspiration for Dostoevsky's novel *The Possessed*, centred around the murder of a member of his conspiratorial organization, a student Ivanov who was falsely accused by him of planning to betray the group to the police. Nechaev's real motive was to bind the other members together more closely by their complicity in the crime.

Populism, which by the seventies had largely superseded 'nihilism', certainly had its violent elements and was, in theory at all events, dedicated to revolution. But it was distinguished by its spiritual content, its essentially religious dedication to service to 'the people'. The populists were, above all, conscious of their duty to repay the debt which they owed to the suffering poor for the privileges which they had long enjoyed at their expense. The young revolutionaries at the end of the sixties and early seventies were no longer inspired by Chernyshevsky so much as by Peter Lavrov, whose 'Historical Letters', published in 1868 and 1869, were a 'direct appeal to the conscience of the intelligentsia' and formed 'the fundamental ideological document in the attack against the ideas that were later to find expression in Nechaev's venture'.[104] Part of the service to the people urged by Lavrov was education, and it was mostly in propaganda among workers and peasants that many populists saw their immediate duty in preparing for the revolution which was to come. This propaganda movement found its culmination in the famous 'going to the people' in 1874, when thousands of young men and women went into the villages to live with the peasants and share their dress, their lives, and their suffering, in order both to serve them and to prepare them for their future political role. It was a romantic dream and ended, as could have been foreseen, in disaster. But in its inception it was a great spiritual revelation. As Stepnyak recalled in later years:

Nothing like it had ever been seen before or after. . . . It was a powerful cry that arose no one knows whence and that called living souls to the great work of redeeming the Fatherland and the human race. And the living souls, when they heard this cry, arose, overflowing with grief and indignation for their past. And they gave up their homes, their riches, honours and families. . . . It was not yet a political movement. Rather it was like a religious movement, with all the infectious nature of such movements. Men were trying not just to reach a certain practical end, but also to satisfy a deeply felt duty, an aspiration for moral perfection.[105]

Turgenev was in Russia when this extraordinary movement which dominates *Virgin Soil* (though the action in that novel is stated to take place in 1868) first exploded, but it was probably not until later that he was able to study it, along with the many centres in Russia where before 1874 the preparation and apprenticeship for 'going to the people' had taken place.[106] He also tried to get to know about the more violent elements in the populist movement, just as he had closely followed the reports of the Nechaev affair from Paris. While in St. Petersburg in 1874 he had an opportunity of observing (if not actually witnessing) the trial of the Dolgushin group, a populist organization which was inspired by Bakunin's inflammatory ideas, and which had attempted unsuccessfully to raise a revolt among the peasants.[107] All these aspects of revolutionary activity were to find an echo in *Virgin Soil*.

Turgenev's attitude to the revolutionaries remained fairly constant throughout his life. He deplored the use of violent means to achieve political ends, and not only because he detested brutal methods: he did not believe that desirable ends could be achieved in this manner. This outlook had determined his approach to the insurgents in 1848 in France, and to the Polish rising of 1863, to the Paris Commune (and also to the sadistic cruelty with which it was put down by General Gallifet), and to Nechaev and his like. He remained a convinced monarchist, so far as Russia was concerned (France was a different matter). The attempts on the life of Alexander II, by Karakozov in 1866 and by a Pole in Paris in 1867, filled him with horror and indignation. But he admired, venerated almost, the dedication and self-sacrifice of the revolutionaries. Something of this attitude explained his love for Bazarov; Turgenev throughout his life remained a Hamlet who wished he had been born a Don Quixote. This feeling about the revolutionaries became even more evident in the seventies – particularly so far as the women were concerned.*

What he thought of radical youth is best revealed in his correspondence in 1874 with A. P. Filosofova, an active member of the woman's movement whom he got to know well in St. Petersburg. She supplied him with her diary and with many other documents on populist activities in order to acquaint him with the nature of the 'new men and women' of her generation (she was twenty-seven). The diary apart, the material did not much impress him – these were not, he wrote to her, the true new men and women – he knew many more young people to whom the description applied much more aptly. (One young man in particular, V. G. Dekhterev, impressed him so unfavourably with his pretentious vanity and lack of talent that he satirized him in *Virgin Soil*.) What he objected to in Filosofova's young friends was their grandiose claim to intellectual eminence which they lacked; not that any special talent or brain was now needed, only the ability to sacrifice oneself, 'to teach the peasants to read and write, to organize hospitals'. It was a question of a good heart and of true patriotism, that was all.[109]

For Turgenev, who had greeted the great reforms of the sixties

---

* He actually planned in 1873 a visit to the Zurich Colony of radical young girl students, but the project came to nothing, in part because the Russian government succeeded in getting them expelled by the Swiss authorities before he arrived there. The girls, incidentally, did not relish the prospect of being 'inspected'.[108]

with hope and eager expectations there was reason enough, some ten years later, for disillusionment. The experience of a decade no longer justified the optimism with which he had welcomed the emancipation of the peasants in 1861. Nikitenko records in his diary the substance of an official report in 1873 of a commission on the plight of the peasants, set up by the Minister of the Interior, Valuev. While their condition had generally improved since the emancipation, their mode of life was still very unsatisfactory. They suffered from ignorance and backwardness, from meagre allotments of land in some provinces and from the obligation to pay excessive compensation for them, and from high taxes. The communal system of land ownership resulted in constant re-division of their holdings; both the administration and the special courts to which the peasants were subject were deplorable.[110] The other reforms had fared little better.

The activities of the 'nihilists' in the sixties, the Polish rebellion of 1863, Karakozov's attempt to kill the Emperor in 1866 – all had helped to stimulate the enemies of peaceful evolution among Alexander's advisers. It would be difficult to point to a more loyal supporter of the monarchy and of public order than Nikitenko, who in his criticism of radicalism was usually far more extreme than Turgenev. Yet the diary of this liberal-minded conservative reveals growing despair, not at the repression of revolution, but at the unimaginative stupidity of official measures and practices which in the end could only help to encourage its growth.

Our most dangerous internal enemies are not the Poles, not the nihilists, but those government figures who create nihilists by ... arousing indignation and disgust for the administration. ... The main things we lack in implementing our so-called reforms are sincerity and good faith. ... We establish new procedures and immediately hasten to invalidate them as soon as they begin to produce the necessary results. ... In the early years of the present reign I was enthralled by its splendid and noble beginnings. ... It wasn't very long before I became bitterly disillusioned and convinced that it was our fate to begin fine deeds but not to carry them through to their conclusion.[111]

He witnessed with fear and apprehension the growing alienation of the intelligentsia from the government. But he also blamed them for their 'disgusting' propaganda, like advocacy of the abolition of the family and private property, which hurt the cause of freedom and progress. They should, he believed, concentrate their fire on the abuses practised by the administration.

A constant theme in Turgenev's correspondence, as in Nikitenko's diary, is the growing repressiveness of the censorship, which at times seemed to him to be little different from what it had been in the age of Nicholas I. He was also appalled at the educational reforms initiated in 1871 by Count D. A. Tolstoy, the Minister of Education, which had been strongly influenced by M. N. Katkov. The proposal which was discussed at great length, and eventually adopted by the Emperor against the majority view of the State Council, amounted in essence to a restriction of admission to the university to those who had completed a course of Greek and Latin in a classical gymnasium. This policy was primarily designed to safeguard the universities from the influence of the radicals, since they generally inclined towards the natural sciences. The products of the non-classical Schools (*real* schools) were only to be allowed access to the various higher technical institutions. Turgenev, who had been prematurely delighted by the defeat of the 'vile' Katkov in the State Council, was very critical of what he regarded as an unfair pre-eminence being given to classical education.[112] His correspondence bristles with abuse of Katkov, whose influence on government policy he may well have exaggerated.

Symptomatic of Turgenev's dislike of the growing repressiveness in Russia was his quarrel with his old friend, the poet A. A. Fet. For years he had poked fun at Fet for his reactionary views which he regarded as little more than an echo of the *Moscow Chronicle*, the paper of which Katkov had become the editor in 1863. But in November 1874 he broke with him when he heard from his friend Polonsky that Fet (who had, incidentally, been allowed by the Emperor to take the surname of his natural father, Shenshin) had asserted that he, Turgenev, had in Fet's presence tried to inspire a couple of young boys with a 'thirst for Siberia' – in other words had tried to make revolutionaries of them. Fet did not admit to making the remark in the form alleged by Turgenev. But what he claimed he had said amounted to much the same.[113] The two men were reconciled in 1878, but did not meet again until 1881.[114]

CHAPTER FIFTEEN

Virgin Soil

Virgin Soil, the longest and last of Turgenev's novels, is also the most complicated. At one level it is a subtle, romantic love story: at another it is a penetrating analysis of the Russian revolutionary movement. Although the date of the action appears in the author's plan as 1868, the political activity portrayed corresponds much more closely (though not exactly) to the 'going to the people' period of 1874 and 1875. As usual Turgenev drew all the characters from real life (and indeed his detailed preliminary plans often reveal who the prototypes were); however none of them is the exact portrait of a single individual.

The story opens at the poor lodgings of some young revolutionaries, around whom the plot is to revolve. One of them, Mashurina, a tense, rather plain young woman, is soon disclosed as the blind and obedient follower of a shadowy figure (who never appears in person) but who is clearly identifiable as the terrorist Nechaev, whose trial in 1871–3 Turgenev had closely followed. In fact all the revolutionaries depicted seem to be under 'Nechaev's' orders at one time or another, though not all show the same unquestioning obedience as Mashurina. Nezhdanov, the illegitimate son of a nobleman, for example, with whom Mashurina is secretly in love, is much too sensitive and introspective to be the tool of anyone. In the opening chapter Nezhdanov is engaged by Sipyagin to come down to his country house to act as tutor to his son, and it is in the Sipyagin household that the story develops. Sipyagin is portrayed with evident dislike: he is a distinguished government servant, on the way up, anxious to display himself as a man of enlightened, liberal views, and at the same time completely loyal to the government – in fact, occupying what many would have said was Turgenev's own political position. He is described in the conspectus as 'the type of Russian *juste milieu*', and as modelled on liberal bureaucrats like Valuev and

Abaza,[1] but the author leaves us in no doubt that the main characteristics of Sipyagin are hypocrisy, self-interest, and futility. Sipyagin's
neighbour, Kallomeitsev, a wealthy landlord, is drawn with particular malevolence: his views are so illiberal as to draw protests even
from Sipyagin.*

Sipyagin's wife is a vain and beautiful man-eater. Her brother,
Markelov, is an ascetic, fanatical, dedicated, and completely uncompromising revolutionary – according to the conspectus he is 'convenient and ready soil for the Nechaevs and company'.[3] He believes
implicitly (like Nechaev and Bakunin) that the people are ripe for
a rising and only need a 'spark' to set them off. When the inevitable
arrest follows on his attempt to raise a revolt, to which the peasants
respond by seizing him and handing him over to the police, he
behaves with courage, defiance, and dignity. He betrays none of his
accomplices. Markelov is in love with the heroine of the novel,
Marianna, who rejects his suit. Marianna, Madame Sipyagin's impoverished niece whose father has fallen into disgrace in the past, has
been brought up in humiliating charity by her aunt. She hates her,
despises her uncle, and pines for freedom. She is immediately drawn
to Nezhdanov, and when he confides to her his involvement in revolutionary activities she longs to join her life with his and to devote
it to service to the people. They decide to escape together from the
Sipyagin household. Marianna is ready to become Nezhdanov's
mistress, but only if he is sure that he loves her. But Nezhdanov is
as uncertain of his love as he is of his dedication to revolution; it
is the tragedy which dogs him throughout his short life. He is,
according to Turgenev, a 'romantic of realism'. Just as the romantics
sought for poetry in the ideal, the 'romantic of realism' seeks poetry
in the real, 'which is nonsense; real life is prosaic, and must be such'.
From the earliest plan of the novel dated 1870, he is destined for suicide.[4]

The escape of Marianna and Nezhdanov is made possible by Solomin, the real hero of the novel, and one of the most extraordinary
of all Turgenev's characters. He is the manager of a nearby paper
factory. He provides the pair both with shelter in the factory com-
pound and with contact with the local peasants. Although sceptical
of revolutionary activity, he is completely loyal to those who partici-

---

*He is modelled on several prominent public men whom Turgenev disliked,
including one of Katkov's collaborators, B. M. Markevich; and M. N. Longinov,
once a contributor to the *Contemporary* and a friend of Turgenev, who had long
since abandoned his youthful liberalism. His appointment in 1871 as director responsible for the public press was greeted by Turgenev with dismay.[2]

pate in it and determined to shield them from the authorities. The rather pathetic attempts at revolution which follow come to nothing. Nezhdanov dresses up as a peasant and sets off to distribute propagandist literature. He does not get very far: drawn into the local drinking establishments by his desire for union with the people, he is incapacitated by vodka. Marianna, meanwhile, is persuaded by Solomin that she can more usefully serve the peasants by tending the local children and teaching them their letters than by spreading pamphlets. Turgenev's miniature of the 'going to the people' is moving and ennobling: its essential naive absurdity is redeemed by the devotion, enthusiasm, and dedication of these scions of the Russian gentry who deliberately adopt the most spartan mode of living and dress – 'become common' in the words of a peasant woman at Spasskoe which had imprinted themselves on Turgenev's memory while *Virgin Soil* was germinating in his mind. Markelov's arrest throws suspicion on Solomin, Marianna, and Nezhdanov. Nezhdanov shoots himself, leaving a long letter to Marianna and Solomin, urging them to marry, and survives for long enough to join their hands. His motive for suicide is not fear of arrest but the culmination of the tragic indecision of his life – doubts about his dedication to the cause, and about his love for Marianna – the bitter predicament of the man, and especially a Russian, who is by his nature denied the capacity for positive action, the tragedy of a Hamlet who longs to be a Don Quixote. There is also a suggestion that Nezhdanov feels he is overshadowed in Marianna's regard by Solomin, although neither of them has in any way been disloyal to the unhappy young man. The two now go into hiding until the storm blows over, and eventually marry. Although we are not told this, we can assume that Marianna, by her husband's side, devotes herself to the kind of realistic, practical service to the people which is Solomin's (and Turgenev's) version of revolution.

Solomin was from the start intended as a contrast to Nezhdanov – he is 'a real practical, in the American manner, who goes about his business as calmly as a peasant ploughs and sows. ... He has his own religion – the triumph of the lowest class, in which he wishes to participate. A Russian revolutionary.'[5] This is how he was conceived in 1870. Two years later the character became more detailed. He is the son of a minor church officiant, who studied mathematics and science and worked in England. He sympathizes with revolutionaries, but keeps his distance because he does not believe that a revolution can be achieved so long as it is something totally strange to the people. His faith is in slow, patient education, not in the sudden saviours or panaceas in which Russians so readily believe.[6] There was at least one other preparatory sketch for the character of Solomin, in which his main quality was stated to be 'sobriety', but no such version is extant.[7]

The person of Solomin epitomizes the central message of the novel. Its epigraph is a quotation from the notes of an agronomist: 'Virgin soil must be worked not with a superficial wooden plough but with one that raises the depths,' and, as Turgenev explained to his editor, the 'plough' was not meant to be revolution, but enlightenment.[8] Those who interpreted Turgenev's new work as a sign of his conversion to the revolutionary cause were very wide of the mark. He rejected violent insurgency, as he had all his life, as pointless and harmful, and continued to believe that in Russia any reform other than from above was 'unthinkable'.[9] As one of the characters in *Virgin Soil* says of Solomin: 'The main thing about him is that he is no instant healer of our social wounds. Because, look at us Russians – we are always waiting. There, something, or someone will turn up – and will cure all our wounds in a moment. . . . Who will this magician be? Darwinism? The village? . . . A foreign war? Anything you please. . . .' But at the same time, there is deep sympathy in the novel and indeed constantly in Turgenev's correspondence, for the sincerity, the self-sacrifice, and the dedication of the young revolutionaries. This sympathy is especially shown for the women. It is worth recalling that before the trial in February and March 1877 of fifty young people accused of revolutionary activities of whom sixteen were girls, the Russian public had remained unaware of the important role which women played in the movement, and dismissed Marianna as a figment of Turgenev's imagination.[10] There is, of course, an appealing charm about Marianna, even if she appears as a rather pale and weak figure besides the great Turgenev heroines like Liza or Elena. But the gauky Mashurina also comes in for a good deal of sympathy from her creator. Throughout his life Turgenev regarded women as superior beings: 'A brilliant future', he said once in conversation, 'awaits only those peoples who will place woman not only on a basis of equality with men, but higher' – and he cited as examples of countries where the first signs of this tendency were becoming evident England, the United States of America, and – of all places on earth – Australia.[11]

Turgenev explained his attitude to the young revolutionaries in a letter to his editor, Stasiulevich:

The young generation has up to now been portrayed in our literature either as a riff-raff of rogues and rascals – which is in the first place unjust and secondly could only be insulting to young readers as a lie and a slander; or else this generation was as far as possible idealized, which was again unjust, and besides, harmful. I decided to choose the middle road, to take up a position which is nearer to the truth: to depict young people who are for the most part good and honest, and to show that their honesty notwithstanding, their very enterprise is so untrue and remote from life that it can only lead them to a complete fiasco.[12]

There was nothing new in all this, so far as Turgenev's outlook was concerned. What seemed to be a new note in *Virgin Soil* was the rejection of the liberal gentry as the mainstay of reform. In his arguments with Herzen in the sixties he had repeatedly stressed that only its educated class could save Russia – in other words, mainly the nobility. A few years earlier he had taken as active a part as he could in putting through the Emancipation Act. The freeing of the peasants had certainly filled him with hopes that other necessary reforms would follow in its wake. But ten years later these expectations had been disappointed, and with this disillusionment came his faith in men of different social origin and of an entirely distinct breed – the Solomins. In the course of a discussion in which Sipyagin attempts to persuade Solomin to enter his employment and manage his factory, Solomin tells him that the landed gentry are incapable of running any enterprise. Turgenev takes great pains to show Sipyagin as inefficient and unserious, and to emphasize the rise of what he regards as a new breed of landlords – moneylenders who are merciless in their exploitation of the peasants. Evidently Turgenev now believed that the future of Russia lay in the hands of practical, efficient men of ambition and enterprise who were emerging out of a hitherto dormant lower social stratum. This was so, he explained in conversation, because (unlike the revolutionaries, government ministers, and the liberal gentry) they have both roots in the soil and support among the people. But it would depend on themselves whether they degenerated in the end into avaricious members of the bourgeoisie.[13] In later years, according to Lavrov who was generally truthful, Turgenev frequently asserted that his fellow-liberals in Russia, although full of the best intentions and ideals, lacked the courage to act, and were incapable of any self-sacrifice. However, he retained until the end of his life the greatest respect for the outstanding liberal figures of the past, like N. A. Miliutin.[14]

After a number of years of preparatory study and cogitation about *Virgin Soil*, and the jotting down of notes, plans, and conspectuses, Turgenev first began to write in earnest (having just overcome one of his bouts of severe gout, or 'Katkovitis', as he called it) in Paris, on 1 February 1876. The work on the first draft did not progress too well and he felt increasingly the need to return to Russia for inspiration. In nearly six weeks which he spent in Spasskoe (from 6 June until 15 July), he worked on the novel with great intensity, often until the small hours, and completed the first version; 302 out of the 490 manuscript pages were written in Spasskoe.[15] He then returned to Bougival, and embarked on 'transcribing' the manuscript – a process which, as usual with Turgenev, entailed substantial alteration. This task was completed early in October. The text was then submitted to Annenkov for comment and dispatched to Stasiulevich after further alterations in November. The novel was published in the first two issues of the *European Herald* for 1877.

Both Turgenev and Annenkov were particularly anxious that Stasiulevich should print the novel, for all its length, in one issue of his journal, for fear that a double publication might encourage the censor to make difficulties over the second instalment. Their very natural apprehension of possible trouble with the censor increased after some student revolutionaries had held a demonstration in front of the Cathedral of Our Lady of Kazan in St. Petersburg on 6 December – an incident described by Turgenev as the limit of stupidity. As it turned out, the publication in two parts worked in Turgenev's favour. Having passed the first, the censorship committee was evenly divided on the question of sanctioning the second. The matter was decided in favour of publication by the Minister of the Interior who ruled that it would be an insult to the public (in other words, would make the censors look ridiculous) to ban the sequel after allowing the original half to appear.[16]

The numerous alterations made to the first draft fall mainly into three categories: variations introduced into its reworking, changes made in the course of copying the manuscript in Bougival, and emendations consequent on Annenkov's criticisms. These alterations, which take up nearly 116 pages in the edition of *Virgin Soil* published under the auspices of the Soviet Academy of Sciences, provide further evidence of the detailed care which the author devoted to his novel. In reworking his draft Turgenev was mainly concerned with two aims: improvements in style, to which he always devoted the greatest attention, and underlining, through his characters, the main political message. For example, a number of additions to the passages dealing with 'going to the people' are designed to stress the hostility and incomprehension of the peasants in face of the propagandists.* The satire on Sipyagin and Kallomeitsev was made more

---

* Materials based on police archives, such as intercepted letters and reports of

bitter in the course of revision, and Solomin's views were given greater emphasis.

Annenkov, in general, warmly approved of the novel, but criticized what he described as its pamphleteering nature in some instances. Turgenev took account of most, but not all, of Annenkov's strictures. For example, he removed, on Annenkov's advice, a remark by one of the characters which recalled the judgement by Joseph de Maistre that the Russians were unfitted for the natural sciences, as the Romans had been incompetent in the fine arts, but were none the worse for that. This remark (palpably untrue, incidentally, so far as the Russians were concerned) did not in fact represent Turgenev's views, nor was he acquainted with the writings of de Maistre.[18] There is no doubt that *Virgin Soil* retained a good deal of its pamphleteering character in spite of revision; Professor Freeborn goes so far as to describe it as a forerunner of the Soviet 'socialist realist' novel.

Virgin Soil was not at first well received. According to Turgenev himself, writing in 1879,

With the exception of two or three judgements – written, not printed – I heard nothing from anyone except abuse [of *Virgin Soil*]. At first it was generally asserted that I had invented it all, that living almost permanently abroad I had lost all understanding of Russian life, and Russian men and women. . . . Later, after a certain trial which vindicated the great part of what had been described as my fabrications, my judges changed their line. It was now alleged almost that I had participated in all those ill-intentioned plots and certainly knew about them, since otherwise how could I have foreseen and foretold it all in advance, and so on and so forth.

However, he adds that two years after publication of *Virgin Soil*, on his recent visit to Russia, the judgement on his novel had completely changed.[19]

The initial reaction to the book was certainly universally hostile. The right-wing critics resented the adverse judgements on Russia, expressed or implied, and especially the satire on Sipyagin and Kallomeitsev. The radical critics, in general, found the picture of the revolutionaries false, and dismissed the 'gradualist' Solomin as a 'kulak' or 'bourgeois'. The trial of the Fifty in February and March 1877 (to which Turgenev refers) which revealed the nature of the current revolutionary movement, particularly to those who sympathized with it, but knew little about it, brought about a change in the tone

---

the participants in the 'going to the people', published by Soviet scholars nearly 100 years later, fully bear out Turgenev's picture.[17]

of some critics. The revolutionaries themselves gave the novel a mixed reception. G. Lopatin and the younger populists were generally hostile, though there were some exceptions among them. The veterans, like Kropotkin and Lavrov, were more favourably disposed. Lavrov in particular argued that the picture of the movement painted by Turgenev, though objective, was incomplete.[20]

The positive judgements referred to by Turgenev included those of the legal historian K. D. Kavelin, and of his brilliant young daughter Sofia, also an historian. Kavelin's letter is lost, but his daughter's views appear from a long article which she wrote, but which was not published at the time, presumably for reasons of censorship. This article is a most perceptive study both of the novel and of the mood of the enlightened younger generation, written in the perspective of the trial of the Fifty of 1877. It understands the motives and frustrations of the revolutionaries, without approving their actions: 'Each one of us has his or her moment when one inclines towards revolution, as well as certain moments when one places one's hopes on reform.' History has many examples of the beastliness perpetrated by tsars, but they have never yet set out to strangle primarily the younger generation. What are we doing liberating Slavs from the Turkish yoke? We are very nearly worse off than the Sultan's subjects because 'with every reign we are tantalized by reforms which are then undermined by scoundrels who crush under the ruins of these very reforms those who created them'. She then discusses the novel and its characters with great insight, particularly the image of Solomin. Although she does not recognize him in existing persons (rightly – the prototypes of Solomin are most nebulous in Turgenev's notes), he is not false; and Russia needs such men to transform her. When six out of ten Russians become Solomins, the government will have to yield on reform, and if it does not the Solomins will carry out the revolution. She concludes that Turgenev 'now stands solitary, rejected by the extreme left and the extreme right sides. . . . Let us see what the future will say'.[21] Around the same time Turgenev commented in a letter to Ralston describing the trial of the Fifty (and pointing out that some of the defendants resembled Marianna and Solomin), 'Russian statesmen ought . . . to come to the conclusion that the only way of stopping the progress of revolutionary propaganda in Russia is to grant a constitutional reform.'[22]

Virgin Soil was an instant success outside Russia. It was rapidly translated into many languages including French, German in four versions, English, Italian, Swedish, Polish, Czech, Serbian, and Hungarian – all within seven or eight months of its publication in

Russia.[23] It also won high praise from those whose opinion Turgenev respected, like Flaubert, Ralston, and Julian Schmidt.[24] This, however, was small consolation to him for the general rejection of the novel by the Russian public. In a letter to his editor Stasiulevich, he accepted the justice of much of the critical comment: 'No! one cannot attempt to drag into the open the essence of Russia while living almost permanently far away from the country. I took upon myself a task beyond my strength. ... In the fate of every Russian writer of any prominence there has always been a tragic aspect – mine was absenteeism. ...'[25] How far this was his real or consistent opinion is another question. Thus, writing at the end of 1876 to Kavelin (who had expressed warm approval of *Virgin Soil* before publication), he had asserted that whatever the ultimate fate of the novel ('I already know, I know for certain that I have not wasted my time'), he had done good service to his generation.[26]

For some years after the appearance of the novel Turgenev kept on assuring his correspondents that he had given up creative writing, that he would now confine himself to translations, and so forth. Indeed he did not publish a great deal, apart from a few stories and the *Prose Poems* (though he did embark at the end of the seventies on several more substantial works which were never completed). He was often subject to fits of depression and melancholy, and fear of death (that 'dumb, dead abyss')[27] as the years advanced upon him. The attacks of the all too familiar gout became more frequent and more severe. He was probably beginning to exhibit some symptoms of the cancer of the spine of which he was to die in 1883. The doctors whom he consulted were able to do little for him, although for a time sodium salicylate (or 'the wonderful pills' of François-Joseph) seems to have provided some relief. 'From my observations over the past year,' he wrote to his friend Polonsky at the end of 1876, 'I have derived the conviction that depression, melancholy, and hypochondria are all nothing else but fear of death. It is self-evident that this fear must increase with every year.'[28] (Turgenev was then fifty-eight.) An entry in his diary, dated midnight, 17 March 1877, is full of despair: 'I am once again sitting at my desk. Below my poor friend is singing something with her completely cracked voice. My spirit is darker than the dark of night. It is as if the grave were in a hurry to swallow me up. The day flies past like some instant – empty, purposeless, colourless. Before you know where you are it is time to fall into bed. I have neither the right nor the inclination to live; there is nothing more to do, nothing to wait for, nothing even to wish for. ...'[29] 'Life becomes completely egoistic and on the defensive against death,' he wrote to Flaubert eighteen months later;[30] and again, in the summer of the following year, 1879, he commented to Flaubert on his mood in characteristic fashion: '... I am physically very well. As for the condition of my spirit you can give yourself an exact image of it by raising the lid of a cesspool privy and looking inside it. But it must not be an English water-closet, since they are usually clean.'[31]

However, as always, Turgenev's depressions must not be over-estimated, in the sense that they did not too much interfere either with his enjoyment of the things that gave him pleasure, or with his avid interest in political events. His correspondence shows a keen and con-stant absorption in French politics and in the struggles which de-veloped after 1875 between the monarchical and right-wing Presi-dent MacMahon, the republican majority in the Chamber of Deputies, and the various groups of the left which developed within it. Turgenev's sympathy lay with this republican majority and par-ticularly with Gambetta, during the attempts which were made by the President, with the Senate's support, to wage a struggle against it. He detested MacMahon, whom he saw as plotting to restore Bonapartism, and was elated when in October 1877, contrary to his expectations, the victory of the left in the elections brought about MacMahon's resignation.

His most passionate interest was, naturally enough, centred on Russia's Balkan policy of protecting the Slav minorities living under Turkish rule, and the conflict with Turkey to which this eventually led. After the declaration of war on 24 April 1877 he followed the fortunes of his country with eager enthusiasm, lamenting the reverses which followed on initial successes both in Bulgaria and in the Cau-casus, and rejoicing in the subsequent victories of the Russian forces.★[32] Turgenev's patriotism was untinged by the Pan-Slav emotions which in part motivated Russian Balkan policy, but he was outraged by Turkish repressions, and warmly approved of the war when it was declared. His national pride was certainly hurt by the hostility to Russia shown by Great Britain and France, and especially by the British government's support for Turkey and failure to put an end to Turkish atrocities against the Serbian and Bulgarian minorities, in spite of popular agitation inside Great Britain for such action.[33] His resentment at British Near Eastern policy evoked from him in 1876 a bitter poem of some forty lines entitled 'A Game of Croquet at Windsor'. In these verses Queen Victoria is depicted

★ One of his prose poems, 'The Blackbird', written in August 1877, laments the fate of his compatriots who were dying in the battles.

watching a family game of croquet, when to her horror she realizes that the balls are in fact the bloodstained and disfigured heads of the Bulgarian and Serbian victims of Turkish atrocities. One such head of a golden-locked child, propelled towards her by her daughter, causes her to scream with horror; her dress is stained with blood. The poem ends with a rhetorical cry that all the rivers of Great Britain cannot wash away the bloodstains.

The poem was written in the train between Moscow and St. Petersburg in the night of 19 to 20 July 1876. When he arrived in the capital, Turgenev tried to have his verses published, but the censor objected. However, the satire circulated in manuscript, and became widely known. It was printed in Russian in the same year in the form of a flysheet, published in a Bulgarian paper and, in a French translation, in *Le XIXe Siècle* on 3 September 1876. There was some attempt to print a prose translation into English in the *Daily News* (the liberal paper which had made public the first account of the massacre of the Bulgarians) but nothing came of this. An English version did eventually appear in Baden in 1882, in a volume of 'Translations from Russian and German Poets by a Russian Lady', but (like the rest of Turgenev's poetry) not in England. It was first published in Russia in 1881.[34]

*   *   *   *   *

For a number of years after the marathon effort to finish *Virgin Soil* in Spasskoe in 1876, Turgenev returned annually to Russia, usually in order to attend to his financial affairs which had entered upon another disastrous phase. The events which took place on his visit in 1879 proved as momentous as they were unexpected. He arrived in St. Petersburg on 9 February and left for Moscow four days later. There the first surprise awaited him: one of the brilliant young professors at Moscow University, the historian and sociologist M. M. Kovalevsky, gave a dinner for some twenty scholars who collaborated on a learned journal which he edited. Speeches and toasts were declaimed and their flattering terms reduced Turgenev to tears. In reply he proposed a silent toast to the memory of Belinsky.[35] This was, however, only the beginning. On 18 February Turgenev attended a public meeting of the Society of the Lovers of Russian Literature which took place in the largest lecture theatre of Moscow University: it was crammed with an audience which included many students. To his complete surprise Turgenev was greeted with an ovation: as reported in the press there was applause for several minutes and shouts of 'hurrah!' A medical student, P. P. Viktorov, delivered an address of welcome, which, however, mainly stressed the merits of the author of the *Sketches from a Sportsman's Notebook*. Viktorov ended by saying that the time had come for another kind of *Sketches*, but that Turgenev would not write them. Turgenev, deeply moved, replied that he took the praises directed to him as pertaining to his intentions rather than his achievements. In spite of the very qualified eulogy delivered by Viktorov, there could be no doubt after the Moscow visit that whatever discord had been sown between Turgenev and the younger generation by *Virgin Soil* was now healed or forgotten. For the three weeks he remained in Moscow the apartment of his friend I. I. Maslov (with whom he habitually stayed when in the city) was thronged daily by students and other young admirers.

On 4 March another public gathering took place, this time in the Assembly Hall of the Nobility, for a concert in aid of needy students, at which Turgenev read one of the *Sketches* ('The Surly Fellow'). He described his reception in a letter to Pauline:

Picture to yourself more than a thousand students in this colossal hall. I enter, an uproar enough to bring the building down, shouts of 'hurrah', hats flying in the air.... Then two enormous wreaths, then a speech shouted at me by a young student delegate – a speech bordering on the forbidden in every sentence, an outburst. The rector of the university in the front row, pale with fear. Myself, trying to reply in a manner which would not set a light to the powder keg, while at the same time trying to utter something more than platitudes. Then, after I had finished my reading, the whole crowd following me into the adjacent halls, recalling me 20 times in a frenzy, young women seizing my hands ... to kiss them!!! It was a mad scene. If a colonel of the *gendarmerie* had not come to escort me out, in the most polite manner, and got me into my carriage, I believe I should still be there.[36]

The speech of welcome greeted Turgenev as the last major representative of the generation of Belinsky, Granovsky, and Bakunin. In reply Turgenev evaded controversy by praising the spiritual enlightenment of Moscow University. It was only at a dinner given to him by a group of professors and writers on 6 March that he spoke of the need to finish the work of the generation of the forties in 'an upright, honest and open manner', and added the hope that the young generation would avoid 'unnecessary enthusiasms' as well as any steps backward.

The frenzied homage of youth continued in St. Petersburg; as in Moscow, his hotel room was thronged by a series of deputations and by countless students. On 15 March he was welcomed with wild enthusiasm when he appeared at an evening organized by women students for the benefit of needy undergraduates, and on the following day at a reading in aid of the charitable Literary Fund, the women medical students crowned him with a wreath. He was also pressed by the students of St. Petersburg University and of the Institute of Mines to take part in musical and literary evenings. He refused on the grounds of health. But it was believed, on the basis of what he was reported to have told one undergraduate, that the authorities had intervened and forbidden him to appear. His letter to the students stated that 'this generation, so far as I can judge, is on a good road, a road which alone can lead to the aims which we all desire: to the flourishing and strengthening of our dear country, Russian thought, and Russian life'.

It is quite evident from what has been recorded of Turgenev's speeches that he did not find it necessary to express any warning of any kind to the young generation against the adoption of violent means to achieve their ends, and indeed did not regard the acts of terrorism which were occurring by now with some frequency as of much importance. He referred to this theme in a speech at a dinner which was given in his honour in St. Petersburg on 13 March by a group of distinguished professors and writers. After stressing that in contrast to the position in the forties, there was now common ground between the generations, he continued: 'It is idle to point to certain criminal over-exuberant excesses. These manifestations are deeply distressing. But to see in them signs of convictions which are held by the majority of our youth would be an injustice, a cruel injustice, and in every degree as criminal.' The ultra-conservative K. P. Pobedonostsev, in a letter dated a few days later, commented: 'This grey-haired madman Turgenev, like the crow praised to the skies by the fox, dissolves with emotion, and makes speeches in which he bows down with enthusiasm before the younger generation,' and indeed it would seem that Turgenev was living in cloud cuckoo land so far as the political scene in Russia in 1879 was concerned.[37]

He was quite certain that he knew what was going on. 'I understand perfectly the reason for all this [i.e. the students' enthusiasm]. On the eve of reforms which are always promised and always postponed, on the eve of the birth of political life, all this youth is charged with electricity like a Leyden jar, and I play the part of the device which discharges it. . . . If these poor young people did not demonstrate they would burst!'[38] There was certainly truth in the fact that the country was in a ferment of expectation of an imminent constitution. The Third Department (security) said so in a secret report on

Turgenev's appearances in Moscow.[39] The students of Moscow University, in spite of the fact that several of their number had close links with the revolutionary Land and Liberty organization, had in the past year or two accepted the advice of more moderate leaders to press for reforms and had ignored the hot-heads who urged them to spill out into the streets in violent demonstrations.[40] Lavrov was probably right that the overwhelming majority of the students who thronged to welcome Turgenev were liberal rather than revolutionary in outlook though, as the reaction of the members of the People's Will to his death in 1883 was to show, he had won considerable respect among them too.

It was also true that in the country as a whole pressure for reform was gaining ground. In 1878 and 1879 a number of *zemstva* had responded to the government's appeal for support against the mounting wave of terrorism by stressing that this violence was just a symptom of the unhealthy political state of Russia, and could only be cured by constitutional changes in a liberal direction. Most remarkable of all was the fact that in spite of the growing disorder, which included several attempts on his life, Alexander II eventually approved the proposal of his ministers for a very limited and moderate form of representative government, the so-called Loris-Melikov 'Constitution'. The rescript summoning the Council of Ministers to prepare the necessary communication of the proposed reform to the public was signed by him on the morning of 1 March 1881. In the afternoon of the same day he was killed by an assassin's bomb.

It was of course true, even if Turgenev did not perceive it at the time, that side by side with the mood of relatively peaceful agitation for constitutional change there was a growing terrorist movement. This rejected outright any and all forms of compromise, and saw the only possible solution for Russia's ills in the forcible overthrow of the entire imperial regime. Turgenev was, no doubt, right in regarding acts of violence as the work of a minority: but in revolutions it is the minority that counts. Turgenev had depicted the revolutionary scene in Russia as it was around 1874 or 1875 with substantial accuracy in *Virgin Soil* – the naive idealistic 'going to the people', with terrorism and stirring up revolt as a fringe activity with not much future, and with the only hope for revolution lying in patient, long-term educational activity. But much had happened since then – indeed, it was as a reaction against the futility of 'going to the people' that the revolutionary organization, which adopted the old name 'Land and Liberty' (first used in 1861) came into existence in 1876.

Its aim, as set out in its statute, was revolution and towards that end it proclaimed as its main tasks the forging of links between revolutionary elements among the people and existing revolutionary organizations, and the 'disorganization' of the power of the government. This, apart from recruitment of adherents in the Civil Service and in the armed forces, included the 'systematic destruction' of the more malevolent or outstanding government figures, to be followed by the mass destruction ' on the day of reckoning' of all those on whom the existing hated order rested. A revision of the statute in 1878 (echoing the views of the leading theorist of Russian Jacobinism, P. N. Tkachev) stressed that the sole possible course was violent overthrow of the government as soon as possible, since otherwise the rapid development of capitalism threatened to bring about stability of the bourgeois order.[41]

The vice of the imperial regime, like that of most authoritarian governments, was that it could not distinguish between peaceful agitation and violent subversion, and thus by its own policy helped to nurture terrorism. But it was equally the case that the extremists of the revolutionary movement did not want compromise, and would settle for nothing less than the complete extermination of the existing order. The mass trials of 1877 of the demonstrators before the Cathedral of Our Lady of Kazan in January, and of the participants of the 'going to the people' – the Fifty, followed in October by the Hundred and Ninety-Three – were intended to win over popular support by exposing the fanaticism of the revolutionaries. They achieved the opposite. The skill of the defendants and the severity of some of the sentences won them public sympathy. The incompetence of the police led to the acquittal of some of the leading figures, who later planned the assassination of Alexander II. The trials marked the end of 'going to the people' and the beginning of systematic terrorism. An analysis of those arrested in connection with the 'going to the people' (at least 1,611, of whom 15 per cent were women) shows that the Russian revolutionary movement of the seventies was not mainly motivated by class hatred: of 425 described as 'especially criminal' nearly half were nobles or sons of high officers; while of the 193 accused only 44 belonged to the category of 'commoners' (*raznochintsy*). The overwhelming majority were young – under twenty-five – and Russians or Ukrainians.[42] A revolution led by fanatics was in preparation.

The event which sparked off a wave of terrorism was the acquittal of Vera Zasulich by a jury on 31 March 1878. She had shot the Governor General of St. Petersburg, General Trepov, at point-blank range, though he did not die. Trepov, with the agreement of the Minister of the Interior, had ordered the flogging of a political prisoner who had failed to remove his cap when the Governor General passed him on a visit to the prison. Vera Zasulich's act was in revenge for this, and she did not deny the shooting. When the jury acquitted her, in defiance of the evidence, a wave of exultation, voiced as openly as was possible in Russian conditions, spread within liberal society. Hardly anyone of those who welcomed the acquittal – least of all Turgenev – paused to think of the blow which had been dealt to the reformed legal system that was beginning to take root. ('As the call is, so is the echo' was Turgenev's comment.) A series of violent acts now followed. Leading government officials were assassinated in August 1878 and February 1879, and there were three attempts on the life of the Emperor in 1879. Even while Turgenev was in Russia, Land and Liberty was moving towards a split. In June 1879 an executive committee of extremists was formed within the organization which shortly afterwards, on 26 August 1879, voted to assassinate ('execute', as they expressed it) Alexander II. Around the same time the organization split into two: the People's Will, which now engaged in the duel with the Emperor which culminated on 1 March 1881; and All-round Repartition, which still adhered to the old tenet of Land and Liberty that a revolution can only be accomplished by 'the people' and feared that the isolation of the People's Will from the people would lead to the replacement of one dictatorship by another. Russian marxist social-democracy would before long evolve from All-round Repartition.

Turgenev was almost certainly unaware of the growing tide of an uncompromising policy of terrorism within the revolutionary organization. But the increase in the number of successful and attempted assassinations was evident enough; he dismissed this as a deplorable but inevitable reaction to the repressive policy of the government. In many cases this was true. But it did not alter the fact that the Russian revolutionary movement was reaching the stage where, if it succeeded, it would destroy not only the imperial regime, but along with it all the aspects of civilized life which were so dear to Turgenev. It was in this respect that he seems on this memorable visit to have been ruled by his heart rather than his head. Part of the euphoria was undoubtedly induced by the invitation extended to him by the students, in many addresses presented to him in Moscow and St. Petersburg, to come back, settle in Russia, and become the leader of all shades of progressive opinion. According to one not very reliable account, Turgenev accepted the invitation while in Russia. This is improbable. But it seems likely that for some time after this visit he was considering the possibility of some kind of political activity – he told Lavrov so. According to what he confided in Annenkov, he had been invited by the students 'not, of course, to become a leader (which is not in my nature) ... but a central point, a banner'. A few months before his departure for Russia in 1880 Turgenev wrote that he was going 'without knowing in the slightest when I shall return. The reasons which have induced this step are various – personal ... and others. We will talk about it when we meet. I cannot say that the decision which I took was easy – it is even very difficult ... and I am in a certain condition of melancholia.'[43]

Whatever the reasons, they could not have been connected with Pauline, with whom his friendship was completely serene. The political ambition, if indeed it was such, was eventually abandoned; the vision of Turgenev as a radical leader does not inspire confidence. It was to remain yet another dream of the Don Quixote *manqué*.

Turgenev's activities in Russia in 1879 had naturally aroused deep suspicion in the minds of the police. They were increasingly displeased by his friendship with Lavrov, with whom he corresponded regularly, and whom he often saw when the veteran revolutionary moved to Paris from London in the spring of 1877. They remained on fairly close terms until Turgenev's death. Turgenev occasionally contributed funds for Lavrov's activities, subscribed 500 francs a year to his journal *Vpered*, and once even procured him an invitation to a concert in aid of indigent Russian artists living in Paris, organized by the charitable society of which Turgenev was a leading member. Representatives of the Russian aristocracy attended and heated protests at Lavrov's presence ensued, so that Turgenev was very nearly obliged to resign from the society. The matter was smoothed over by the ambassador, Prince Orlov, but the rules were altered to make the repetition of so scandalous an occurrence impossible. Turgenev seems to have been under the impression that Lavrov's interest in revolution was really a pose (which it was not): 'He is a dove, who tries in every way to make himself out to be a hawk,' he wrote to Annenkov early in 1879. 'One has to hear him cooing about the necessity for Pugachevs and Razins. . . . The words are very terrible – but his looks are benevolent and he has the kindest of smiles ... even that enormous, shaggy beard looks gentle and idyllic.'[44] According to Lavrov, Turgenev's motive in supporting his organization was not belief in revolution, but his conviction that the necessary reforms from above would only come about as the result of pressure from below.[45]

Turgenev was also on friendly terms with a number of other revolutionaries, many of whom later published their memoirs. These included Kropotkin and German Lopatin. When Turgenev met the latter in Russia in 1879, he warned him of rumours that his arrest was impending, and after Lopatin had been imprisoned, interceded for him with Prince Orlov. He also stood surety for the release on bail of Elena Kulesheva (Anna Rozenshtein), a Bakuninist revolutionary arrested by the French police, and persuaded Prince Orlov not to hand her over to the Russian authorities.[46] What seems to have aroused especial ire in official Russian circles was the fact that Turgenev wrote a Preface (in which he made it clear that he did not approve of the author's views) to the prison memoirs of I. Pavlovsky, a revolutionary who had escaped from exile, and was befriended by Turgenev when he arrived in Paris.[*][47] Prince Orlov did not seem to take the affair very seriously, because Turgenev was still invited in October 1879 to meet the heir to the throne, the future Alexander III, when he visited Paris.[48] There was at least one denunciation to the embassy by an informer of Turgenev's supposed links with terrorists.[49]

Shortly before his departure for Russia early in 1880, an attack on Turgenev by B. M. Markevich, who had been singled out for special insult in *Virgin Soil*, appeared in Katkov's paper, accusing him of expressing revolutionary sympathies in order to curry favour with the young generation. Turgenev published a letter in the *European Herald* denying that he had ever changed his views from that of a liberal gradualist, and asserting that he had made them clear to the students when in Russia.[50] (This was not strictly true.) He left for Russia, where he was to spend five months this time, on 22 January 1880. He told Flaubert, whom he was not destined to see again, that he was apprehensive of being exiled to his estate once more.[51]

★   ★   ★   ★   ★

One of the main purposes of Turgenev's visits to Russia in the second half of the seventies was the need to attend to his financial affairs, which were once again in a disastrous state. The cause of the trouble was, as in the past, the manager of his estates. Uncle Nicholas's successor, Kishinsky, turned out to be equally unreliable. Turgenev's suspicions were aroused in the spring of 1876: by the summer he was 'almost certain' that he was being robbed,[52] and he replaced Kishinsky with the son of his neighbour, M. A. Shchepkin, to whom

---

[*] This was the same Pavlovsky whose memoirs about Turgenev were so much to distress Daudet.

he had leased Spasskoe shortly before. Intended as temporary, the arrangement with the young Shchepkin lasted till Turgenev's death. It is difficult to assess the extent of Kishinsky's depredations, although they were, no doubt, considerable: 'over half' of his fortune, a 'substantial part' and 'one quarter' were the various estimates given by Turgenev.[53] The new manager set about, as best he could, repairing the family fortunes by selling and leasing properties, but the process of recuperation was to take some time.

Turgenev's financial problems figured largely in his correspondence with his brother Nikolai. The two had little in common. Nikolai was everything that Ivan was not: a shrewd, even avaricious business man (not above lending capital on usury), very close with his money, and a complete philistine in his tastes. When not concerned with finance, the two brothers' correspondence generally dealt with questions of health. Yet, in spite of occasional fairly acrimonious disputes over money, there were some ties of affection between them which ensured harmony on the comparatively rare occasions when they met. Nikolai even from time to time showed some interest in his brother's literary activities, while Ivan took pains to maintain the family bond intact, and was warmly sympathetic in times of need – in 1872, for example, when Nikolai's wife (whom Ivan disliked) died. Whatever the exact extent of Kishinsky's misdeeds, there remained the fact, from what Ivan wrote to his brother, that in spite of being the owner of Spasskoe and of seven major and minor estates (two of the largest leased), his net income, even as late as the autumn of 1878, was only 6,000 roubles. He endeavoured, in vain, to persuade his brother to help. Nikolai had lent him 15,000 roubles on which Ivan paid him an annual interest of 1,350 roubles. He now proposed that Nikolai should remit the debt in return for his foregoing his claim to the 100,000 roubles which Nikolai had undertaken to leave him under his will. He argued that if Nikolai should survive him, the sale of Spasskoe would yield more than enough to cover the debt as well as the provision which he had made, in the event of his predeceasing his brother, for Pauline and Paulinette.[54] Various alternative proposals were made over the years, none of which Nikolai was prepared to accept – including an offer of the nude painting by Blanchard in satisfaction of the interest due on the debt for 1878.

The immediate purpose of Turgenev's memorable visit to Russia in 1879 had been to deal with the estate of his brother, who died quite suddenly on 7 January of that year. Turgenev was, it seems, genuinely distressed by the death: 'We seldom met, we had no interests in common ... but still, a brother! There is here an unconscious bond of blood, which is stronger than many others,' he wrote to Annenkov, and in similar terms to Flaubert–his two closest friends.[55] He was particularly upset by the fact that the serious nature of his brother's last illness had been concealed from him – it would seem deliberately. This was because of an intrigue by relatives of Nikolai's dead wife under whose influence he had fallen in his last years. These people were determined (or so Turgenev claimed) to do Ivan out of his inheritance as far as they could. Nikolai had frequently assured his brother that he had left him 100,000 roubles in his will. But it turned out in the end that he had only left him 60,000 roubles out of an estate of 520,000 roubles. Turgenev also inherited under the will the contents of his brother's house but gave the proceeds of the sale (up to a maximum of 2,000 roubles) to a cousin.[56]

Turgenev was now able to command high fees for his writings and his literary earnings were quite a considerable part of his total income. Stasiulevich paid him 500 roubles a printer's sheet (instead of 400, as originally agreed), which yielded 9,000 roubles in all for *Virgin Soil*. A further 2,000 roubles were paid when the novel appeared in volume form. He also contracted in May 1879 for the publication of the fourth collected edition of his works, in 5,500 copies, to be sold at 15 roubles a set, for a total royalty of 22,000 roubles, payable in instalments over two years.[57] However, for some years the effects of his manager's depredations left Turgenev in serious financial difficulties, and he was forced to sell his collection of pictures. The sale took place on 20 April 1878 in the Hôtel Drouot in Paris; Turgenev was too disabled by gout to attend. He realized only half of what he had paid for his paintings, which was 50,000 francs, a surprisingly modest sum for a collection which included, apart from modern French paintings, pictures by such Dutch masters as Teniers, Van der Neer, and van Ruysdael. He did not put his favourite Rousseau into the sale, and was able to keep it for a few years longer. The Blanchard nude (to which he was so devoted) was sold in Russia for 1,500 roubles – he had paid the equivalent of 1,700 for it.[58]

The financial situation was further aggravated by the disastrous state of his son-in-law's business. Paulinette's dowry had all disappeared, the glass factory proved to be worthless and there were debts which Turgenev only discovered when he was importuned by his daughter to come to the rescue. There was much acrimonious correspondence between father and daughter, although Turgenev, who gave his daughter a monthly allowance of 400 francs and had even lent Gaston capital, had not been ungenerous. The worst part of the situation was that Gaston was unco-operative and, in particular, rejected his father-in-law's sensible advice to find someone who would take over the factory without payment in order to cut losses. Gaston was eventually reduced to complete destitution.[59]

Meanwhile, by 1879 Turgenev's fortunes were temporarily improved, probably as the result of the inheritance from his brother. The increased prosperity was celebrated by the purchase of a horse and carriage, with the assistance of the son of his old friend N. I. Turgenev. For reasons which are difficult to discern he also acquired a she-ass. The ass proved useless, and there were frequent veterinary expenses with the horse.[60]

Two short stories were published by Turgenev shortly after the appearance of *Virgin Soil*, in 1877. Both deal with somewhat fantastic or supernatural themes; most of Turgenev's literary activity to the end of his life was now to centre around such inventions. His interest in these matters was not entirely new. It had shown itself in such earlier works as 'Three Portraits', 'Three Meetings', 'Faust', 'Ghosts', and 'The Dog'. Turgenev's method of treating these subjects (reminiscent of some of Hoffmann's tales) usually, but not always, took the form of leaving the reader wondering whether the events described were really, after all, outside the bounds of rational explanation.

'The Dream', written, with long interruptions, in the course of 1875 and 1876 in Paris, evidently did not please Stasiulevich, because it was published in another journal, *Our Age* (*Nash vek*). It is in truth, as Turgenev's young admirer Sophie Kovalevskaia (Briullova) described it, 'fantastic . . . and very strange'. The narrator, a young boy, lives in a seaside town with his mother, to whom he is devoted. His father is long dead – or so he believes. But he has a recurrent dream in which someone is identified as his father, though totally unlike the man whom he believes to be his real father. In the dream the father is not dead, but in hiding: he is very striking and sinister in appearance. Shortly afterwards the boy meets and talks to the man, who shows an interest in his family. Meanwhile, his mother becomes seriously ill, stricken with terror at some recent secret experience. Half delirious, she tells her son the story of her marriage (thinly disguised as the experience of a friend), and recalls a terrifying night when her husband was playing cards at his club and she was alone. (The narrator had not been born at the time.) A sinister man entered her room, overpowered her and removed her wedding ring. She and her husband soon left for another town, but shortly before this they

came upon a man with his head broken, obviously dead, lying on
a stretcher in the street. It was her frightening assailant. Having heard
his mother's story the boy goes off in search of the stranger, but learns
that he has left for America. Wandering aimlessly along the coast
he comes upon the corpse of the stranger, washed ashore. He is now
convinced that this is the body of his real father. His mother's wedding ring (which he knows from her description) is on the dead man's
finger. He removes it. He runs home and tells his mother of his experience, and gives her the ring. She insists on going with him to
see the dead man. When they reach the spot, the body is gone. All
inquiries by the boy fail to discover the explanation of its disappearance.

The second tale, 'The Story of Father Alexis', was written in one
night, at the end of January 1877 in Paris, and revised during the
following months. Turgenev was therefore working on it while the
furious debate over *Virgin Soil* was getting under way. The village
priest Alexei was a real character, from one of Turgenev's estates.
In the story the priest's son, after some time in the seminary, decides
that he wishes to go to university and adopt a secular life. His father
is saddened by the decision, but agrees. On the boy's first visit home
his parents find him completely changed, and in a state of obvious
terror. The father worms the reason out of him: he is possessed with
visions of the devil. Eventually, with much prayer and fasting, the
dread apparition is seemingly laid and father and son set off for confession and prayer at the nearest cathedral, in Voronezh. The son,
while taking communion after confession, is suddenly seized with
a fit of blind terror, and rushes from the church, with his father in
hot pursuit. He follows him for days on the pilgrimage route home
and eventually catches up with him and begs him in tears to explain.
The boy, in despair, reveals that as he was taking communion, the
devil appeared to him and whispered: 'Spit it out and grind it into
the ground.' The boy did this, and was now facing certain damna-
tion. Father and son drag themselves home, and the boy dies soon
after. The story is told with compassion and reverence. The editors
of 'The Story of Father Alexis' in the Academy of Sciences Complete
Works suggest that the theme may have been inspired by Dostoevsky's 'Vlas'.[61] But according to what Turgenev told Henry
James his story was based on fact.[62]

'The Story of Father Alexis' was rather unwisely published first
in an authorized French translation, and was then promptly, to Turgenev's fury, retranslated into Russian and published in *Novoe
vremia*. This was the second time that an unscrupulous editor had

treated him in this manner, so Turgenev should have known better. He sent a letter of protest to *Nash vek* (which had just published 'The Dream') but seems to have taken no steps against the editor of *Novoe vremia*, A. S. Suvorin. Suvorin attempted to justify what would seem to have been an act of gross editorial dishonesty by accusing Turgenev of vanity and lack of patriotism for publishing his story in a French paper before the Russian text had appeared. 'The Dream' also appeared first in French translation, but was not pirated in Russia. However, Turgenev found it necessary to write letters to the Russian and French press repudiating suggestions which had been circulated that the story had originally been written in French: 'I have never written a line (in the literary sense) in any language other than Russian.'[63]

A year later, in 1878, an idea for a story was jotted down by him: 'N.B. Some day it should be possible to compose a story about a man who has killed his wife, and who is thereafter pursued by her shadow, her ghost, *which he has never seen himself*, but which others see.... This must reduce him to despair, to self-accusation, to suicide. ... I had such a dream—something could be made of it.'[64] Turgenev's preoccupation with the supernatural, or its borders, was often to remain evident in what time was left to him for writing. It was, perhaps, to be explained by the continuous reflection on death with which he approached his old age. Towards the end of the seventies, as his Paris manuscripts revealed, Turgenev was engaged on preliminary work on a novel, and on a long short story. The action in the novel takes place in Paris, and was apparently intended to describe the bohemian *demi-monde* with which Turgenev was acquainted. The heroine, Salina Monaldeschi, the daughter of a Neapolitan, has hypnotic powers and extra-sensory gifts. The other characters of whom detailed descriptions have survived include exiled Russians, Frenchmen, a German Jew brought up in France, Italians, and a negress. There is no mention of this planned novel in Turgenev's correspondence or in accounts of his conversations in memoirs, except for one possible reference in a letter written in 1881, describing his intention to resume work on an idea which he had abandoned; and a remark in the memoirs of Lukanina, a young writer friend of Turgenev, that she had heard rumours that he was engaged on a new novel about 'a woman attractive in all respects whom, however, no one loves'.[65] Of a novelette, entitled 'Silaev', one completed fragment is extant, which describes the appearance to an old acquaintance of the narrator of the ghost of his uncle, in the shape of a black cat.[66]

A form of writing which belongs distinctively to the last years of Turgenev's life was that exemplified by the *Prose Poems*. Sixty-nine out of the total eighty-three of these miniature pieces were written in the years from 1877 to 1879, though much revised later in the process of recopying. Only fifty of them were published in Turgenev's lifetime, in 1882. The remainder (apart from one which was printed in 1905) appeared many years after his death when the manuscript was discovered: the first complete scholarly Russian edition is dated 1931. Although uneven in quality, the *Prose Poems* include examples of Turgenev's art at its best, and detailed study of them has shown the extent to which they reflect his literary experience and vast reading of a lifetime. A glance at the main themes dealt with in the *Poems* reveals Turgenev's private preoccupations between 1877 and 1879 (between the ages of fifty-nine to sixty-one), since at that date he certainly had no intention of publishing these fragments. A large number of the poems are concerned with death, usually his own, and his lost youth – twenty-seven out of the sixty-nine. Two very moving pieces of great simplicity are obviously addressed to Pauline. One extols the beauty which she expresses and personifies, thereby achieving the only immortality which it is possible to achieve: the other implores her not to visit his grave, but to read a favourite passage from one of the books which they once read together, and think of him – 'Oh, thou, my only friend, oh thou whom I love so deeply and so tenderly!' In some cases the purpose of the story related is to underline the long-suffering submission of the Russian peasant in the face of disaster – a favourite theme of Turgenev. An example of this is the sketch entitled 'Masha', which was based on experience, because Turgenev had related the facts to Goncourt some years before. It is a very simple and touching account of a conversation with a peasant cab driver whose much loved wife had been carried off by cholera some months before. Another is a shattering story of the war in 1805, told in a couple of pages. The narrator's military servant is accused of robbing a woman, who complains to the general who happens to be passing. The servant, who is in fact innocent, is so overcome with fear at the sight of the general that he cannot utter a word when asked what he has to say in his defence, and is ordered to be hanged. The woman is now frantic with remorse, as the stolen hens have been found. She begs all and sundry to spare the wretched servant, but the general has departed and the military machine rolls on inexorably. Just before he is hanged the servant turns to the narrator, his officer, and says: 'Tell her not to distress herself, your excellency. . . . After all, I have forgiven her.'

Some of the poems record personal events and emotions such as taking leave of the dying Nekrasov; or the tribute to the memory of Baroness Vrevskaia. There are bitter satires, little paeans of hatred – one might not have guessed that Turgenev could hate so fervently. The satire on a pharisee ('The Egoist') is written with particular venom: the entry of 'Viardot' in brackets in the manuscript (not in the published version), if really intended to signify what it appears to convey, reveals sentiments towards Louis which one would not otherwise have suspected Turgenev of harbouring. There are some poems which deal with revolutionary themes, such as the conversation between two workers who, on hearing that a revolutionary is to be hanged, are concerned solely to obtain a piece of the hangman's rope which brings luck; or the famous 'Threshold' which Stasiulevich would not publish in 1882 without alterations which Turgenev refused to make. Following Lavrov, 'Threshold' was widely believed by the revolutionaries to have been inspired by the hanging of one of the assassins of Alexander II, Sophie Perovskaia in 1881. But since Turgenev dated it May 1878 it seems likely that it was prompted by the trial of Vera Zasulich. It was first printed illegally in a broadsheet produced for Turgenev's funeral in September 1883 by the People's Will, clandestinely circulated subsequently, and first legally published in 1905.[67] A young girl is being examined on joining the revolutionaries – is she prepared for all the forms of hardship and suffering which her life will bring? She is. 'Are you prepared to commit a crime?' The girl drops her head. 'I am prepared for that too.' As she steps over the threshold one voice cries 'Fool!' and another 'Saint!'

This was typical of Turgenev's romantic mood at that date. Saint? The assassin who threw the first bomb at Alexander II on 1 March 1881 missed, and killed a small boy who was standing by. The Emperor left his carriage to attend to the child, and was mortally wounded by the assassins' second bomb. Who was the 'Saint'?

Finally, there are poems which deal with two of Turgenev's favourite themes: the blind, impersonal force of nature, which pursues its own ends of ensuring procreation and survival and is quite indifferent to men's aspirations; and the overriding importance of love in human relations. For example, a sketch of a terrified sparrow defending its fledgling which has fallen from the nest against Tresor (one of Turgenev's gun dogs) ends with the words, 'Love, I thought, is stronger than death and the fear of death. Only by it, by love, does life persist and move forward.' The *Prose Poems* are uneven in

quality and some are of little merit. At their best they are among
Turgenev's most exquisite and most conscious artefacts.

But the prose poems were a private affair and for some years after
the appearance of *Virgin Soil* Turgenev kept to his declared intention
that he would publish no more works of fiction. There were, however,
other literary activities. One of these was his edition of Pushkin's
letters to the girl who became his wife. These letters which were in
the possession of Pushkin's daughter, Countess Mehrenberg, the
morganatic wife of the Prince of Nassau, had by 1876, when the
question of Turgenev's participation as editor was first raised by the
Countess, been hawked around by her in Russian literary circles. The
conventions relating to the exhibition for prying eyes of the intimate
correspondence of the great were not then what they are now, and
there was reason for apprehension over the way readers would react.
Annenkov, Pushkin's first editor and biographer, had read the letters,
and when consulted by Turgenev about publication, replied in scathing, even violent terms – the Countess was only interested in money,
he wrote; it was disgraceful to expose private family discourse to
the vulgar gaze of the stranger, and the like. None the less Turgenev
persuaded Stasiulevich to print the letters in the *European Herald*, with
appropriate excisions – a restriction which the Countess herself had
originally insisted on when she first approached Turgenev. The project was delayed by Turgenev's preoccupation with *Virgin Soil*, but
he completed it by the end of 1877. The passages which worried
both Annenkov and Turgenev were the occasional somewhat
obscene remarks, the frank comments on individuals who were still
alive, and the rough political jibes. Turgenev made numerous
excisions, some of which Stasiulevich (to his intense annoyance)
ignored. The verdict of scholars who have subsequently worked on
the originals was that Turgenev did his work as editor competently
and conscientiously; his versions were the only ones available until
the full texts were partly published in 1935, and the remainder in
1938. In his Preface, Turgenev was mainly concerned to justify the
publication of such intimate correspondence and, with more tact
than truth, thanked Countess Mehrenberg for sanctifying 'our right
to raise the whole question [of making the letters available] to a more
exalted and impersonal sphere', and for a decision which she 'of
course, took not without a certain hesitation'. In spite of this Preface
and Turgenev's reputation, the Pushkin correspondence provoked
a good deal of indignation among the Russian reading public when
it appeared in print.[68]

Another literary effort, also in 1877, was his translation of two of Flaubert's recent minor works, which he considered to be master-pieces – 'La Légende de Saint-Julien l'Hospitalier', and 'Hérodias'. He persuaded Stasiulevich to publish them in the *European Herald*. There was also some suggestion that Turgenev should translate *Un Cœur simple*, but Flaubert dissuaded him, probably suspecting, rightly, that he did not admire this work so much as the two stories.[69] The friendship between the two men became warmer and more intimate as they grew older. Flaubert did not come to Paris very often, but Turgenev visited him fairly frequently in the country, at Croisset – although his habitual unpunctuality left Flaubert bewildered. 'This custom of always failing to keep his word makes my head swim. I don't begin to understand it,' he wrote to his niece in 1879.[70] But Flaubert's correspondence leaves no doubt that he became increas-ingly affectionate towards Turgenev in the last years of his life, always concerned for his health, anxious to hear from him and, above all, eager to know his Russian friend's opinion of his work. Tur-genev, for all the unpunctuality of a Russian *grand seigneur*, cer-tainly returned the affection; there are few correspondents, Annen-kov and the poet Polonsky apart, to whom he wrote in such warm terms, or showed so much consideration, remembering to bring him gifts from Russia (although never inviting him to Spasskoe) and sending salmon and caviar from Paris (how, in 1879, these delicacies could arrive in perfect condition is a mystery).[71]

Turgenev's efforts in 1879 to help Flaubert when the latter fell into serious financial difficulties, were very unsuccessful, though not for want of trying. A post fell vacant in one of the Paris libraries, which was in the gift of Gambetta, President of the Chamber of Deputies, whom Turgenev much admired. Erroneously convinced that Gam-betta would recommend Flaubert for the post, Turgenev persuaded him to accept it, incidentally misinforming him about the salary, and conveying an over-confident picture of Gambetta's intentions. Humiliation came both for Flaubert and for Turgenev. After much rather undignified lobbying Turgenev succeeded in securing an invi-tation to a reception in a *salon* at which leading political figures, in-cluding Gambetta, were present, but he was told by his hostess that the library post had been given to someone else, and that Gambetta had refused to meet him. The whole story immediately appeared in the *Figaro*, to the bitter distress of Flaubert.[72]

The news of Flaubert's sudden death on 8 May 1880, which reached Turgenev in Spasskoe, grieved and shocked him. 'After your family and Annenkov this was, I believe, the man whom I loved above all others on earth,' he wrote to Marianne Viardot.[73] He was

later active as a vice-president of the committee which was organizing the collection of funds for the erection of a monument to the
French writer. His attempts to raise money in Russia met with some
hostility, 'which I bear with great equanimity'.[74]

Turgenev's relations with Flaubert were based on a degree of intimacy which he did not readily offer to his many friends – not, for
example, to the other French authors whose company he enjoyed
to the end of his life, Zola, Daudet, Edmond de Goncourt, and Maupassant among others. Turgenev revelled in conversation and in con-
vivial company, he liked being admired for his wit and he was always
eager for the society of those who had something interesting to say.
One such was Henry James. The young American writer (thirty-
two when he first met Turgenev) was an enthusiastic admirer of the
Russian's work and had described him in an article devoted to his
novels as 'the first novelist of the day'. On arrival in Paris in 1875
James sought out Turgenev (who was not only twenty-five years
his senior but head and shoulders taller) and immediately fell under
his spell. He was to remain a hero-worshipper of the older man to
the end. The memorial article which he devoted to him in 1884 is
one of uncritically ebullient admiration: 'The most approachable . . .
man of genius it has been my fortune to meet. . . . He had not a par-
ticle of vanity. . . . His humour exercised itself as freely upon himself
as upon other subjects.'[75]

James venerated Turgenev, and Turgenev certainly seems to have
enjoyed his company and, while James remained in Paris, introduced
him to the Viardot circle and to some of his closest Russian friends –
in particular the painter P. V. Zhukovsky and Princess Urusova. He
was invited to the Viardot Thursday and Sunday parties – the former
he described as 'rigidly musical and to me therefore, rigidly bore-
some' except when Pauline herself sang. The less formal Sunday
parties he found 'rather dingy', but to see 'poor Turgenev' acting
charades, sometimes on all fours, and 'dressed out in old shawls and
masks' was both strange and sweet. It was 'a striking example of that
spontaneity which Europeans have and we have not'. (James did not
add, and probably did not know, that Turgenev's Russian friends
often found this 'spontaneity' embarrassing.) The American
remained very unimpressed with Turgenev's Paris friends. As he
wrote a few years later, 'I can't get over the sense that the people
he was with [meaning the Viardot circle] are a rather poor lot, and
that to live with them is not living like a gentleman.'[76] One would
have liked to hear Pauline's comment on this judgement!

According to Henry James, Turgenev had no high opinion of his fellow writer's work. There is certainly nothing in Turgenev's letters to suggest the contrary. 'A very amiable, sensible, and talented man' was how he described him to William Ralston in 1877, when James had moved to London. James sent him several of his works to read – *The American* and *Confidence* among others – but no detailed comment on them by Turgenev exists, although he did say of the first volume of *Confidence* that he liked it, and that 'Your style has become tighter (*plus ferme*) and simpler.'[77] He made a point of see-ing James whenever they coincided in Paris, and on his visits to Lon-don in 1879 and 1881. In 1879 James arranged a dinner party for him on 20 June at the Reform Club, to which Ralston and James Bryce were invited.* Turgenev's last meeting with Henry James was in 1882, nine months before Turgenev died.

Death was taking its toll both of old friends and enemies. Nekrasov died at the end of 1877, after a long and wasting illness. He and Turgenev had quarrelled in 1860,[79] and in spite of Nekrasov's assurance after their break that 'I remain, as ever, one who loves you and is grateful to you for much',[80] Turgenev had declined to renew the friendship. His references to Nekrasov in subsequent years had been scathing and contemptuous – both of the man and of his poetry (which he had never liked). The suggestion that they should meet apparently came from Nekrasov, in conversation with the historian A. N. Pypin, in January 1877. Baroness Vrevskaia may have learnt of this, or perhaps she herself suggested a letter of sympathy to Tur-genev, who was then in Paris. As he told her, 'I would willingly write to Nekrasov: in the face of death everything is wiped out. Besides, which of us is right and which wrong?' but he went on to say that such a letter from him might read like a messenger of death.[81]

Towards the end of May 1877, according to what Pypin told Sta-siulevich, Nekrasov sent a message to Turgenev to the effect that he had always loved him and expressed a wish to see him. At the beginning of June Turgenev, who was then in Russia, called on the sick man, accompanied by Annenkov.[82] He was deeply affected by the change in Nekrasov's appearance and, overcome by emotion, was only able to touch his hand. No word was spoken during the

* No comment on the occasion by Turgenev exists, but during this visit to Eng-land he was also entertained to lunch at the 'magnificent' Reform Club, with its 'horrible portraits' and 'no less horrible' busts. Curiously enough he only singles out 'white beans' for mention, notwithstanding the great gastronomic reputation then enjoyed by the Club, to say nothing of his interest in food. His host was Hall, on whose estate at Six Mile Bottom he had shot partridge the year before.[78]

visit by either man. In his prose poem describing the scene Turgenev wrote: 'Death reconciled us'.[83] Reconciliation did not mean that he had changed his judgement of Nekrasov. Shortly after the poet's death, Turgenev declined an invitation to speak at an evening dedicated to his memory. 'I cannot speak the whole truth about Nekrasov, whom I knew very intimately; I do not wish to say what is untrue; to limit myself to banalities would be indecent.'[84]

Having virtually decided to abandon writing for publication, Turgenev found himself with more time to spare. Much of this increased leisure was devoted to promoting the works of others. He took a detailed interest in the contents of the *European Herald* and encouraged Stasiulevich to publish the work of new authors whose writing he admired.

Of Russian authors, three young women particularly benefited from Turgenev's bombardment of Stasiulevich with their manuscripts and entreaties to read their works. One of them, to whose recollections of life at Bougival (under the name E. Ardov) reference has already been made, was Elena Blaramberg (later Apreleva), whose novel *Guilty but Blameless* was published, after much pressure by Turgenev, in the *European Herald* (Stasiulevich rejected a second novel *Apollon Markevich*, in spite of Turgenev's eulogies). Another protégée was Liubov Stechkina, whose novel *Varin'ka Ul'mina*, in a form much reworked on Turgenev's advice, also appeared in the journal. Adelaida Lukanina, in addition to being the author of novels (a number of which were published in the *Herald*) was also a doctor of medicine of the Philadelphia Medical School. Lukanina saw a great deal of Turgenev, and left a record of their meetings in memoirs which she published in 1887, and which were based on the diary which she kept. The particular interest of these recollections lies in the conversations which they describe on the subject of Russian poetry and the Russian language. It is small wonder that a master of Russian prose like Turgenev should have passionately loved the language of his craft. But throughout his life, as many who met him recalled, the subtle beauty of Russian seemed to him proof of the virtues of those who spoke it, and a promise that the darker sides of Russian life could never in the end prevail. 'What a strange thing!' he had written to Countess Lambert in 1859, 'These four qualities – honesty, simplicity, freedom and strength – are not to be discerned in the people, but are present in the language. ... This means they will eventually be found in the people too.' Twenty-three years later the same sentiment was expressed in his prose poem, 'The Russian Language'.[85]

The greater amount of free time which Turgenev enjoyed after the completion of *Virgin Soil* no doubt also accounted for the growth in the numbers of his letters; of nearly 7,000 items of his published correspondence covering a period of 52 years, more than one-third are dated in the six years of 1877–83. The number of his public engagements also increased considerably. He was active on committees of several charities devoted to indigent Paris Russians of one category or another. He appeared at innumerable concerts organized for such benevolent purposes to read some extract from his works. In 1878, he presided (very incompetently, according to one account) over an international congress of writers which met in Paris, devoted to the subject of authors' rights. Turgenev had been elected Vice-President, Victor Hugo President. The congress was totally ineffective, according to Turgenev. His speech was received with great enthusiasm by the French, but rather badly by some Russian critics, who considered that he had exceeded the call of courtesy by exaggerating French influence on Russian literature.[86]

Turgenev's sixtieth birthday on 28 October 1878 has left no trace in his correspondence, beyond a reference to a telegram from Professor Friedlaender. It was certainly not made the occasion for any special celebration or ceremony. In general Turgenev seems to have been indifferent to the marks of distinction which accompany literary success, such as his election as an honorary member of the St. Petersburg Society of Painters, or of the University of Kiev in the course of his triumphant reception in Russia in 1879. But he was inordinately pleased (as he delightedly informed numerous correspondents) when the University of Oxford decided to confer on him the honorary degree of Doctor of Civil Law. (Doctor of 'Common Law', as he for some time mistakenly supposed.) The official proposal to the Hebdomadal Council of the University was made on 2 June 1879 by the Master of Balliol College, Benjamin Jowett, whom he had met eight years before. But the first move to promote an honorary degree for him at Oxford was made in 1874 by William Ralston, who told him about the possibility. Turgenev was delighted – 'but is it not too ambitious, and would not the public ask: who is this man and wherefore this honour?'[87] Nothing came of Ralston's efforts at the time, but he renewed them with success in 1879. He was able then to enlist the support of Professor Friedrich Max-Müller, the philologist, whom Turgenev had met in Oxford on his first visit at the end of October 1878, when he stayed with the Master of Balliol (in a large room, 'a little cold, with an open fire that stinks more than it warms one's back').[88]

Strange to relate, Turgenev was the first novelist ever to be honoured by Oxford in this fashion, although poets, including Wordsworth and Longfellow, had had this distinction conferred on them. Apart from members of the imperial family and court (who included, in 1839, V. A. Zhukovsky, the poet, who was tutor to the heir apparent) the last Russian to have had a doctorate bestowed on him by Oxford was the astronomer V. Ya. Struve, in 1844. Among those similarly honoured with Turgenev in the Encaenia on 18 June were the Bishop of Durham, Sir Frederic (later Lord) Leighton, the painter, and the Ambassador in St. Petersburg, Lord Dufferin. Turgenev had some apprehensions that there might be disturbances at the ceremony because of the unpopularity of Russia as a result of the recent Balkan events, but all went very smoothly. The Public Orator, James Bryce, in presenting Turgenev in Latin referred both to his accomplishments as a writer and to the part which he had played in furthering the emancipation of the serfs. Turgenev stayed with Jowett and, as usual, left a most favourable impression on the many people who met him.[89] On his return to Bougival Turgenev wrote accounts of the ceremony to several friends in Russia, who knew nothing of the matter: there was no mention of it in the Russian papers, according to Annenkov.[90] Turgenev was delighted with the reception accorded to him in Oxford, and particularly by the fact that his scarlet robes had been presented to him by the dons at Balliol.[91] According to Jowett he was 'as pleased as a child'.[92] Of course, Turgenev always enjoyed dressing up. But, as he wrote to Annenkov, the red gown and black mortar-board hat were 'somehow inappropriate for a Russian face'.[93]

CHAPTER SIXTEEN

'Bliss and Hopelessness'

Before leaving for Russia in 1880 Turgenev confided to his friend Annenkov that there were both personal and political motives for his impending journey. Little was to be heard again of the romantic dream of leading the student protest movement, which had turned his head in 1879. In fact Turgenev was in love – gripped by that last and most tender passion in a man's life which Tiutchev in one of his memorable poems apostrophizes as 'at once bliss and hopelessness'.

The object of Turgenev's infatuation was Maria Gavrilovna Savina, twenty-five years old when he first met her in 1879. She was an actress of outstanding charm and talent who, since her début in 1874, had won universal acclaim for her appearances on the stage of the St. Petersburg Alexandrine Theatre, and elsewhere in Russia. Turgenev had seen her in her first role in 1874: she was not without talent, he wrote to Pauline, she was pretty and intelligent, but had a 'ghastly voice which recalled a Russian servant girl'.[1] A strange judgement. Savina, to judge by numerous photographs, though certainly clever, captivated by her charm and vivacity rather than her looks, which were somewhat coarse; and accounts by contemporary critics refer to her voice as sympathetic and clearly audible.*[2]

Their meeting came about as the result of Savina's decision to play the part of Vera in Turgenev's *A Month in the Country*. This, at the time almost forgotten play, published in 1850, had never been staged until 1872, when it ran for five nights in Moscow, and was not a success. Early in 1879 Savina, looking for a suitable work for her

---

* Turgenev's opinions on acting were generally somewhat idiosyncratic. There are repeated attacks in his letters on Sarah Bernhardt, for example, 'this insolent and affected mountebank, totally devoid of talent, whose only asset is a delightful voice', as he wrote to Madame Polonsky. He delivered himself much in the same style to Savina, with the additional embellishment of a rather improper joke.[3]

bénéfice night happened upon *A Month in the Country*, and in particular on the part of Vera – the young girl who clashes with her
employer over the love of the young student tutor, and is transformed before the eyes of the audience from a child into a woman.
Savina realized that the play had to be abridged, and telegraphed
a request to this effect to the author, who was then in Paris: he replied
on 22 or 23 January agreeing, but adding that the play was not
written for the stage and is 'unworthy of your talent'.[4] *A Month in
the Country* was a great success when it was staged later in January,
and a triumph for Savina. On 15 March, after his boisterous reception
in Moscow, Turgenev attended a performance in St. Petersburg and
was overwhelmed, both by Savina and by her performance. (He had,
incidentally, assumed that she would be acting the role not of Vera,
but of the older woman, Natalia Petrovna.)

It is not easy to define the precise nature of their relations. There
are seventy-nine letters from him to her, meticulously treasured by
Savina, and published in 1918 (three years after her death) reverently
edited by the distinguished jurist, A. F. Koni, and by Savina's third
husband. But her letters to him are lost; they were not returned to
Savina by Pauline after Turgenev's death, as was customary at the
time, at any rate by Russian conventions. The editors of his letters
made a number of significant excisions in the interests, as they
believed, of Savina's reputation. The complete texts were only
published by the Soviet Academy of Sciences in 1967 and 1968. The
omitted passages strengthen the accepted view that Turgenev was
in love with this young girl: they do not support any suggestion
that the two were lovers. It is not even certain that Turgenev was
by 1879 capable of physical love – though in older men there is often
little relation between desire and potency.

The most intimate stage of the friendship did not develop until
Turgenev's trips to Russia in 1880 and in 1881. During his short time
in St. Petersburg in March 1879 he called on her, and she visited
him at his hotel. They also gave a joint public reading from *The
Provincial Lady*, with Turgenev rather inadequately impersonating
the pompous and susceptible Count Liubin. They did not correspond
for the rest of the year, but maintained contact through a common
friend – Turgenev's factotum in St. Petersburg, A. V. Toporov.
When Turgenev first met Savina Toporov tried to protect him from
her supposedly mercenary ambitions, and accused him of being
deceitful about her. He was treated to one of the angriest letters Turgenev ever wrote.[5] It was from Toporov that he heard that Savina
had expressed a wish for his photograph. He sent one on 27 October,

addressing her in what at that time was an intimate form between a man and a woman, and ending in the manner reminiscent of his letters to Vrevskaia – 'and, meanwhile, stretch out both of your pretty little hands so that I can kiss them with that tender (half-fatherly, half- ... something else) feeling'.*[6] During his long stay in Russia in 1880 (nearly five months) he was in constant correspondence, increasingly intimate in its terms, with Savina and seeing her whenever possible, on or off the stage.

His letters to Pauline and Claudie from Russia in 1880 and 1881, only recently made available by Pauline's descendants, suggest irresistibly that, on the one hand, he was secretive about Savina in writing to Pauline and her daughter, and, on the other, that 'his ladies' were aware of the infatuation and rather resented it. Within a day or two of his arrival in St. Petersburg he called on Savina, who had had a slight accident on the stage and was confined to her house. 'I owed it to her as author,' he wrote to Pauline.[7] One can surmise that the motives were more than those of formal courtesy. There are a number of enthusiastic references to her acting and Turgenev was assiduously attending every new role which she played, although on one occasion – how truthfully is another matter – he complained that her voice was 'monotonous, unpleasing and had a common tone'.[8] A little later he referred to 'some friendly chidings'[9] in Pauline's letters (which are not available for this period).

Claudie seems to have been persistent in reproaching him about Savina on his visit to Russia in the following year, because the subject is mentioned repeatedly in his letters to her (none of her apparently frequent letters to him are known). It is difficult to believe a word of the following passage in a letter to Claudie dated 22 May 1881 from St. Petersburg, at a time when he was trying to persuade Savina to pay a visit to Spasskoe: 'You wicked girl! You speak to me of Savina! She appeared for a moment and has disappeared again. My thermometer as far as she is concerned has dropped to below "warm". Her fish mouth, her plebeian nose and her vulgar voice make me forget her eyes, which are beautiful and lively, but not kind. She is forgotten and soon never to be heard of. Ah, these men, these men – as you say.'[10] A few weeks later he wrote that Savina had not visited him in Spasskoe, and would not now do so. This, he claimed, was a relief to him: although her conversation was interesting the theatre had spoilt her 'to the marrow', and besides she

---

* Turgenev had a fetish for women's hands, and detailed descriptions of kissing them in imagination always figured in his letters to Countess Lambert and Baroness Vrevskaia – to say nothing of Pauline and Claudie.

would have interfered with his work.[11] A few weeks later he wrote once again that Savina would not be coming to Spasskoe, but even if she did 'it would be no great credit to me to keep the promise which I made you: this tiny little flame went out a long time ago'.[12] But Savina did come – as we shall see. One may be forgiven for doubting whether the letter to Pauline in which he says he described the visit was a complete picture. To Claudie he retailed Savina's matrimonial and career complications and promised to provide a fuller version when they were all reunited at Bougival. 'But I have no need to think of the promise which I gave you. So all is for the best.'[13]

Since we do not know what promise he made to Claudie, we cannot know whether he did indeed keep it, or how much he told the ladies when he returned to Bougival. But his letters to Savina leave no doubt that his friendship with her was of the same nature as his *amitié amoureuse* with Vrevskaia. As with Vrevskaia, the erotic elements were largely in the realm of the imagination, 'what might have been'; and as with all his love affairs, fictional as well as real, the first move always had to come from the woman. If the letters to Savina are more outspoken and suggestive than those written to Vrevskaia the explanation must have lain in the character of the two women: the nun-like personality of Vrevskaia recoiled, as the correspondence between them showed, from any hints which he gave of feeling physical attraction for her. Savina, more temperamental, robust, and bohemian probably found a feminine delight in leading Turgenev on a little – if only innocently. She was even perhaps in love with him herself. There is a passage in one of his letters to her written when he was already in the throes of his last illness, on 19 June 1882, which strongly suggests this: 'Oh my dear friend, I am so chastened in spirit that I do not even allow myself to think about the meaning of the following words in your letter: "Remember from time to time how difficult it was for me to say goodbye to you in Paris, and *all that I then experienced emotionally!*" I know for certain that if only our lives had come together sooner. . . . But what is the point of all this? Like my German Lemm in *A Nest of the Landed Gentry*, I am staring at my coffin, not at a rosy future.'[14]

Turgenev saw Savina frequently during his stay in 1880 in St. Petersburg: 'Of all my St. Petersburg memories,' he wrote to her from Moscow, 'the most precious and the best is you.'[15] A number of letters refer to an arrangement to meet: Savina was due to travel from Moscow to Kiev, Turgenev, now in Spasskoe, was to meet her in Mtsensk and travel with her as far as Orel, a distance of about thirty miles. The meeting took place, and was often recalled by him –

there is an oblique reference which recurs in his letters to a 'bolt' which she shut, or kept shut. Possibly this symbolized some resistance, or impediment, to physical consummation of love. He had failed to persuade her to come to Spasskoe; otherwise, he writes, they would be sitting on the terrace and he would 'in a passion of gratitude (the bolt . . .) repeatedly in his thoughts be kissing her feet'. She was due later to come to Paris, and he gave her directions to write to him (poste restante). 'But if the bolt must remain closed you had better not write. . . . You know what the predicament of Tantalus was. . . . I kiss your little hands, your feet, and all that you will allow me to kiss . . . and even what you will not allow me.' This letter includes a lighthearted imaginary scene of the kidnapping and carrying off of Savina at Orel station, and of the press comments on the incident. It ends with the following words: 'I assume that none but you will read this letter? That is why I seal it with Pushkin's ring – the talisman.'*

A day or two later a note of sadness, perhaps reality, creeps in. He wrote to her from Spasskoe:

Suddenly I notice that my lips whisper 'what a night we could have spent together! And afterwards? The Lord only knows!' And immediately I realize that this will never happen, and that I will in the end depart for that 'unknown bourn' without taking with me the memory of something that never happened to me. . . . You are wrong to reproach yourself, to call me your 'sin'. Alas! I will never be that. . . . My life is behind me, and that hour spent in the railway compartment, when I almost felt like a twenty-year-old youth, was the last burst of flame. It is even difficult for me to explain to myself what kind of feeling you have aroused in me. Am I in love with you? I don't know: it was different on past occasions. This insurmountable longing for fusion, for possession and for the surrender of oneself, when even sensation disappears in a kind of thin fire. . . . I suppose I am talking nonsense – but I would be happy beyond words if only . . . if only. . . . And now that I know it is not to be, it is not that I am unhappy . . . but I am deeply sorry that this beautiful night is thus lost forever and has not touched me with its wing. . . .

And he adds that this is a farewell letter: he hopes that they will continue to meet and correspond but 'the door behind which there was something mysterious and wonderful has closed forever'. And again there is a reference to that bolt.[17]

* This ring, a gold and cornelian signet, always worn by Pushkin, was given on his deathbed to the poet Zhukovsky, and inherited by Zhukovsky's son, who gave it to Turgenev. It passed after Turgenev's death to Pauline, who presented it to the Museum of the Alexandrine Lycée in St. Petersburg, whence it was stolen in the course of 1917. The ring bore a Hebrew inscription.[16]

Savina was in 1880 in the course of obtaining a divorce, and when she came to Paris in the summer it was to meet her future second husband. She did not inform Turgenev about her arrival ('evidently she does not wish to see me – which I am not at all grieved about,' he wrote to Toporov. 'She has ceased to exist for me.') They did meet, but formally.[18] Savina, who had doubts about the marriage, kept putting it off. Something of the old intimacy between her and Turgenev was renewed in Russia in 1881. Before going he had written to her on 1–3 March (under the impact of the news of the assassination of the Emperor): 'You say, at the end of your letter "I kiss you warmly". How? Do you mean as you did then, on that June night, in the railway compartment? If I live a hundred years I will never forget those kisses. . . . I love you very much – much more than I should, but that is not my fault.'[19]

Once again she promised, when they met in St. Petersburg and Moscow, to come to Spasskoe. This time she kept her word, and stayed for five days in July. Turgenev made feverish preparations for her arrival. His old friend Polonsky was staying at the house with his wife and children. There was much champagne, piano thumping, dancing, a peasant festivity. He went to church with her – Savina was religious. There were romantic walks and kisses, in the dark, in the great park. Savina swam in the pond in a specially constructed en-closure (and was glimpsed on one occasion in her bathing suit by Polonsky, to the envy of Turgenev). There was also much discussion about her projected marriage on which she was reluctant to embark. But the 'door' remained closed and bolted. One evening Turgenev read to her and to Polonsky his, as yet unpublished, 'Song of Triumphant Love'. He also read privately to Savina what she de-scribed as one of his intimate prose poems which he said would never be published. (He does indeed refer to this in a letter.) The poem she described in later years is not recognizable as any of the known *Prose Poems*, but from her description, it must have been addressed to Pauline, and was full of reproaches for ruining his life. But did he really ever write down such thoughts about Pauline to whom he wrote two prose poems of a very different nature?[20]

Savina married soon after: the marriage proved a disaster. Tur-genev continued to write to her until the last year of his life. The tone of his letters remained the same to the end – affectionate, much concerned for her welfare and happiness, and even with occasional erotic hints. 'Just imagine the following picture,' he wrote to her on 30 October 1881 from Bougival, 'Venice, perhaps, in October (the best month in Italy) or Rome. Two strangers in travelling clothes walk the streets – or sail in a gondola. One tall, clumsy, white-haired and long legged – but very pleased. The other a trim little madam with wonderful black eyes and the same hair – well, let us suppose she too is pleased. They go around the galleries, the churches etc., dine together, spend the evening in the theatre – and later. ... Here my imagination stops respectfully. ... Is that because there is something to hide here ... or because there is nothing to hide?'[21]

Turgenev never returned to Russia after 1881, and never saw Savina again on the stage. They last met in Paris, in 1882, when she was ill: Turgenev, who had a whole squadron of distinguished doctors among his contacts, helped her to obtain the necessary advice. His letters continued to show affection, interest in her career, her health, and her frame of mind. But the short-lived affair was over. 'I am resigned, dear Maria Gavrilovna, resigned,' he wrote on 5 November 1882, when he was already in the grip of his last, fatal illness, 'so that recalling the gaiety at Spasskoe last year I ask myself: is it really possible that I am that young, even if grey-haired, man who was capable of becoming all aflame from a kiss from a pair of delightful lips, etcetera, etcetera?'[22] Was he really in love with Savina? What is quite certain is that there had been no change in his feelings for Pauline and the Viardot family who remained the pivot of his life – his letters to Pauline and Claudie throughout his last visits to Russia leave no possible doubt about this. But passion had long vanished from his life with Pauline. And the young and temperamental Russian girl with her peasant face awakened in him, probably against his better judgement, an instinctive desire which he did not even try to suppress.

Although, perhaps, not as stirring as in 1879, Turgenev's two last visits to Russia in 1880 and in 1881 were very memorable (quite apart from the interlude with Savina). As usual, he made the rounds of St. Petersburg, Moscow, and Spasskoe, spending a much longer time on his estate on these occasions than he had usually done in the past – six weeks on the first visit in 1880, and nearly two months in the following year. In St. Petersburg, where he spent a great deal more time than in Moscow, he was plunged into a round of social activities which, one would have thought, would have daunted a younger man, even one not plagued by recurrent attacks of gout.

He sent Pauline an account of his engagements on 20 March 1880, which was presumably not untypical of his daily life: after expressing concern that he has had no letter from her for *five* days he proceeds with the catalogue of his social life in the recent past, in what he calls 'telegraphic' language, in order to save time. (The emphasis on *five* days is his: he had written no fewer than twenty-six letters since his departure from Paris on 3 February.) He had dined with his editor and some friends, who had locked him up and forced him to write an article. He had also spent a family evening with the Polonskys, to whom he was becoming increasingly attached. Then there were some grand, aristocratic dinners. One, in Princess Worontzoff's superb house, when there were violent diatribes against the depravity of the modern radical girl: 'High society understands NOTHING about what is happening below and around itself.' The second, rather boring, at the Grand Duchess Catherine's, attended by the ambassador in Paris, Prince Orlov. Then there was a dinner at the house of Princess Paskevich; and, gastronomically the best, (*ceps* fried in cream and Tilsit cheese!) a banquet at Prince Worontzoff's mansion.

Apparently the attacks on Turgenev mounted from time to time by conservative journalists like Katkov for his alleged revolutionary activity, had not succeeded in frightening off the St. Petersburg aristocracy. On the other hand, the attempt on the life of the Emperor, which had taken place five weeks before, and was followed soon after by an enormous public manifestation of loyalty and affection, may have shaken the revolutionary ardour which had inspired him to write 'Threshold' two years before. He described the panic in St. Petersburg in detail in his letters to Pauline, expressing approval of the rumoured appointment of Loris-Melikov to pacify public excitement. He also gave her an account of the execution of the young Polish Jew who had tried to kill the Emperor, expressing fear that the public might react to it by carrying out anti-Jewish pogroms, 'all the more unjust because the Jews have always given evidence of their very loyal feelings towards the government and the Emperor's person'.[23] There were no pogroms that year. When they did occur, in the following year, Turgenev repeatedly refused requests from Jewish public figures to protest openly against them.[24] One of the highlights of the visit to St. Petersburg in 1880 was an invitation, by which he felt very honoured, to the dinner commemorating the emancipation of the serfs on 19 February. Many of the statesmen who had been most active in bringing the momentous act into being were now dead. But Turgenev heard much conversation on the conditions of the peasantry from the high government officials who were present, and came away almost convinced that the era of reform 'so unhappily halted' was not yet over.[25]

He seems to have derived more pleasure from his last two visits to Spasskoe than ever before in his life. The estates were conscientiously, and it would seem efficiently, managed by young Shchepkin, and

Turgenev was on the friendliest terms with him and his wife – whose detailed memoirs form one of the most important sources of the period.[26] His friend Polonsky was also staying in Spasskoe with his family most of the time that Turgenev was there and Turgenev also became closely attached to Polonsky's wife, Josephina, with whom he maintained a regular and a rather intimate correspondence when he returned to France. She was an amateur sculptor, whom Turgenev constantly encouraged in her art (she eventually modelled the bust which was placed on his grave). He seems also to have been attached to her two young boys, made up imaginative little stories for them, and wrote some letters to the older one when back in France.

The two summers in Spasskoe provided him with an opportunity to enjoy once again the kind of Russian country life which he had so long missed. He could indulge his habit of snuff-taking – strictly forbidden by his 'ladies', even in his own apartments in Paris or Bougival. There was a little shooting, but not a great deal. There was much talk on every conceivable subject – on the state of Russia, on revolution, on the Russian peasant, on his childhood, on his views of himself. ('Can you describe my character in five letters?' he once asked Polonsky. When Polonsky gave up, he told him the answer to the riddle – 'T – R – U – S – hard sign'★ – which is the Russian word for 'coward'.)[27] Above all, there were visitors: old friends like Grigorovich, the novelist, and new friends, like Evgenii Garshin, who was the brother of the writer, Vsevolod Garshin, whom Turgenev regarded as the rising star of Russian literature, indeed, as his own 'heir'.[28] There was an ex-enemy, with whom he had become reconciled – Leo Tolstoy; and above all, in 1881, there was Savina.

For all these forthcoming visits Turgenev had already made preparations from Paris by instructing his manager to hang new curtains in the main living-room of the old house, to instal a bath, to procure a good cook, and to lay in wine.[29] He was able while in Spasskoe to take his responsibilities as landlord more seriously than he could do when in Paris – his numerous pensioners, the school, the almshouse, and peasant welfare generally. When the local drinking establishment was by a fortunate chance burnt down, he had a chapel built near the site for which he ordered an icon to be painted. This, as he intended, prevented a new tavern from going up in the neighbourhood, since the law prohibited the building of drink shops within a certain distance of a church. But although Turgenev was probably a better landlord than many, certainly more generous in frequent small acts of assistance, and always fair in his dealings, the conditions

★ The hard sign was a letter of the pre-revolutionary alphabet.

of the peasants on his estates according to Polonsky were far from exemplary. The peasants' average holdings of three and a half *desiatins* (about nine and a half acres) were insufficient to preserve them from near starvation in the winter, and there was much disease – though Turgenev did eventually pay for regular visits by a doctor to look after the sick.[30] He was also able to attend to the business side of his estate – though how far his interventions in practical matters were of any material benefit is another question.

Turgenev and Tolstoy had not met since their quarrel in 1861, but the older man always retained his high regard for the younger writer whom he considered foremost in Russian letters – at least so far as the works of which he approved were concerned. He did all he could with considerable energy to encourage and promote in France and in Germany *War and Peace* and *The Cossacks*.[31] Early in 1878 Tolstoy, in one of his moods of Christian forgiveness, wrote warmly to Turgenev offering to forget the quarrel. Turgenev replied expressing genuine delight that 'the misunderstandings between us are a thing of the past'.[32] In the course of the next few years the two men met as often as circumstances allowed: Turgenev visited Yasnaia Poliana twice in 1878 and again in 1880 and 1881; Tolstoy stayed at Spasskoe in 1881 on his return from a spiritual retreat at Optyna Pustyn, a monastery not far from Kaluga, and a visit to the sectarians.[33]

The reconciliation seems to have been as complete as was possible between two men of very different temperament. Tolstoy at first kept some of his reservations – as he wrote to Fet, '... we know the degree of intimacy which the two of us can achieve'; and there was now and again a sign of the old irritation. When on one occasion Turgenev demonstrated the ancient form of the cancan and fell down in the process, Tolstoy recorded in his diary: 'Turgenev – cancan. Sad.'[34] But these were matters of minor importance. 'Undoubtedly a genius, and the kindest of men', Turgenev called him in a letter to Grigorovich.[35] In 1881, before visiting Spasskoe, Tolstoy wrote to him: 'I felt so happy in your company, at our last meeting [in Yasnaia Poliana] as never before.'[36] The correspondence between them continued right to the end of Turgenev's life. Turgenev shows a constant interest in Tolstoy's writing – as did Tolstoy in his, as well as affectionate concern for his failing health. 'I embrace you, my old and most dear and very precious person and friend,' he wrote in May, 1882.[37] Turgenev's well-known letter, urging Tolstoy to return to literature (as distinct from the religious and philosophical writings to which he had recently devoted himself) was, even if more dramatic as coming from a dying man, in essence the continuation of what Turgenev had been urging for some time past on one whom he regarded as the greatest living Russian writer.[38]

Among other Russian authors he praised the work of Vsevolod Garshin and also of Saltykov-Shchedrin and Grigorovich, whose earlier fiction he had disliked, and the writings of Gleb Uspensky. On a number of occasions he read stories by Uspensky at one of the numerous Paris literary evenings in aid of charity in which he participated.* He liked the later plays of Ostrovsky a good deal less than the earlier ones; and continued to speak of Polonsky as the last living poet. Turgenev's high regard for Pisemsky remained unchanged. He referred to N. S. Leskov's talent as 'beyond dispute'. There is no evidence that the two writers ever met, although Turgenev wrote to the younger man, correcting some inaccuracies in a memoir of Benni written by Leskov, who had been friendly with him. Turgenev wrote in terms of unrestrained praise for the long-forgotten novels of his young women protégées – Lukanina, Blaramberg, and Stechkina. But then he was occasionally prepared to admit to his friends, who were sometimes sceptical about his literary enthusiasms, that his judgement could sometimes be of dubious value. On the other hand, his criticism of the literary efforts which were often sent to him for comment by strangers could be very scathing indeed.

On the work of Dostoevsky he hardly ever expressed an opinion. He could scarcely have failed to discern its quality of genius, but Dostoevsky's Slavophile and nationalist outlook, to say nothing of *The Possessed*, could hardly have endeared even the author of *The Idiot* and *The Brothers Karamazov* to Turgenev. When Dostoevsky died in 1881 Turgenev contributed twenty-five roubles to a subscription to erect a monument to him, and seems to have contemplated writing an article on him, but he never did.[39] In a letter to Saltykov after Dostoevsky's death, he pointed to what he considered were elements of de Sade in Dostoevsky's writings: 'And to think that all the archpriests in Russia celebrated requiem masses for our de Sade....'[40]

Turgenev devoted his main critical effort to Pushkin in the summer of 1880. This was the result of the decision of the Society of Lovers of Russian Literature to organize festivities in Moscow in honour of Pushkin. A monument erected to the poet was to be un-

---

* He also wrote a preface to the translation by Uspensky's wife of a collection of tales by Leon Cladel, published in 1877. It was indeed Turgenev who recommended to her that she should produce a Russian version of these tales which were of a very 'populist' character.

veiled in the course of a ceremonial session lasting several days. A committee of the Society was set up to organize the proceedings. Turgenev became a member of it, and was charged to attend the Moscow ceremonies as a delegate of the Society for Assistance to Writers and Scholars in Need, which he had helped to found some twenty years before.[41] He spent some time assisting with the arrangements and persuading some of the leading authors of the day – like Annenkov (successfully) or Tolstoy (unsuccessfully) – to participate. The aim of the organizers, as Turgenev reported to the President of the Society, was to include all the leading literary figures from Moscow and St. Petersburg and to ensure that, on the one hand, all outlooks should be represented – that is to say, both the more nationalist and the more cosmopolitan – but that, on the other hand, the 'bad element' (which for Turgenev always meant Katkov) should not be given an opportunity to make a speech. Another 'bad element', Count Dmitry Tolstoy, had, to Turgenev's great delight, been removed from his post as Minister of Education and Procurator of the Holy Synod, around the time of Turgenev's arrival in Moscow from St. Petersburg on 18 April 1880. Among those invited to speak at the Pushkin celebrations were Grigorovich, Pisemsky, Annenkov, Dostoevsky, Turgenev, and the historian of literature Grot, from St. Petersburg; and Ostrovsky and Ivan Aksakov, among others, from Moscow. Goncharov was invited, but was prevented by illness from attending.[42]

On 2 May Turgenev left Moscow for Spasskoe, spending two days on the way at Yasnaia Poliana with Tolstoy. Once at Spasskoe, he spent only a few days preparing his speech on Pushkin.★ This lecture is not among his outstanding works. A nation, Turgenev said, only succeeds in asserting its right to a place in history when it achieves full, conscious, and distinctive expression in its art. Homer, Goethe, and Shakespeare did this for their countries: Pushkin won this claim for Russia. His genius lay in his ability to blend both foreign and national influences, but without becoming submerged by either.

★ His mind seems to have been preoccupied with Savina while he was thus engaged: he was trying to arrange the meeting on the railway train for the journey from Mtsensk to Orel, but she did not answer his letters. He was originally invited by the organizing committee to write a popular short brochure on Pushkin which could be distributed in print in the course of the festivities as well as being delivered orally. But he found that he was incapable of writing for the people ('which in any case knows nothing of Pushkin') and informed the chairman that he would only give the speech. Having made a fair copy, he sent his text to Stasiulevich and ask him to suggest some cuts, and to consult Pypin and Annenkov on the question. In the end, Turgenev accepted all the suggested omissions – one of them of some political significance.[43]

He produced true Russian national art – not popular art, which consciously imitates models emanating from the common people and is false. Pushkin's great achievement was to create a living, superb language, essentially Russian in its character, because, as Mérimée had once said to Turgenev, the true quality of Russian poetry is that it seeks truth in the first instance, and leaves beauty to look after itself. Pushkin was, indeed, at the very innermost core of Russian life. If he did not become a world poet, this was because he was killed when he was only thirty-seven. Turgenev then referred to the temporary decline of Pushkin's influence and popularity, which had now happily been halted. 'It is said of Shakespeare that everyone who has just achieved literacy inevitabily becomes a new reader of Shakespeare's works. So let us hope it will be with Pushkin: that each of our descendants, as he stands lovingly before this statue of the poet ... will by that very act become more Russian, more educated, more free!'[44]

After a postponement occasioned by the death of the Empress on 22 May, the monument was unveiled on 6 June. The festivities lasted for three days, during which period there were various speeches, and Turgenev, along with Annenkov and Professor Grot, was elected an honorary member of the Council of Moscow University. This was followed by a dinner and a concert in the course of which Turgenev read some of Pushkin's poems.* On the following day Turgenev delivered his lecture. It was not too well received. According to Kovalevsky it was too subtle and too moderate to appeal strongly to a very nationalistically inclined public. At the dinner given by the Society of the Lovers of Russian Literature Katkov, who had, of course, been invited, stretched his champagne glass towards Turgenev in a gesture of reconciliation, but his overture was rejected – as was noted by the representatives of the press who were present.[45]

The highlight of the proceedings was, beyond doubt, Dostoevsky's famous speech which was delivered the following day, 8 June, and was greeted with ovations almost without precedent, even in highly-charged Moscow audiences. His praise of the universality of Pushkin's genius won much greater acclaim than Turgenev's modest doubt whether he was a poet of world stature. Dosteovsky's Messianic proclamation that the Russian soul, as symbolized by Push-

---

* There were some who criticized his choice of poems, suggesting that his aim had been to draw attention to himself rather than to exalt Pushkin. But then the whole course of these celebrations was shot through with cross-currents of emotionalism.

kin, strove towards the ultimate goal of universal man struck a deep
response. At one moment in his speech, while praising the chastity
and modesty of Pushkin's Tatiana he linked with hers the name of
Turgenev's Liza. Turgenev was visibly moved, and blew Dosteovsky a kiss – according to some accounts he went up and embraced
him.[46]

Turgenev was not a vain man, despite the frequent accusations
by those who disliked him. Besides, there had been enough adulation
accorded to him too, including a spontaneous demonstration of
cheering by school pupils who recognized him on his way to the
hall and a laurel wreath solemnly presented to him after one of his
readings from Pushkin's poems. But he could scarcely be blamed
for feeling some resentment at what he recognized as a victory for
the nationalist, anti-Western view which he disliked and associated
with Moscow. No description of the Pushkin celebration sent to Pauline or to Claudie has come down to us, which is a pity, because
he always wrote most frankly to them. In a long letter to his editor,
Stasiulevich, he was severely critical of the speech, and in particular
rejected a remark which Aksakov had made that he, Turgenev, had
fully approved what Dostoevsky had said. The speech was 'clever
and brilliant, and cunningly skilful' but totally false. Tatiana had been
subtly described – but did only *Russian* wives remain faithful to their
old husbands? And this universal man, whom the public had
applauded with such unrestrained enthusiasm – what is the point of
him? 'It is much better to be an original Russian than this depersonal-
ized all-man.' He urged his editor to print something of this kind
to show that 'Messrs. the Slavophiles have not yet swallowed us up.'
(Stasiulevich did print the substance of his comments.) When Dostoevsky's speech was later published, Turgenev felt tempted to write
a reply to it (as he told Annenkov), but resisted the impulse.[47]

Turgenev was beginning to shed some of his more naive infatuation for the revolutionaries which he had experienced so strongly
in 1879, when he blamed all their violence, which he deplored,
squarely on the government. In part this change of outlook was due
to the mounting wave of terrorist acts, of which the attempt to blow
up the Emperor in February 1880 was only one. The great demonstrations in St. Petersburg in support of Alexander II must have
brought home to him once again the moral which he sought to stress
in *Virgin Soil*, that revolution in Russia is doomed to failure because
there is no point of contact between the people and the self-appointed
champions who seek to liberate them. He was also favourably
impressed with the liberal trends which the Emperor was showing

in 1880 in spite of the mounting violence: for example, the replacement of Count Tolstoy by a more enlightened Minister of Education, Saburov, and the choice of another liberal, Abaza, as Minister of Finance. Above all, there had been the appointment in 1880 of General M. T. Loris-Melikov, an Armenian and a hero of the Turkish War, to head a commission to examine the whole course of revolutionary activity, to attempt some kind of reform, and to promote reconciliation with the radical youth. Turgenev greatly admired Loris-Melikov (who was indeed one of the most liberal-minded statesmen of the reign), and often praised him in his letters.

He had such high hopes in 1880 of Loris-Melikov's administration that he included a passage in the original draft of his Pushkin memorial lecture expressing praise for the fact that, in spite of the 'lamentable events' (he meant the recent attempt on the life of the Emperor), the 'almost exhausted confidence of the government is being reborn' and is appealing to the healthy elements in society. This was the passage which Stasiulevich and Annenkov advised him to excise – not, of course, because they did not approve of reforms or of liberal ideas, but because they regarded the judgement as inappropriate in the kind of speech he was to deliver, and perhaps also as unnecessarily subservient to the government.[48] Turgenev was, as one can imagine, deeply shocked by the events of 1 March 1881, which not only put an end to the most beneficial reign that Russia had ever known under the Romanovs, but set back for a long time to come all prospects of reform. He was particularly outraged by the letter addressed to Alexander III by the Executive Committee of the People's Will offering to stop terrorist acts if the Emperor granted political and civil freedom.[49] On 26 March 1881 he published an unsigned article on the new Emperor in a French journal. It was moderate in tone, very well informed, not optimistic about the prospects of far-reaching constitutional reform, but hopeful that Alexander II's policies would be continued. As for the nihilists, his successor 'will not wish to avenge, but he will know how to forestall and to punish'.[50] A talk with Polonsky in the summer of 1881 was very revealing of Turgenev's attitude. This was now considerably different from that of the romantic who, in 1878, had heard a voice cry 'Saint' as the young woman revolutionary stepped over 'the threshold'. In this conversation Turgenev contrasted the fate of Antigone as depicted by Sophocles, with that of the revolutionaries executed on 3 April for the murder of the Emperor. Antigone's death, as punishment for disobeying the law and giving her dead brother's body decent burial, is tragic. What she has done is against King Creon's edict, but it has the full approval of the entire Theban population. This is not so in the case of the revolutionaries, to whose life and death the people of Russia are completely indifferent.[51]

*   *   *   *   *

Passing through Berlin in 1880 Turgenev examined an altar of Zeus which had been recently excavated in the ancient city of Pergamon, acquired by the Prussians, and was now on exhibition in the Berlin Museum. He was enormously impressed by these classical reliefs and described them in terms of the highest praise in a letter to Pauline from Berlin, dated 26 January: 'I have seen, seen with my own eyes, the immortal, the god-like, the incomparable fragments of the colossal high reliefs of Pergamon picturing the war of the Gods against the giants.' The sculpture was as perfect as that of the Parthenon. He described the various scenes in detail – the beauty had made him weep.[52] At lunch at his editor's office in St. Petersburg, when A. F. Koni was also present, he discoursed so eloquently about these sculptures that the two of them persuaded him to write an article. He was shut up in a neighbouring room (leaving his tie as a pledge that he would not try to escape) and within an hour produced an essay which was shortly afterwards published in the *European Herald*.[53] The description of the reliefs, which runs to nearly six pages, is superb both in the picture which it conveys, and in its imaginative comment: 'Victory is undoubted and final: it is on the side of the Gods, on the side of light, beauty, and reason. But the dark, wild forces of the earth still resist – and the battle is not over.' There follows a detailed account of the figures and the action. At the conclusion he refers to the debate on whether this sculpture is to be regarded as 'classical' or 'romantic', and dismisses the discussions as irrelevant. There is realism, of course, as shown in much of the detail, just as there is romanticism in the great freedom of movement. But the realistic details as well as the 'stormy freedom of romanticism' is so penetrated by the highest and clearest order of 'ideal thought of the highest artistry' that one càn only pause and wonder, try humbly to learn, and feel grateful for having lived to see those marvellous works.[54]

Although Turgenev did not fully carry out his threat to give up all creative writing after *Virgin Soil*, he wrote very little in the last years of his life. Two stories, one entitled 'Old Portraits', the other 'The Desperado', were published with an overall title *Fragments from Reminiscences – My Own and Those of Others*. The first 'fragment' appeared in 1881, in *Poryadok*, a short-lived liberal daily newspaper which was launched and edited by Stasiulevich. By the time 'The Desperado' was ready for publication, *Poryadok* had ceased to exist, and the story was published, as usual, in the *European Herald* in January 1882. While he was working on the first of the two sketches, Turgenev seems to have had in mind embarking on a series comparable to the *Sketches from a Sportsman's Notebook*; this had also developed accidentally out of the success of 'Khor and Kalinych'. 'It would be a miracle,' he wrote to Annenkov on 22 November 1880, 'if "Old Portraits" were also to prove as fruitful at the end of the same career.'[55] But it was not to be: the intended cycle never got beyond the two stories, a list of characters which suggests that Turgenev was contemplating a third,[56] and finally 'Une Fin' which he dictated to Pauline in 1883. Both stories are founded on personal experience, or on incidents related to the author.

In 'Old Portraits' the action takes place many years ago, in the time of serfdom. Most of the narrative is taken up with a charming picture of the life and death of an old, devoted, rather simple pair – a country landlord Aleksei Telegin and his wife Malania. (The prototype for Telegin was an uncle whom Turgenev had known many years before.)[57] But the story ends with a bombshell, which shatters the idyll and shows up serfdom in its true light. The narrator describes the scene of his last visit. One of Telegin's serfs appeals to him in despair: it appears that the new owner of a neighbouring estate, notorious for his brutality, has discovered that this particular man belongs to him and not to Telegin, and demands his return. He refuses the princely price offered to him by the kindly Telegin and there is no help for it: the serf has to be returned. The man in desperation vows that he will kill his new master, and indeed some time later splits his head open with an axe, surrenders to the police, and disappears to penal servitude. 'Yes, the good old times – well, let them be!' is Turgenev's final comment, quoting Telegin. Annenkov advised him to end the story with the suicide of the serf but Turgenev, with greater psychological insight into the mind of the Russian peasant, would not agree.

'The Desperado', which describes the exploits of a restless and disappointed scion of the nobility, is a faithful portrait of Turgenev's first cousin, Mikhail Alekseevich Turgenev, his father's brother's son. The cousin ended up as a drunkard, living largely on charity, and Ivan Sergeevich made repeated small contributions to his upkeep. Neither story can rank among Turgenev's best work. Both met with moderate approval from Russian critics, and were published in a number of translations soon after their appearance in Russian.

The longest among these late stories was 'Song of Triumphant Love', which he started to write at the end of 1879, and completed, after an interruption of eighteen months, in June 1881, and then revised. (It was, thus, written in the aftermath of the affair with Savina.) It was published in the *European Herald* in November 1881. The story, which is dedicated to the memory of Flaubert and which in style reminds one of Flaubert's *Legends*, which Turgenev translated in 1877, is cast in the form of an account supposedly discovered in an ancient Italian manuscript. It is set in Ferrara in the middle of the sixteenth century. Like the other tale which he was able to complete, 'Clara Milič', it has a supernatural theme which leaves the reader in some doubt whether there may not, after all, be a rational explanation for the strange happenings. Two friends, Mucius and Fabius, both handsome, rich, well-bred, and talented (the one in music, the other in painting), fall in love with the beautiful and accomplished Valeria. They vow to accept her choice: the loser will leave Ferrara, and only return when he is certain that his passion is a thing of the past. Valeria (on her mother's advice) chooses Fabius, and Mucius departs. The young couple live for five years in complete happiness, marred only by their failure to have children. Then Mucius returns: he is welcomed and installed in a pavilion in the garden. Accompanied by a mysterious and dumb Malay servant, he is laden with exotic Eastern objects including an Indian violin, on which he plays a stirring, triumphant melody, which he describes as a song from Ceylon, a song of satisfied love.

The effect on Valeria is disastrous. Mucius comes to her by night in a dream, and haunts her by day. One scene, when Fabius finds Valeria in the garden, seems to convey Turgenev's interpretation of the intrusion of animal, sexual passion, which is seen almost as a desecration of true love: 'Fabius ran into the garden, and there, in one of the most distant alleys, he saw Valeria. She was sitting on a bench. Her head had sunk to her breast, her hands were crossed on her lap. Behind her, emerging from the dark green of the cypresses, appeared a marble satyr, his face distorted by a smile of malicious contempt, his outstretched lips laid close to the pan-pipes. ...' There follow nocturnal encounters between the two which are discovered by Fabius (or so it seems – it is never made quite clear whether these encounters are real or merely imagined). Fabius stabs Mucius to death, as he believes. But Mucius is revived by the magic art of the Malay, and leaves the house, though moving more like a corpse than a man. Valeria appears as much relieved by his departure as she was oppressed by his presence when she could not shake off his influence. (There is no suggestion at any time that she was in love with him.) Life returns to normal. Then, one day, Valeria is sitting idly by the organ, her fingers gliding over the keys. Suddenly, the sounds of the song of triumphant, satisfied love burst, unintended, from the organ. At the same moment she feels, for the first time since her marriage, the stirring of a new life within her womb. The story ends abruptly at this point.

The theme of blind, uncontrollable sexual passion, intruding on helpless victims unable to resist it was, of course, not a new one for Turgenev, and had recurred in his writings throughout his life. Turgenev did not expect 'this piece of nonsense' to win much approval either from his friends or from the critics. Yet Polonsky and Annenkov were delighted with the story, and the majority of critics, even when dubious about the supernatural elements, were won over by the beauty of the language.*

In the course of 1882, on a visit to Bougival, when Turgenev was already very ill, Stasiulevich discovered that for some years past Turgenev had been privately writing *Prose Poems*, without any intention of publishing them. With some difficulty he persuaded Turgenev to let him print some of them. Turgenev made a selection in the sense that (as he told Grigorovich) he removed all the personal poems. Later he replaced 'Threshold', which he had originally included, with another item, and the selection of *Prose Poems* (the only one to appear in his lifetime) was published in the *European Herald* in December 1882.[59] The title *Senilia* was first used in a separate edition in the Russian Library series in Leipzig, in 1883, though it had been originally suggested by Turgenev and rejected by Stasiulevich. For the most part, the *Prose Poems* were favourably received in spite of their uneven quality – possibly the fact that Turgenev was known to be so ill may have influenced some of the more malicious critics. Turgenev was particularly delighted to receive a letter from Tolstoy praising 'some' of the *Prose Poems* – this letter is lost, so we do not know which poems Tolstoy liked.[60]

Apart from the new edition of his Collected Works, which was being prepared in 1883 while he was still alive, though published after his death, the only work of his to appear in that year was a story for children, entitled 'The Quail'. This was written in September

---

* It was promptly translated; in English it first appeared in New York soon after the Russian publication in 1882. The first French translation was made by Turgenev himself with the help of Pauline.[58]

and October 1882, for Tolstoy. Originally intended to appear in a magazine for children which was published by Countess Tolstoy's brother and Prince L. D. Obolensky, it was in the end included in a volume of Tolstoy's stories for children, lavishly illustrated by well-known artists. The story is about a ten-year-old boy who is out shooting quail and partridge with his father. The dog puts up, and kills, a quail who is practising the age-old 'broken wing' trick in an attempt to divert the dog from her nest. When the father explains the mother's sacrifice of her life, the boy is very distressed and insists on burying the dead bird near her fledglings. After the incident he loses his passion for shooting.* Turgenev was delighted both with the production of the book in which his story appeared and with the association with Tolstoy. He was too ill to write when he received a copy in January 1883, but dictated a very warm and affectionate letter to Tolstoy.[61]

Around the same time, in the autumn of 1882, Turgenev completed a story which had been in his mind for nearly a year. This was 'Clara Milič', which bore the subtitle 'After Death' – the name it was originally intended to bear. The tale was based on an account which he had originally heard from Madame Polonsky, although the facts were widely known and discussed. These concerned an actress, E. P. Kadmina (whom Turgenev once saw act) who committed suicide, for unknown reasons, by taking poison during a performance. One V. D. Alenitsyn, a zoologist whom Turgenev used to meet at the Polonskys', either saw Kadmina once and fell in love with her, or, according to other versions of the affair, only fell in love with her after her death; but, at all events, his love for her after she died took the form of a mental disturbance. It was out of these materials that Turgenev created his story in which, once again, the supernatural plays a large part: when he first heard the extraordinary account of Alenitsyn's posthumous infatuation he wrote to Madame Polonsky that 'this would make a semi-fantastic story in the manner of Edgar Poe'.[62] 'Clara Milič' was warmly approved both by Turgenev's friends and by most of the critics, and was translated into several languages during his lifetime.[63]

In Turgenev's version, the young actress commits suicide by taking poison on the stage, as in real life. Aratov, the fictional equivalent of Alenitsyn, is a recluse, mollycoddled by an old aunt who lives with him, and completely at a loss in feminine company. He is persuaded by a friend to come to a concert at which a new star of the

* Turgenev had described in a letter to Pauline as far back as 1849 his own experience with the 'broken wing' trick, but on that occasion the brave bird was spared.

theatre, Clara Milič, is due to appear. (She is a singer, as well as an actress and, incidentally, sings one of Pauline's favourite pieces composed by Tchaikovsky.) He is not very much impressed with the celebrity, except that she gazes at him fixedly during her performance, with her hypnotic eyes. The following day he receives an unsigned note, which he guesses is from Clara, urging him to come to a place appointed by her in the city in the afternoon. When they meet, the girl is confused. She has so much to tell him, she says, she does not know how to say what she has in mind. He makes a pompous, severe, and unsympathetic reply; the girl is appalled, disillusioned, humiliated, and leaves in a hurry. Some time later he reads in a newspaper which is some days old the account of Clara's suicide; according to rumour her motive was an unhappy love affair. From this time on he becomes obsessed with the girl. He questions his friend about her, then sets off for the provincial town from which she came in order to interview her mother and sister, and acquires her diary and other relics. By this time he is in love with her – hopelessly, irrevocably. His health goes into a decline. He hears her voice in the night, and eventually she appears to him, seated in his bedroom. He begs her forgiveness. She turns her eyes on him, they kiss. His illness becomes worse. After a few days he dies in a state of bliss.

Turgenev's imagination remained vigorous and fertile to the end. Apart from sketches and plans for stories and novels which have come down to us in his manuscripts, he frequently outlined ideas to friends, often to the Polonskys in the summer of 1881 when they were together in Spasskoe. A fragment has survived which would have formed part of one of the ideas which he sketched to Polonsky. From what Turgenev told him he had just started to write a short novel entitled 'The Two Old Doves'.

Only a few introductory pages were found among his papers. The story, as related to Polonsky, was to be about two young men – the son of the manager of a large estate and his friend – both rather cynical and lighthearted on the subject of women. The owner of the property arrives. He is quite old, and has recently married a wife only slightly younger than himself, whom he had loved since his youth. The young men laugh at this romantic love affair of two old people. For a bet the son begins to pay court to the wife, and discovers to his amazement that the love of the old couple is deeper and more real than anything that he has yet met with. He ends by falling in love with the wife and, of course, being rejected by her.[64] It is not difficult to discern some personal moments in this plot.

Of the plans which he jotted down on paper, those belonging to an earlier period (1879) have already been mentioned. Not long before his death he dictated to Pauline in French, a list of nine characters, which (as she later told Stasiulevich in a letter) were intended by him to form the basis of a new, long novel. The novel was apparently intended to be about revolutionaries, and in particular about what is described as 'a new type in Russia. A cheerful (*gai*) revolutionary'. It is difficult to be certain exactly what Turgenev had in mind. According to Kropotkin what Turgenev generally meant by the 'new type' was one totally devoid of Hamlet-like qualities, and personified by Myshkin, who was the hero of the trial of the 193, in 1877–8. Myshkin was one of the earliest revolutionaries to advocate the need for a properly organized social revolutionary party which would prepare for the new society that would have to be constructed after the inevitable overthrow of the autocracy.[65] In this sense he may be described as one of the few and earliest constructive revolutionaries – but why 'cheerful'?

Around the same time, about 10 August 1883 according to one of his visitors[66] (this was a few weeks before he died) Turgenev dictated to Pauline a story entitled 'Une Fin'. This was concerned with the survival of the habits of serf owners after the emancipation and relates the fate of a coarse and violent landlord who continues to abuse and brutalize his peasants as if nothing had changed, and is eventually found dead on the highway with his head broken open. The story, in French, was passed on by Pauline to Stasiulevich, who, however, did not publish it in the *European Herald*, partly because he doubted its authenticity and partly because he refused to pay the large fee requested by Pauline. After lengthy negotiations it was published in a Russian translation by Grigorovich in the journal *Niva* in 1886.[67] There seems no reason to doubt its authenticity, since it appears to belong to the series which Turgenev was planning towards the end of his life of which he only had time to write 'Old Portraits' and 'The Desperado'.

In June 1883, less than three months before his death, Turgenev dictated to Pauline in French an account of the fire at sea which had happened just over fifty years before (see Chapter 2). Since this account was intended to be printed as a hitherto unpublished item in Volume 10 of the new edition of his Collected Works, then in course of preparation, it was translated into Russian by Lukanina (his literary protégée) and checked by the author. The decision to write about this painful episode of his youth dated from the summer of 1882.[68]

There seems little doubt that at some time there existed – and perhaps survives to this day – an unpublished autobiographical novel, or simply an autobiography, by Turgenev, entitled *Life for Art*, and dedicated to Pauline. A number of circumstantial accounts which appeared in the Russian and French press soon after Pauline's death, at the age of eighty-nine, on 18 May 1910, stated that information from a relative of Pauline had disclosed that a manuscript in two parts, in Turgenev's own hand, bearing this title, had been found in a secret drawer of one of Pauline's tables. 'Three pages are missing from the middle of the manuscript. Appended to the manuscript is a note from Pauline Viardot with the request that the novel should not be published until ten years after her death.' In spite of repeated rumours and attempts by scholars to discover it, no conclusive information about this work has ever been garnered. Unless it was destroyed, it must still be reposing among those portions of Turgenev's papers which Pauline Viardot's heirs have hitherto refused to make public.[69]

The first collected edition of Turgenev's works had appeared, with Annenkov's co-operation, in 1856. Thereafter collected editions came out at intervals of approximately five years. In 1879 Turgenev sold the right to publish his works to the Salaev Brothers in Moscow for 22,000 roubles, but reserved for himself the entitlement to print in popular format a separate edition of the *Sketches from a Sportsman's Notebook*. It sold 6,000 copies in three years. The Salaev edition was nearly exhausted by 1882, and besides Turgenev frequently complained about the misprints which it contained. After protracted negotiations in which his friends in Russia, especially Toporov and Stasiulevich, played a major part, a new contract was concluded with the St. Petersburg firm of Glazunov. But Turgenev was anxious in the last months of his life to conclude an outright sale of his copyright for a capital sum; it may be that he had in mind that money in hand after his death would provide better for Pauline and Paulinette than an income from royalties, or would present fewer problems from the legal point of view. At any rate, in August of 1883, the contract with Glazunov was altered to one of outright sale of copyright for 80,000 roubles. Against this sum had to be set 20,500 roubles which were still owing under the agreement signed with Glazunov the previous year, leaving a total due of 59,500 roubles. Since Turgenev estimated his annual earnings at 7,000 roubles (about £1,200) in 1882, the capital sum agreed upon could hardly be regarded as excessive.[70] The Glazunov edition entitled *Complete Works, Second Edition* (the Salaev edition of 1880 being reckoned the first) appeared in 1884. In spite of his illness Turgenev was able to look through all the volumes, except one, as they were printed, and to decide on the order of items and on the contents of each.[71]

CHAPTER SEVENTEEN

The End

For some six months after his return to Bougival from Russia (on 13 September 1881) Turgenev enjoyed excellent health – even the perennial gout seems to have left him in peace. He made plans to spend the summer months of the following year in Spasskoe and pressed Savina to pay a second visit. ('Surely your future husband will allow it?')[1] A month later he took a short trip to England, shot partridge on Henry Hall's estate at Six Mile Bottom, saw Henry James, who was just about to sail for America, and attended a dinner studded with literary celebrities which Ralston organized in his honour. He was given to read on this visit a translation into English verse of *Eugene Onegin* by Lieutenant Colonel Spalding, published that year, 'improbably, amazingly accurate, and at the same time amazingly dunderheaded'.[2]

He planned to leave Paris for St. Petersburg in early April 1882, and to stay in Spasskoe until October. He invited Ralston to come out and visit him – and, perhaps, to translate the (as yet unwritten) novel about the Russian and French revolutionaries,[3] which had been talked about on Ralston's previous journey to Russia. He seems to have been in good spirits: as he wrote to Madame Polonsky on January 1882 he had not after all died the previous year, as someone had foretold, 'and I am becoming convinced that one should not peer into the future'.[4] There were causes for worry, of course, as he wrote to Savina on 14 March: Louis Viardot had nearly died, and was still in danger, and Paulinette's matrimonial affairs were in a disastrous state. On the other hand, Marianne (who in 1881 had married a young composer, Duvernoy, of whom Turgenev thoroughly approved) had been safely delivered of a daughter after very difficult labour.[5] He now intended to leave Paris at the end of April and spend May to September in Spasskoe, but shortly afterwards he postponed his departure until May because of various commitments. One of them may have been the arrival of Savina in Paris early in April. She was ill, though not very seriously, and needed to consult the local medical celebrities – an undertaking in which Turgenev provided expert assistance. But he himself was no longer in the excellent state of health of which he had boasted. 'I wrote to Toporov some days ago, that I am as fit as an ox. Alas, I am now not even as fit as a calf,' he wrote to Madame Polonsky on 11 April. 'For about a week I have had neuralgic (or perhaps gouty) pain in the heart and near it. I can scarcely walk and climbing the stairs is especially uncomfortable.'[6] It was the first sign of the cancer of the spinal marrow which was to carry him to his grave eighteen months later.

None of the many doctors whom he consulted ever diagnosed his disease correctly. The famous Charcot decided on 17 April that he was suffering from angina pectoris, not the usual form, but a kind of neuralgia of the heart, brought on by gout. He prescribed immobility, observed that 'medical science is virtually impotent in the case of this disease', and refused to say when the patient would be able to move again – certainly in not less than a month's time. Turgenev was forced to remain in a lying position, because of the severe pains in the shoulder and chest if he attempted to stand up.[7] For the time being there was no question of going to Spasskoe as planned, although he did not give up hope of getting there later in the year. His lady friends in Russia such as Madame Polonsky and his half-sister Zhitova (with whom he had recently become reunited) were convinced that he was languishing in squalor, and he had to dampen their ardour in order to stop them from rushing to Paris to nurse him. Savina was the source of these rumours of the neglect of Turgenev,[8] though it did not take much for his Russian friends to believe anything discreditable to Pauline Viardot. He made careful arrangements with his manager for the Polonskys' proposed stay in Spasskoe, and still hoped to get there himself by August.[9]

How far these optimistic hopes were genuine is another matter. On 6 June he was moved to Bougival: as he wrote to Savina the next day he was beginning to get used to the thought that he would never again be able to stand and walk as others do; if only this illness had waited a year or so, 'I had so many plans – literary and business, all kinds of plans. ... It is time to write me off.'[10] Life in Bougival was fairly happy in spite of illness: for a time the young people were there – Claudie and her husband and two daughters aged seven and three, Marianne, with her husband and three-month-old baby, and the unpopular Paul. Even after they had all left in August 1882, life was tolerable for 'the sort of oyster I have now become'. There was whist in the evening, and a little music. The severity of the pains was no longer so acute.[11] This was, presumably, the result of the efforts of the numerous doctors whose advice Turgenev sought. In Bougival there was Dr. Magnin. But Turgenev was also advised to consult the famous Dr. Jaccoud by a Russian physician, Dr. Belogolovy, who had visited him when passing through France. This was eventually arranged, and Dr. Jaccoud prescribed a diet consisting of nothing but milk. Turgenev apparently ignored his advice (which had cost him the large sum of 400 francs) until about a month later when a distinguished Russian physician, Dr. L. B. Bertenson, saw him on a visit to France, examined him, and confirmed Dr. Jaccoud's prescription – but strictly forbade the use of morphia to which Turgenev had been having recourse in order to make it possible for him to sleep.[12] (He did, however, continue to seek relief in morphia from unbearable pain right to the end.) He was able to get some benefit from a German contraption called *Baunscheidts Lebenswecker*, which was said to relieve rheumatic and similar pains by pressure on and puncturing of the affected parts.[13]

Turgenev was completely unaware at this time that he was fatally ill: he regarded his pain and virtual immobility as incurable, but not dangerous, and repeatedly said so in letters to his friends to whom he described his condition in detail. 'One can live twenty years like this,' he wrote to Madame Polonsky on 11 July 1882, 'the question is, is it worth it?'[14] There is certainly no thought of dying in his correspondence in 1882, and indeed optimism was never far below the surface: 'I have no intention of dying' (16 August); 'I have not lost hope of getting to Spasskoe, if not in the autumn, then in the winter' (17 August); 'I have not the remotest intention of selling Spasskoe' (22 August); 'I am certain that I will live another twenty years' (25 August); 'There is now some hope that I will get to Petersburg in the winter' (27 August).[15] In August he resumed writing, working on 'Clara Milič'. He retained his lively interest in art, in politics, and in all the things that absorbed him.

Whether as the result of the milk diet or of the German machine, there was an improvement in his condition by September, as he informed several of his friends. Perhaps the explanation was mainly that Turgenev was learning to practise the kind of resignation and acceptance of suffering which he had so often praised in the Russian peasant. This is how he described his state to Madame Polonsky (who had, apparently, complained that he had not told her enough about his health) on 29 October:

Imagine a man who is perfectly well ... but he can neither stand nor walk nor ride without a sharp pain, rather like toothache, attacking his left shoulder. What would you have me do in these circumstances? To sit, to lie down, then to sit again and know that in such conditions it is impossible to move to Paris, let alone to Russia. ... However, my state of mind is very peaceful. I have accepted the thought [i.e. that his condition would not get any better] and even find that it is not so bad ... it is not too bad to be an oyster. After all I could have gone blind. ... Now I can even work. Of course, my *personal* life is at an end. But still – I will be sixty-four in a few days' time.[16]

And a few months later he wrote to Polonskaia, who was always very much concerned about him: 'I have completely adapted myself to my state,' and he quotes Tiutchev's verse 'A day lived through – thanks be to God.'[17] Nevertheless, his health did occasionally improve, and by 18 November he was well enough to remove to Paris. Henry James, who had called on him in Bougival, accompanied him on his journey.[18]

Illness apart, the end of Turgenev's life was clouded by unhappy relations with his daughter. Early in 1882 Paulinette's marriage came to a dramatic end: Gaston had even squandered the capital which Turgenev had intended should be settled on his grandchildren (as by French law he could do), had taken to drink, and had threatened to kill himself or kill Paulinette. She was forced to flee with the children; Turgenev told her to bring them to Paris, until he could find a safe haven for them all, out of the reach of Gaston. Money was needed at once, and he raised some by selling his remaining pictures and his horse and carriage. Mother and children duly arrived in Paris, and were settled shortly afterwards (with the assistance of the Viardots' housekeeper, Mademoiselle Arnholt) in Soleure in Switzerland.[19] This was, however, only the beginning of the trouble between Turgenev and Paulinette.

The main cause of disagreement was money which became for a year thereafter the subject of acrimonious and at times angry letters from father to daughter. Turgenev had not been tight-fisted. He allowed her 5,000 francs a year. In order to ensure the regular payment of the monthly amount he had transferred 40,000 roubles of his capital to the Viardots, so that they could pay the allowance out of the interest. The securities remained the property of the Viardots, but their value (100,000 francs) was eventually transferred to Paulinette.* Turgenev claimed to have provided half a million francs in all, for Gaston and Paulinette – around £25,000.[20]

* The statement sometimes seen that Turgenev left Paulinette 100,000 francs in

In spite of repeated threats that he would not provide a penny over and above the monthly allowance, it is clear from his letters and from his diary that he occasionally did. Paulinette was, no doubt, improvident and unreasonable. But, as he had often admitted to friends in the past, his feelings for his daughter were those of duty rather than of deep affection and he showed little sympathy for this unfortuante young woman whose life had known little happiness. Money apart, there were other causes for paternal irritation; her refusal to be examined by a doctor for a minor gynaecological complaint, for example, and his suspicions of the attentions shown to her by a young man. ('I must admit I believed you to have arrived at an age when certain demands cease to make themselves felt.'[21] Paulinette was forty.) His last letters to her, in January 1883, are angry diatribes about money – 'I stop here, not wishing to lose my self-possession.' After that there was only a note of two lines enclosing the monthly 400 francs.[22] At the same time he wrote gentle and affectionate little letters to his ten-year-old granddaughter Jeanne, of whom he was genuinely fond.

On 30 April 1883, four months before he died, the unhappy Paulinette wrote her father a desperate, imploring letter – it is one of the only two of her letters which are known to exist. In it she begs him to provide the money to enable her to leave Soleure – she wants to find work and to earn her living. (On an earlier occasion when she had raised the question of earning some money by giving lessons, he had replied that she had better first learn French orthography.) She seemed to have run into debt: 'You have done so much for me up till now that you can't abandon me in this way. Give me the means to escape from a difficult situation and leave Soleure in a decent and upright manner. My father, my kind father, be kind and forgive me once more! I await a word from you. I am writing to Madame Viardot in order to explain my plans and in order to ask her pardon for what I may have said. I am so embittered, so unhappy, and my life is so dreadful at the moment that I don't know where to turn. Oh, send me a reply, I beg of you. P.B.' He sent no answer so far as is known. The reference to apologizing to Pauline relates back to a long and very angry and bitter letter from her father of 11 September accusing her, as often before, of impoliteness towards Pauline Viardot and ingratitude towards Mademoiselle Arnholt, and apparently of complaining that he spent all his money on presents for the Viardot household. It was a familiar picture.[23]

---

his will is wrong – he left everything to Pauline Viardot. Had he left anything to Paulinette, Gaston would in French law have become entitled to it.

Paulinette remained solitary, with two young children on her hands, and with her sole income the interest on the 100,000 francs until such time as Jeanne was able to earn. After Gaston's death in 1895, she was able to move to Paris, where she died of cancer in 1919. Jeanne, who unlike her mother was musical and a good linguist, with a talent for painting, had evidently inherited some of her grandfather's gifts. She venerated his memory, and carefully preserved all relics connected with him, including his letters to her mother, which she sold to the Soviet authorities in 1933 – whether from financial need or from a sense of duty is not recorded. She supported herself all her life by giving lessons, and never married. She died in 1952 without issue. Of the grandson Georges Albert nothing is known, save that he also died unmarried and without issue in Paris on 23 June 1924.[24]

By a fortunate chance we can form a detailed picture of Turgenev's life for two months after he returned to Paris from Bougival on 18 November 1883. This is because of the survival among his papers, now in the Bibliothèque Nationale in Paris, of a notebook which contains his diary for the period of 9 December 1882 to 29 January 1883. This was discovered by Professor André Mazon in 1930, but only published by Professor I. S. Zilbershtein in 1961. There is no doubt that Turgenev kept a diary all his life, from 1851 onwards – there are repeated references to it in memoirs and in correspondence, nearly always accompanied by the statement that all his personal papers, including his diary, were to be burnt after his death. Whether Pauline destroyed the whole diary (except for this one notebook) or whether it still survives in the possession of one of her descendants is, up to the present, unknown.[25]

The most significant fact revealed by the notebook is the remarkably full, and even occasionally active life that Turgenev was able to lead, in spite of his condition being 'the same as ever – neither stand, nor walk . . .'. He was, moreover, threatened with an operation for the removal of a neuroma. In the space of a few weeks he attended a performance of an opera composed by Marianne's husband, called *Sardanapalus* and was very pleased with its success, though the music was 'mediocre'. A number of 'moribund' Russians called to see him – including Pavlovsky and his protégée, Stechkina, who was dying of consumption, and for whom he had made arrangements for her travel to Italy. He spent one evening at the artists' benevolent club; 'applause, champagne' greeted him. Music on other evenings, (Beethoven and Haydn) and cards. Among later visitors were Augier, Maupassant who read his 'remarkable novel' (*Une Vie*), the

American former Secretary of State, John Hay, who had been given a note of introduction by Henry James, two unimportant Russians, and Princess Urusova with her daughter. He paid another social call, this time to the 'three-quarters dead' Prince Gorchakov.

In the course of the next three weeks he went out again, to watch (from a window), the funeral of Gambetta: 'I have never seen anything like it – a whole people was burying its leader.' Turgenev sent a wreath and a telegram in the name of the Russian colony in Paris. There were again many visitors: the painter Pakhitonov, who was doing his portrait, the Grand Duke Constantine, Taine, the historian of the French language Gaston Paris, a distinguished woman psychiatrist, a famous explorer (Miklukho-Maklay), Natalie Herzen, Prince Meshchersky. On the eve of the Russian New Year he went out again to a party at the Russian artists' club, and gave a reading. There was unpleasantness over the translation of Maupassant's *Une Vie* for the *European Herald*; Turgenev, out of charitable impulses, had entrusted it to an *émigré* revolutionary, who made a mess of it. It had to be done again by the competent Lukanina, and Turgenev paid the fee originally agreed out of his own pocket. There were lengthy discussions with Claudie, who was being pursued by the diplomat Maurice Paléologue, who had fallen madly in love with her – and she, indeed, was not indifferent to him. ('Of no importance. No female life can escape this kind of thing.')[26] And so forth.

On 14 January 1883 the operation for the removal of the neuroma the size of a walnut in his lower abdomen was performed by the young surgeon, Paul Segond (in whom Turgenev had great confidence).* The doctors had decided that he could not stand chloroform, so all he was given to dull the pain was ether. It was an excruciating experience, not only at the time, but for days afterwards. As he recorded in his diary, he followed the advice of Kant during the operation and tried to note in detail exactly what he felt, and as a result neither screamed nor moved during the twelve minutes.[27] He recovered fully from this operation, but his former condition remained unaltered, and gradually grew worse. His sufferings were particularly severe in the course of March and April, and affected his mind. He demanded poison, accused everyone of conspiring against him, even turned on Pauline Viardot.[28] Up to the end his many doctors were unable to diagnose what was the matter with

* A number of letters to this doctor, dated between May 1882 and January 1883, have recently been published. They contain a wealth of medical detail. In spite of the great pain which Turgenev was suffering, his style is witty and light-hearted.

him, although the Russian doctor Belogolovy who saw him and examined him in June suspected cancer (so he wrote a few months after his death), but said nothing about it as it was too late to do anything to save him.[29]

Dr. Belogolovy found Turgenev completely rational, except that he was still convinced that he had been poisoned. However, he seems to have been in full possession of his mental faculties right up to the end: during the last months of his life in the intervals when he was sufficiently free from pain, he continued to receive visitors, and to deal with business matters, dictating letters in Russian or in French when he could no longer write. It is not easy to determine the moment when he realized that he was dying. On 24 May, shortly after he had been moved from Paris (where Louis Viardot had died nineteen days earlier) to Bougival, he wrote a short letter to the Polonskys: 'My illness is getting worse, the suffering is constant and unbearable ... there is no hope. My longing for death keeps growing.' Yet a few days later he is 'waiting impatiently' for improvement in his health, on 10 June he 'seems to be better', and during the following few weeks he is sending out requests to friends to call on him. But in his farewell letter to Tolstoy dated 11 July, he wrote 'to speak plainly, I am on my deathbed';[30] and indeed it is clear from the text of the letter, written in his own hand, that he knew he had not long to live.

Despite Turgenev's lifelong fear of death, there is nothing in the records of his last weeks on earth to suggest that he was gripped by any kind of terror, when once he faced the knowledge that the end was imminent. Stasiulevich found him in fair condition and lucid on 13 July: next day he was very low, and the two friends said good-bye, believing it to be forever. But on the third visit, a month later, around the middle of August, he found him in better condition mentally, though fully aware that he had not long to live. He was much concerned about what would happen to his literary property after his death, and expressed the wish to be buried near Belinsky.[31] The painter V. V. Vereshchagin, who saw Turgenev two weeks before he died, recorded that he was much worried by the thought that because of his dilatoriness he had not sold Spasskoe, and that now goodness knows who would inherit the estate in Russian law – certainly not Pauline or his daughter.[32] These repeated anxieties before death are confirmed by what has survived of his correspondence for the last weeks of his life. On 2 August a letter offering to sell his literary property outright for 80,000 roubles (this deal was completed by Toporov in Russia); and on 23 August instructions to his manager (followed six days later by a telegraphic reminder) to forward all the documents relating to Spasskoe and other estates to Ginzburg's Bank. A draft power of attorney to his friend and banker Baron Ginzburg to sell the properties was also prepared, but was not executed. It was dated six days before he died.[33] It seems probable that these belated efforts to sell Spasskoe were made under Pauline's persuasion who, according to Shchepkin's wife, 'bombarded' Turgenev's manager with telegrams urging him to speed up the sale of the estate.[34]

Accounts of the last days of Turgenev by his Russian friends and acquaintances must be treated with caution. Allegations by some of them that he was neglected by the Viardot family in his last hours are about as reliable as the suggestion that his Jewish doctor was deliberately trying to kill him. There is no doubt at all that Pauline and her daughters with their husbands, cared for Turgenev throughout his last illness with utter devotion, and, so far as they could, comforted and sustained him to the end.[35] Members of the family were in his sick-room day and night, taking turns to sit with him. Attacks of pain became particularly violent a week before his death: by the Thursday his mind was wandering, and he talked or raved incoherently in the intervals between unconsciousness. On Sunday he recovered consciousness, at any rate in part. Prince A. A. Meshchersky, a geographer with whom Turgenev had been intermittently friendly, and who called a number of times during these last days, came to Bougival at ten o'clock that morning, and remained to the end. Since he was the only one present who could understand Russian, apart from Pauline who knew a little, and since Russian was the language which the dying man most frequently used, Meshchersky's is the only available account of Turgenev's last hours. He published his story a week later in the Russian press, and soon after sent a detailed description of what he had witnessed in a long letter to Natalie Herzen, which has only recently been discovered.[36] As one would expect, the two versions (the letter to Natalie is by far the fuller) do not tally in every respect. What is beyond doubt is that the thoughts uppermost in Turgenev's mind as his life came to an end were those that had always guided him, even if he could not always live up to his ideals – love, kindness, honesty, and truth.

As Meshchersky entered the room, Pauline (the entire family was there) asked Turgenev if he recognized him: he made a slight sign, but said nothing. He caught sight of Claudie's husband, and said to him, in Russian: 'Yes, you (thou) have a Russian face, well, kiss me in the Russian way and believe me. Everyone must believe me because I always loved sincerely and lived honestly. ... The time has come to say goodbye, as the ancient Russian tsars used to do.' As Pauline drew closer to him he recognized her and said (still in Russian): 'And here is the queen of queens, and how much good she has done.' All the family now crowded round the bed, and he was trying to gather all their hands in his. Pauline spoke to him: 'Turéfi, nous vois-tu?' (It is the only recorded instance of the use of the intimate form of address between them – even in their letters they used 'vous'.) He answered her in French: 'You are not all here yet, come closer, I want to see you all. Warm me with your bodies.' Claudie embraced him and lay across his breast. At this point his mind began to wander again. He kept making signs, like those of benediction, and repeating (in French), 'Yes, the Tsar Alexis dux [or 'deux'] dux, Alexis. ...' and seemed angry because he could not make himself understood. He became more restless, more incoherent. He appeared to imagine himself as a dying Russian peasant or patriarch, giving advice to his daughter on the upbringing of her son: 'Yes, this is your sin [or, perhaps, 'even if he is feckless']. It doesn't matter, as long as he is good, is good ... is honest. ... Bring him up in truth, let him be loving. ...' There was one phrase which he uttered towards the end, which Prince Meshchersky could not understand: 'Farewell my dear ones, my whitish [*belesovatye*] ones.'[37] Was he unconsciously recalling the phrase which he had used in the death scene in *Virgin Soil*, where the dying Nezhdanov 'sought Marianne with his gaze, but some kind of grim whitishness [*belesovatost*] already clouded his eyes from within'? Nothing more could be made out after that. He died on the following day, Monday 3 September 1883, at exactly two o'clock in the afternoon.

Appendix

In a letter dated 13 May 1882 Turgenev had appointed Annenkov his literary executor in respect of all his papers and correspondence, without exception. He confirmed this on 10 January 1883 and added that he would inform the Viardots of his decision. Be that as it may, after his death the only papers entrusted by Pauline to Annenkov were the numerous letters which had been received by Turgenev throughout his life – but not any letters from her, or members of her family and probably some others, including Savina. The Russian correspondence in due course found its way from Annenkov into various archives, and much of it has since been published. Pauline retained all the personal papers and all literary remains, as well, of course, as Turgenev's letters to her and to her family. This material, unless any of it was destroyed, passed to her descendants.[1]

Turgenev left at least three wills. One, dated 1 May 1879, bequeathed the chalet in the grounds of Bougival and its contents to Pauline, and her children after her.[2] There seems to have been no litigation about this document. Two further wills are known. One, in French, dated 17 June 1883, left his entire property to Pauline Viardot. This may, in law, have been deemed to include his literary and personal papers, but whether Turgenev had intended this result is another question. The second will, in Russian, was earlier in date, 29 March 1883, and left Pauline his entire rights in his literary property. This disposition was, however, overtaken by the sale shortly before his death of his copyright to Glazunov. Pauline at first attempted to get both wills validated, but in the end only the French one was proved in the St. Petersburg court, on 11 October 1883.

This was, however, only the beginning of her troubles. An attempt by Gaston Bruère to upset the will in the French courts failed. The real difficulty was on the Russian side, since by Russian civil law Spasskoe–Lutovinovo, being a so-called 'patrimonial' estate, could not be devised by testament at all, and the representatives of two remote descendants of Turgenev's mother obtained an order in the Orel court declaring their rights to the property, valued at 165,000 roubles – a very low figure indeed. There were thus two, not entirely consistent, court orders. Fortunately for Pauline, she still retained a receipt by Turgenev in respect of 50,000 francs borrowed from her in 1864 when he was starting to build his grand villa in Baden. The loan had almost certainly been wiped out when Louis took over the villa, if not before, but Pauline had kept the receipt. And so, after protracted negotiations between the lawyers of both sides, Pauline's claim on the estate (balanced by that which the legal heirs to Spasskoe were entitled to make in respect of a proportionate part of the moveable property which she inherited) was eventually settled for around 25,000 roubles.[3] The moveable property, apart from money and personal belongings left in France and in Spasskoe, presumably consisted of whatever amount was still owing from Glazunov for the sale of the copyright in Turgenev's works. Thus, Pauline could not have inherited much more than about 85,000 roubles in all (assuming that the entire sum of 59,500 roubles due from Glazunov still remained owing at Turgenev's death), of which, no doubt, the lawyers had their share.

Turgenev was no sooner dead than there began a display of calumny, official stupidity, and individual malice which did credit to none. He had expressed the wish to be buried near Belinsky, in the Volkovo cemetery at St. Petersburg, and there was in any case never any doubt that he was to be buried in Russia. A few days after his death however, with true revolutionary zeal, hoping to embarrass the Russian government and prevent it from claiming Turgenev as a loyal son, Lavrov published in the French press a statement (true in itself) that Turgenev had subsidized his paper *Vpered*. Katkov, ever enthusiastic about damaging Turgenev's reputation, alive or dead, reprinted Lavrov's letter in Russian translation without comment. Stasiulevich immediately published a denial of Lavrov's allegations, stating (in complete good faith) that it was a slanderous invention. All this had the intended effect on the Russian authorities, and there was some delay before they even authorized the transport of the coffin with the remains to Russia.[4] Meanwhile in France, a private service for the dead at Bougival, attended among others by Prince Orlov, was followed by a second service at the Russian church in the rue Daru (which for all his agnosticism, Turgenev frequently attended). A party of 'nihilists', headed by Lavrov, entered the church to lay a wreath from 'Les réfugiés Russes' in Paris, and then waited outside the doors in order to pay their respects to the coffin when it was brought out.[5] The remains were then transferred to a specially arranged mourning chapel on the Gare du Nord to await transport to Russia. Many hundreds came to bid farewell, including prominent figures in French literature and music. There were, of course, speeches, including a long and moving tribute by Ernest Renan, for whose work Turgenev had always had a high regard.

Permission to transport the coffin to Russia eventually arrived. The Russian authorities were, however, very worried about the possibility of demonstrations at the intermediate stations on the journey. There was a feverish exchange of telegrams with the local governors and frantic instructions of the kind that characterize a police state always unsure of its authority. Neither the government nor representatives of high society attended a memorial service for Turgenev at the Cathedral of Our Lady of Kazan on 10 September, which showed that the efforts of Lavrov and Katkov had not been in vain. According to Stasiulevich who, together with Pauline's two sons-in-law, Chamerot and Duvernoy, and Claudie, accompanied the coffin on its slow journey to St. Petersburg, he was faced with so many obstructions and difficulties on the way that one might imagine (as he wrote to his wife) that he was bringing back the remains of Solovei the Robber (a figure in Russian legend) and not those of a great writer. Nevertheless, crowds gathered at the stations as the train bearing the body stopped, and usually religious services were held. There were further official restrictions and regulations concerning the funeral itself and, on the day of the burial, 27 September, the procession and the cemetery teemed with police agents. Actually the magnificent ceremony ran its course with dignity and solemnity, and there were no unpleasant incidents of the kind which often marred funerals of writers in Russia. There were no fewer than 176 deputations from literary, learned, artistic, national, and other societies, each bearing a grand wreath with a suitable inscription. Specially composed poems were read, and three speeches were held at the graveside – by the Rector of the University, by Professor Muromtsev (later to become the first President of the Duma), and by the writer Grigorovich. Neither the government nor the conservative press was represented.

On the day following the funeral a memorial literary evening was held. Savina read from 'Faust', Kavelin recited 'Enough', Annenkov made a speech which was generally dismissed as colourless, and Grigorovich recited garbled versions of some of the *Prose Poems*, having forgotten the texts. Polemics on Turgenev continued after his funeral. Katkov's paper and similar journals attacked his reputation, the People's Will in its illegal press and in clandestine pamphlets defended it with similar vigour ('He was not, of course, a revolutionary, but ...'). The city duma voted 3,000 roubles towards the cost of transporting the coffin and of the funeral, the city mayor, or *nachal'nik*, issued a protest, and litigation and wrangling on the question dragged on for nearly ten years. The whole matter was in the end abandoned. Only Gogol could have done justice to these proceedings.[6]

Bibliography

In the Notes, works are generally cited by the name of the author. Where an abbreviation is used this is indicated at the side of the work listed.

I EDITIONS OF WORKS AND LETTERS USED	*Cited as*
Russkaia Biblioteka, *Senilia. Stikhotvoreniia v proze I. S. Turgeneva* (Leipzig, 1883)	
I. S. Turgenev, *Polnoe sobranie sochinenii*, vtoroe izdanie, 10 vols. (in 6) (St. Petersburg, 1884)	
I. S. Turgenev, *Polnoe sobranie sochinenii i pisem v dvadtsati vos'mi tomakh*. Sochineniia v piatnadtsati tomakh (Moscow-Leningrad, 1960–8)	W., I, II, etc.
I. S. Turgenev, *Polnoe sobranie sochinenii i pisem v dvadtsati vos'mi tomakh*. Pis'ma v trinadtsati tomakh (Moscow-Leningrad, 1961–8)	L., I, II, etc.
Turgenevskii sbornik. Materialy k polnomu sobraniiu sochinenii i pisem I. S. Turgeneva, 5 vols. (Moscow-Leningrad, 1964–9)	T. sb., Vol. I, Vol. II, etc.
Alexandre Zviguilsky (ed.), *Ivan Tourguénev. Nouvelle Correspondance Inédite*. 2 vols. (Paris 1971, 1972)	Zv., Zv. II
Henri Granjard et Alexandre Zviguilsky, *Ivan Tourguénev. Lettres inédites à Pauline Viardot et à sa famille* (Paris, 1972)	G. & Zv.
Patrick Waddington, *The Dodillon Copies of Letters by Turgenev to Pauline and Louis Viardot* (The Queen's University, Belfast, July 1970)	
'Pauline Viardot as Turgenev's Censor', *Times Literary Supplement* (1 January 1970), p. 16	

II GENERAL SOURCES

E. Abbott and L. Campbell, *The Life and Letters of Benjamin Jowett, M.A.*, Vol. II (New York, 1897)

E. D. J. Lyon-Dalberg Acton, *Alexander Herzen and the role of the intellectual revolutionary, 1847–1863*, unpublished dissertation submitted for the degree of Ph.D., University of Cambridge, 1975

Addressbuch der Grossherzoglichen Stadt Baden. Amtliche Ausgabe (Baden-Baden, 1867)

Leonid Afonin and Aleksei Mishchenko, *Na rodine Turgeneva* (Moscow, 1968)

M. P. Alekseev (ed.), *I. S. Turgenev (1818–1883—1958)*, Stat'i   Alekseev,
i materialy (Orel, 1960)   *I. S. Turgenev*

'Turgenev v sporakh o pyese E. Ozhye', in *T. sb.*, Vol. III, pp. 240–54

'Stikhotvornye teksty dlia romansov Poliny Viardo', in *T. sb.* Vol. IV, pp. 189–204

N. V. Alekseeva, 'Vospominaniia P. P. Viktorova o Turgeneve' in Alekseev, *I. S. Turgenev*, pp. 288–343

P. V. Annenkov, *Literaturnye vospominaniia* (Moscow, 1960)

E. Ardov (pseudonym for Apreleva, *née* Elena Blaramberg), 'Iz vospominanii ob I. S. Turgeneve' in *Turg. v vosp.*, Vol. 11 (Moscow, 1960), pp. 172–200

O. Argamakova, 'Semeistvo Turgenevykh' in *Istoricheskiy vestnik* (1884), No. 2

M. A. Arzumanova, 'Zaveshchaniie I. S. Turgeneva', in Alekseev, *I. S. Turgenev*, pp. 264–86

Nikolai Barsukov, *Zhizn' i trudy M. P. Pogodina*, 22 vols. (St. Petersburg, 1888–1910)

V. G. Belinsky, *Polnoe sobranie sochinenii*, 13 vols. (Moscow, 1953–9)

N. A. Belogolovy, *Vospominaniia i drugiia stat'i*, 3rd ed. (Moscow, 1898), written in 1883.

Isaiah Berlin, *Fathers and Children*, Romanes Lecture 1970 (Oxford University Press, 1972)

Bibliografiia literatury ob I. S. Turgeneve 1918–1967 (Leningrad, 1970)

D. Blagoi, 'Turgenev-redactor Tiutcheva' in N. L. Brodskii (ed.), *Turgenev i ego vremia* (Moscow-Petrograd, 1923), pp. 142–63

M. Ya. Blinchevskaiia, 'Ob odnom pis'me Turgeneva k Nekrasovu (k istorii razryva Turgeneva s "Sovremennikom")', *T. sb.*, Vol. III, pp. 234–8

Nadezhda Bogdanova, 'Dva intimnykh pisem I. S. Turgeneva' in *T. sb.*, ed. Piksanov

N. L. Brodskii, *I. S. Turgenev i russkiie sektanty* (Moscow, 1922)

' "Premukhinskii roman" v zhizni i tvorchestve Turgeneva. Pis'ma T. A. Bakuninoi k. I. S. Turgenevu' in

Dokumenty po istorii literatury i obschestvennosti. Vyp'usk vtoroi. I. S. Turgenev (Moscow-Petrograd, 1923)

T. I. Bron', 'Turgenev i ego doch' Polina Turgeneva-Bruer' in *T. sb.*, II, pp. 324–38

Oscar Browning, *Life of George Eliot* (London, 1890)

N. F. Budanova (ed.), 'Statya G. K. Briullovoi o romane "Nov'"', *L.N.*, Vol. 76, pp. 277–320

'Roman "Nov'"' i protsess dolgushintsev' in *T. sb.*, Vol. II, pp. 182–5

V. Burtsev (ed.), *Za sto let (1800–1896)* (London, 1897), reprinted The Hague, 1965

G. A. Byalui (ed.), *Ivan Sergeevich Turgenev v portretakh, illiustratsiakh, dokumentakh* (Moscow-Leningrad, 1966)

N. G. Chernyshevskii, *Sobranie sochinenii v piati tomakh* (Moscow, 1974)

I. S. Chistova, 'Turgenev i muzikal'nye utrenniki v Baden-Badene', *T. sb.*, Vol. I, pp. 315–19

D. I. Chizhevskii, *Gegel' v Rossii* (Paris, 1939)

Alphonse Daudet, *Trente ans de Paris.* A travers ma vie et mes livres (Paris, 1925). First published in the Century Magazine, New York, in 1880

A. G. Dement'ev, A. V. Zapadov, M. S. Cherepakhova (eds.), *Russkaiia periodicheskaiia pechat'* (1702–1894). Spravochnik (Moscow, 1959)

The Diary of Tolstoy's Wife, translated by A. Werth (London, 1928)

M. I. Dikman i Yu. D. Levin, 'I. S. Turgenev i M. L. Mikhailov' in Alekseev, *I. S. Turgenev*, pp. 201–18

N. A. Dobroliubov, *Sobranie sochinenii v deviati tomakh* (Moscow-Leningrad 1961–4)

N. A. Dobroliubov v vospominaniiakh sovremennikov (Moscow, 1961)

F. M. Dostoevsky, *Pis'ma*, Vol. I, 1832–67, A. S. Dolinin (ed.) (Moscow-Leningrad, 1928)

Polnoe sobranie sochinenii v tridtsati tomakh, Vol. I, Vol. XII (Leningrad, 1972, 1975)

S. Wayne Dowler, *The 'Native Soil' (Pochvennichestvo) Movement in Russian Social and Political Thought 1850–1870*, unpublished dissertation for the degree of Ph.D., University of London, 1973

A. Dunin, 'Delo o buystve I. S. Turgeneva', *Istoricheskii vestnik* (1912), No. 2, pp. 629–31

Leon Edel, *Henry James.* The Conquest of London 1870–83 (London, 1962)

G. Z. Eliseev, 'Iz vospominanii' in *I. S. Turgenev v vospo-*

minaniiakh sovremennikov, Vol. II (Moscow, 1968), pp. 373–8

B. M. Engel'gardt (ed.), *I. A. Goncharov i I. S. Turgenev* (St. Petersburg, 1923)

Victor Erlich, *Gogol* (New Haven-London, 1969)

E. M. Feoktistov, *Vospominaniya za kulisami politiki i literatury* (Leningrad, 1929); reproduced Cambridge, 1975

A. A. Fet, *Moi vospominaniia*, Vols. I & II (Munich, 1971); reproduced from Russian edition of 1890

April Fitzlyon, *The Price of Genius*. A life of Pauline Viardot (London, 1964)

Gustave Flaubert, *Lettres inédites à Tourgeuéneff*, ed. Givard Gailly (Monaco, 1946) — Flaubert, *Lettres inédites*

Œuvres Complètes. Correspondance. Nouvelle Edition. Vols. 6 & 7 (Paris, 1930) — Flaubert

Œuvres Complètes. Correspondance. Supplément, 4 vols. (Paris, 1954) — Flaubert, *Supplément*

Richard Freeborn, *Turgenev. The Novelist's Novelist*. A Study (Oxford University Press, 1963)

'Turgenev at Ventnor' in *Slavonic & East European Review*, Vol. LI (1973), pp. 387–412

L. Fridlender, 'Vospominaniia o Turgeneve' in *Vestnik Evropy*, Vol. 41 (1906), No. 10, pp. 829–36

M. O. Gabel, 'Tvorcheskaiia istoriia romana *Rudin*' in *L.N.*, Vol. 76, pp. 9–70

M. Gershenzon, *Mechta i mysl' I. S. Turgeneva* (Moscow, 1919); reproduced Munich, 1970

A. I. Gertsen (Herzen), *Sobranie sochinenii v tridtsati tomakh* (Moscow, 1954–66)

Royal A. Gettmann, *Turgenev in England and America* (Westport, Connecticut, 1974); reprint of 1941 edition

Edmond et Jules de Goncourt, *Journal*. Mémoires de la Vie Littéraire, Vols. 5 & 6, 1872–84 (Paris, 1935)

V. N. Gorbacheva, *Molodye gody Turgeneva* (Kazan', 1926)

Edmund Gosse, 'A Memory of Tourgenieff', the *London Mercury*, Vol. XVII, No. 100, p. 403

Henri Granjard, *Ivan Tourguénev La Comtesse Lambert et 'Nid de Seigneurs'* (Paris, 1960) — Granjard, *Le Nid*

Ivan Tourguénev et les courants politiques et sociaux de son temps (Paris, 1954) — Granjard, *Tourguénev*

'Lettre de A. A. Meščerskij à Natalie Herzen', *Cahiers du Monde Russe et Soviétique*, Vol. XI (avril–juin 1970), pp. 259–77 — Granjard, 'Meščerskij

A. S. Griboedov, *Sochineniia v dvukh tomakh*, 2 vols (Moscow, 1971)

Apollon Grigoriev, *Vospominaniia* (Moscow, Leningrad, 1930)

D. V. Grigorovich, *Literaturnye vospominaniia* (Leningrad, 1928)

L. G. Grinberg (ed.), *Materialy dlia bibliografii vospominanii o Turgeneve* in *L.N.*, Vol. 73 (ii), pp. 412–60

K. Ya. Grot, 'Vospominaniia K. Ya. Grota ob O. A. Turgenevoi i N. M. Eropkinoi. (K voprosu o prototipakh personazhei "Dyma")' in *T. sb.*, Vol. I, pp. 299–303.

N. M. Gutiar, *Ivan Sergeevich Turgenev* (Iuriev, 1907)

Wilhelm Haage, *Iwan Sergejewitsch Turgenev*, Vortrag (Baden-Baden, 1904)

Rolf Gustav Haebler, *Geschichte der Stadt und des Kurortes Baden-Baden*, Vol. II (Baden-Baden, 1969)

Heinrich Heine, *Gesammelte Werke*, ed. Gustav Karpeles, Vol. VII, 2nd edn. (Berlin, 1893)

N. Ikonnikov, *La Noblesse de Russie* (Paris, 1962)

Innostrannaia kritika o Turgeneve (St. Petersburg, 1884)

B. S. Itenberg (ed.), *Revoliutsionnoe narodnichestvo 70–kh godov XIX veka*, Vol. I, 1870–5 gg (Moscow, 1964)

N. V. Izmailov, 'Turgenev – izdatel' pisem Pushkina k N. N. Pushkinoi' in *T. sb.*, Vol. V (Leningrad, 1969), pp. 399–416

Eva Kagan-Kans, *Hamlet and Don Quixote. Turgenev's Ambivalent Vision* (The Hague-Paris, 1975)

N. M. Karamzin, *Izbrannye sochineniia v dvukh tomakh*, 2 vols. (Moscow-Leningrad, 1964)

Vl. Karenin, 'Turgenev i Zhorzh Sand' in *Turgenevskii sbornik* ed. A. F. Koni (St. Petersburg, 1921), pp. 87–130

Martin Katz, *Mikhail N. Katkov*. A Political Biography (The Hague, 1966)

E. M. Khmelevskaia, 'Utrachennye pis'ma I. S. Turgeneva (1838–1856)' in *T.Sb.*, I, pp. 344–78.

M. K. Kleman, *Letopis' zhizni i tvorchestva I. S. Turgeneva* (Moscow-Leningrad, 1934)

'Otets Turgeneva v pis'makh k synoviam' in *T. sb.*, ed. Koni, pp. 131–44 — Kleman in *T. sb.*, ed. Koni

V. Kolontaeva, 'Vospominaniia o sele Spasskom' in *Istoricheskii vestnik* (1855), No. 10, pp. 41–65 — Koni

A. F. Koni (ed.), *Turgenev i Savina* (Petrograd, 1918)

'Pokhorony Turgeneva. Vospominaniia' in *T.sb.*, ed. Koni, pp. 57–85

A. A. Kornilov, *Gody stranstvii Mikhaila Bakunina* (Leningrad-Moscow, 1925)

Cited as

Aleksandr I. Koshelev, *Zapiski*, 1806–83 (Berlin, 1884), photographic reprint Newtonville, Mass., 1976

M. M. Kovalevskii, 'Vospominaniia ob I. S. Turgeneve', in *Turg. v vosp.*, Vol. II, pp. 139–54

P. M. Kovalevskii, *Vstrechi na zhiznennom puti*, reprinted in Grigorovich, pp. 287–452

B. P. Koz'min, *Iz istorii revoliutsionnoi mysli v Rossii. Izbrannye trudy* (Moscow, 1961)

L. V. Krestova, 'Tatiana Bakunina i Turgenev' in *Turgenev i ego vremiia. Pervyi sbornik*, ed. N. L. Brodskii (Moscow–Petrograd, 1923), pp. 31–50

Peter Kropotkin, *Memoirs of a Revolutionist* (New York, 1971)

N. E. Krutikova, 'Pis'ma M. A. Markovich', (Marka Vovchka), 1859–64, *L. N.*, Vol. 73 (ii), pp. 249–302

P. L. Lavrov, 'Iz stat'i "I. S. Turgenev i razvitie russkogo obshchestva"' in *Turg. v vosp.*, Vol. I (Moscow, 1960), pp. 389–425.

M. Lemke, *Politicheskie protsessy* (St. Petersburg, 1907)   Lemke, *Protsessy*

Ocherki osvoboditel'nago dvizheniia shestidesiatykh godov (St. Petersburg, 1908)   Lemke, *Ocherki*

Nikolaevskie zhandarmy i literatura 1826–1855 godov (St. Petersburg, 1908)   Lemke, *Zhandarmy*

K. Leontiev, *Sobranie sochinenii*, Vol. IX (St. Petersburg, 1913)

N. A. Leontyevskii, *Turgenev v dome Viardo*, Vospominaniia Batista Fori, *L.N.*, Vol. 76, pp. 489–502

Letters and Memorials of Jane Welsh Carlyle, ed. J. A. Froude, 3 Vols. (London, 1883)   *Letters, Carlyle*

Letters and Private Papers of William Makepeace Thackeray, ed. Gordon N. Ray, Vol. IV (London, 1946)   *Letters, Thackeray*

Yu. D. Levin, 'Neosushchestvlennyi istoricheskii roman Turgeneva' in Alekseev, *I. S. Turgenev*, pp. 96–131

Ya. I. Linkov, *Revoliutsionnaia bor'ba A. I. Gertsena i N. P. Ogareva i tainoe obshchestvo 'Zemlia i volia' 1860–kh godov* (Moscow, 1964)

N. M. Lisovskii, *Novye materialy dlia biografii I. S. Turgeneva* (St. Petersburg, 1892)

Literaturnoe nasledstvo, Vol. 73 (i), 73 (ii), 76, 86 (Moscow, 1964, 1964, 1967, 1973)   *L.N.*, Vol. 73 (i), etc.

Percy Lubbock (ed.), *Letters of Henry James* Vol. I (London, 1920)

N. M., 'Cherty iz parizhskoi zhizni I. S. Turgeneva', in *Turg. v vosp.*, Vol. II (Moscow, 1960), pp. 155–71

Raymond T. McNally, *Chaadayev and His Friends* (Tallahassee, Florida, 1971)

Marion Mainwaring (ed.), *Ivan Turgenev. The Portrait Game* (London, 1973)

I. M. Malysheva, 'Pis'ma materi. (Iz neizdannoi perepiski V. P. Turgenevoi s synom)' in *T. sb.*, ed. Piksanov, pp. 24–48

André Mazon, *Manuscrits Parisiens d'Ivan Tourguénev. Notices et Extraits* (Paris, 1930)

'Rabota Turgeneva nad romanom "dva pokoleniia"' in *L.N.*, Vol. 73 (1), pp. 39–51

A. A. Meshchersky, 'Predsmertnye chasy I. S. Turgeneva' in *Turg. v vosp*, Vol. 2, pp. 441–4

K. Mochul'sky, *Dukhovnyi put' Gogolia* (Paris, 1934, reprinted 1976)

Dostoevskii. Zhizn' i tvorchestvo (Paris, 1947)

George Moore, 'Tourguéneff', the *Fortnightly Review*, Vol. XLIII, 1888, pp. 237–51

L. N. Nazarova, 'K istorii tvorchestva I. S. Turgeneva 50–60 kh godov' in Alekseev, *I. S. Turgenev*, pp. 132–46

'O romane "dva pokoleniia"' in *L.N.*, Vol. 73 (i) pp. 52–8

'Turgenev i O. A. Turgeneva' in *T. sb.* Vol. I, 293–9

M. Nechkina, 'Novye materialy o revoliutsionnoi situatsii v Rossii (1859–1861 gg.)' in *L.N.*, Vol. 61, pp. 459–522

N. A. Nekrasov, *Sobranie sochinenii v vos'mi tomakh* (Moscow, 1965–7)

N. A. Nekrasov v vospominaniiakh sovremennikov (Moscow, 1971)

L. F. Nelidova, 'Pamiati I. S. Turgeneva' in *Turg v vosp.*, Vol. II, pp. 235–55

A. V. Nikitenko, *Moia povest' o samom sebe ... Zapiski i dnevniki* (1804–1877 gg.) 2nd edn., 2 vols. (St. Petersburg, 1904–5)

Yu. Nikol'skii, *Turgenev i Dostoevsky. (Istoriia odnoi vrazhdy)* (Sofia, 1921)

N. N. Novikova, *Revoliutsionery 1861 Goda. 'Velikoruss' i ego komitet v revoliutsionnoi bor'be 1861.g.* (Moscow, 1968)

N. P. Ogarev, *Izbrannye sotsial'no-politicheskie i filosofskie proizvedeniia*, 2 vols. (Moscow, 1952, 1956)

Yu. G. Oksman, 'I. S. Turgenev na sluzhbe v ministerstve vnutrennykh del' in *Uchenye zapiski saratovskogo universiteta*, Vol. LVI A (Saratov, 1957), pp. 172–83.

Opisanie rukopisei i izobrazitel'nykh materialov pushkinskogo doma, Vol. IV, I. S. Turgenev (Moscow-Leningrad, 1958)

N. A. Ostrovskaia, *Vospominaniia o' Turgeneve*, in *T. sb.*, ed. Piksanov, pp. 62–134

A. Ostrovskii, *Turgenev v zapisiakh sovremennikov* (Leningrad, 1929)

D. N. Ovsianiko-Kulikovskiy, *Sobranie sochineniy*, Vol. 2 (St. Petersburg, 1910; reprinted 1969); Vol. 8 (St. Petersburg, 1911; reprinted 1969)

I. I. Panaev, *Literaturnye vospominaniia*, ed. Yampol'sky (Leningrad, 1950 – the fullest edition)

A. Ya. Panaeva (Golovacheva), *Vospominaniia* (Moscow, 1956)

Maurice Parturier, *Une Amité Litteraire*. Prosper Mérimée et Ivan Tourguéniev (Paris, 1952)

Blaise Pascal, *Pensées* (London, 1908, 1943)

Isaac Pavlovsky, *Souvenirs sur Tourguéneff* (Paris, 1887)

Perepiska Nikolaia Vladimirovicha Stankevicha 1830–1840, ed. Aleksei Stankevich (Moscow, 1914)

Ludwig Pietsch, 'Iz vospominanii' in *Turg. v vosp.*, Vol. II, pp. 259–73

Richard Pipes, *Russia under the Old Régime* (London, 1974)

D. I. Pisarev, *Sochineniia*, 4 vols. (Moscow, 1953)

Izbrannye proizvedenia (Leningrad, 1968)

Alexis E. Podgorelskin, *The Career of M. M. Stasiulevich 1850–1882*, unpublished Ph.D. thesis, Yale University, December, 1976

Ya. P. Polonsky, *Povesti i rasskazy*, Chast' II, Section 10, 'I. S. Turgenev u sebia v ego poslednii priezd na rodinu' (St. Petersburg, 1885)

M. V. Portugalov, *Po Turgenevskim mestam* (Sputnik ekskursanta) (Moscow, 1924)

A. S. Pushkin, *Polnoe sobranie sochinenii v desiati tomakh* (Moscow-Leningrad, 1949)

P. G. Pustovoit, *Roman I. S. Turgeneva 'Otsy i deti' i ideinaiia bor'ba 60-kh godov XIX veka* (Moscow, 1965)

N. P. Puzin, 'Turgenev i M. N. Tolstaiia' in *T. sb.*, Vol. II, pp. 248–58

Raduga, Al'manakh pushkinskago doma (St. Petersburg, 1922)

William Ralston, 'Ivan Serguévitch Tourguénieff', in the *Athenaeum*, No. 2916, 15 September 1883 (London)

Horst Rappich, 'Turgenev i Bodenshtedt', in *L.N.* Vol. 73 (ii), pp. 333–52

I. E. Repin, 'Vospominaniia ob I. S. Turgeneve' in *Turg. v vosp.*, Vol. II, pp. 118–22

Lady Ritchie, *Blackstick Papers* (London, 1908)

Geroid Tanquary Robinson, *Rural Russia under the Old Régime. A History of the Landlord–Peasant World and a Prologue to the Peasant Revolution of 1917* (New York, 1949)

S. Romm, 'Iz dalekago proshlago. Vospominaniia ob Ivane Sergeeviche Turgeneve' in *Vestnik Evropy* No. 12 (1916), pp. 95–132

M. E. Saltykov-Shchedrin, *Sobranie sochinenii v dvadtsati tomakh*, Vol. VI (Moscow, 1968)

Leonard Schapiro, 'The *Vekhi* Group and the Mystique of Revolution' in *Slavonic & East European Review* (December, 1955), pp. 56–76

Shchepkina. *See* 'I. S. Turgenev v Spasskom-Lutovinove' below

Arthur Schopenhauer, *The World as Will and Idea*, translated by R. B. Haldane and J. Kemp, 3 vols. (London, 1948)

Gregor Schwartz, 'Predstavleniia operetty "Poslednii koldun"' in *L.N.*, Vol. 73 (i), pp. 208–24

P. A. Sergeenko, *Turgenev i Tolstoi*, Literary etc. supplements to the magazine *Niva* (St. Petersburg, April–September 1906)

N. A. Serno-Solovievich, *Publitsistika, pis'ma*, ed. I. B. Volodarskii and G. A. Kaikova (Moscow, 1963)

Hugh Seton-Watson, *The Russian Empire 1801–1917* (Oxford University Press, 1967)

N. V. Shcherban', 'Tridsat' dva pis'ma I. S. Turgeneva i vospominaniia o nem', *Russkii vestnik* (1890), No. 7 p. 13

I. Shneiderman, *Maria Gavrilovna Savina 1854–1915* (Moscow, 1956)

A. E. Shol'p, 'I. S. Turgenev i "Evgeny Onegin" P. Chaikovskogo' in Alekseev, *I. S. Turgenev*, pp. 159–83

John Simmons, 'Turgenev and Oxford' in *Oxoniana*, Vol. XXXI (1966), pp. 146–51

E. A. Shtakenshneider, *Iz dnevnika*, reprinted in Grigorovich, pp. 455–60

Sochineniia N. V. Gogol'a, ed. N. Tikhonravov. 10th edn., Vol. IV (Moscow, 1889)

M. M. Stasiulevich, 'Iz vospominanii o poslednikh dniakh I. S. Turgeneva' in *Vestnik Evropy* (1883), Vol. V, pp. 847–54

                                                         Cited as
M. M. Stasiulevich i ego sovremenniki v ikh perepiske, ed.
M. K. Lemke, Vol. III (St. Petersburg, 1912)
V. V. Stasov, 'Iz vospominanii ob I. S. Turgeneve' in *Turg.
v vosp.*, Vol. II, pp. 98–117
V. N. Stefanovich, '"Kroket v Vindzore" K istorii in-
ostrannykh perevodov stikhotvoreniia' in *T. sb.*, Vol.
V, pp. 305–10
G. V. Stepanova, 'K istorii izdaniia sbornika "Turgenev
i Savina"' in *T. sb.*, Vol. III, pp. 271–9
M. P. Sultan-Shakh, 'Turgenev i semia dekabrista N. I.
Turgeneva'. Iz dnevnikov F. N. Turgenevoi 1857–
1883, in *L.N.*, Vol. 76, pp. 359–414
Tagebücher von K. A. Varnhagen von Ense, Aus dem Nach-
lass Varnhagen's. Vierter Band (Leipzig, 1862)
Abram Terts, (pseudonym for Andrei Siniavsky), *V teni
Gogolia* (London, 1975)
William Makepeace Thackeray, a Biography, by Lewis Mel-
ville, Vol. 1 (London, 1910)
A. F. Tiutcheva, *Pri dvore dvukh imperatorov*. Vospo-
minaniia-Dnevnik (Moscow, 1928)
L. N. Tolstoy, *Perepiska s russkimi pisateliami*, ed. S.
Rozanova (Moscow, 1962)
S. L. Tolstoy, *Ocherki bylogo*. 2nd edn. (Moscow, 1956)
N. A. Tuchkova-Ogareva, *Vospominaniia* (Moscow, 1959)
A. I. Turgenev, *Khronika russkogo*. Dnevniki (1825–1826),
ed. M. I. Gillel'son (Moscow, 1964)
Turgenev i ego vremia. Pervyi sbornik, ed. N. L. Brodskii   *T.sb.* ed.
(Moscow-Petrograd, 1923)   Brodskii
Turgenev i krug 'Sovremennika', Neizdannye materialy   *Turg. i krug*
(Moscow-Leningrad, 1930)
'I. S. Turgenev v Spasskom-Lutovinove', (Vospominaniia   Shchepkina
S. G. Shchepkinoi'), in Krasnyy arkhiv, No. 3 (1940), pp.
195–228
I. S. Turgenev v vospominaniiakh revoliutsionerov-semi-   *Turgenev v*
desiatnikov, ed. M. K. Kleman and N. K. Piksanov   *vosp. rev.*
(Moscow-Leningrad, 1930)
I. S. Turgenev v vospominaniiakh sovremennikov, 2 vols.   *Turg. v vosp.*
(Moscow, 1969)
Turgenevskii sbornik, ed. A. F. Koni (St. Petersburg, 1921)   *T. sb.*, ed. Koni
Turgenevskii sbornik, ed. N. K. Piksanov (Petrograd, n.d.)   *T. sb.* ed.
L. Utevskii, 'Smert' Turgeneva' in *T. sb.*, ed. Koni   Piksanov
pp. 13–56
N. Valentinov, *Vstrechi s Leninym* (New York, 1953)
Franco Venturi, *Roots of Revolution*. A History of the
Populist and Socialist Movements in Nineteenth Cen-

tury Russia, translated from the Italian by Francis Haskill (London, 1960)

V. V. Vereshchagin, *Ocherki, nabroski, vospominaiia* (St. Petersburg, 1883)

Paul Viardot, 'Iz vospominanii artista', in *Turg. v vosp.*, Vol. II, pp. 304–11

E. N. Vodovozova, 'Iz knigi "Na zare zhizni"' in *Turg. v vosp.*, Vol. II, pp. 379–88

Vospominaniia Borisa Nikolaevicha Chicherina. Moskva sorokovykh godov, ed. S. V. Bakhrushin (Moscow, 1929

Alexander Vucinich, *Social Thought in Tsarist Russia*. The Quest for a General Science of Society, 1861–1917 (Chicago and London, 1976)

Patrick Waddington, 'Turgenev & George Eliot: a Literary Friendship', *Modern Language Review*, No. 4 (1971), pp. 751–9

Andrzej Walicki, *The Slavophile Controversy* (Oxford University Press, 1975)

T. Wemyss Reid, *The Life, Letters and Friendships of Richard Monckton Milnes, First Lord Houghton*, 2 vols. (London, 1890)

Harry T. Willetts, 'The Agrarian Problem', in George Katkov, Erwin Oberländer, Nikolaus Poppe, and Georg von Rauch (eds.) *Russia Enters the Twentieth Century 1894–1917* (London, 1971), pp. 111–37

David Alec Wilson and David Wilson MacArthur, *Carlyle in Old Age* (1865–1881) (London, 1934)

R. B. Zaborova, 'Turgenev i ego diadia N. N. Turgenev' in *T. sb.*, Vol. III (Leningrad, 1967), pp. 221–34

A. V. Zapadov (ed.), *Istoriia russkoi zhurnalistiki* XVIII–XIX vekov, 2nd edn. corrected & enlarged (Moscow, 1966)

Nicholas G. Zekulin, 'Turgenev in Scotland', *Slavonic & East European Review*, Vol. LIV, No. 3 (July 1976), pp. 355–70

V. N. Zhitova, *Vospominaniia o semye I. S. Turgeneva* (Tula, 1961)

I. S. Zilbershtein, 'Poslednii dnevnik Turgeneva' in *L.N.*, Vol. 73 (i), pp. 365–424

Notes

References are given in full in the Bibliography, pp. 333–43.

CHAPTER ONE

[1] Arzumanova, p. 284.

[2] *T. sb.*, I, p. 218.

[3] L., X, p. 161.

[4] Malysheva, p. 38.

[5] According to Ostrovskaia, p. 122, T. told her that his father only kissed him once in his life.

[6] W., IX, pp. 30–1.

[7] *T. sb.*, ed. Koni, pp. 135–6.

[8] Portugalov, p. 25.

[9] See L. Krestova.

[10] *T. sb.*, V, pp. 347–351; cf. Argamakova.

[11] Polonsky, pp. 497–8.

[12] Portugalov, pp. 23–4.

[13] W., I, p. 438.

[14] 'I. S. Turgenev na vechernei besede', *Russkaia starina*, 1883, No. 10.

[15] Polonsky, pp. 494–5.

[16] W., XV, p. 232 – from an inscription in an album.

[17] On the impact of Kheraskov on the boy see a letter of 3–8 September 1840, L., I, p. 202.

[18] L., IX, p. 133.

[19] Portugalov, pp. 27–31.

[20] L., I, p. 423.

[21] I have followed the chronology of the editors of Turgenev's 'Memorial', in *L.N.*, Vol. 73 (i) p. 347 which I find convincing.

[22] L., I, pp. 147–8.

[23] L., I, p. 665.

[24] L., III, p. 74.

[25] See a long letter about this to S. T. Aksakov of 22 January 1853, L., II, pp. 111–12, from which it is evident that Turgenev had not lost his enthusiasm for this novel over twenty years after first becoming acquainted with it. Zagoskin was, incidentally, a close friend of Turgenev's father.

[26] *L.N.*, Vol. 73 (i) pp. 342, 347.

[27] *Journal des Goncourt. Mémoires de la vie littéraire. Tome sixième, 1878–1884*, Paris, 1892, p. 10.

[28] See *L.N.*, Vol. 73 (i) p. 342. Petrovskoe was a village belonging to his mother.

CHAPTER TWO

[1] L., I, pp. 424–6.
[2] See Kleman in *T. sb.*, ed. koni, pp. 142–3.
[3] *L.N.*, Vol. 76, p. 340.
[4] W., XV, p. 207.
[5] *L.N.*, Vol. 73 (i) pp. 342, 349.
[6] *T. sb.*, V, pp. 354–5.
[7] Ostrovskaia, p. 97.
[8] W., XIV, pp. 11–21.
[9] L., X, p. 213.
[10] L., III, p. 62 (from a letter to Leo Tolstoy).
[11] W., XIV, p. 23.
[12] L., I, p. 164. This work is now lost.
[13] W., XIV, pp. 15–16, footnote.
[14] W., XIV, pp. 75–6.
[15] W., VI, pp. 7–17.
[16] Zhitova, Kolontaeva, Argamakova.
[17] Annenkov, p. 387.
[18] *T.sb.*, I, pp. 270–6.
[19] Kolontaeva, pp. 52–3.
[20] A. Dunin 'Delo o buystve I. S. Turgeneva', *Istoricheskii vestnik*, 1912, No. 2 – based on police records – the incident probably dates from 1834.
[21] L., I, p. 171.
[22] Turgenev's account is in W., XIV, pp. 186–202, the letter in W., XV, pp. 147–8. For the rumours see the notoriously unreliable Panaeva, pp. 95–6.
[23] Khmelevskaia, *T. sb.*, I, pp. 348, 350.
[24] L., I, p. 189.
[25] W., VI, p. 373.
[26] *Perepiska*, p. 707.
[27] Kornilov, p. 25.
[28] W., VI, p. 393.
[29] L., I, p. 195.
[30] A. I. Turgenev, p. 494.
[31] For the draft see L., I, pp. 211–4.
[32] L., VI, p. 114.
[33] L., I, p. 197.
[34] Annenkov, p. 200.
[35] Letter of 8 October 1868, L., XIII (2), p. 210.
[36] Gorbacheva, pp. 13–14.
[37] See *T. sb.*, II, pp. 92–9.
[38] L., I, p. 190.
[39] *Istoriia russkoi zhurnalistiki*, p. 263.
[40] L., I, p. 279.
[41] W., I, p. 344.
[42] Zhitova, pp. 13–15.
[43] See W., I, p. 52. Written in 1843, when little Varvara was ten.
[44] See Malysheva; and Khmelevskaia.
[45] Malysheva, p. 26.
[46] Kornilov, pp. 64, 68.

CHAPTER THREE

[1] Kornilov, p. 73.

[2] L., IX, p. 246.

[3] L., I, p. 397.

[4] 8 May 1842, West European Calendar, 26 April by the Russian Calendar, according to official documentation – see a letter to Madame Viardot of 13 May 1853, L., II, p. 154.

[5] See Kornilov, Chapter III; Krestova: and Brodskii. The poems are in W., I.

[6] Belinsky, Vol. XII, pp. 152–3.

[7] Belinsky, Vol. XI, p. 247.

[8] Kornilov, pp. 107–8, footnote.

[9] L., I, pp. 219–20.

[10] W., I, pp. 342–3.

[11] Krestova, pp. 46–8.

[12] *Andrei* is in W., I: 'Andrei Kolosov' in W., V.

[13] L., I, pp. 222, 544–5.

[14] For the order to the bankers despatching 2,000 roubles see L., I, p. 428. The correspondence reprinted in Kornilov is much occupied with money matters – see especially pp. 248–9, 251–2, 255, 260–2.

[15] Annenkov, pp. 383–4, 394–5. Ostrovskii, p. 65, quoting a speech by Annenkov.

[16] *L.N.*, Vol. 73 (i), pp. 343, 351.

[17] Gutiar, pp. 53–68.

[18] W., XIV, p. 64.

[19] Annenkov, pp. 240–1.

[20] Annenkov, p. 382.

[21] Herzen (see Gertsen), Vol. XXII, p. 176.

[22] *Perepiska*, p. 692.

[23] Belinsky, Vol. XII, p. 151.

[24] W., I, pp. 481, 542–4.

[25] *L.N.*, Vol. 73 (i) p. 357; Gutiar, pp. 55–8.

[26] Details of the examination and the texts of the written essays are in *T. sb.*, II, pp. 87–108. See also Lisovskii.

[27] Kornilov, pp. 140–1.

[28] Kleman, p. 32, based on Varvara Petrovna's letters.

[29] L., I, pp. 194–208.

[30] Kleman, p. 32.

[31] W., XV, p. 207; Kleman, p. 34.

[32] The request and the reply are quoted in Kleman, p. 33.

[33] W., I., p. 629.

[34] *L.N.*, Vol. 73 (i) p. 344; Oksman.

[35] W., XIV, pp. 8–9.

[36] First published in 1884. Reprinted in *I. S. Turgenev v vospominaniiakh*, Vol. I, p. 90.

[37] W., I, pp. 459–72.

[38] Kleman, p. 34. 'Collegiate Secretary' was the fifth from the bottom in the official table of fourteen ranks, equivalent to the rank of army lieutenant.

[39] L., X, p. 349 (letter of 11 January 1875).

[40] L., I, pp. 232, 233.

[41] Belinsky, Vol. VII, pp. 65–80. The influential P. A. Pletnev, the editor of the *Contemporary (Sovremennik)* also praised *Parasha* highly.

[42] Belinsky, Vol. XII, p. 139.

[43] Panaev, p. 254.

[44] W., XIV, pp. 49–50.

[45] This is evident from two letters to Aksakov, written in April 1843 and April 1844, which are extant – see L., I, pp. 232, 236.

[46] Belinsky, Vol. XII, p. 151.

[47] L., XII (i) p. 90. cf. W., XIV, p. 210, written in 1860.

[48] Panaev, quoted in Ostrovskii, pp. 60–61. This passage seems to have been almost omitted in the only edition of this book available to me, the third, of 1888.

[49] L.N., Vol. 73 (i) p. 344; Panaeva, p. 95, where the date of her meeting with Turgenev is mistakenly given as 1842. On Panaeva see Chapters 3 and 7.

[50] Kolontaeva, p. 63.

[51] Quoted in Ostrovskii, p. 58.

CHAPTER FOUR

[1] Heine, p. 231.

[2] For information on Pauline Viardot, here and elsewhere in this book, I have relied heavily on *The Price of Genius* and gratefully acknowledge my debt. Mrs. Fitzlyon's study is particularly admirable on Turgenev's side of his life-long friendship with Pauline.

[3] L., II, p. 82, letter of 1 Nov. 1852 to Pauline Viardot.

[4] See e.g. Zhitova, p. 30.

[5] Though it must be recalled that many of the more ridiculous stories emanate from the memoirs of that incorrigible chatterbox, Madame Panaeva, whose tendency to embroider is well known.

[6] W., I, p. 309.

[7] Kleman, p. 36.

[8] Zv., II, p. 4.

[9] L., I, p. 430.

[10] Quoted in Kleman, p. 36.

[11] Zv., p. 5.

[12] W., I, pp. 102–27, 533–9.

[13] W., V, p. 35.

[14] Belinsky, Vol. VIII, p. 483; Vol. X, p. 345.

[15] L., III, pp. 101, 501.

[16] W., I, pp. 229–30.

[17] *ibidem*, p. 238.

[18] Fitzlyon, p. 181.

[19] L., I, p. 430; Kleman, p. 38.

[20] Zhitova, p. 71. The date given by Zhitova, 1846, is obviously wrong, since Madame Viardot did not sing in Moscow in 1846.

[21] L., I, p. 240.

[22] L., I, p. 431.

[23] Kleman, p. 39. Oksman, pp. 181–3.

[24] L.N., Vol. 73 (i) p. 344.

[25] For the text of this article and the argument in favour of Turgenev's authorship see L.N., Vol. 73 (i) pp. 271–80.

[26] Zv., p. 6., footnote 4.

[27] Quoted in Nikol'skii, pp. 3–4.

[28] Dostoevsky, Vol. I, p. 497.

[29] W., I, pp. 360–1, 609.

[30] L.N., Vol. 86, p. 301. For an objective account of these events see Grigorovich, pp. 143–4. Grigorovich and Dostoevsky were living together at the time.

[31] See L., I, p. 558.

[32] Zv., p. 6.
[33] 21 October, Zv., p. 12.
[34] May 1846, Zv., p. 8.
[35] L., I, pp. 249–52.
[36] Khmelevskaia, *T. sb.* I, p. 353.
[37] Zhitova, pp. 95–99.
[38] *Turgenev i krug*, pp. v–xv.
[39] L., I, p. 254.
[40] Nekrasov, VIII, p. 62. And cf., p. 83.
[41] G. & Zv., p. 5.
[42] Kleman, p. 41.

CHAPTER FIVE

[1] Herzen (see Gertsen), Vol. XXIII, p. 82.
[2] *ibidem*, p. 103.
[3] Tuchkova-Ogareva, pp. 279–83.
[4] *I. S. Turgenev v vosp.*, Vol. I, pp. 107–8.
[5] W., I, pp. 314–15.
[6] 'Tatiana Borisovna and her Nephew', W., IV, p. 204.
[7] L., I, p. 274.
[8] *Tagebücher*, Vol. IV, pp. 32, 45.
[9] Herzen (see Gertsen), XXIII, pp. 9, 342.
[10] For a full discussion of Kavelin's article and Slavophile criticism of it see Walicki, pp. 404–12.
[11] *Turg. v vosp.*, Vol. II, pp. 259–62.
[12] Belinsky, Vol. XII, pp. 333–63; L., I., pp. 256–8.
[13] Belinsky, Vol. XII, pp. 366–7.
[14] Annenkov, p. 336.
[15] Belinsky, Vol. XII, p. 340.
[16] Belinsky, Vol. X, p. 214.
[17] Annenkov, pp. 361–3.
[18] See e.g. Mochul'sky, and the very recent 'V teni Gogolia' by Abram Terts (Siniavsky).
[19] W., XIV, p. 68.
[20] Barsukov, Vol. VIII, p. 618.
[21] L., II, p. 144.
[22] L., I, p. 259.
[23] Tuchkova-Ogareva, p. 283.
[24] L., I, pp. 296–7.
[25] Lemke, *Ocherki*, p. 162; Gutiar, p. 83.
[26] Herzen (see Gertsen), Vol. XXIII, p. 113.
[27] W., V, p. 351; G. & Zv., p. 315.
[28] G. & Zv., No. 2.
[29] Zv., No. 14; cf. L., I, pp. 389, 393–4, etc.
[30] *T. sb.*, I, pp. 453–4.
[31] G. & Zv., No. 2.
[32] L., I, p. 281.
[33] Erlich, pp. 80–94.
[34] Waddington, p. 2.
[35] L., I, p. 325.
[36] L., I, p. 282.
[37] Zv., No. 9.

38 G. & Zv., No. 3.
39 Waddington, *T.L.S.*, p. 17.
40 L., I, pp. 299–304.
41 W., XIV, pp. 136–46.
42 Zv., No. 10.
43 Waddington, *T.L.S.*, p. 17.
44 Waddington, p. 3.
45 L., I, p. 283.
46 Waddington, *T.L.S.*, p. 17.
47 Zv., No. 6.
48 W., IV, pp. 474–87.
49 Annenkov, p. 267.
50 See e.g. Gutiar, p. 165.
51 *Alien Bread* is printed in W., II; the details of publication appear in the commentaries. The review of Gedeonov's play is in W., I, pp. 257–71. On meetings with Chaadaev see Gutiar, p. 63.
52 L., X, p. 256.
53 L., I, p. 375.
54 Zv., Vol. II, p. 9.
55 Zhitova, pp. 107–8.
56 L., I, p. 378.
57 Zv., No. 11.
58 Zv., No. 5.
59 L., I, p. 287.
60 Zv., No. 7.
61 *L.N.*, Vol. 73 (i) p. 344.
62 L., I, p. 327.
63 G. & Zv., No. 7. The journey from Paris to London took about twelve and a half hours in 1850, so Pauline had left Paris the previous night at about half past nine.
64 G. & Zv., No. 3, of 13 October 1848.
65 G. & Zv., Nos. 7 & 8.
66 Zv., No. 10.
67 Fitzlyon, pp. 250–51.
68 Herzen (see Gertsen), Vol. XXIII, p. 325.
69 Zv., No. 13.
70 G. & Zv., p. 313.
71 Zv., p. 68.
72 G. & Zv., No. 10.
73 Unpublished; referred to in Zv., pp. 42–3, footnote 2.
74 Zv., No. 15.
75 G. & Zv., pp. 309–10. The editors' dating 'entre le 15 et le 20 juin 1850' cannot be right: this letter is obviously in reply to a letter of 20 June, and can scarcely be dated earlier than 22 June.
76 G. & Zv., pp. 310–15.
77 Letter of 1 December from Moscow – G. & Zv., No. 20.
78 The letter is in the Bibliothèque Nationale, bound in Volume N.A.F. 16273.
79 G. & Zv., No. 20, p. 50.
80 For details of the omissions insisted on by the censor see *Turg. i krug*, pp. 255–66.
81 Quoted in W., III, p. 406. The information on the writing of the play is derived from the detailed annotation to the play in W., III.
82 W., III, p. 145.
83 L., I, pp. 386–7.

84 Zv., No. 16.
85 G. & Zv., No. 11.
86 Kolontaeva, p. 65; Fet, Vol. I, p. 5.

CHAPTER SIX

1 Entry for 25 April 1848.
2 Annenkov, pp. 529–48.
3 Zv, No. 18; Zhitova, pp. 128ff.
4 L., II, pp. 8–9.
5 See Chapter 17.
6 For extracts relating to her daughter see Zhitova, pp. 11–12.
7 Ostrovskii, pp. 91–2, quoting the account of L. Pietsch, with whom Turgenev was on intimate terms.
8 Zv., No. 19; and *ibidem*, p. 346 for Pauline's reply.
9 G. & Zv., No. 20, p. 50.
10 L., I, pp. 400–1.
11 G. & Zv., No. 15, p. 37.
12 Fet, Vol. I, p. 271.
13 G. & Zv., No. 19.
14 Zhitova, pp. 147–52.
15 L., I, pp. 411–13.
16 Malysheva, p. 48.
17 L., II, p. 13.
18 L., II, p. 21.
19 L., IX, p. 225.
20 Dowler – *passim*, especially Chapter II.
21 W., V, pp. 387–96.
22 See W., III, pp. 435–7 for a long extract from his article.
23 Grigoriev, p. 530.
24 L., II, pp. 137–8.
25 For an account of the career of Countess Sailhas de Tournemire see Feoktistov, pp. 362ff.
26 G. & Zv., p. 46.
27 W., V, pp. 415–16, 647.
28 G. & Zv., No. 18, p. 42.
29 Alekseev, pp. 137–8.
30 See W., IV, pp. 503–6 for full details of this story.
31 L., II, pp. 99, 465.
32 L., II, pp. 142, 491.
33 L., II, p. 100.
34 L., II, p. 356.
35 L., II, p. 99.
36 Alekseev, pp. 132–3.
37 L., II, p. 24.
38 L., II, p. 37.
39 L., II, pp. 71–2.
40 L., II, p. 144, dated 21 April 1853.
41 L., II, p. 77.
42 L., II, p. 159. This novel, of which only one chapter and the detailed plan of the whole have survived, is discussed in the next chapter.
43 Barsukov, Vol. XI, pp. 533–4.
44 Erlich, pp. 202–9.

[45] Letter to I. S. Aksakov of 3 March 1852, L., II, pp. 49–50.

[46] See also Nikitenko's entry for 24 February 1852. Nikitenko was also at the meeting and heard many details of Gogol's death from Turgenev based on these letters. The letters from Feoktistov are in *L.N.*, Vol. 58, pp. 743–4.

[47] Zv., No. 23, pp. 63–5.

[48] Diary entry for 20 April 1852.

[49] L., II, p. 59.

[50] W., XIV, p. 72.

[51] Lemke, *Zhandarmy*, pp. 203–8; Feoktistov, pp. 17–20.

[52] L., II, pp. 55–7.

[53] Zv., No. 29.

[54] L., XI, p. 290, where Turgenev's drawing of the house is reproduced.

[55] Zv., No. 27, p. 72.

[56] 8 September 1853, G. & Zv., No. 29.

[57] Panaeva, pp. 211–12.

[58] L., I, pp. 412–13.

[59] L., II, pp. 171, 176.

[60] Letter of 1 November 1852, L., II, p. 83. Cf. his letter of 13 May 1853, L., II, p. 155.

[61] Letter to Pauline of 4 February 1853, G. & Zv., p. 64.

[62] On Gluck see letter of 12 October 1853 to S. A. Miller, L., II, pp. 188–9.

[63] G. & Zv., No. 26.

[64] L., II, p. 63.

[65] L., II, p. 210.

[66] L., II, pp. 163, 198–201.

[67] Leontiev, Vol. IX, pp. 69–153.

[68] L., II, p. 104.

[69] L., II, p. 298, 580.

[70] L., II, p. 185.

[71] L., II, p. 169.

[72] L., II, pp. 109–10. Marlinsky and Ozerov were both practitioners of what Turgenev used to call the 'pseudo-majestical' literary manner.

[73] L., II, p. 172.

[74] L., II, pp. 144–5.

[75] L., II, p. 197.

[76] L., II, pp. 79, 152.

[77] L., II, p. 184.

[78] Portugalov, pp. 31–8.

[79] L., II, p. 39.

[80] Bogdanova, pp. 50–2.

[81] L., VI, pp. 9–11.

[82] L., II, pp. 276, 285; *Turg. i krug*, pp. 268, 270.

[83] Feoktistov, pp. 13–17; L., II, pp. 30–1. Cf. also *Turg. i krug*, pp. 146–8.

[84] *T. sb.*, III, pp. 238–9.

[85] G. & Zv., p. 50.

[86] Zv., p. 66.

[87] G. & Zv., p. 67, footnote 1.

[88] Herzen, (see Gertsen) Vol. XXV, p. 69, letter to M. K. Reikhel of 4 June 1853.

[89] L., II, pp. 211, 523–4.

[90] L., II, p. 212.

CHAPTER SEVEN

[1] W., V, p. 423.

[2] L., III, pp. 123–4, 128.

[3] For Turgenev's relations with Botkin see Gutiar, pp. 285–300.

[4] Zv., p. 148, footnote 3; L., IV, p. 170.

[5] *Turg. i krug*, p. 212.

[6] W., XV, pp. 217–22. The squeamish Soviet editors of the Academy edition of Turgenev replace all the rude words with dots, but the rhyme enables the reader with a knowledge of Russian scatological idiom to reconstruct them.

[7] Gutiar, pp. 208–9; L., II, p. 246; Zv., No. 30, letter of 18 October 1854.

[8] L., III, p. 131. See Chapter 9 for the sequel to the story.

[9] *Turg. i krug*, pp. 358–9.

[10] L., II, p. 315.

[11] L., II, pp. 333–4.

[12] *Turg. i krug*, pp. xxvii–xxxii.

[13] L., III, Nos. 496, 498, 502.

[14] W., XV, pp. 127–9.

[15] *Vospominaniia ... Chicherina*, pp. 136–44.

[16] e.g. L., II, p. 220, to K. Leontiev.

[17] On the evidence for identifying Kapitolina Markovna and Tatiana in *Smoke* with Eropkina and Olga see Grot.

[18] L., II, p. 364.

[19] L., II, p. 362.

[20] Zv., No. 32.

[21] L., IX, p. 282. Details about Olga Turgeneva are to be found in Nazarova and Grot.

[22] Zv., No. 30, letter of 18 October 1854.

[23] Zv., No. 31, p. 79, letter of 10 February 1855. The French word used is *taquiner*.

[24] Leontiev, IX, pp. 125–6.

[25] Letter of 3 December 1855, L., II, p. 324.

[26] L., II, p. 360.

[27] L., II, p. 238.

[28] Puzin, p. 254.

[29] W., VII, p. 50.

[30] L., II, pp. 315–17.

[31] L., II, p. 328.

[32] L., II, p. 337.

[33] Fet, Vol. I, pp. 106–7; cf. Grigorovich, pp. 250–4.

[34] See Chapter 10.

[35] Sergeenko, issue for May, columns 78–80.

[36] L., III, p. 235.

[37] L., II, p. 299.

[38] G. & Zv., p. 69.

[39] L., II, p. 262.

[40] Grigorovich, pp. 232–7.

[41] Fet, Vol. I, pp. 104–5, 126–7.

[42] See Blagoi.

[43] W., VI, p. 598.

[44] Nazarova, 'O romane ...', pp. 55–6.

[45] L., III, pp. 91–2.

[46] W., VI, pp. 7–17.

[47] For a discussion of the plan of this novel see Mazon, 'Rabota ...'.

[48] W., VI, p. 190.
[49] W., VI, p. 80.
[50] W., VI, pp. 204, 206, 540.
[51] W., VI, pp. 337–8.
[52] L. II, p. 340.
[53] W., VI, p. 371.
[54] Nekrasov, Vol. 8, p. 166, letter of 24 November 1855.
[55] L., II, Nos. 389 and 462.
[56] L., II, p. 354.
[57] Herzen (see Gertsen), Vol. XXVI, p. 24.
[58] Nekrasov, Vol. VIII, p. 176, letter of 15 (or 17) June 1856.

CHAPTER EIGHT

[1] Herzen (see Gertsen), Vol. XXVI, pp. 22, 24.
[2] L., III, pp. 8–9.
[3] Zv., p. 83.
[4] In *British Quarterly Review*, Vol. 50, 1869, pp. 424–47.
[5] *Letters, Carlyle*, Vol. II, p. 356.
[6] L., III, pp. 199–201, 552.
[7] L., III, p. 129.
[8] I am indebted for this information to the Secretary of the Athenaeum.
[9] *Annual Register*, 1857, pp. 80–5.
[10] The identification in Zv., p. 87 would seem to be erroneous.
[11] This account is based on a letter to Pauline of 10 June 1857, which has only recently become available – see Zv. No. 34.
[12] G. & Zv., No. 33.
[13] L., III, p. 217.
[14] Wemyss Reid, Vol. II, p. 28.
[15] W., XIV, pp. 239–45.
[16] *Letters, Thackeray*, p. 392.
[17] *Turg. v vosp.*, Vol. II, p. 22.
[18] L., IV, p. 210.
[19] L., V, p. 284; L., XII (i) No. 4642: Ralston, p. 338.
[20] *Turg. v vosp.*, Vol. II, pp. 327–8.
[21] L., III, p. 20. The date in Kleman, p. 86, is wrong.
[22] Zv., No. 137, 11 June 1880.
[23] L., III, pp. 15, 24–5.
[24] See *L.N.*, Vol. 73, (i), pp. 427–567. This meticulous research has also formed the basis for Mainwaring, in English.
[25] Fet, Vol. I, pp. 149–62.
[26] L., III, pp. 42–3.
[27] L., II, p. 352.
[28] L., III, pp. 91–2.
[29] L., III, p. 117.
[30] L., III, p. 143. The original, in the State Tolstoy Museum in Moscow, was not available to me.
[31] L., III, pp. 75, 103.
[32] Nekrasov, Vol. VIII, p. 221.
[33] L., III, p. 178.
[34] Fitzlyon, pp. 314–16.
[35] L., III, p. 132.
[36] L., III, p. 118.

[37] See, for example, a letter to S. T. Aksakov of 8 January 1857, L., III, pp. 67–8.

[38] L., III, p. 113.

[39] L., III, p. 76.

[40] L., IV, p. 167.

[41] *T. sb.*, Vol. I, pp. 276–8.

[42] L., III, p. 53.

[43] L., III, p. 73.

[44] L., III, p. 117.

[45] L., III, pp. 137–8.

[46] L., III, p. 293.

[47] L., V, p. 71.

[48] L., III, pp. 364–6, 371–2.

[49] L., III, pp. 321–2.

[50] L., III, p. 145.

[51] L., III, pp. 54–5.

[52] W., XIV, pp. 85–96.

[53] For an excellent account of the whole course of emancipation, from delineation to decision, see Seton-Watson, pp. 334–48.

[54] Zv., No. 37.

[55] *L.N.*, Vol. 73 (i) p. 416.

[56] W., XV, pp. 235–44.

[57] W., XV, pp. 136–7, 361–2.

[58] The letter was written at the request of Prince Cherkassky – L., III, p. 192.

[59] Seton-Watson, p. 346.

[60] L., III, pp. 163–4, 170–1.

[61] L., IV, pp. 28–9.

[62] L., III, p. 627.

[63] L., IV, pp. 254–5.

[64] L., III, p. 213.

CHAPTER NINE

[1] L., III, pp. 218, 561.

[2] W., XV, pp. 7–12.

[3] For a masterly analysis of the manuscript which is in the Bibliothèque Nationale, see W., VII, pp. 427–33.

[4] W., VII, p. 80.

[5] L., III, p. 163.

[6] L., III, pp. 300, 607.

[7] 'A Russian at a rendezvous', Chernyshevskii, Vol. III, pp. 398–421.

[8] L., III, p. 283.

[9] L., III, p. 298.

[10] Granjard, *Le Nid*, p. 72.

[11] L., III, p. 321.

[12] Countess Lambert's surviving letters to Turgenev, together with his letters to her, are reprinted with an introduction and commentaries in Granjard, *Le Nid*.

[13] L., III, p. 23.

[14] This date has been established by the recently published letter from Turgenev to Pauline Viardot, dated 18 November, which says that he had arrived in St. Petersburg four days before, and that the novel had already been read and approved – Zv., No. 38.

[15] W., VII, pp. 461–2.

[16] L., III, pp. 253–4.

[17] Granjard, *Le Nid*, pp. 60–1.

[18] L., III, p. 292.

[19] L., IV, pp. 306, 312.

[20] L., IV, p. 383.

[21] L., I, pp. 295–6.

[22] G. & Zv., No. 39.

[23] W., VIII, p. 323; Pascal, pp. 55–6.

[24] *Raduga*, pp. 181–96, where Turgenev's attitude to religion is discussed.

[25] W., XII, pp. 303–10.

[26] W., VIII, pp. 502–4.

[27] Granjard, *Tourguénev*, pp. 255–6.

[28] See a letter from Feoktistov of 5 September 1851, quoted in W., VIII, p. 553.

[29] W., VIII, p. 14.

[30] L., III, pp. 238–9.

[31] For a concise guide to the vast literature which grew up around *A Nest of the Landed Gentry* see W., VII, pp. 488–95.

[32] Annenkov, p. 426.

[33] L., VIII, p. 323.

[34] Based on the memoirs of Zhivkova, quoted in W., VIII, pp. 514–5.

[35] W., VIII, pp. 517–19.

[36] Granjard, *Le Nid*, p. 89.

[37] L., III, pp. 379–80.

[38] Annenkov, pp. 433–4.

[39] For a summary of contemporary criticism of *On the Eve*, see W., VIII, pp. 523–41.

[40] *Dobroliubov v vospominaniiakh*, pp. 171–2.

[41] Nekrasov, Vol. 8, p. 248.

[42] *Turg. i krug*, pp. xxviii–xxx.

[43] Panaeva, pp. 273–81.

[44] L., III, pp. 60–1.

[45] *Turg. i krug*, pp. xxiii–xxiv; and cf. L., II, pp. 345, 347.

[46] L., II, pp. 290, 293, 300–1.

[47] L., III, pp. 258, 583–4; Blinchevskaiia, p. 235.

[48] L., III, p. 276.

[49] Dobroliubov, Vol. 4, p. 167.

[50] L., II, p. 317–18.

[51] Shcherban', p. 13.

[52] Herzen (see Gertsen), Vol. XIII, p. 363.

[53] For the texts of the two letters see Barsukov, Vol. XV, pp. 246–57, 261–8.

[54] Herzen (see Gertsen), Vol. XII, p. 436.

[55] Dobroliubov, Vol. IV, pp. 307–43. Published in the *Contemporary*, No. 5, for May 1859.

[56] Herzen (see Gertsen), Vol. XIV, p. 116, published on 1 June 1859. For a summary of the storm which Herzen's attack produced in intellectual circles see *ibidem*, pp. 492–7.

[57] Koz'min, pp. 606–37.

[58] Dobroliubov, Vol. VI, pp. 96–140, published in the *Contemporary* No. 3 for March 1860. There were difficulties with the censor, and the article was eventually published with cuts. The censor also disallowed the title, which was only restored on republication in the collected edition in 1862. For the argument that the version printed in this volume is the original version, restored by Chernyshevsky in 1862 from the manuscript, see *ibidem*, pp. 492–3.

[59] L., IV, p. 41.

[60] Gabel, p. 64.
[61] L., IV, pp. 137, 139.
[62] *Turg. i krug*, p. 111.
[63] Nekrasov, Vol. 8, pp. 280–1.
[64] W., XV, p. 142. Turgenev's reply to Nekrasov is lost, but he referred to it in a subsequent open letter to the press.
[65] W., XIV, pp. 108–9 (written in 1868–9).
[66] L., V, p. 10.
[67] See Chapter 15.

CHAPTER TEN

[1] L., III, p. 306.
[2] L., III, p. 321.
[3] L., IV, p. 133.
[4] L., IV, p. 166.
[5] L., IV, p. 171.
[6] L., IV, p. 97.
[7] L., III, p. 270.
[8] L., V, pp. 29–30.
[9] L., IV, p. 183.
[10] Mme. Markovich's letters are reprinted, excellently edited, in Krutikova.
[11] See the photograph opposite page 307.
[12] L., IV, p. 301.
[13] Nikol'skii, pp. 25–9.
[14] L., X, p. 250.
[15] Engel'gardt, pp. 9–63; Nikitenko, entry for 29 March 1860; (Nikitenko was very much impressed with Turgenev's dignified behaviour, unlike, it would seem, the more critical Annenkov). Annenkov, pp. 441–3. (The posthumously published paranoid account of Goncharov's version of the plagiarism from which he had allegedly suffered was not yet available to Engel'gardt.)
[16] L., IV, p. 209.
[17] Fet, I, pp. 369–71; there is also a short account set down many years later by Countess Tolstoy, and based on what her husband told her.
[18] Ostrovskaia, p. 100.
[19] L., IV, p. 266.
[20] See L., IV, pp. 247–9, and 291–3, for Turgenev's letters to Tolstoy; and L., IV, p. 587 where Tolstoy's diary entries and his curt reply to Turgenev's challenge are reprinted. Also Sergeenko, pp. 339–53.
[21] Fet, II, pp. 304–5.
[22] L., VI, p. 216.
[23] Kleman, p. 120.
[24] W., XV, pp. 245–52, 425–7; Annenkov, pp. 448–54.
[25] L., IV, pp. 393–5.
[26] See Chapter 12.
[27] L., V, p. 50, letter of 8 October 1862.

CHAPTER ELEVEN

[1] L., IV, Nos. 1043, 1047, 1048, 1049.
[2] Seton-Watson, pp. 347–8.
[3] See e.g. Koshelev, p. 131.
[4] L., IV, pp. 242–4.

[5] Ogarev, Vol. I, pp. 527–36.

[6] See Nechkina. Nechkina's conclusions both on the extent of Chernyshevsky's participation and the degree of preparation are challenged in Lin'kov, pp. 134–9, and indeed, in view of the strained relations between Herzen and Chernyshevsky, her theory seems, on the face of it, unconvincing.

[7] For a detailed study of this early revolutionary organization by a Soviet scholar see Novikova.

[8] L., IV, pp. 606–7; Dikman i Levin.

[9] The text is in Burtsev, pp. 40–6.

[10] L., XI, p. 191.

[11] Diary for 12 June 1862.

[12] Lemke, *Ocherki*, pp. 17–230.

[13] Lemke, *Protsessy*, pp. 201–421.

[14] Herzen (see Gertsen), Vol. XVI, pp. 199–205.

[15] Acton, Chap. 8; Herzen (see Gertsen), Vol. XX (2), p. 590.

[16] Herzen (see Gertsen), Vol. XXVII (1), pp. 145–6.

[17] L., IV, p. 116.

[18] L., IV, p. 137, letter to Annenkov.

[19] W., VIII, p. 571.

[20] W., VIII, pp. 246, 453.

[21] W., VIII, pp. 304, 463, 574.

[22] W., VIII, pp. 446, 576–7.

[23] L., IV, p. 313.

[24] For one such conjecture see Pustovoit, pp. 143–57.

[25] L., IV, p. 300.

[26] L., IV, p. 383.

[27] L., X, p. 325.

[28] The main basis for the analysis attempted above is the concordance of the various texts – the MS., the fair copy, the subsequent alterations, the text as first published and the text as revised for publication in book form – in the Academy edition of Turgenev's novels. See W., VIII, pp. 446–88.

[29] Zilbershtein, in *L.N.*, Vol. 73 (i) p. 368.

[30] L., X, p. 281.

[31] Eliseev, p. 374; Vodovozova, pp. 381–5.

[32] *Raduga*, p. 216.

[33] Pisarev, *Izbrannye*, p. 95.

[34] Pisarev, Vol. III, p. 294 (written in 1865).

[35] *Raduga*, pp. 207–25; cf. Ostrovskaiia, pp. 94–5.

[36] W., XII, p. 314.

[37] See quotations from memoirs in Pustovoit, pp. 217–28.

[38] Vucinich, pp. 12–13.

[39] W., XIV, pp. 97–8; a slightly different version is related by Ostrovskaia, pp. 79–83.

[40] L., IV, p. 385.

[41] Dostoevsky, *Sobranie sochinenii*, 1956, Vol. IV, pp. 79–80; L., IV, pp. 358–9.

[42] Herzen (see Gertsen), Vol. XXVII (i) p. 217.

[43] Kropotkin, p. 301.

[44] L., V, p. 120.

[45] L., V, p. 129.

[46] Valentinov, p. 103.

[47] Vodovozova, p. 381.

[48] Serno-Solovievich, pp. 277–355.

CHAPTER TWELVE

[1] See Pietsch in *Innostrannaiia kritika*.

[2] For details of the Viardots' life in Baden see Fitzlyon, Chapter XXV; Haebler, pp. 98–9.

[3] Zv., p. 355 (letter dated 1869); L., VII, p. 170 (1898).

[4] Zv., No. 42, No. 43; G. & Zv., No. 43; G. & Zv. pp. 320–1.

[5] Now in the Houghton Library, Harvard University, and referred to by kind permission.

[6] See Chistova for details, where a number of programmes are reprinted, including one in Turgenev's writing.

[7] L., VI, p. 28.

[8] W., XIV, p. 178.

[9] L., V, p. 133.

[10] L., XIII (2), p. 22.

[11] L., V, p. 337.

[12] L., V, p. 262.

[13] L., V, p. 309.

[14] L., V, p. 319.

[15] L., X, p. 174; L., VIII, pp. 308, 524.

[16] L., V, pp. 340, 374.

[17] L., V, p. 316.

[18] L., V, p. 347.

[19] L., IV, p. 335.

[20] Lemke, *Ocherki*, pp. 168–71.

[21] L., V, p. 60.

[22] Herzen (see Gertsen), Vol. XVI, pp. 129–98.

[23] L., V, pp. 51–2.

[24] L., V, pp. 64–5.

[25] L., V, pp. 67–8.

[26] L., V, pp. 48–50, 513–16.

[27] L., V, 54–6.

[28] Herzen (see Gertsen), Vol. XXVII (i) p. 266.

[29] L., V, pp. 73–5.

[30] L., V, pp. 94–5.

[31] Herzen (see Gertsen), XXVII (i) p. 293.

[32] L., V, p. 146.

[33] L., V, pp. 82–3, 537–8.

[34] L., V, pp. 382–3. The letter as finally sent was toned down, presumably by the ambassador, by the omission of some of the more emotional sentences – see L., V, pp. 387–9 for the draft.

[35] L., V, pp. 390–401; Lemke, *Ocherki*, p. 162.

[36] In fact the *Bell* only began to appear in 1857.

[37] L., VI, pp. 327, 584.

[38] W., XV, pp. 145–6, 366–7.

[39] G. & Zv., No. 45.

[40] L., V, p. 196.

[41] Zv., No. 46.

[42] Zv., No. 47.

[43] Zv., No. 48.

[44] Lemke, *Ocherki*, pp. 220–3.

[45] L., V, pp. 241–2.

[46] Herzen (see Gertsen), Vol. XXVII (ii) pp. 453–5.

[47] L., IV, p. 201.

[48] L., V, pp. 90, 94–5.
[49] See my *Vekhi*.
[50] L., V, p. 206.
[51] Rappich. Bodenstedt's letters to Turgenev, edited by Henri Granjard, are in *L.N.*, Vol. 73 (ii) pp. 303–32.
[52] Alekseev, 'Stikh. teksty', pp. 189–92.
[53] L., V, p. 279, dated 3 September 1864.
[54] L., VIII, p. 23.
[55] W., IX, pp. 480–1.
[56] Flaubert, p. 3.
[57] *Turg. v vosp.*, Vol. II, pp. 54–61. The author of the memoirs, designated by the intials M. P. S–ova, cannot be identified with certainty.
[58] Kleman, p. 149.
[59] L., V, p. 157.
[60] L., I, pp. 365–6, dated 11 to 14 August 1849.
[61] Dostoevsky, *Pis'ma*, pp. 343, 352.
[62] L., VIII, p. 172.
[63] W., IX, p. 106; Schopenhauer, Vol. II., p. 163.
[64] W., IX, p. 379.
[65] Pascal, Paragraph 347, p. 97.
[66] L., XII (i) p. 322.
[67] W., IX, pp. 497–8.
[68] W., IX, pp. 499–503.

CHAPTER THIRTEEN

[1] W., IX, pp. 396 (the 1862 conspectus); 515–20.
[2] See Nazarova and Grot in *T. sb.*, Vol. I.
[3] *Raduga*, pp. 214–20.
[4] L., VI, p. 258.
[5] W., XIV, pp. 305, 572–4; L., XIII (i) p. 272.
[6] L., VI, p. 335.
[7] Parturier, p. 191.
[8] For some typical quotations see W., IX, pp. 532–41.
[9] Letter to Pauline of 28 March 1867, L., VI, No. 1797.
[10] L., X, p. 7 (letter to Annenkov); p. 475.
[11] L., VI, No. 1832.
[12] For Herzen's views see Herzen (see Gertsen), Vol. XIX, pp. 261–2 (an article).
[13] L., VI, p. 355; L., VII, p. 13.
[14] L., VIII, Nos. 2452, 2453.
[15] L., VIII, p. 299; L., XI, p. 205; L., XII (2), 4924.
[16] Mochul'sky, pp. 197–8.
[17] Virtually the whole text of this letter is reproduced in Nikol'skii, pp. 30–43.
[18] *L.N.*, Vol. 86, p. 411.
[19] L., VII, No. 1955.
[20] See e.g. his letters to Pauline written after his first visit to Spasskoe for some years – G. & Zv., No. 75, L., VII, nos. 2094 and 2101.
[21] L., X, No. 3016. The most balanced account of the relations between the two men is that by Dostoevsky's biographer Mochul'sky – see Mochul'sky, pp. 267–9, 384–5. See also Dostoevsky, Vol. 12, pp. 165–78.
[22] L., XI, pp. 224, 579.
[23] Ostrovskaia, p. 105; L., IX, p. 95.
[24] W., XIV, p. 171.

[25] L., VII, p. 16 (letter to Annenkov of 3 January 1868).

[26] For Turgenev's interest in dissenters see Brodskii.

[27] See Parturier, pp. 179–229 for the relevant letters from Mérimée. See also the study by Levin.

[28] L., VI, p. 211.

[29] L., VIII, No. 2567.

[30] For a bibliography of translations of Turgenev's works into English, published up to 1934 in England, and up to 1924 in the United States, see Gettman, pp. 187–9.

[31] L., VIII. No. 2337 and No. 2340 (letter to Ralston).

[32] L.. VII, pp. 246–7, 527–8; W., XV, p. 149.

[33] See L.. VII, No. 1992.

[34] Fet, II, p. 118.

[35] Zaborova, pp. 229–30, based on Uncle Nicholas's unpublished correspondence.

[36] L., VI, Nos. 1773 and 1803.

[37] L., VI, pp. 208, 531.

[38] L., VI, No. 1733.

[39] G. & Zv., No. 66.

[40] Fet, II, p. 119.

[41] L., XII (i) p. 283.

[42] Fet, II, p. 357. This account is mainly based on many letters written in the course of 1867 and 1868 by Turgenev to his new manager and to friends. References are too numerous to list, but will be found in Zaborova.

[43] L., VII, p. 114.

[44] L., VI, pp. 133, 159, 166.

[45] L., VIII, pp. 41, 53.

[46] L., VIII, pp. 77, 209.

[47] L., VII, No. 2217; p. 541.

[48] The texts, which are not included in the recent Complete Works published under the auspices of the Soviet Academy of Sciences are reprinted, with Russian translation, in *L.N.*, Vol. 73 (i) pp. 91–207.

[49] L., VIII, p. 47.

[50] cf. L., VI, pp. 329–30. *L.N.*, Vol. 76, p. 372.

[51] W., XIV, pp. 286–96, 563–4; Alekseev in *T. sb.*, IV, pp. 199–200, note 24.

[52] L., VIII, No. 2468; *L.N.*, Vol. 73 (i) pp. 220–3. See also in my translation of *Spring Torrents* the note on p. 157.

[53] L., VIII, No. 2474.

[54] See Zv., pp. 364–73. Two further poems, possibly by Turgenev, but not signed, are printed *ibidem* on pp. 374–5.

[55] Zv., no. 61.

[56] Zv., II, pp. 99–101.

[57] L., VIII, pp. 238, 248.

[58] L., VII, p. 104.

[59] L., VI, p. 17.

[60] Zv., No. 60.

[61] Zv., No. 66.

[62] G. & Zv., p. 148.

[63] L., VII, p. 162.

[64] G. & Zv., No. 75.

[65] L., VII, p. 172.

[66] L., VIII, p. 312.

[67] G. & Zv., No. 79.

[68] His letters to her, or a selection of them, have only very recently been made

available from archives hitherto closed, and published – see Zv., pp. 247–314 (where two very charming drawings of Claudie are reproduced), and G. & Zv., pp. 243–93.

[69] L., VIII, No. 2518; G. & Zv., No. 82; Zv., No. 89.
[70] L., VIII, p. 89.
[71] Fet, Vol. II, pp. 216–17. Relations with Fet were already becoming somewhat strained.
[72] See Ralston.
[73] Zv., Nos. 70 & 71; Pietsch, p. 269.
[74] L., X, p. 252.
[75] W., XV, p. 154.
[76] L., XI, p. 149.
[77] L., VII, pp. 277–8, 279.
[78] See, for example, L., VII, Nos. 2001, 2012, 2021, 2036, 2054, 2099, 2233, 2273; L., VIII, No. 2478.
[79] L., VII, p. 122. The original letter is, apparently, lost – p. 486.
[80] W., XIV, pp. 212–13.
[81] Sultan-Shakh, pp. 368–74, for the years 1865–70.
[82] L., VII, pp. 230, 521.
[83] L., VII, p. 240.
[84] L., VIII, No. 2328.
[85] L., VIII, No. 2492.
[86] L., VIII, Nos. 2536, 2537.
[87] L., VIII, pp. 263–4.
[88] W., XV, pp. 14–33.
[89] L., VIII, p. 274.

CHAPTER FOURTEEN

[1] Zv., No. 168.
[2] L., IX, Nos. 2669, 2675, 2811.
[3] Zv., No. 169.
[4] Zv., pp. 191–2, and note 2.
[5] Wilson & MacArthur, p. 236; Polonsky, p. 534; L., IX, No. 2603.
[6] L., X, No. 2972; Moore, p. 237.
[7] Kovalevsky, pp. 141–2.
[8] See Waddington, in *M.L.R.*; L., XII (1), No. 4637.
[9] Zekulin; Zv., No. 92; G. & Zv., Nos. 89–92; Simmons.
[10] See, for example, Daudet, pp. 331–2.
[11] Fitzlyon, pp. 412–15; L., X, Nos. 3482, 3491.
[12] Kovalevsky, p. 150.
[13] L., IX, No. 2895; Flaubert, Vol. III, p. 34.
[14] Flaubert, Vol. VII, p. 71, letter to his niece of 5 October 1873.
[15] Flaubert, Vol. VI, p. 128.
[16] L., X, p. 669.
[17] L., XI, No. 3569.
[18] See Daudet, pp. 343–4; Pavlovsky, p. 73; and e.g. L., XI, No. 3673; L. XII (i) No. 4449; L., XII (ii) No. 4992 ('a very big talent'); L., XII (i) p. 726.
[19] Moore, p. 237.
[20] As recorded in the 'Memorial', *L.N.*, Vol. 73 (i) p. 344.
[21] Karenin, pp. 88–9, p. 103; L., X, p. 9.
[22] W., XIV, p. 233; Zv., No. 90.
[23] L., IX, No. 2954; L., X, No. 2986; L., X, No. 3199.

24 W., XIV, p. 233.

25 The entry in the Goncourt Journal is for 5 March 1876. For masterly analysis of the whole incident in its full context see Alekseev in *T. sb.*, Vol. III. See also Browning, pp. 128–9.

26 W., XIV, p. 306, from an unfinished article on *La Tentation de St Antoine*; cf. a letter to Flaubert of 17 June 1874, explaining why the novel had not found a publisher in St. Petersburg. L., X, No. 3361.

27 L., XI, No. 3746; p. 524; No. 3766.

28 L., XI, p. 25; p. 80.

29 L., XI, p. 230.

30 L., X, pp. 206–7, 587; W., XV, pp. 106–7.

31 L., X, No. 3363, and p. 616.

32 L., XII (i) p. 347.

33 L., XI, Nos. 3532, 3533, 3553; pp. 436, 445–6.

34 L., X, 3473.

35 See illustration facing page 306.

36 W., XIV, pp. 214–23.

37 L., X, No. 3062.

38 L., XI, No. 3600.

39 L., XIII (2), Nos. 5908, 5911, 5925.

40 L., IX, No. 2872, pp. 569–70.

41 L., IX, 2623; Zv., No. 95.

42 L., X, No. 3090, L., XI, No. 3536.

43 e.g. L., IX, No. 2619; G. & Zv., No. 85; W., XIV, pp. 246–9.

44 L., XII (i) pp. 216, 607; No. 4499.

45 L., IX, Nos. 2621, 2623.

46 L., IX, pp. 463–4.

47 Repin, pp. 118–19.

48 G. & Zv., No. 86.

49 Stasov, p. 99.

50 L., IX, p. 31.

51 Zv., p. 292; Shol'p.

52 Zv., No. 98.

53 Zv., No. 87.

54 Stasov, p. 112.

55 L., IX, No. 2770, and p. 525.

56 See below, Chapter 16.

57 Repin, p. 119.

58 Kovalevsky, p. 153.

59 Nelidova, pp. 244–5.

60 N.M., p. 158.

61 Ardov, pp. 187–8.

62 Paul Viardot, p. 310; cf. Romm.

63 Ardov, pp. 183–8.

64 G. & Zv., Nos. 150, 151.

65 See an extract from the memoirs of Sergei Volkonsky, quoted in *L.N.*, Vol. 73 (i) p. 407.

66 *L.N.*, Vol. 73 (i) p. 394.

67 Zv., Nos. 86, 88.

68 L., IX, pp. 157–8.

69 Zv., No. 84.

70 L., IX, No. 2934; L., X, No. 2992.

71 L., X, No. 3451.

72 For details on the finances of the Bruère family see Bron'.

[73] See Zapadov, pp. 496–8; Podgorelskin, pp. 217–18, 224–49.

[74] L., IX, p. 157.

[75] L., IX, p. 195.

[76] Fridlender, pp. 830–1. (There are also some supposed autobiographical reminiscences related by the very unreliable Pavlovsky, pp. 89–90.)

[77] L., IX, p. 261.

[78] L., X, p. 136.

[79] L., IX, pp. 184, 197.

[80] G. & Zv., Nos. 93 and 94.

[81] L., XIII (i) p. 196; W., IX, pp. 462–3, 374–5.

[82] L., X, Nos. 3398, 3399; L., XI, Nos. 3762, 3838.

[83] W., XI, pp. 471–3.

[84] L., X, pp. 60, 47–8.

[85] W., XI, pp. 464–8.

[86] See, for example, Ostrovskaiia, pp. 86–7.

[87] L., X, p. 282.

[88] L., X, No. 3268.

[89] L., X, No. 3331; L., VII, p. 138, where he refers to 'the cripple Evpraksia' as having once been a beauty with whom he had had sexual relations as a boy. The girl in the story is called Lukeria.

[90] Zv., Nos. 87, 88; L., XI, No. 3994.

[91] L., IX, No. 2645; Alekseev, in *T. sb.*, Vol. IV, p. 201; L., XI, No. 3596. (Translations by Turgenev of seven German poems, set to music by Pauline, and published in 1869 and 1871, were ascribed to him on the title-page. See W., XIII, pp. 298–303.)

[92] L., IX, p. 193.

[93] L., IX, p. 292.

[94] L., X, No. 3342, p. 607.

[95] Zv., No. 100.

[96] L., IX, No. 2656; Zv., No. 96.

[97] G. & Zv., No. 103; L., X, No. 3380, dated 26 June – 'when you left this morning'.

[98] L., XI, No. 3741.

[99] L., XI, p. 323.

[100] L., XI, No. 3974.

[101] L., XII (i) Nos. 4190, 4208.

[102] Shchepkina, p. 202; W., XIII, p. 167.

[103] L., XII (i) No. 4499.

[104] Venturi, p. 449.

[105] From his 'Underground Russia', quoted in Venturi, p. 503.

[106] For a description of one such centre, very relevant to *Virgin Soil*, see Venturi, p. 504.

[107] See Budanova.

[108] L., X, Nos. 3128, 3136; Lavrov p. 300, note; W., XII, p. 484, note 1.

[109] L., X, Nos. 3407, 3417, 3436.

[110] Entry for 2 August 1873. The best account in English of the condition of the peasants after the emancipation is Willetts.

[111] Entries for 12 June 1867, 19 May 1869, 4 February 1871.

[112] L., IX, pp. 101, 133.

[113] L., X, No. 3497; Fet, Vol. II, pp. 302–6.

[114] L., XII (i) pp. 348, 671.

CHAPTER FIFTEEN

[1] W., XII, p. 322.
[2] L., IX, p. 196.
[3] W., XII, p. 320.
[4] W., XII, pp. 314–15.
[5] W., XII, pp. 314–15.
[6] W., XII, pp. 323, 295.
[7] L., XII (1) p. 14.
[8] L., XI, p. 299.
[9] L., XII (2) p. 61.
[10] e.g. L., XII (1) p. 103.
[11] Gintovt-Dzievaltovsky in *Turg. v vosp. rev.*, p. 328.
[12] L., XII (i), p. 44.
[13] Krivenko in *Turg. v vosp. rev.*, pp. 240–1; Lavrov *ibidem* pp. 41–3.
[14] W., XV, p. 52; L., XIII (2) p. 65.
[15] W., XII, p. 492.
[16] L., XII (1) p. 88; Kleman, p. 255.
[17] See Itenberg, Vol. I *passim*.
[18] For a detailed analysis of the reworking of *Virgin Soil* see W., XII, pp. 342–462, 493–510.
[19] W., XII, pp. 308–9, from the 'Preface' to the 1880 edition of his novels.
[20] For a full summary of reviews and comments see W., XII, pp. 524–40.
[21] For the text and an important introduction see Budanova.
[22] L., XII (1) p. 136.
[23] L., XII (i) p. 222.
[24] Flaubert, *Supplément*, Vol. 3, pp. 308–9, 344–5; W., XII, pp. 543–51.
[25] L., XII (i) p. 116.
[26] L., XII (i) p. 39.
[27] L., XII (i) p. 218.
[28] L., XI, pp. 339–40.
[29] Quoted in a letter to Polonsky, L., XII (i) p. 135. On Turgenev's diary which is virtually all lost, see Chapter 16.
[30] L., XII (i) p. 385.
[31] L., XII (ii) p. 109.
[32] For an account of Russian policy in the Balkans between 1875 and 1878 see Seton-Watson, pp. 445–59.
[33] This question of British policy is fully discussed in Robert Blake, *Disraeli*, (London, 1966); for Turgenev's views on Russian policy see L., XI, p. 349.
[34] W., XIII, pp. 292–3, 691–4; L., XI, p. 349; L., XI, pp. 318, 647–8; Stefanovich.
[35] Kovalevsky, p. 144.
[36] Zv., pp. 224–5.
[37] The literature on the 1879 fêting of Turgenev is immense. See especially Kovalevsky, Lavrov, and above all Alekseeva; also W., XV, pp. 308–20, and 57–63, where the surviving texts of the speeches are reprinted.
[38] Zv., p. 225.
[39] *L.N.*, Vol. 76, p. 325.
[40] Alekseeva, pp. 301–2.
[41] Itenberg, Vol. II, pp. 27–32.
[42] Venturi, p. 595.
[43] L., XII (2) pp. 65, 177.
[44] L., XII (1) p. 411.
[45] Lavrov, p. 391.
[46] L., XII (1) p. 315.

[47] W., XV, pp. 116–17, 353–4.
[48] L., XII (2) p. 178.
[49] Kleman, p. 288.
[50] W., XV, pp. 184–5.
[51] Flaubert, Vol. 8, p. 334.
[52] L., XI, p. 272.
[53] L., XI, pp. 295, 301, 302.
[54] L., XI, p. 293; XII (1) pp. 347–8.
[55] L., XII (2) pp. 15, 12.
[56] L., XII (2) pp. 37–8; 112; 188.
[57] L., XI, p. 344; XII (1) p. 66; XII (1) p. 180; XII (2) pp. 78, 330–2.
[58] L., XII (1) pp. 211, 282–3, 306–7, 310–11, 312; XII (2) p. 90; XIII (1) p. 200.
[59] L., XII (1) 153; XII (2) 165–6, 497–8; Bron', pp. 329–31.
[60] L., XII (2) pp. 83, 86, 90, 127, 210.
[61] W., XI, p. 532.
[62] L., XII (i) p. 98.
[63] W., XV, pp. 168–76, 379–83.
[64] W., XIII, p. 601.
[65] Mazon, pp. 120–47; W., XIII, pp. 325–47, 710–18.
[66] Mazon, pp. 156–63; W., XIII, pp. 318–24, 709–10.
[67] W., XIII, p. 652.
[68] Izmailov; W., XV, pp. 114–15, 351–2.
[69] Flaubert, *Supplément*, Vol. III, p. 290; W., XIII, pp. 682–8.
[70] Flaubert, Vol. XIII, p. 260.
[71] Flaubert, *Supplément*, Vol. IV, pp. 8–9, 292–3.
[72] L., XII (2) pp. 27, 28, 30, 31–2, 34; Flaubert, Vol. 8, pp. 214–330.
[73] G. & Zv., p. 297.
[74] L. XIII (1), p. 20.
[75] *Atlantic Monthly*, Vol. 53 (Boston 1884), pp. 42–55. The letters of appreciation to American critics are in L., XIII (2) pp. 216–17.
[76] Letter to his father of 11 April 1876, Lubbock, pp. 45–6; Edel, p. 437.
[77] L., XII (1) p. 63; XII (2) p. 200.
[78] Edel, pp. 367–8; G. & Zv., p. 211.
[79] See Chapter 9.
[80] Nekrasov, Vol. 8, p. 284.
[81] L., XII (1) p. 70.
[82] *Nekrasov v vosp.*, pp. 459–60; L., XI (1) p. 261.
[83] W., XIII, p. 168. For a description of the scene by the common law wife of Nekrasov, see *Nekrasov v vosp.*, p. 456.
[84] L., XII (1) p. 260.
[85] L., III, p. 386; W., XIII, p. 198.
[86] Kovalevsky, pp. 139–40; L., XII (1) pp. 333, 664–5; W., XV, pp. 53–4, 307.
[87] L., X, p. 198.
[88] Zv., pp. 289–90 (letter to Claudie).
[89] See Simmons, for a full account and references.
[90] L., XII (2) p. 461.
[91] L., XII (2) p. 91.
[92] Abbott and Campbell, p. 150.
[93] L., XII (2) p. 126.

CHAPTER SIXTEEN

[1] Zv., p. 202.
[2] Shneiderman, p. 41.
[3] L., XIII (1) pp. 151, 156.
[4] Koni, *Turgenev i Savina*, p. 63; L., XII (2) pp. 14–15.
[5] L., XIII (2), pp. 222–3.
[6] L., XII (2), No. 4997.
[7] Zv., No. 106.
[8] G. & Zv., No. 110.
[9] Zv., No. 111.
[10] Zv., No. 139.
[11] Zv., No. 140.
[12] G. & Zv., No. 141.
[13] G. & Zv., No. 142.
[14] L., XIII (1) p. 278.
[15] L., XII (2) p. 235.
[16] L., XII (2) pp. 258–9, 555–6.
[17] L., XII (2) pp. 260–1.
[18] L., XII (2) Nos. 5242, 5248, 5290.
[19] L., XIII (1) p. 72.
[20] Koni, *Turgenev i Savina*, p. 74, pp. 26–8 footnote. L., XIII (2) p. 43.
[21] L., XIII (1) p. 137.
[22] L., XIII (2) pp. 78–79.
[23] Zv., No. 109; G. & Zv., No. 109; G. & Zv., No. 110; Zv., No. 107.
[24] See e.g. L., XIII (1) pp. 99–100, 219, 268–9, 457–8.
[25] G. & Zv., No. 110.
[26] Shchepkina, *passim*.
[27] Polonsky, p. 577.
[28] L., XII (2) No. 5204.
[29] L., XIII (1) No. 5445, No. 5450.
[30] Polonsky, pp. 590–4; L., XIII (2) No. 5966, 8 October 1882.
[31] L., XII (1) No. 4663, 4709; and numerous letters to Tolstoy and others in L., XIII (1) and L. XIII (2).
[32] Tolstoy, *Perepiska*, pp. 113–14; L., XII (1), p. 323.
[33] Polonsky, pp. 550–3.
[34] Fet, Vol. II, p. 354; S. L. Tolstoy, pp. 314–15.
[35] L., XIII (1) No. 5698.
[36] Tolstoy, *Perepiska*, p. 127.
[37] Tolstoy, *Perepiska*, p. 128.
[38] L., XIII (2) No. 6168, dated 'The beginning of July, Russian style' – in fact postmarked 11 July, Western style, i.e. 29 June, Russian style – *ibidem*, p. 378.
[39] L., XIII (2) pp. 55–8.
[40] L., XIII (2) p. 49.
[41] Kleman, p. 292.
[42] L., XII (2) Nos. 5142, 5143; pp. 543–4.
[43] L., XII (2) Nos. 5150, 5158, 5159, 5160, 5183.
[44] W., XV, p. 76.
[45] Kovalevsky, p. 147; Kleman, p. 294; Koni, *Pokhorony*, pp. 67–8.
[46] There are accounts in the contemporary papers. Recently several versions of the events by participants, not intended for publication, have appeared, rescued from the archives – see *L.N.*, Vol. 86 (F. M. Dostoevsky), Moscow, 1973, pp. 501–7, 511–12, 514–16.
[47] L., XII (2) pp. 272, 565; 298, 578. Annenkov was scathing about the speech.

[48] W., XV, pp. 268–9, 324–5.
[49] Burtsev, pp. 173–9.
[50] W., XIV, p. 274.
[51] Polonsky, pp. 524–5.
[52] G. & Zv., No. 106.
[53] Stasiulevich, in *Vestnik Evropy*, No. 5, 1884, pp. 421–2.
[54] W., XV, pp. 34–9.
[55] L., XIII (1) p. 15.
[56] W., XIII, p. 352.
[57] Lukanina, p. 225.
[58] W., XIII, pp. 567–72.
[59] Stasiulevich in *Vestnik Evropy*, 1883, pp. 849–50; L., XIII (2) p. 116.
[60] L., XIII (2) p. 133; cf. the entry in his diary, *L.N.*, Vol. 73 (1) p. 394.
[61] L., XIII (2) p. 151.
[62] L., XIII (1) p. 168.
[63] W., XIII, pp. 582–7.
[64] W., XIII, pp. 348–51, 718–21.
[65] W., XIII, pp. 353–8; Stasiulevich, III, pp. 268–9; Kropotkin, pp. 412–13; Venturi, pp. 589–90.
[66] Lukanina, p. 234.
[67] W., XIII, pp. 729–30.
[68] W., XIV, pp. 505–7.
[69] The whole question of the existence of this novel has been most meticulously investigated and documented by I. S. Zilbershtein in *L.N.*, Vol. 73 (1) pp. 376–84, but valuable additional analysis will be found in April Fitzlyon, 'Un roman inédit d'Ivan Tourguéniev?', in *Cahiers Ivan Tourguéniev Pauline Viardot Maria Malibran*, No. 1 (Paris, October 1977), pp. 9–16.
[70] L., XIII (1) p. 246; L., XIII (2) pp. 183, 379–80.
[71] Stasiulevich in *Turgenev, 1884*, Vol. I, pp. i–xi.

CHAPTER SEVENTEEN

[1] L., XIII (1) p. 131.
[2] L., XIII (1) Nos. 5546, 5560, 5563, 5575.
[3] L., XIII (1) Nos. 5590, 5603.
[4] L., XIII (1) No. 5625.
[5] L., XIII (1) No. 5674.
[6] L., XIII (1) No. 5704.
[7] L., XIII (1) Nos. 5714, 5715, 5722, 5731.
[8] L., XIII (1) Nos. 5768, 5769, 5784.
[9] L., XIII (1) No. 5788.
[10] L., XIII (1) No. 5777.
[11] L., XIII (1) p. 325.
[12] L., XIII (1) Nos. 5814, 5845, 5847.
[13] L., XIII (1) No. 5803.
[14] L., XIII (1) No. 5820.
[15] L., XIII (1) Nos. 5867, 5871, 5879, 5880, 5884.
[16] L., XIII (2) No. 5980.
[17] L., XIII (2) p. 114.
[18] Edel, pp. 486–7. James mistook the date of the journey (17 November) and did not, it would seem, realize that Turgenev was actually removing from Bougival on this day. L., XIII (2), Nos. 6015, 6016, 6017.
[19] L., XIII (1) Nos. 5659, 5660, 5665, etc.

[20] L., XIII (1) Nos. 5723, 5736; Bron', pp. 332–3, where the mistake about the legacy is repeated; L. XIII (2), No. 5907.

[21] L., XIII (2) Nos. 6012, 6033.

[22] L., XIII (2) Nos. 6081, 6095, 6135.

[23] Bron', p. 337; L., XIII (2) No. 5907. Professor Bron''s misreading of 'ma maitresse' for 'ta maitresse' in this letter makes a nonsense of the whole incident.

[24] Bron', pp. 333–4, based in part on official French records.

[25] See Zilbershtein for a detailed study of the surviving portion of the diary, and for the text.

[26] Zilbershtein, pp. 393–8.

[27] Zv., Vol. II, pp. 37–54; L., XIII (2) Nos. 6100, 6104, 6105, etc.; Zilbershtein, pp. 397–8.

[28] Utevsky, pp. 25–6 – based on the report of one of his doctors and on Annenkov's recollections.

[29] Belogolovy, pp. 409–19.

[30] L., XIII (2) Nos. 6155 to 6168.

[31] Stasiulevich, in *Vestnik Evropy*, 1883, Vol. V, pp. 847–54.

[32] Vereshchagin, p. 137.

[33] L., XIII (2) Nos. 6173–5; pp. 185–6.

[34] Shchepkina, pp. 218–19.

[35] For the evidence see Utevsky, pp. 37–8.

[36] Meshchersky; Granjard, 'Meščerskij'.

[37] Vereshchagin, p. 141.

APPENDIX

[1] See L., XIII (1) No. 5741; L., XIII (2), No. 6090; Stasiulevich, III.

[2] Quoted from unpublished papers in Granjard, 'Meščerskij', pp. 263–4, footnote 2.

[3] Arzumanova.

[4] Granjard, 'Meščerskij', pp. 265–7.

[5] Ralston, p. 337.

[6] Koni, 'Pokhorony ...'; Stasiulevich, III, pp. 232 *et seq*.

Index of Turgenev's Works

The following works by Turgenev are mentioned in the text

General Index

Compiled by Patricia Utechin

About the Author

LEONARD SCHAPIRO, Emeritus Professor of Political Science at the London School of Economics and a Fellow of the British Academy, is the author of numerous articles and books on the Soviet Union, including a translation of Turgenev's *Spring Torrents*. Born in Glasgow in 1908, he was educated at University College, London, and after practicing at the Bar for many years, joined the staff at the L.S.E. in 1955.